James E. Stenger
T. McLemore 12-15-92

The Journal of
GEORGE FOX

EDITED WITH AN INTRODUCTION

AND NOTES BY

Rufus M. Jones

*With an Essay on the Influence
of the* JOURNAL *by* HENRY J. CADBURY

CAPRICORN BOOKS   NEW YORK

Introductory Essay © 1963, by Henry J. Cadbury

CAPRICORN BOOKS EDITION, 1963

Manufactured in the United States of America

CONTENTS.

Contents.

THE INFLUENCE OF
The Journal of George Fox

HENRY J. CADBURY

That the *Journal* of George Fox is a religious classic would be admitted by many persons who have no special reason to praise it, or no substantial acquaintance with it. As religious autobiography of an Englishman, it has been considered in the same class as Wesley's *Journal* and Newman's *Apologia pro Vita Sua,* and according to at least one historian's judgment, Fox's contribution is the most original of the three.

The first edition of Fox's *Journal* contained testimonies and memorials of him, including one by Thomas Ellwood, the editor, one by Fox's widow and, most valuable of all, one by William Penn.* Modern editors of the *Journal* have retained these testimonies, but have usually compiled their own appreciations of Fox's character and significance. For the present edition it has seemed suitable to attempt instead something that has perhaps never been undertaken before, namely a review of the traceable historical, religious and literary influence of this ancient autobiography. The influence of the *Journal* can be studied at all only with difficulty, and in isolation from other factors. The first prefaces to which I have just alluded were written by persons that had known Fox directly: Margaret Fell since 1652, Thomas Ellwood since (he says) 1660, and William Penn, as we now know, since at least 1669 and, as he says, "not only by report of others, but from my own long and most inward converse and intimate knowledge of him." Indeed there is little evidence that any of these writers, except Thomas Ellwood, had read the Journal to which their testimony was prefixed. To them, and to the whole of that generation, the living and remembered Fox, "dear George," as

---

* This last, under the title "A Brief Account of the Rise and Progress of the People Called Quakers," has merited and received independent publication. All the more surprising is it to learn that one of Fox's heirs, William Meade, succeeded in having Penn's piece excluded from many of the first bound copies of the volume. Meade's motives were probably political criticism of Penn.

they called him, had been communicated directly and not by a written medium.

As this sharp, personal impression faded, there remained two less immediate forces operating to keep the memory of Fox green: the *Journal* and his other works published or republished (the two folio volumes of epistles and doctrinal writings, for example, issued respectively in 1698 and 1704), and the Society of Friends which Fox had founded. Emerson has said that an institution is the lengthened shadow of one man ". . . as Quakerism of George Fox," but how were men like Emerson and others outside the Society of Friends (or even inside it) to differentiate between the unwritten legacy of Fox and the man himself, at least that portrait of himself painted by Fox in the *Journal*? Is it not possible for the institution to overshadow the one man that it derives from?

The influence of Fox's *Journal* even within Quakerism is very difficult to estimate. That it was from the first widely circulated we know. Fox had left instructions that it be printed at the expense of his estate and free copies sent to every organized community of Friends in the world. (The book, I may add, eventually weighed four and a half pounds). In many meetings are preserved minutes noting the receipt of these books promptly in 1694. Each copy was to be made available for members of the meeting to borrow in turn. In some meetings the copy was chained in the house. When in August the central meeting in London received word of possible exaggeration in one passage they printed a substitute leaf to insert in all undistributed copies, and they tried to insert it in distributed copies, particularly those in the university libraries at Oxford and Cambridge. To judge from dozens of copies I have seen, they succeeded more often than they failed.

The *editio princeps* of 1694 was followed by many other editions. The *Journal* was not translated as early or as completely into continental languages as other Quaker books. But for two centuries the society kept the work—the whole work—in print, both in England and in America.

Even so, the influence of the book on Quakers is more easily inferred than proved. Actual references to its being read are sparse. Of course, Fox's *Journal* was not the first autobiography of a Friend. Many records of Friends who predeceased him had been printed, some of them at his instigation, and with contributions written by him. Fox's *Journal* is much longer than any of these, however, for many of them are much more like religious confessions than extended autobiographies. The *Journal* has a more detailed account of Fox's years of service, for example, than it is customary to find in these other works.

For the influence of Fox's *Journal* one would have to look at Quaker autobiographies written later. Many of those of his contemporaries bear some resemblance to Fox's book, but the resemblance is due either to coincidence or to the influence of the central publishing authorities of Friends. After Fox's death it became evident that other Journals of Friends would be published; the authors of these in that expectation would standardize their manuscripts as they prepared them to be left with their heirs. More detailed or exact imitation of Fox's *Journal* is far to seek in these Journals, though they have received a good deal of attention from modern scholars.

The earliest and most vocal reaction to the publication of Fox's *Journal* came, as might be expected, not from the Friends themselves nor from the authorities in church and state who since 1688 had adjusted to tolerate Quakerism, but from the renegade Quakers and other individuals critical of the Society of Friends; few other persons than these entertained any personal dislike of Fox. One of these critics of longest standing was Francis Bugg. From 1680 when he became disaffected to Quakerism to his death more than forty years later he poured out a stream of attacks—over sixty publications in all. Beginning with the very year the Journal was published it was the object of sundry and repeated criticism.* He was suspicious of the printed *Journal* partly because of its excellence of style. Bugg knew that Fox's original style was not polished, just as his handwriting was crude. (He and his fellow critics published *literatim* some of Fox's holograph letters and a testamentary memorandum which they called his "will"; presumably they saw the original of the latter in the Prerogative office, though even that copy is less uncultivated than the text that they circulated.) But Bugg was fully justified in suspecting that the *Journal* as printed had been edited and corrected; it was common knowledge that thirteen Friends had been entrusted with the task. Referring to this editorial committee Bugg wrote:

> You see what persons G. Fox reposed his trust in to print his books, papers and manuscripts. I know some of them well, and I suppose the rest are like them or else they left the work to them, for there is not one book of Fox's that I can find that was printed as it was writ, nor do I think there is four lines of G. Fox's manuscript called his Journal printed as wrote by him.

* A marked copy owned by Bugg is still extant in Trinity College Library, Cambridge.

We now know that very few lines of Fox's *Journal* were written by him at all; most were dictated to others. We know that Thomas Ellwood and the rest of the editorial committee *did* smooth the written text; that was to be expected, but it hardly justifies Bugg's complaint. The *Journal* was a better edited book than he wanted to see, and by the standards of the time the editing process was quite justified. When Bugg found fault with other features of the *Journal* he was quite willing to blame them on Fox himself. Thus the *Journal* was criticized both because it *was* and because it *was not* couched in what seemed to the critics the natural idiom of Fox.

Beginning almost at once Bugg inserted in successive publications a caricature of "The Quakers Synod." Conspicuous on the desk was "ye Journal of G. Fox." It had long been complained that Friends did not have or read a Bible in their meetings. Obviously the *Journal* seemed a blasphemous substitute. Bugg quotes a Friend who declared "this Journal of Fox's is a better book than the Bible," and he tells us that at their schools they read "a certain portion every day of Geo. Fox's Journal." This is repeated from Charles Leslie's *The Snake in the Grass,* but it is denied by James Barkays, who had for four years been French Master in the school referred to.

Another criticism of the *Journal* was of a different character. Nowhere in its hundreds of pages did either the *Journal* or the other volumes of his collected works indicate any confession of sin on Fox's part. Such an omission became more evident when the complete journal was published. It seemed to justify all the suspicions of his opponents that he claimed superhuman purity of life without due modesty or any note of repentance.

Pehaps the most persistent of all Bugg's criticisms have to do with Fox's claim to work cures. Under the heading "Miracles," the Index to the *Journal* pointed conveniently to at least a dozen apparent cases of such. Evidently Bugg thought they were insufficiently attested and without contemporary confirmation, but were paraded in the journal now that they could not be confirmed or refuted. Above all, none of them are said to have been done in the name of Jesus but "in Fox's own name and power like Simon Magus."

What would Francis Bugg and his associates have thought if they had known that the editors of the manuscript journal had already omitted as many such stories as they retained, and had softened the latter by writing in credit to God? And what would the critics have said if they had known of the manuscript of Fox's *Book of Miracles,* which was then in the hands of his literary executors and which contained not merely a dozen but a dozen dozens of miracle tales?

Probably the criticisms levelled at the few miracles in the *Journal* partly explain why the executors ultimately did not publish the larger collection.

Of subsequent objections to Fox's *Journal* no doubt a considerable list could be made. There is a long catalogue of books adverse to Quakerism and written by persons who, unlike Francis Bugg and George Keith, had never been members of the Society of Friends. After 1694 most of these writers would have had access to the *Journal* and could select items in it according to their own grounds for hostility, as well as some repeating the traditional grounds on which members of other churches usually found fault with Quakerism and with its founder. The *Journal* provided abundant, varied and firsthand targets for attack.

The *Journal* of George Fox has from time to time come to the attention of men of letters, both eminent and less eminent. Fox's place in history was felt to be significant, and after so full and varied an autobiography was in print, sundry literary persons were likely to come upon it accidentally or to seek it out in libraries or borrow it from contemporary Quakers of their acquaintance.

Daniel Defoe was a neighbor and acquaintance of some Friends of London. His haunts overlap the districts of the city that are prominent in Quaker annals, and Quakers play a conspicuous rôle in his fiction. His active literary career falls in the years just following the publication of Fox's *Journal* and well within the time that Francis Bugg was reiterating his charges against it. Certainly Defoe was involved in current debate on Quakerism pro and con, and in 1705-6 he was involved (in his *Review of the State of the British Nation*) in a literary altercation with Francis Bugg. Defoe here as elsewhere defends the Quakers, or rather, he expresses his hostility to Francis Bugg and to his past and future literary attacks upon them. He referred to him as "the learned Mr. B— who has done more by raving at them to make any man turn Quaker than all the authors I have met with." Neither this nor other allusions to Bugg and the Quakers prove that Defoe was acquainted with Fox's *Journal* at first hand. Francis Bugg could have provided him with indirect knowledge of it. However, a voracious reader like Defoe very likely handled the *Journal* itself.

On the continent of Europe, the *Journal* of Fox had very little direct influence, though in Holland and later in France there was much curiosity about Quakerism. This absence of direct influence was due to the size and to the language of the *Journal*. Curiously enough, the first continental writer of Quaker history—indeed the first author of Quaker history in any language—had anticipated any possible translation of the *Journal*. This was Gerard Croese, whose *Historia Quakeriana* was published first in Latin in 1695 and soon after in English and German. Where it overlaps the contents of Fox's *Journal* the parallels are not due to last-minute consultation of the new folio, but to a parallel brief manuscript account (extant but still unpublished) that Fox had himself dictated. A Dutch Friend had solicited by letter such a record from Fox and it evidently was dictated and sent a very short time before Fox's death. The letter ends its request with the words, "It [the proposed Quaker history] will be something as is like to be spread almost all the world over, and that first in Latin." As far as Europe was concerned that prophecy was largely true: Croese's history was to a generation and more of later writers the chief source of knowledge of Fox's life.

The second original history of Quakerism came also from Holland. That was written by William Sewel of Amsterdam. He was a Friend, not an outsider like Croese, and his work was much larger than Croese's, and more accurate. Like all Quaker histories since, it depended heavily, not only for the life of Fox but for the general outline of Quaker beginnings, on Fox's *Journal*. Published in 1717 in Dutch, in 1722 in English, and often later, and in other languages, this is the medium through which the contents of Fox's own journal, or at least part of it, have become most widely known. Sewel himself was aware of the composite character of that work, as the preface to the Dutch edition makes clear. Although Sewel diligently assembled other materials during the score of years he was preparing it, and although modern historians have had access to much ancient and unpublished manuscripts, Sewel was right in relying as a historian upon the *Journal*. Fox was without predecessor in the spread of Quakerism, and not one of the sixty-odd early associates in the movement—the so-called first publishers of Truth—left a biographical record at all comparable.*

Sewel's history in English rivalled the *Journal* in size and in circulation, and I believe that it excelled it in popularity. At any rate, it transmitted much of the best of the contents of its rival to English-speaking readers. On the continent its influence was less marked. After Croese the most accessible account of Fox is contained in a much briefer English work than Sewel's but one which

* When every meeting in England was asked to report the facts of its first settlement, several referred to Fox's account of his first visit in the *Journal*.

like it was based upon Fox's *Journal*. This was the twenty pages
by Thomas Clarkson in the Introduction to his *Portraiture of
Quakerism* (1806). Clarkson was, like Croese, not a Friend, but his
knowledge of Quakerism was intimate. After his work was translated
into French as *Histoire des Quakers* (1820), this account of Fox
became at least in France the principal (if indirect) channel of
influence of the *Journal*.

Perhaps the most famous French author to deal with the early
Quakers was Voltaire. They are the subject of the first four of his
Lettres sur les Anglais ou lettres philosophiques (1734). There are
references to Fox in the third of these, though these are not as
favorable as the allusions to Barclay and Penn. Some of these
references, no matter how sketchy they are, must rest upon knowledge of Fox's *Journal,* though it is not certain whether directly
from that volume or indirectly from other books, including non-
Quaker books in French, or even if they come from his British
Quaker informant, Andrew Pitt of Wandsworth, whom he consulted
when in England.

About a century after the time of Daniel Defoe Quakerism
entered more fully into the stream of British literature. This was
evident in the works of the group associated with Wordsworth and
Coleridge. As has been lately shown, "it would . . . scarcely be an
exaggeration to say that an atmosphere of Quakerism was felt
among the literary celebrities of the Lake School of Poets and
Writers."

This interest was due less to intensive reading of Quaker books
than to philosophic sympathy with aspects of Quakerism. It was
also due to the fact that most of these writers had personal acquaintance with Friends. There were in fact several minor Quaker poets at
the time who were also personal acquaintances of those who over-
shadowed them. Thomas Wilkinson was an intimate Quaker neighbor
of Wordsworth and, less so, of Coleridge. Both exchanged poems
with him. Robert Southey was another Lake neighbor, and he was
a friend of Bernard Barton, the Quaker poet. More intimate than
Southey with Barton was Charles Lamb, and both Lamb and
Coleridge were each for a period in close touch with Charles Lloyd,
the poet, who had Quaker parentage. Edward Fitzgerald was for
years another friend of Barton. Barton himself as a Quaker must
have long had knowledge and memory of Fox's *Journal*. Charles
Lamb wrote to Barton that he had read through the ponderous
folio of George Fox. He had borrowed it for six months but says,
"I think I was about as many days in getting through it, and do

not think that I skipped a word of it." * According to Caroline Fox, John Sterling read the *Journal* with interest in 1842, while John Stuart Mill had read Sewel before he was ten years old.

Strangely enough, though, it was Southey, the poet laureate, that was drawn to use the *Journal* more than any of the others had. His attraction to Quakerism had begun perhaps in 1803 when he met Thomas Clarkson, a great admirer of Quakerism, though not a Friend, and then engaged in writing his *Portraiture of Quakerism*. This preceded Southey's acquaintance with Barton and with Joseph John Gurney. He was probably never in sympathy with certain phases of Quakerism, (its pacifism, for example), but two undertakings (both left unfinished at his death) long occupied him. One was a poem placed in New England at the time of King Philip's War, with a Quaker hero, Oliver Newman. The other was a biography of George Fox and history of Quakerism on the same plan as his *Life of Wesley and the Rise and Progress of Methodism*. He wrote to a Friend in 1820: "My intention in writing the life of your founder and the rise and progress of your society is to do it diligently, faithfully and fully and charitably in a Christian spirit, not dissembling my own opinion but rendering ample justice to the opinions of others." Friends who knew him did not encourage him in the project, not so much because of any unfriendliness in his minor references to Quakerism, but because they could not trust to his freedom and independence. The unfinished and unpublished manuscript of his prose *Life of Fox* is extant at Friends Library, London.

Perhaps the loudest echo of Fox's *Journal* in *belles-lettres* is in Carlyle's *Sartor Resartus*. In this Philosophy of Clothes the alleged Teutonic source takes up the passing reference to Fox's leather breeches and defines the making of them as "perhaps the most remarkable incident in modern history." In a personal letter to his mother Carlyle applies this same symbol of freedom to his own current independence. There are, however, more extensive evidences of Carlyle's interest in Fox's career. It was an attraction to him among the mental portraits for his narrative of the civil war and background for his work on Cromwell's letters and speeches. "George's huge journal to our regret has no dates," he wrote, and yet he expressed to a friend who proposed writing a life of Lilburne a

* February, 1823. The actual copy with a record of the transaction is now at Friends Library, London. A poem on Fox by William Howitt, long contemplated, was also left unfinished. Coleridge twice projected volumes to include Fox, once along with Hooker, Baxter and Biddle, and later along with Behmen, Bruno and Spinoza.

somewhat limited preference for George Fox as "a much worthier subject" in the field of English history. "Take his own huge monster of a Journal: select with rigorous candid insight what is still interesting and alive to a man of the year 1848—which will not probably equal the hundredth part, I should guess."

Macaulay entertained a very low opinion of Fox. Like some other readers of the *Journal* he found Fox's scruples petty and absurd. Macaulay ranked Fox morally and intellectually not above Lodowicke Muggleton or Johanna Southcott—"with an intellect in the most unhappy of all states—that is to say, too much disordered for liberty and not sufficiently disordered for Bedlam." This verdict on Fox, less well known than Macaulay's misjudgment of William Penn, occupies a few pages in *The History of England,* Vol. VI. However, Macaulay admits that some of Fox's followers, though still regarding him with reverence, polished his rude doctrines and translated his gibberish into English. Over against Macaulay's unsympathetic appraisal of Fox stands the quite favorable verdict of his great nephew, George Macaulay Trevelyan, given in his *England Under the Stuarts,* Chapter 10, and in later writings.

More famous as Quaker poet than Barton was the American John Greenleaf Whittier. Brought up in a simple Quaker home in New England, the few Quaker books supplied a large fraction of his early reading. He has left two lists in verse of this household's library which he had read before his middle teens. "Fox," (presumably the *Journal*), was one of them, and for him as for many others this was reinforced by the full derivative account in Sewel's *History* ". . . painful Sewel's ancient tome; / Beloved in every Quaker home." As is to be expected, there are a number of references to Fox in his correspondence and prose. But Whittier was acquainted with other early Quaker Journals and episodes and felt the fabric of the wider Quaker history as suitable for poetic exploitation. Two poems, "Revelation" and "The Shadow and the Light," are based upon early religious experiences of Fox, originally related in the *Journal* and retold in Sewel. Another famous poem, "The King's Missive," though not about Fox nor based on his memoranda, is derived (I believe) from the account of Samuel Shattuck's return to Massachusetts included in Fox's *Journal* as printed and thence in Sewel.

The interest in Quakerism was shared by Whittier's non-Quaker literary friends. They too inherited and wrote upon the narratives of New England Quaker persecution though these accounts were not derived from Fox's *Journal.* However, there are letters showing that Whittier lent this volume to Longfellow in 1859 and to Emerson in 1852. But Emerson's interest in Quakerism was already of long standing. He had had occasion to mention Fox frequently, and Fox was an old favorite with him when he decided to include him in an early series of lectures in biography in 1835. This, first published in 1959, shows dependence directly or indirectly on Fox's Journal and on the notes Emerson had taken from reading in Fox and Sewel. A copy of Sewel's *History,* still in the Emerson house at Concord, was given to Charles Emerson, Waldo's brother, in 1832, as an inscription in it shows. The same year Emerson's Journals show he was taking notes about Fox from Sewel.

Emerson's interest in Quakerism was early nourished by his contact with living Friends, liberal Friends in New Bedford, and by one chance conversation with Edward Stabler of Virginia. Another "Friend of the Friends" was Walt Whitman whose knowledge of Elias Hicks led him to write some reminiscences and impressions of him sixty years later and to follow these with a few pages on Hicks' predecessor, George Fox. Both men had local connections of interest for the Long Island-born Whitman, and he read the published Journal of each of them. That Hicks himself knew Fox's *Journal* goes without saying; it would be available in the libraries of the local meeting and in those of Friends in the neighborhood. A copy which Elias Hicks himself owned is preserved in the Friends Historical Library at Swarthmore College.

Without pursuing other clues to the influence of Fox's *Journal* we have already seen clearly that the influence has been quite varied and sometimes contradictory. Samuel Newton, the Presbyterian churchman, found something bizarre in Fox's early exploits, citing especially his walking without his shoes through "the bloody city of Lichfield"; and it is precisely this same event that is cited at the beginning of William James' *Varieties of Religious Experience* as the best concrete example of a trait of religious genius—"symptoms of nervous instability," as "subject to abnormal psychical visitation," "peculiarities which are ordinarily classed as pathological."

"The Quaker religion which [Fox] founded," continues Professor James, "is something which it is impossible to overpraise. In a day of shams, it was a religion of veracity rooted in spiritual inwardness, and a return to something more like the original gospel truth than men had ever known in England. . . . No one can pretend for a moment that in point of spiritual sagacity and capacity, Fox's mind was unsound. . . . Yet from the point of view of his nervous constitution Fox was a psychopath or *détraqué* of the deepest dye. His Journal abounds in entries of this sort." He proceeds to quote at length the Lichfield episode (see pp. 132-134). But Professor James exaggerates the abundance of parallels. His subsequent quotations from Fox are not of this sort, nor in his own copy of Fox's *Journal,* now in the Harvard Library, does he repeat the kind of emphatic marking with which he showed his interest in the Lichfield incident.

Another "abnormal" feature of Fox's *Journal* has already been noted, the absence of a sense of sin. This was particularly offensive to orthodox Eighteenth Century piety. Again and again Francis Bugg, taking the Journal with its 632 folio pages (actually 732), complains that there is not a single confession of sin or guilt or prayer for forgiveness in the name of Jesus. Fox speaks of temptation and oppression. But there is no admission of yielding to temptation, or of the need or fact of his own conversion. Some may set this down as an example of what William James called the "once-born soul." It is more than one expects of Fox's phrases about his youth. "In my young years I had gravity and stayedness of mind and spirit, not usual in children." "When I came to eleven years of age I knew pureness and righteousness; for while a child I was taught how to walk to be kept pure" (see p. 66).

Not merely the early critics of Quakerism have been bothered by this profession of innocence: it does not suit the ideas on conversion of later evangelical Friends. Joseph John Gurney writing (probably about 1820) to his uncle Joseph, notes this lack of expression of "spiritual weakness, conflict, doubtfulness or depression [in Fox]. To be sure he was sorely exercised in early life, but when he was well hardened and polished, he seems to have taken leave of all imperfection. Were it not for the confidence which undoubted evidences respecting his life and character inspire, this trait in his Journal would inject into my mind no slight suspicion that all was not right with him."

The influence of Fox's Journal has been summarized by one writer from one incident, by another writer from another. More correctly it has been appraised for some obvious traits of the author's character shining through his artless narrative. He was a man of independence and courage, of directness of speech and action, original and sincere. He insisted on reality, on the inwardness and contemporary character of true religion. The opposition he received was from traditionalism or formalism, whether Anglican or

Puritan. His emphasis on direct revelation made him a favorite of secular independent thinkers quite outside the framework of conventional religion. They have found in his *Journal* support for their own unorthodoxy and anti-clericalism. Bernard Shaw once planned to write a play on Fox, and did include him in his *In Good King Charles' Golden Days.*

There is, however, another feature of the book that has given it a strangely ambivalent effect within the Society of Friends. Fox's language is fundamentally Biblical, and he retains alongside of his revolutionary ideas a great deal of traditional terminology. Immediate guidance is identified with historical revelation. The Light within is not detached from Christ or the Holy Spirit. It is the same spirit as gave forth the Scriptures. He leaves the reader in no doubt —or if he does, his opponents leave none—that he put inner experience above scripture record, religion today above divine acts in the past. But he acknowledged the past much as more orthodox folk did. It was the same God or spirit at work in history as today, in the life and death of Jesus as in the inspired and empowered lives of Fox and the early Quakers.

This unresolved ambivalence in Fox's message has given his *Journal* a strange effect among his followers. These followers, generation after generation, have divided their own emphasis. Beside the mystical—or, if you prefer, the prophetic—understanding of religion like Fox's understanding, in every generation some Friends have clung to an evangelical emphasis similar to that of Fox's own opponents. There is in the *Journal* enough of this common Christian theology for them to claim that their own position is identical with Fox's. Thus in a curious and unsuspected way Fox's *Journal* is honestly believed by quite contrasting groups of Friends to justify precisely their own understanding of Quakerism and not its opposite. They naturally claim on both sides to be in accord with the message of their founder.

There is a sense in which the impression made by Fox's *Journal* upon its readers discloses more about the readers than about the *Journal* itself or about its author. Hence readers, modern as well as ancient, outside Quakerism or within it, professional historians and laymen, find in their own response to it more information about themselves than about the book they are reading. The degree of their own sensitivity to the sincerity—the "enormous self-confidence"—of Fox determines how they will receive and transmit the tremendous impact of the personality of George Fox.

INTRODUCTION.

There are mysterious moments in the early life of the individual which we call "budding periods." They are incubation crises, when some new power or function is coming into being. The budding tendency to creep, to walk, to imitate, or to speak, is an indication that the psychological moment has come for learning the special operation.

There are, too, similar periods in the history of the race, mysterious times of gestation, when something new is coming to be, however dimly the age itself comprehends the significance of its travail. These racial "budding periods," like those others, have organic connection with the past. They are life-events which the previous history of humanity has made possible, and so they cannot be understood by themselves.

The most notable characteristic of such times is the simultaneous outbreaking of new aspects of truth in sundered places and through diverse lives, as though the breath of a new Pentecost were abroad. This dawning time is generally followed by the appearance of some person who proves to be able to

be the exponent of what others have dimly or sub-
consciously felt, and yet could not explicitly set forth.
Such a person becomes by a certain divine right the
prophet of the period because he knows how to interpret its ideas with such compelling force that he
organizes men, either for action or for perpetuating
the truth.

In the life history of the Anglo-Saxon people few
periods are more significant than that which is commonly called the Commonwealth period, though the
term must be used loosely to cover the span from
1640 to 1660. It was in high degree one of these
incubation epochs when something new came to
consciousness, and things equally new came to deed.
This is not the place to describe the political struggles which finally produced tremendous constitu-
tional changes, nor to tell how those who formed the
pith and marrow of a nation rose against an anti-
quated conception of kingship and established principles of self-government. The civil and political commotion was the outcome of a still deeper commotion.
For a century the burning questions had been
religious questions. The Church of that time
was the result of compromise. It had inherited a large stock of mediæval thought, and
had absorbed a mass of mediæval traditions. The

men of moral and religious earnestness were bent on some measure of fresh reform. A spirit was abroad which could not be put down, and which would not be quiet. The old idea of an authoritative Church was outgrown, and yet no religious system had come in its place which provided for a free personal approach to God Himself. It has, in fact, always been a peculiarly difficult problem to discover some form of organization which will conserve the inherited truth and guarantee the stability of the whole, while at the same time it promotes the personal freedom of the individual.

The long struggle for religious reforms in England followed two lines of development. There was on the one hand a well-defined movement toward Presbyterianism, and on the other a somewhat chaotic search for freer religious life—a movement towards Independency. The rapid spread of Presbyterianism increased rather than diminished the general religious commotion. It soon became clear that this was another form of ecclesiastical authority, as inflexible as the old, and lacking the sacred sanction of custom. Then, too, the Calvinistic theology of the time did violence to human nature as a whole. Its linked logic might compel intellectual assent, but there is something in a man as real as his intellect, which is not satisfied with this clamping of eternal truth into inflexible propositions. Personal soul-hunger, and the necessity which many individuals feel for spiritual quest, must always be reckoned with. It should not be forgotten that George Fox came to his spiritual crisis under this theology.

Thus while theology was stiffening into fixed form with one group, it was becoming ever more fluid among great masses of people throughout the nation. Religious authority ceased to count as it had in the past. Existing religious conditions were no longer accepted as final. There was a widespread restlessness which gradually produced a host of curious sects. Fox came directly in contact with at least four of the leading sectarian movements of the time and there can be no question that they exerted an influence upon him both positively and negatively. The first " sect " in importance, and the first to touch the life of George Fox, was the Baptist—at that time often called Anabaptist. His uncle Pickering was a member of this sect, and, though George seems to have been rather afraid of the Baptists, he must have learned something from them. They already had a long history, reaching back on the continent to the time of Luther, and their entire career had been

marked by persecution and suffering. They were
" Independents," i. e., they believed that Church and
State should be separate, and that each local church
should have its own independent life. They stoutly
objected to infant baptism, maintaining that no act
could have a religious value unless it were an act
of will and of faith. Edwards, in his " Gangræna,"
1646, reports a doctrine then afloat to the intent that
" it is as lawful to baptize a cat, or a dog, or a chicken
as to baptize an infant." Their views on ministry
were novel and must surely have interested Fox.
They encouraged a lay ministry, and they actually
had cobblers, leather-sellers, tailors, weavers and at
least one brewer, preaching in their meetings. John
Bunyan, who was of them, proved to general satisfaction that " Oxford and Cambridge were not necessary to fit men to preach." Still stranger, they
had what their enemies scornfully called " She-
preachers." Edwards has recorded this dreadful error in his list of one hundred and ninety-nine " distinct errors, heresies and blasphemies ": " Some say
that 'tis lawful for women to preach, that they have
gifts as well as men; and some of them do actually
preach, having great resort to them "!

Furthermore, they held that all tithes and all set
stipends were unlawful. They maintained that

preachers should work with their own hands and not " go in black clothes." This sad error appears in Edwards's chaotic list: " It is said that all settled certain maintenance for ministers of the gospel is unlawful." Finally many of the Baptists opposed the use of " steeple houses " and held the view that no person is fitted to preach or prophesy *unless the Spirit moves him.*

The " Seekers " are occasionally mentioned in the Journal and were widely scattered throughout England during the Commonwealth. They were serious-minded people who saw nowhere in the world any adequate embodiment of religion. They held that there was no true Church, and that there had been none since the days of the apostles. They did not celebrate any sacraments, for they held that there was nobody in the world who possessed an anointing clearly, certainly and infallibly enough to perform such rites. They had no " heads " to their assemblies, for they had none among them who had " the power or the gift to go before one another in the way of eminency or authority." William Penn says that they met together " not in their own wills " and " waited together in silence, and as anything arose in one of their minds that they thought favored with a divine spring, so they sometimes spoke."

We are able to pick out a few of their character-istic " errors " from Edwards's list in the " Gan-græna." " That to read the Scriptures to a mixed congregation is dangerous." " That we did look for great matters from One crucified in Jerusalem 1600 years ago, but that does no good; it must be a Christ formed *in* us." " That men ought to preach and ex-ercise their gifts without study and premeditation and not to think what they are to say till they speak, because it shall be given them in that hour and the Spirit shall teach them." " That there is no need of human learning or reading of authors for preach-ers, but all books and learning must go down. It comes from want of the Spirit that men write such great volumes."

The " Seekers " expected that the light was soon to break, the days of apostasy would end and the Spirit would make new revelations. In the light of this expectation a peculiar significance attaches to the frequent assertion of Fox that he and his follow-ers were living in the same Spirit which gave forth the Scriptures, and received direct commands as did the apostles. " I told him," says Fox of a " priest," " that to receive and go with a message, and to have a word from the Lord, as the prophets and apostles had and did, and as *I had done*," was quite another

thing from ordinary experience. A much more chaotic " sect " was that of the " Ranters." There was
probably a small seed of truth in their doctrines, but
under the excitement of religious enthusiasm they
went to wild and perilous extremes, and in some
cases even fell over the edge of sanity. They started
with the belief that God is in everything, that every
man is a manifestation of God, and they ended with
the conclusion which their bad logic gave them that
therefore what the man does God does. They were
above all authority and actually said: " Have not *we*
the Spirit, and why may not *we* write scriptures as
well as Paul ? " They believed the Scriptures " not
because such and such writ it," but because they
could affirm " God saith so in me." What Christ did
was for them only a temporal figure, and nothing external was of consequence, since they had God Himself in them. As the law had been fulfilled they held
that they were free from all law, and might without
sin do what they were prompted to do. Richard
Baxter says that " the horrid villainies of the sect did
speedily extinguish it." Judge Hotham told Fox
in 1651 that " if God had not raised up the principle of Light and Life which he (Fox) preached, the
nation had been overrun with Ranterism." Many of
the Ranters became Friends, some of them becoming

substantial persons in the new Society, though there were for a time some serious Ranter influences at work within the Society, and a strenuous opposition was made to the establishment of discipline, order and system. The uprising of the " Fifth-monarchy men " is the only other movement which calls for special allusion. They were literal interpreters of Scripture, and had discovered grounds for believing in the near approach of the millennium. By some system of calculation they had concluded that the last of the four world monarchies—the Assyrian, Persian, Greek and Roman—was tottering toward its fall, and the Fifth universal monarchy—Christ's —was about to be set up. The saints were to reign. The new monarchy was so slow in coming that they thought they might hasten it with carnal weapons. Perhaps a miracle would be granted if they acted on their faith. The miracle did not come, but the uprising brought serious trouble to Fox, who had before told these visionaries in beautifully plain language that " Christ *has* come and has dashed to pieces the four monarchies."

The person of genius discovers in the great mass of things about him just that which is vital and essential. He seizes the eternal in the temporal, and all that he borrows, he fuses with creative power into

a new whole.   This creative power belonged to
George Fox.   There was hardly a single truth in the
Quaker message which had not been held by some
one of the many sects of the time.   He saw the spiritual and eternal element which was almost
lost in the chaos of half truths and errors.   In
his message these scattered truths and ideas were
fused into a new whole and received new life from
his living central idea.

It is a strange fact that, though England had
been facing religious problems of a most complex sort since the oncoming of the Reformation, it had produced no religious genius.   No
one had appeared who saw truth on a new level,
or who possessed a personality and a personal message which compelled the attention of the nation.
There had been long years of ingenious, patchwork
compromise, but no distinct prophet.   George Fox
is the first real prophet of the English Reformation,
for he saw what was involved in this great religious
movement.*   Perhaps the most convincing proof of

---

* " But of ' prophets ' there are very few.   The good God does not
seem to need many.   Centuries pass, as He orders history, in which there
are none.   So we call them Dark Ages.   Then comes some John in the
desert, and the world is wakened ; some Wesley in the Church of England, and there is a revival of religion.

" For our English races, since there were English races, I count three
or four such prophets ; for the world of Europe I count perhaps eleven

this is not the remarkable immediate results of his labors, though these are significant enough, but rather the easily-verified fact that the progress of religious truth during the last hundred years has been toward the truth which he made central in his message.* However his age misunderstood him, he would to-day find a goodly fellowship of believers.

The purpose of this book is to have him tell his own story, which in the main he knows how to do.

worthy of our gratitude to-day. I mean the gratitude of all mankind. Saint Paul and Saint John are two; Augustine of Hippo is three; Dante and Francis of Assisi are two more; Thomas à Kempis and Jacob Böhme, two more ; and, coming across to England, Wiclif, John Milton, George Fox, and John Wesley."—*Edward Everett Hale, in an Address at the Wesley Bicentennial Celebration in People's Temple, Boston.*

" The three most influential Englishmen of the last three centuries were George Fox, John Wesley and John Henry Newman. Those who wish really to understand those three centuries must read, mark, learn, and inwardly digest Fox's Journal, Wesley's Journal, and Newman's Apologia. The entire future of England and the English Empire depends upon the answer to this question : Will Newman defeat Fox and Wesley, or will Fox and Wesley defeat Newman ? "
Editorial in " The Methodist Times."

* " The Quaker religion which he (George Fox) founded is something which it is impossible to overpraise. In a day of shams, it was a religion of veracity rooted in spiritual inwardness, and a return to something more like the original gospel truth than men had ever known in England. So far as our Christian sects to-day are evolving into liberality, they are simply reverting in essence to the position which Fox and the early Quakers so long ago assumed. No one can pretend for a moment that in point of spiritual sagacity and capacity, Fox's mind was unsound. Every one who confronted him personally, from Oliver Cromwell down to county magistrates and jailers, seems to have acknowledged his superior power."
James's "Varieties of Religious Experience," page 6.

It will, however, be of some service to the reader to
develop in advance the principle of which he was the
exponent. The first period of his life is occupied
with a most painful quest for something which would
satisfy his heart. His celebrated contemporary,
Bunyan, possessed much greater power of describing
inward states and experiences, but one is led to
believe on comparing the two autobiographical
passages that the sufferings of Fox, in his years of
spiritual desolation, were even more severe than were
those of Bunyan, though it is to be noted that the
former does not suffer from the awful sense of personal sin as the latter does. " When I came to eleven
years of age, *I knew pureness and righteousness*," is
Fox's report of his own early deliverance from the
sense of sin. His "despair," from which he could find
no comfort, was caused by the extreme sensitiveness
of his soul. The discovery that the world, and even
the Church, was full of wickedness and sin crushed
him. " I looked upon the great professors of the
city [London, 1643], and I saw all was dark and
under the chain of darkness." This settled upon him
with a weight, deep almost as death. Nothing in the
whole world seemed to him so real as the world's
wickedness. " I could have wished," he cries out, " I
had never been born, or that I had been born blind

that I might never have seen wickedness or vanity; and deaf that I might never have heard vain and wicked words, or the Lord's name blasphemed."

He was overwhelmed, however, not merely because he discovered that the world was wicked, but much more because he discovered that priests were "empty hollow casks," and that religion, as far as he could discover any in England, was weak and ineffective, with no dynamic message which moved with the living power of God behind it. He could find theology enough and theories enough, but he missed everywhere the direct evidence that men about him had found God. Religion seemed to him to be reduced to a system of clever substitutes for God, while his own soul could not rest until it found the Life itself.

The turning point of his life is the discovery— through what he beautifully calls an "opening"— that Christ is not merely an historic person who once came to the world and then forever withdrew, but that He is the continuous Divine Presence, God manifested humanly, and that this Christ can "speak to his condition."

At first sight, there appears to be nothing epoch-making in these simple words. But it soon develops that what he really means is

that he has discovered within the deeps of
his own personality a meeting place of the human
spirit with the Divine Spirit. He had never had any
doubts about the historical Christ. All that the
Christians of his time believed *about* Christ, he, too,
believed. His long search had not been to find out
something *about* Christ, but to find *Him*. The
Christ of the theological systems was too remote and
unreal to be dynamic for him. Assent to all the
propositions about Him left one still in the power
of sin. He emerges from the struggle with an absolute certainty in his own mind that he has discovered a way by which his soul has immediate dealings
with the living God. The larger truth involved in
his experience soon becomes plain to him, namely,
that he has found a universal principle, that
the Spirit of God reaches every man. He finds
this divine-human relation taught everywhere in
Scripture, but he challenges everybody to find
the primary evidence of it in his own consciousness. He points out that every hunger of the
heart, every dissatisfaction with self, every act of
self-condemnation, every sense of shortcoming shows
that the soul is not unvisited by the Divine Spirit,
To want God at all implies some acquaintance with
Him. The ability to appreciate the right, to discrim-

inate light from darkness, the possibility of being anything more than a creature of sense, living for the moment, means that our personal life is in contact at some point with the Infinite Life, and that all things are possible to him who believes and obeys.

To all sorts and conditions of men, Fox continually makes appeal to " that of God " within them. At other times he calls it indiscriminately the " Light," or the " Seed," or the " Principle " of God within the man. Frequently it is the " Christ within." In every instance he means that the Divine Being operates directly upon the human life, and the new birth, the real spiritual life, begins when the individual becomes aware of Him and sets himself to obey Him. He may have been living along with no more explicit consciousness of a Divine presence than the bubble has of the ocean on which it rests and out of which it came; but even so, God is as near him as is the beating of his own heart, and only needs to be found and obeyed.

Instead of making him undervalue the historic revelations of God, the discovery of this principle of truth gave him a new insight into the revelations of the past and the supreme manifestations of the Divine Life and Love. He could interpret his own inward experience in the light of the gathered revelation of the ages. His contemporaries used to say that, though the Bible were lost, it might be found in the mouth of George Fox, and there is not a line in the Journal to indicate that he undervalued either the Holy Scriptures or the historic work of Christ for human salvation. Entirely the contrary. As soon as he realized that the same God who spoke directly to men in earlier ages still speaks directly, and that to be a man means to have a "seed of God" within, he saw that there were no limits to the possibilities of a human life. It becomes possible to live entirely in the power of the Spirit and to have one's life made a free and victorious spiritual life. So to live is to be a "man"—for sin and disobedience reduce a man. The normal person, then, is the one who has discovered the infinite Divine resources, and is turning them into the actual stuff of a human life. That it happens now and then is no mystery; that it happens so seldom is the real mystery. "I asked them if they were living in the power of the Spirit that gave forth the Scriptures" is his frequent and somewhat naïve question, as though everybody ought to be doing it.

The consciousness of the presence of God is the characteristic thing in George Fox's religious life. His own life is in immediate contact with the Divine

Life. It is this conviction which unifies and gives direction to all his activities. God has found him and he has found God. It is this experience which puts him among the mystics.

But here we must not overlook the distinction in types of mysticism. There is a great group of mystics who have painfully striven to find God by a path of negation. They believe that everything finite is a shadow, an illusion—nothing real. To find God, then, every vestige of the finite must be given up. The infinite can be reached only by wiping out all marks of the finite. The Absolute can be attained only when every "thing" and every "thought" have been reduced to zero. But the difficulty is that this kind of an Absolute becomes absolutely unknowable. From the nature of the case He could not be *found*, for to have any consciousness of Him at all would be to have a finite and illusory thought.

George Fox belongs rather among the *positive* mystics, who seek to realize the presence of God in this finite human life. That He transcends all finite experiences they fully realize, but the reality of any finite experience lies just in this fact, that the living God is in it and expresses some divine purpose through it, so that a man may, as George Fox's friend, Isaac Penington says, " become an organ of the life and power of God," and " progagate God's life in the world." The mystic of this type may feel the light break within him and know that God is there, or he may equally well discover Him as he performs some clear, plain duty which lies across his path. His whole mystical insight is in his discovery that God is near, and not beyond the reach of the ladders which He has given us.

But no one has found the true George Fox when he stops with an analysis of the views which he held. Almost more remarkable than the truth which he proclaimed was the fervor, the enthusiasm, the glowing passion of the man. He was of the genuine apostolic type. He had come through years of despair over the wickedness of the world, but as soon as the Light really broke, and he knew that he had a message for the world in its sin and ignorance, there was after that nothing but the grave itself which could keep him quiet. He preached in cathedrals, on hay stacks, on cliffs of rock, from hill tops, under apple trees and elm trees, in barns and in city squares, while he sent epistles from every prison in which he was shut up. Wherever he could find men who had souls to save he told them of the Life and Truth which he had found.

Whether one is in sympathy with Fox's mystical view of life or not, it is impossible not to be impressed with the practical way in which he wrought out his faith. After all, the view that God and man are not isolated was not new; the really new thing was the appearance of a man who genuinely practiced the Divine presence and lived *as though he knew* that his life was in a Divine environment.

We have dwelt upon the fundamental religious principle of Fox at some length, because his great work as a social reformer and as the organizer of a new system of Church government proceeds from this root principle. One central idea moves through all he did. His originality lies, however, not so much in the discovery, or the rediscovery, of the principle as in the fearless application of it. Other men had believed in Divine guidance; other Christians had proclaimed the impenetration of God in the lives of men. But George Fox had the courage to carry his conviction to its logical conclusions. He knew that there were difficulties entailed in calling men everywhere to trust the Light and to follow the Voice, but he believed that there were more serious difficulties to be faced by those who put some external authority in the place of the soul's own sight. He was ready for the consequences and he proceeded to carry out both

in the social and in the religious life of his time the
experiment of obeying the Light within. It is this
courageous fidelity to his insight that made him a
social reformer and a religious organizer. He belongs, in this respect, in the same list with St. Francis
of Assisi. They both attempted the difficult task of
bringing religion from heaven to earth.

1. In the light of his religious discovery Fox rein-
terpreted man as a member of society. If man *has*
direct intercourse with God he is to be treated with
noble respect. He met the doctrine of the divine
right of kings with the conviction of the *divine right
of man.* Every man is to be treated as a man. He
was a *leveler,* but he leveled up, not down. Every
man was to be read in terms of his possibilities—if
not of royal descent, certainly of royal destiny.
This view made Fox an unparalleled optimist. He
believed that a mighty transformation would
come as soon as men were made aware of this divine
relationship which he had discovered. They would
go to living as he had done, in the *power* of this conviction.

He began at once to put in practice his principle of
equality—*i. e.*, equality of privilege. He cut straight
through the elaborate web of social custom which
hid man's true nature from himself. Human life

had become sicklied o'er with a cast of sham, until man had half forgotten to act as *man.* Fox rejected for himself every social custom which seemed to him to be hollow and to belittle man himself. The honor which belonged to God he would give to no man, and the honor which belonged to any man he gave to every man. This was the reason for his "thee" and "thou." The plural form had been introduced to give distinction. He would not use it. The Lord Protector and the humble cotter were addressed alike. He had an eye for the person of great gifts and he never wished to reduce men to indistinguishable atoms of society, but he was resolved to guard the jewel of personality in every individual—man or woman.

2. His estimate of the worth of man made him a reformer. In society as he found it men were often treated more as things than as persons. For petty offenses they were hung,* and if they escaped this fate they were put into prisons, where no touch of man's humanity was in evidence. In the never-ending wars the common people were hardly more than human dice. Their worth as men was well nigh forgotten. Trade was conducted on a system of sliding prices— high for this man, low for some other. Dealers were

---

* At this epoch there were more than two hundred capital offenses.

honest where they had to be; dishonest where they could be. The courts of justice were extremely uncertain and irregular, as the pages of this journal continually show. Against every such crooked system which failed to recognize the divine right of man George Fox set himself. He himself had large opportunities of observing the courts of justice and the inhuman pens which by courtesy were called jails. But he became a reformer, not to secure his own rights or to get a better jail to lie in, but to establish the principle of human rights for all men. He went calmly to work to carry an out-and-out honesty into all trade relations, to establish a fixed price for goods of every sort, to make principles of business square with principles of religion. By voice or by epistle he called every judge in the realm to "mind that of God" within him. He refused ever to take an oath, because he was resolved to make a plain man's "yea" weigh as heavy as an oath. He was always in the lists against the barbarity of the penal system, the iniquity of enslaving men, the wickedness of war, the wastefulness of fashion and the evils of drunkenness, and by argument and deed he undertook to lead the way to a new heroism, better than the heroism of battlefields.

3. The logic of his principle compelled him to value education. If all men are to count as men, it is a man's primal duty to be all he can be. To be a poor organ of God when one was meant for a good one belongs among the high sins.* If it was " opened " to him that Oxford and Cambridge could not make men ministers, his own reason taught him that it is not safe to call all men to obey the voice and follow the light without broad-basing them at the same time in the established facts of history and nature. Fox himself very early set up schools for boys and girls alike in which " everything civil and useful in creation " was to be taught. It is, however, quite possible that he undervalued the æsthetic side of man, and that he suffered by his attempt to starve it. In this particular he shared the puritan tendency, and had not learned how to hold all things in proportion, and to make the culture of the senses at the same time beautify the inner man.

---

* " Dear friends and brethren that have gone into Americ   the islands thereaway, stir up the gift of God in you and improve your talents. Let your light shine among the Indians, the blacks and the whites, that ye may answer the truth in them and *bring them to the standard and ensign that God hath set up, Jesus Christ. Grow in the faith and grace of Christ that ye be not like dwarfs,* for a dwarf shall not come near to offer upon God's altar."

From an Epistle of George Fox written in 1690.

4. On the distinctively religious side his discovery of a direct divine-human relationship led to a new interpretation of worship and ministry. God is not far off. He needs no vicar, no person of any sort between Himself and the worshipper. Grace no more needs a special channel than the dew does. There is no special holy place, as though God were more *there* than *here*. He does not come from somewhere else. He is Spirit, and needs only a responsive soul, an open heart, to be *found*. Worship properly begins when the soul discovers Him and enjoys His presence—in the simplest words it is the soul's appreciation of God. With his usual optimism, he believed that all men and women were capable of this stupendous attainment. He threw away all crutches at the start and called upon everybody to walk in the Spirit, to live in the Light. His house of worship was bare of everything but seats. It had no shrine, for the shekinah was to be in the hearts of those who worshipped. It had no altar, for God nee no appeasing, seeing that He Himself had made the sacrifice for sin. It had no baptismal font, for baptism was in his belief nothing short of immersion into the life of the Father, Son and Holy Spirit—a going down into the significance of Christ's death and a coming up in newness of life with Him.

There was no communion table, because he believed that the true communion consisted in partaking directly of the soul's spiritual bread—the living Christ. There were no confessionals, for in the silence, with the noise and din of the outer life hushed, the soul was to unveil itself to its Maker and let His light lay bare its true condition. There was no organ or choir, for each forgiven soul was to give praise in the glad notes that were natural to it. No censer was swung, for he believed God wanted only the fragrance of sincere and prayerful spirits. There was no priestly mitre, because each member of the true Church was to be a priest unto God. No official robes were in evidence, because the entire business of life, in meeting and outside, was to be the putting on of the white garments of a saintly life. From beginning to end worship was the immediate appreciation of God, and the appropriate activity of the whole being in response to Him.

William Penn says of him: " The most awful, living, reverent frame I ever felt or beheld was his in prayer." And this was because he realized that he was in the presence of God when he prayed. He believed that the ministry of truth is limited to no class of men and to no sex. As fast and as far as any man discovers God it becomes his business to make Him known to others. His ability to do this effectively is a gift from God, and makes him a minister. The only thing the Church does is to recognize the gift. This idea carried with it perfect freedom of utterance to all who felt a *call* to speak, a principle which has worked out better than the reader would guess, though it has been often sorely tested.

In the Society which he founded there was no distinction of clergy and laity. He undertook the difficult task of organizing a Christian body on which the priesthood of believers should be an actual fact, and in which the ordinary religious exercises of the Church should be under the directing and controlling power of the Holy Spirit manifesting itself through the congregation.

Not the least service of Fox to his age was the important part which he took in breaking down the intolerable doctrine of predestination, which hung like an incubus over men's lives. It threw a gloom upon every person who found himself forced by his logic to believe it, and its effect upon sensitive souls was simply dreadful. Fox met this doctrine with argument, but he met it also with something better than argument—he set over against it two facts: that Divine grace and light are free, and that an inward

certainty of God's favor and acceptance is possible
for every believer. Wherever Quakerism went this
inward assurance went with it. The shadow of dread
uncertainty gave place to sunlight and joy. This was
the beginning of a spiritual emancipation which is
still growing, and peaceful faces and fragrant lives
are the result.

No reader of the Journal can fail to be impressed
with the fact that George Fox believed himself to be
an instrument for the manifestation of miraculous
power. Diseases were cured through him; he fore-
told coming events; he often penetrated states and
conditions of mind and heart; he occasionally had a
sense of what was happening in distant parts, and he
himself underwent on at least three occasions striking bodily changes, so that he seemed, for days at a
time, like one dead, and was in one of these times
incapable of being bled. These passages need trouble no one, nor need their truthfulness be questioned.
He possessed an unusual psychical nature, delicately
organized, capable of experiences of a novel sort,
but such as are to-day very familiar to the student of
psychical phenomena. The marvel is that with such
a mental organization he was so sane and practical,
and so steadily kept his balance throughout a life
which furnished numerous chances for shipwreck.

It is very noticeable—rather more so in the complete Journal than in this Autobiography—that "judgments" came upon almost everybody who was a malicious opposer of him or his work. "God cut him off soon after," is a not infrequent phrase. It is manifestly impossible to investigate these cases now, and to verify the facts, but the well-tested honesty of the early Friends leaves little ground for doubting that the facts were substantially as they are reported. Fox's own inference that all these persons had misfortune as a direct "judgment" for having harmed him and hindered his cause will naturally seem to us a too hasty conclusion. It is not at all strange that in this eventful period many persons who had dealings with him should have suffered swift changes of fortune, and of course he failed to note how many there were who did *not* receive judgment in this direct manner. One regrets, of course, that this kindly spiritual man should have come so near enjoying what seemed to him a divine vengeance upon his enemies, but we must remember that he believed in his soul that his work was God's work, and hence to frustrate it was serious business.

He founded a Society, as he called it, which he evidently hoped, and probably believed, would some-

time become universal.* The organization in every
aspect recognized the fundamentally spiritual nature
of man. Every individual was to be a vital, organic
part of the whole; free, but possessed of a freedom
which had always to be exercised with a view to the
interests and edification of the whole. It was mod-
elled exactly on the conception of Paul's universal
Church of many members, made a *unity* not from
without, but by the living presence of the One Spirit.
All this work of organization was effected while Fox
himself was in the saddle, carrying his message to
town after town, interrupted by long absences in jail
and dungeon, and steadily opposed by the fanatical
antinomian elements which had flocked to his standard. It is not the least mark of his genius that in
the face of an almost unparalleled persecution he left
his fifty thousand followers in Great Britain and Ireland formed into a working and growing body, with
equally well-organized meetings in Holland, New
England, New York, Pennsylvania, Maryland, Virginia and the Carolinas. His personality and his message had won men from every station of life, and if
the rank and file were from the humbler walks, there

* " In 1658 there was not a Quaker living who did not believe Quakerism to be the one only true Church of the living God."

Hancock's "Peculium," page 8.

were also men and women of scholarship and fame. Robert Barclay, from the schools of Paris, gave the new faith its permanent expression in his Apology. William Penn worked its principles out in a holy experiment in a Christian Commonwealth, and Isaac Penington, in his brief essays, set forth in rich and varied phrase the mystical truth which was at the heart of the doctrine.

This is the place for exposition, not for criticism. It requires no searchlight to reveal in this man the limitations and imperfections which his age and his own personal peculiarities fixed upon him. He saw in part and he prophesied in part. But, like his great contemporary, Cromwell, he had a brave sincerity, a soul absolutely loyal to the highest he saw. The testimony of the Scarborough jailer is as true as it is unstudied—" as stiff as a tree and as pure as a bell." It is fitting that this study of him should close with the words of the man who knew him best—William Penn: " I write my knowledge and not report, and my witness is true, having been with him for weeks and months together on diverse occasions, and those of the nearest and most exercising nature, by sea and land, in this country and in foreign countries; and I can say I never saw him out of his place, or not a match for every service or occasion. For in all things he acquitted himself like a man, yea, a strong man, a new and heavenly-minded man; a divine and a naturalist, and all of God Almighty's making." *

* From William Penn's " Preface to the Journal of George Fox."

THE TESTIMONY OF WILLIAM PENN CONCERNING
THAT FAITHFUL SERVANT

GEORGE FOX.

The blessed instrument of and in this day of God, and of whom I am now about to write, was George Fox, distinguished from another of that name, by that other's addition of younger to his name in all his writings; not that he was so in years, but that he was so in the truth; but he was also a worthy man, witness and servant of God in his time.

But this George Fox was born in Leicestershire, about the year 1624. He descended of honest and sufficient parents, who endeavoured to bring him up, as they did the rest of their children, in the way and worship of the nation; especially his mother, who was a woman accomplished above most of her degree in the place where she lived. But from a child he appeared of another frame of mind than the rest of his brethren; being more religious, inward, still, solid, and observing, beyond his years, as the answers he would give, and the questions he would put upon occasion manifested, to the astonishment of those that heard him, especially in divine things.

His mother taking notice of his singular temper, and the gravity, wisdom, and piety that very early shone through him, refusing childish and vain sports and company when very young, she was tender and indulgent over him, so that from her he met with little difficulty. As to his employment, he was brought up in country business; and as he took most delight in sheep, so he was very skilful in them; an employment that very well suited his mind in several respects, both for its innocency and solitude; and was a just figure of his after ministry and service.

I shall not break in upon his own account, which is by much the best that can be given; and therefore desire, what I can, to avoid saying anything of what is said already, as to the particular passages of his coming forth; but, in general, when he was somewhat above twenty, he left his friends, and visited the most retired and religious people, and some there were at that time in this nation, especially in those parts, who waited for the consolation of Israel night and day, as Zacharias, Anna, and good old Simeon did of old time. To these he was sent, and these he sought out in the neighboring countries, and among them he sojourned till his more ample ministry came upon him.

At this time he taught and was an example of silence, endeavouring to bring people from self-performances, testifying and turning to the light of Christ within them, and encouraging them to wait in patience to feel the power of it to stir in their hearts, that their knowledge and worship of God might stand in the power of an endless life, which was to be found in the Light, as it was obeyed in the

manifestation of it in man. " For in the Word was
life, and that life was the light of men." Life in the
Word, light in men, and life too, as the light is
obeyed; the children of the light living by the life of
the Word, by which the Word begets them again to
God, which is the regeneration and new birth, without which there is no coming unto the kingdom of
God; and which, whoever comes to, is greater than
John, that is, than John's ministry, which was not
that of the kingdom, but the consummation of the
legal, and opening of the gospel-dispensation. Accordingly, several meetings were gathered in those
parts; and thus his time was employed for some
years.

In 1652, he being in his usual retirement to the
Lord upon a very high mountain, in some of the
hither parts of Yorkshire, as I take it, his mind exercised towards the Lord, he had a vision of the great
work of God in the earth, and of the way that he was
to go forth to begin it. He saw people as thick as
motes in the sun, that should in time be brought
home to the Lord, that there might be but one Shepherd and one sheepfold in all the earth. There his
eye was directed northward, beholding a great people that should receive him and his message in those
parts. Upon this mountain he was moved of the
Lord to sound out his great and notable day, as if he
had been in a great auditory, and from thence went
north, as the Lord had shewn him: and in every place
where he came, if not before he came to it, he had

his particular exercise and service shewn to him, so that the Lord was his leader indeed; for it was not in vain that he travelled, God in most places sealing his commission with the convincement of some of all sorts, as well publicans as sober professors of religion. Some of the first and most eminent of them, which are at rest, were Richard Farnsworth, James Nayler, William Dewsberry, Francis Howgil, Edward Burrough, John Camm, John Audland, Richard Hubberthorn, T. Taylor, John Aldam, T. Holmes, Alexander Parker, William Simpson, William Caton, John Stubbs, Robert Widders, John Burnyeat, Robert Lodge, Thomas Salthouse, and many more worthies, that cannot be well here named, together with divers yet living of the first and great convincement, who after the knowledge of God's purging judgments in themselves, and some time of waiting in silence upon him, to feel and receive power from on high to speak in his name (which none else rightly can, though they may use the same words), felt the divine motions, and were frequently drawn forth, especially to visit the publick assemblies, to reprove, inform and exhort them, sometimes in markets, fairs, streets, and by the highway side, calling people to repentance, and to turn to the Lord with their hearts as well as their mouths; directing them to the light of Christ within them, to see and examine and consider their ways by, and to eschew the evil and do the good and acceptable will of God. And they suffered great hardships for this their love and good-will, being

often stocked, stoned, beaten, whipped and imprisoned, though honest men and of good report where
they lived, that had left wives and children, and
houses and lands, to visit them with a living call to repentance. And though the priests generally set themselves to oppose them, and write against them, and
insinuated most false and scandalous stories to de-
fame them, stirring up the magistrates to suppress
them, especially in those northern parts, yet God
was pleased so to fill them with his living power, and
give them such an open door of utterance in his service, that there was a mighty convincement over
those parts.

And through the tender and singular indulgence of
Judge Bradshaw and Judge Fell, in the infancy of
things, the priests were never able to gain the point
they laboured for, which was to have proceeded to
blood, and if possible, Herod-like, by a cruel exercise
of the civil power, to have cut them off and rooted
them out of the country. Especially Judge Fell, who
was not only a check to their rage in the course of
legal proceedings, but otherwise upon occasion, and
finally countenanced this people; for his wife receiving the truth with the first, it had that influence upon
his spirit, being a just and wise man, and seeing in his
own wife and family a full confutation of all the
popular clamours against the way of truth, that he
covered them what he could, and freely opened his
doors, and gave up his house to his wife and her
friends, not valuing the reproach of ignorant or evil-

minded people, which I here mention to his and her honour, and which will be I believe an honour and a blessing to such of their name and family as shall be found in that tenderness, humility, love and zeal for the truth and people of the Lord.

That house was for some years at first, till the truth had opened its way in the southern parts of this island, an eminent receptacle of this people. Others of good note and substance in those northern countries had also opened their houses with their hearts to the many publishers, that in a short time the Lord had raised to declare his salvation to the people, and where meetings of the Lord's messengers were frequently held, to communicate their services and exercises, and comfort and edify one another in their blessed ministry.

But lest this may be thought a digression, having touched upon this before, I return to this excellent man: and for his personal qualities, both natural, moral, and divine, as they appeared in his converse with his brethren and in the church of God, take as follows.

I. He was a man that God endowed with a clear and wonderful depth, a discerner of others' spirits, and very much a master of his own. And though the side of his understanding which lay next to the world, and especially the expression of it, might sound uncouth and unfashionable to nice ears, his matter was nevertheless very profound, and would not only bear to be often considered, but the more it was so, the more weighty and instructing it appeared. And as abruptly and brokenly as sometimes his sentences would fall from him about divine things, it is well known they were often as texts to many fairer declarations. And indeed it shewed beyond all contradiction that God sent him, that no arts or parts had any share in the matter or manner of his ministry, and that so many great, excellent, and necessary truths as he came forth to preach to mankind, had therefore nothing of man's wit or wisdom to recommend them. So that as to man he was an original, being no man's copy. And his ministry and writings shew they are from one that was not taught of man, nor had learned what he said by study. Nor were they notional or speculative, but sensible and practical truths, tending to conversion and regeneration, and the setting up the kingdom of God in the hearts of men, and the way of it was his work. So that I have many times been overcome in myself, and been made to say with my Lord and Master upon the like occasion, " I thank thee, O Father, Lord of heaven and earth, that thou hast hid these things from the wise and prudent of this world, and revealed them to babes "; for many times hath my soul bowed in an humble thankfulness to the Lord, that he did not choose any of the wise and learned of this world to be the first messenger in our age of his blessed truth to men; but that he took one that was not of high degree, or elegant speech, or learned after the way of this world, that his message and work He sent him to do might come with less suspicion or jealousy of human wisdom and interest, and with more force and clearness upon the consciences of those that sincerely sought the way of truth in the love of it. I say, beholding with the eye of my mind, which the God of heaven had opened in me, the marks of God's finger and hand visibly in this testimony from the clearness of the principle, the power and efficacy of it in the exemplary sobriety, plainness, zeal, steadiness, humility, gravity, punctuality, charity, and circumspect care in the government of church affairs, which shined in his and their life and testimony that God employed in this work, it greatly confirmed me that it was of God, and engaged my soul in a deep love, fear, reverence, and thankfulness for his love and mercy therein to mankind; in which mind I remain, and shall, I hope, to the end of my days.

II. In his testimony or ministry he much laboured to open truth to the people's understandings, and to bottom them upon the principle and principal, Christ Jesus, the light of the world, that by bringing them to something that was of God in themselves, they might the better know and judge of him and themselves.

He had an extraordinary gift in opening the Scriptures. He would go to the marrow of things, and shew the mind, harmony, and fulfilling of them with much plainness, and to great comfort and edification.

The mystery of the first and second Adam, of the

fall and restoration, of the law and gospel, of
shadows and substance, of the servant and son's state,
and the fulfilling of the Scriptures in Christ, and by
Christ the true light, in all that are His, through the
obedience of faith, were much of the substance and
drift of his testimonies. In all which he was wit-
nessed to be of God, being sensibly felt to speak that
which he had received of Christ, and was his own
experience in that which never errs nor fails.

But above all he excelled in prayer. The inwardness and weight of his spirit, the reverence and solemnity of his address and behaviour, and the fewness
and fullness of his words, have often struck even
strangers with admiration, as they used to reach
others with consolation. The most awful, living,
reverent frame I ever felt or beheld, I must say, was
his in prayer. And truly it was a testimony he knew,
and lived nearer to the Lord than other men; for they
that know him most will see most reason to approach
him with reverence and fear.

He was of an innocent life, no busy-body, nor self-
seeker, neither touchy nor critical: what fell from
him was very inoffensive, if not very edifying. So
meek, contented, modest, easy, steady, tender, it was
a pleasure to be in his company. He exercised no
authority but over evil, and that everywhere and in
all; but with love, compassion, and long-suffering. A
most merciful man, as ready to forgive as unapt to
take or give offence. Thousands can truly say, he
was of an excellent spirit and savour among them,

and because thereof the most excellent spirits loved him with an unfeigned and unfading love.

He was an incessant labourer; for in his younger time, before his many great and deep sufferings and travels had enfeebled his body for itinerant services, he laboured much in the word and doctrine and discipline in England, Scotland, and Ireland, turning many to God, and confirming those that were convinced of the truth, and settling good order as to church affairs among them. And towards the conclusion of his travelling services, between the years seventy-one and seventy-seven, he visited the churches of Christ in the plantations in America, and in the United Provinces, and Germany, as his following Journal relates, to the convincement and consolation of many. After that time he chiefly resided in and about the city of London, and besides the services of his ministry, which were frequent, he wrote much both to them that are within and those that are without the communion. But the care he took of the affairs of the church in general was very great.

He was often where the records of the affairs of the church are kept, and the letters from the many meetings of God's people over all the world, where settled, come upon occasions; which letters he had read to him, and communicated them to the meeting that is weekly held there for such services; he would be sure to stir them up to discharge them, especially in suffering cases: showing great sympathy and compassion upon all such occasions, carefully looking

into the respective cases, and endeavouring speedy
relief according to the nature of them; so that the
churches and any of the suffering members thereof
were sure not to be forgotten or delayed in their
desires if he were there.

As he was unwearied, so he was undaunted in his
services for God and his people; he was no more to
be moved to fear than to wrath. His behaviour at
Derby, Litchfield, Appleby, before Oliver Cromwell
at Launceston, Scarborough, Worcester, and Westminster-hall, with many other places and exercises,
did abundantly evidence it to his enemies as well as
his friends.

But as in the primitive times some rose up against
the blessed apostles of our Lord Jesus Christ, even
from among those that they had turned to the hope
of the gospel, and who became their greatest trouble,
so this man of God had his share of suffering from
some that were convinced by him, who through prejudice or mistake ran against him as one that sought
dominion over conscience; because he pressed, by his
presence or epistles, a ready and zealous compliance
with such good and wholesome things as tended to an
orderly conversation about the affairs of the church,
and in their walking before men. That which con-
tributed much to this ill work, was in some a begrudg-
ing of this meek man the love and esteem he had and
deserved in the hearts of the people, and weakness in
others that were taken with their groundless suggestions of imposition and blind obedience.

They would have had every man independent, that
as he had the principle in himself, he should only
stand and fall to that and nobody else; not considering that the principle is one in all, and though the
measure of light or grace might differ, yet the nature
of it was the same, and being so they struck at the
spiritual unity, which a people guided by the same
principle are naturally led into: so that what is evil
to one is so to all, and what is virtuous, honest, and of
good report to one, is so to all, from the sense and
savour of the one universal principle which is common to all, and (which the disaffected profess to be)
the root of all true Christian fellowship, and that
spirit into which the people of God drink, and come
to be spiritually minded, and of one heart and one
soul.

Some weakly mistook good order in the government of church-affairs for discipline in worship, and
that it was so pressed or recommended by him and
other brethren; and they were ready to reflect the
same things that dissenters had very reasonably objected upon the national churches, that have coer-
cively pressed conformity to their respective creeds
and worships: whereas these things related wholly to
conversation, and the outward and (as I may say)
civil part of the church, that men should walk up to
the principles of their belief, and not be wanting in
care and charity. But though some have stumbled
and fallen through mistakes and an unreasonable
obstinacy, even to a prejudice, yet blessed be God, the

generality have returned to their first love, and seen
the work of the enemy, that loses no opportunity or
advantage by which he may check or hinder the work
of God, and disquiet the peace of His church, and
chill the love of His people to the truth, and one to
another; and there is hope of divers that are yet at
a distance.

In all these occasions, though there was no person the discontented struck so sharply at as this good
man, he bore all their weakness and prejudice, and
returned not reflection for reflection; but forgave
them their weak and bitter speeches, praying for
them that they might have a sense of their hurt, and
see the subtlety of the enemy to rend and divide, and
return into their first love that thought no ill.

And truly, I must say, that though God had visibly cloathed him with a divine preference and authority, and indeed his very presence expressed a religious
majesty, yet he never abused it, but held his place
in the church of God with great meekness, and a most
engaging humility and moderation. For upon all
occasions, like his blessed Master, he was a servant to
all, holding and exercising his eldership in the invisible power that had gathered them, with reverence to
the head and care over the body, and was received
only in that spirit and power of Christ, as the first
and chief elder in this age; who as he was therefore
worthy of double honour, so for the same reason it
was given by the faithful of this day; because his

authority was inward and not outward, and that he got it and kept it by the love of God and power of an endless life. I write my knowledge and not report, and my witness is true, having been with him for weeks and months together on divers occasions, and those of the nearest and most exercising nature, and that by night and by day, by sea and by land, in this and in foreign countries: and I can say I never saw him out of his place, or not a match for every service or occasion.

For in all things he acquitted himself like a man, yea a strong man, a new and heavenly-minded man. A divine, and a naturalist, and all of God Almighty's making. I have been surprised at his questions and answers in natural things, that whilst he was ignorant of useless and sophistical science, he had in him the foundation of useful and commendable knowledge, and cherished it everywhere. Civil beyond all forms of breeding in his behaviour; very temperate, eating little and sleeping less, though a bulky person.

Thus he lived and sojourned among us, and as he lived so he died, feeling the same eternal power that had raised and preserved him in his last moments. So full of assurance was he that he triumphed over death; and so even to the last, as if death were hardly worth notice or a mention: recommending to some with him the dispatch and dispersion of an epistle, just before written to the churches of Christ, throughout the world, and his own books; but above

all, friends, and of all friends those in Ireland and
America, twice over: saying, Mind poor friends in
Ireland and America.

And to some that came in and inquired how he
found himself, he answered, " Never heed, the
Lord's power is over all weakness and death, the Seed
reigns, blessed be the Lord ": which was about four
or five hours before his departure out of this world.
He was at the great meeting near Lombard Street on
the first day of the week, and it was the third following about ten at night when he left us, being at the
house of H. Goldney in the same court. In a good
old age he went, after having lived to see his children's children to several generations in the truth.
He had the comfort of a short illness, and the blessing of a clear sense to the last; and we may truly say
with a man of God of old, that " being dead, he yet
speaketh "; and though absent in body, he is present
in Spirit; neither time nor place being able to inter-
rupt the communion of saints, or dissolve the fellowship of the spirits of the just. His works praise him,
because they are to the praise of Him that worked
by him; for which his memorial is and shall be
blessed. I have done, as to this part of my preface,
when I have left this short epitaph to his name:
" Many sons have done virtuously in this day, but,
dear George, thou excellest them all."

CHAPTER I.

𝔅𝔬𝔶𝔥𝔬𝔬𝔡 — 𝔄 𝔖𝔢𝔢𝔨𝔢𝔯.

1624–1648.

That all may know the dealings of the Lord with me, and the various exercises, trials, and troubles through which He led me, in order to prepare and fit me for the work unto which He had appointed me, and may thereby be drawn to admire and glorify His infinite wisdom and goodness, I think fit (before I proceed to set forth my public travels in the service of Truth) briefly to mention how it was with me in my youth, and how the work of the Lord was begun, and gradually carried on in me, even from my child-hood.

I was born in the month called July, 1624, at Drayton-in-the-Clay,[1] in Leicestershire. My father's name was Christopher Fox; he was by profession a weaver, an honest man; and there was a Seed of God in him. The neighbours called him Righteous Chris-

---

[1] Now called Fenny Drayton; a little hamlet about five miles from Nuneaton, in a flat, though beautiful farming country. The house in which George Fox was born has long since vanished, and the few cottages which cluster here about the crossing of two roads are of modern structure. An obelisk, with a long inscription, stands within a hundred yards or so of the site of the birthplace.

ter. My mother was an upright woman; her maiden
name was Mary Lago, of the family of the Lagos, and
of the stock of the martyrs.[2]

In my very young years I had a gravity and
stayedness of mind and spirit not usual in children;
insomuch that when I saw old men behave lightly
and wantonly towards each other, I had a dislike
thereof raised in my heart, and said within myself,
" If ever I come to be a man, surely I shall not do
so, nor be so wanton."

When I came to eleven years of age I knew pureness and righteousness; for while a child I was taught
how to walk to be kept pure. The Lord taught me to
be faithful in all things, and to act faithfully two
ways, viz., inwardly, to God, and outwardly, to man;
and to keep to Yea and Nay in all things. For the
Lord showed me that, though the people of the world
have mouths full of deceit, and changeable words,
yet I was to keep to Yea and Nay in all things; and
that my words should be few and savoury, seasoned
with grace; and that I might not eat and drink to
make myself wanton, but for health, using the creatures[3] in their service, as servants in their places,
to the glory of Him that created them.

---

[2] This martyred ancestor of Mary Lago was probably
a member of the Glover family, of Mancetter, a few
miles north of Drayton. (See article on Fox in Dict.
of Nat. Biog., which refers to Riching's " Mancetter
Martyrs," 1860.)

[3] " Creatures " here and frequently means " created
things."

As I grew up, my relations thought to have made me a priest,[4] but others persuaded to the contrary. Whereupon I was put to a man who was a shoe-maker [5] by trade, and dealt in wool. He also used grazing, and sold cattle; and a great deal went through my hands. While I was with him he was blessed, but after I left him he broke and came to nothing.

I never wronged man or woman in all that time; for the Lord's power was with me and over me, to preserve me. While I was in that service I used in my dealings the word Verily, and it was a common saying among those that knew me, " If George says verily, there is no altering him." When boys and rude persons would laugh at me, I let them alone and went my way; but people had generally a love to me for my innocency and honesty.

---

[4] " Priest " here means clergyman in the established Church, though the " priests " with whom he comes in contact in the early years of his ministry are Presbyterian. The word is usually employed for any minister who receives pay for preaching.

[5] This brief connection with shoemaking has been effectively used by Carlyle in his famous characterization of George Fox. (See " Sartor Resartus," book iii., chapter 1: " An Incident in Modern History.") There is, however, no historical foundation for Carlyle's picture. Sewel denies that there was any connection between Fox's suit of leather and " his former leather-work." Croese says the shoemaker and cattle grazer lived in Nottingham.

When I came towards nineteen years of age, being upon business at a fair, one of my cousins, whose name was Bradford, having another professor [6] with him, came and asked me to drink part of a jug of beer with them. I, being thirsty, went in with them, for I loved any who had a sense of good, or that sought after the Lord.

When we had drunk a glass apiece, they began to drink healths, and called for more drink, agreeing together that he that would not drink should pay all. I was grieved that any who made profession of religion should offer to do so. They grieved me very much, having never had such a thing put to me before by any sort of people. Wherefore I rose up, and, putting my hand in my pocket, took out a groat, and laid it upon the table before them, saying, " If it be so, I will leave you."

So I went away; and when I had done my business returned home; but did not go to bed that night, nor could I sleep, but sometimes walked up and down, and sometimes prayed and cried to the Lord, who said unto me: " Thou seest how young people go together into vanity, and old people into the earth; thou must forsake all, young and old, keep out of all, and be as a stranger unto all."

Then, at the command of God, the ninth of the Seventh month, 1643, I left my relations, and broke off

---

[6] " Professor " means here and everywhere throughout this book a nominal Christian. Our modern substitute for the expression would be " a church member."

all familiarity or fellowship with young or old. I passed to Lutterworth, where I stayed some time. From thence I went to Northampton, where also I made some stay; then passed to Newport-Pagnel, whence, after I had stayed awhile, I went to Barnet, in the Fourth month, called June,[7] in the year 1644.

As I thus traveled through the country, professors took notice of me, and sought to be acquainted with me; but I was afraid of them, for I was sensible they did not possess what they professed.

During the time I was at Barnet a strong temptation to despair came upon me. I then saw how Christ was tempted, and mighty troubles I was in. Sometimes I kept myself retired to my chamber, and often walked solitary in the Chase to wait upon the Lord. I wondered why these things should come to me. I looked upon myself, and said, " Was I ever so before ? " Then I thought, because I had forsaken my relations I had done amiss against them.

So I was brought to call to mind all my time that I had spent, and to consider whether I had wronged any; but temptations grew more and more, and I was tempted almost to despair; and when Satan could not effect his design upon me that way, he laid snares and baits to draw me to commit some sin, whereof he might take advantage to bring me to despair.

---

[7] Until 1752 the English year began in March, so that by the calendar then in use June was the fourth month. This method of reckoning time runs through the entire book, and may be mentioned here once for all.

I was about twenty years of age when these exercises came upon me; and some years I continued in
that condition, in great trouble; and fain I would
have put it from me. I went to many a priest to
look for comfort, but found no comfort from them.

From Barnet I went to London, where I took a
lodging, and was under great misery and trouble
there; for I looked upon the great professors of the
city of London, and saw all was dark and under the
chain of darkness. I had an uncle there, one Pickering, a Baptist; the Baptists were tender [8] then; yet
I could not impart my mind to him, nor join with
them; for I saw all, young and old, where they were.
Some tender people would have had me stay, but
I was fearful, and returned homeward into Leicestershire, having a regard upon my mind to my parents
and relations, lest I should grieve them, for I understood they were troubled at my absence.

Being returned [9] into Leicestershire, my relations
would have had me married; but I told them I was but
a lad, and must get wisdom. Others would have had
me join the auxiliary band among the soldiery,* but

* The Civil War was at its height.

---

[8] " Tender " is one of George Fox's favorite words.
It will come often. It means that the persons to whom
it is applied are religiously inclined, serious, and
earnest in their search for spiritual realities.

[9] From his return home in 1644, George Fox dates
the beginning of his religious society. (See *Epistles*,
Vol. I., p. 10. Philadelphia edition, 1831.)

I refused, and was grieved that they offered such things to me, being a tender youth. Then I went to Coventry, where I took a chamber for awhile at a professor's house, till people began to be acquainted with me, for there were many tender people in that town. After some time I went into my own country again, and continued about a year, in great sorrow and trouble, and walked many nights by myself.

Then the priest of Drayton, the town of my birth, whose name was Nathaniel Stephens, came often to me, and I went often to him; and another priest sometimes came with him; and they would give place to me, to hear me; and I would ask them questions, and reason with them. This priest, Stephens, asked me why Christ cried out upon the cross, " My God, my God, why hast thou forsaken me?" and why He said, " If it be possible, let this cup pass from me; yet not my will, but thine, be done"? I told him that at that time the sins of all mankind were upon Him, and their iniquities and transgressions, with which He was wounded; which He was to bear, and to be an offering for, as He was man; but died not, as He was God; so, in that He died for all men, tasting death for every man, He was an offering for the sins of the whole world.

This I spoke, being at that time in a measure sensible of Christ's sufferings. The priest said it was a very good, full answer, and such a one as he had not heard. At that time he would applaud and speak highly of me to others; and what I said in discourse to him on week-days, he would preach of on First-days,[10] which gave me a dislike to him. This priest afterwards became my great persecutor.

After this I went to another ancient priest* at Mancetter, in Warwickshire, and reasoned with him about the ground of despair and temptations. But he was ignorant of my condition; he bade me take tobacco and sing psalms. Tobacco was a thing I did not love, and psalms I was not in a state to sing; I could not sing. He bade me come again, and he would tell me many things; but when I came he was angry and pettish, for my former words had displeased him. He told my troubles, sorrows, and griefs to his servants, so that it got out among the milk-lasses. It grieved me that I should have opened my mind to such a one. I saw they were all miserable comforters, and this increased my troubles upon me. I heard of a priest living about Tamworth, who was accounted an experienced man. I went seven miles to him, but found him like an empty, hollow cask.

I heard also of one called Dr. Cradock, of Cov-

* Richard Abell.

---

[10] It was a settled custom, in fact, a matter of conscience with Fox, to avoid the names of the days and of the months. He disliked them because they commemorated heathen divinities, and he always makes a point of using numeral adjectives instead of the names. It was not an original scruple with him, but a similar position was taken by some of the leading " Separatists " before the Commonwealth period. (See Barrow's " False Churches," p. 204.)

entry, and went to him. I asked him the ground of temptations and despair, and how troubles came to be wrought in man? He asked me, " Who were Christ's father and mother?" I told him, Mary was His mother, and that He was supposed to be the Son of Joseph, but He was the Son of God.

Now, as we were walking together in his garden, the alley being narrow, I chanced, in turning, to set my foot on the side of a bed, at which the man was in a rage, as if his house had been on fire. Thus all our discourse was lost, and I went away in sorrow, worse than I was when I came. I thought them miserable comforters, and saw they were all as nothing to me, for they could not reach my condition.

After this I went to another, one Macham,* a priest in high account. He would needs give me some physic, and I was to have been let blood; but they could not get one drop of blood from me, either in arms or head (though they endeavoured to do so), my body being, as it were, dried up with sorrows, grief and troubles, which were so great upon me that I could have wished I had never been born, or that I had been born blind, that I might never have seen wickedness or vanity; and deaf, that I might never have heard vain and wicked words, or the Lord's name blasphemed.

When the time called Christmas came, while others were feasting and sporting themselves I looked out poor widows from house to house, and gave them some money. When I was invited to marriages (as

* Of Atherstone.

I sometimes was), I went to none at all; but the next
day, or soon after, I would go and visit them, and if
they were poor I gave them some money; for I had
wherewith both to keep myself from being chargeable to others and to administer something to the ne-
cessities of those who were in need.[11]

About the beginning of the year 1646, as I was
going to Coventry, and approaching towards the gate,
a consideration arose in me, how it was said that
" All Christians are believers, both Protestants
and Papists "; and the Lord opened [12] to me that
if all were believers, then they were all born of God,
and passed from death to life; and that none were
true believers but such; and, though others said they
were believers, yet they were not. At another time,
as I was walking in a field on a First-day morning,

---

[11] It is difficult to find out where George Fox's money
came from. He reports in the original MS. of the
Journal, p. 17, a remark his relatives made about him
when he left home: " When hee went from us hee had
a greate deale of gould and sillver about him." He is
always well supplied. He goes to inns, always has a
good horse, wears clean linen and frequently gives to
charity. In signed papers in the Spence collection he
gives orders for the disposal of money invested " in
ships and trade," as well as of a thousand acres of land
in Pennsylvania which William Penn had assigned to
him.

[12] This expression " opened " has a mystical import,
and will be of frequent occurrence. He means to say
that it was directly revealed in his soul so that he as-

the Lord opened unto me that being bred at Oxford
or Cambridge was not enough to fit and qualify men
to be ministers of Christ; and I wondered at it, because it was the common belief of people. But I saw
it clearly as the Lord opened it unto me, and was
satisfied, and admired the goodness of the Lord, who
had opened this thing unto me that morning. This
struck at priest Stephens's ministry, namely, that "to
be bred at Oxford or Cambridge was not enough to
make a man fit to be a minister of Christ." So that
which opened in me I saw struck at the priest's ministry.

But my relations were much troubled that
I would not go with them to hear the priest; for I
would go into the orchard or the fields, with my Bible,
by myself. I asked them, "Did not the Apostle say
to believers that they needed no man to teach them,
but as the anointing teacheth them?" Though they
knew this was Scripture, and that it was true, yet
they were grieved because I could not be subject in
this matter, to go to hear the priest with them. I saw
that to be a true believer was another thing than they
looked upon it to be; and I saw that being bred at
Oxford or Cambridge did not qualify or fit a man to

---

suredly knew it to be true. Often he uses the expression in reference to some truth which he might easily
have discovered in the Scriptures or have learned from
contemporary sources. But in this solemn way he an-
nounces that this truth has now at length come to be a
living truth for him. It is no longer a mere statement
of fact—it is a principle, the truth of which he *sees*.

be a minister of Christ; what then should I follow such for? So neither them, nor any of the dissenting people, could I join with; but was as a stranger to all, relying wholly upon the Lord Jesus Christ.

At another time it was opened in me that God, who made the world, did not dwell in temples made with hands. This at first seemed a strange word, because both priests and people used to call their temples, or churches, dreadful places, holy ground, and the temples of God. But the Lord showed me clearly that He did not dwell in these temples which men had commanded and set up, but in people's hearts; for both Stephen and the apostle Paul bore testimony that He did not dwell in temples made with hands, not even in that which He had once commanded to be built, since He put an end to it; but that His people were His temple, and He dwelt in them.

This opened in me as I walked in the fields to my relations' house. When I came there they told me that Nathaniel Stephens, the priest, had been there, and told them he was afraid of me, for going after new lights. I smiled in myself, knowing what the Lord had opened in me concerning him and his brethren; but I told not my relations, who, though they saw beyond the priests, yet went to hear them, and were grieved because I would not go also. But I brought them Scriptures,* and told them there was an anointing within man to teach him, and that the Lord would teach His people Himself.

* That is, gave them Scripture references.

I had also great openings concerning the things
written in the Revelations; and when I spoke of
them the priests and professors would say that
was a sealed book, and would have kept me out
of it. But I told them Christ could open the
seals, and that they were the nearest things to
us; for the epistles were written to the saints that
lived in former ages, but the Revelations were written of things to come.

After this I met with a sort of people that held
women have no souls, (adding in a light manner), No
more than a goose.[13] But I reproved them, and told
them that was not right; for Mary said, " My soul
doth magnify the Lord, and my spirit hath rejoiced in
God my Saviour."

Removing to another place, I came among a people
that relied much on dreams. I told them, except
they could distinguish between dream and dream,
they would confound all together; for there were
three sorts of dreams; multitude of business sometimes caused dreams, and there were whisperings of
Satan in man in the night season; and there were
speakings of God to man in dreams. But these people came out of these things, and at last became
Friends.[14]

Now, though I had great openings, yet great trouble and temptation came many times upon me; so

[13] This was one of the many curious religious sects
with which the England of the Commonwealth was
overrun. (See Edwards's " Gangræna.")

[14] " Friends " is here used for the first time in the

that when it was day I wished for night, and when it
was night I wished for day; and by reason of the
openings I had in my troubles, I could say as David
said, " Day unto day uttereth speech, and night unto
night showeth knowledge." When I had openings
they answered one another and answered the Scriptures; for I had great openings of the Scriptures:
and when I was in troubles, one trouble also answered
to another.

About the beginning of the year 1647 I was moved
of the Lord to go into Derbyshire, where I met with
some friendly people, and had many discourses with
them. Then, passing into the Peak country,[15] I met
with more friendly people, and with some in empty
high notions.[16] Travelling through some parts of
Leicestershire, and into Nottinghamshire, I met with
a tender people, and a very tender woman, whose

Journal as the name of the new denomination. It is
not possible to determine when the name was adopted
or why it was chosen. When the Journal was written
the term had already become fixed and Fox uses it
without comment or explanation, referring it back to
a period before it came into use as the name of the
Society. At first the word " friends " was probably
used in an untechnical sense for those who were
friendly, and little by little it hardened into a name.
At the very beginning they called themselves " Children of the Light."

[15] In the northern part of Derbyshire.

[16] These were " Ranters " who will appear again and
often. They claimed to be perfect and above the possibility of sinning. Some even went to the wild extreme

name was Elizabeth Hooton.[17] With these I had some meetings and discourses; but my troubles continued, and I was often under great temptations.

I fasted much, walked abroad in solitary places many days, and often took my Bible, and sat in hollow trees and lonesome places till night came on; and frequently in the night walked mournfully about by myself; for I was a man of sorrows in the time of the first workings of the Lord in me.

During all this time I was never joined in profession of religion with any, but gave up myself to the Lord, having forsaken all evil company, taken leave of father and mother, and all other relations, and travelled up and down as a stranger in the earth, which way the Lord inclined my heart; taking a chamber to myself in the town where I came, and tarrying, sometimes more, sometimes less, in a place. For I durst not stay long in a place, being afraid both

---

of claiming to be Christ, or God. They went on living for the most part much as they chose, and justified their acts on the ground that it was God who was acting in them. It is clearly apparent from this autobiography that such persons were very numerous at the time. It will be noticed that George Fox believes also in the possibility of freedom from sin, but perfection as he holds it means something quite other than this doctrine of the Ranters, as the Journal will show.

[17] Elizabeth Hooton was a woman of good standing, who was born in Nottingham about the year 1600. She was the first person of her sex to become a minister in the newly-gathered Society. The preaching of women

of professor and profane, lest, being a tender young man, I should be hurt by conversing much with either. For this reason I kept much as a stranger, seeking heavenly wisdom and getting knowledge from the Lord, and was brought off from outward things to rely on the Lord alone.

Though my exercises and troubles were very great, yet were they not so continual but that I had some intermissions, and I was sometimes brought into such an heavenly joy that I thought I had been in Abraham's bosom.

As I cannot declare the misery I was in, it was so great and heavy upon me, so neither can I set forth the mercies of God unto me in all my misery. O the everlasting love of God to my soul, when I was in great distress! When my troubles and torments were great, then was His love exceeding great. Thou, Lord, makest a fruitful field a barren wilderness, and a barren wilderness a fruitful field! Thou bringest down and settest up! Thou killest and makest alive! all honour and glory be to thee, O Lord of Glory! The knowledge of Thee in the Spirit is life; but that knowledge which is fleshly works death.[18]

---

at this time was not entirely novel, as it was allowed by several of the religious sects of the period. Elizabeth Hooton had her faith severely tested by persecution and long imprisonment. She performed two religious visits to America and the West Indies and died in Jamaica in 1671.

[18] All profound spiritual teachers contrast *wisdom* and *knowledge*—what is here called " knowledge in the

While there is this knowledge in the flesh, deceit and self will conform to anything, and will say Yes, Yes, to that it doth not know. The knowledge which the world hath of what the prophets and apostles spake, is a fleshly knowledge; and the apostates from the life in which the prophets and apostles were have got their words, the Holy Scriptures, in a form, but not in the life nor spirit that gave them forth. So they all lie in confusion; and are making provision for the flesh, to fulfil the lusts thereof, but not to fulfil the law and command of Christ in His power and Spirit. For that they say they cannot do; but to fulfil the lusts of the flesh, that they can do with delight.

Now, after I had received that opening from the Lord, that to be bred at Oxford or Cambridge was not sufficient to fit a man to be a minister of Christ, I regarded the priests less, and looked more after the Dissenting people.* Among them I saw there

* The "Separatists"—especially here the Congregationalists and Baptists.

Spirit" and "knowledge in the flesh," or, what is perhaps more frequently called "knowledge of the heart" and "knowledge of the head." The latter expression means a knowledge of fact—the knowing that a thing is so by evidence which satisfies the mind. The former expression means the soul's immediate grasp of truth by the test of practical experience. The goal in one case is the establishment of some fact; the goal in the other case is the production of positive life and character by the appreciation of the truth.

was some tenderness; and many of them came afterwards to be convinced, for they had some openings.

But as I had forsaken the priests, so I left the separate preachers also, and those esteemed the most experienced people; for I saw there was none among them all that could speak to my condition. When all my hopes in them and in all men were gone, so that I had nothing outwardly to help me, nor could I tell what to do, then, oh, then, I heard a voice which said, " There is one, even Christ Jesus, that can speak to thy condition "; [19] and when I heard it, my heart did leap for joy.

Then the Lord let me see why there was none upon the earth that could speak to my condition, namely, that I might give Him all the glory. For all are concluded under sin, and shut up in unbelief, as I had been; that Jesus Christ might have the pre-eminence, who enlightens, and gives grace, and faith, and power. Thus when God doth work, who shall hinder it? and *this I knew experimentally.*

My desire after the Lord grew stronger, and zeal in the pure knowledge of God, and of Christ alone, without the help of any man, book, or writing. For though I read the Scriptures that spoke of Christ and of God, yet I knew Him not, but by revelation, as He

---

[19] Compare this great passage where George Fox describes his conversion with Paul's account of the spiritual *fiat lux* in 2 Cor. 4: 6, " For God who commanded the light to shine out of darkness [the first *fiat lux*] *hath shined in our hearts* to give the light of the knowledge of the glory of God in the face of Jesus Christ."

who hath the key did open, and as the Father of Life drew me to His Son by His Spirit. Then the Lord gently led me along, and let me see His love, which was endless and eternal, surpassing all the knowledge that men have in the natural state, or can obtain from history or books; and that love let me see myself, as I was without Him.

I was afraid of all company, for I saw them perfectly where they were, through the love of God, which let me see myself. I had not fellowship with any people, priests or professors, or any sort of separated people, but with Christ, who hath the key, and opened the door of Light and Life unto me. I was afraid of all carnal talk and talkers, for I could see nothing but corruptions, and the life lay under the burthen of corruptions.

When I myself was in the deep, shut up under all, I could not believe that I should ever overcome; my troubles, my sorrows, and my temptations were so great that I thought many times I should have despaired, I was so tempted. But when Christ opened to me how He was tempted by the same devil, and overcame him and bruised his head, and that through Him and His power, light, grace, and Spirit, I should overcome also, I had confidence in Him; so He it was that opened to me when I was shut up and had no hope nor faith. Christ, who had enlightened me, gave me His light to believe in; He gave me hope, which He Himself revealed in me, and He gave me His Spirit and grace, which I found sufficient in the deeps and in weakness.

Thus, in the deepest miseries, and in the greatest sorrows and temptations, that many times beset me, the Lord in His mercy did keep me.

I found that there were two thirsts in me—the one after the creatures, to get help and strength there, and the other after the Lord, the Creator, and His Son Jesus Christ. I saw all the world could do me no good; if I had had a king's diet, palace, and attendance, all would have been as nothing; for nothing gave me comfort but the Lord by His power. At another time I saw the great love of God, and was filled with admiration at the infiniteness of it.

One day, when I had been walking solitarily abroad, and was come home, I was taken up in the love of God, so that I could not but admire the greatness of His love; and while I was in that condition, it was opened unto me by the eternal light and power, and I therein clearly saw that all was done and to be done in and by Christ, and how He conquers and destroys this tempter the devil, and all his works, and is atop of him; and that all these troubles were good for me, and temptations for the trial of my faith, which Christ had given me.

The Lord opened me, that I saw all through these troubles and temptations. My living faith was raised, that I saw all was done by Christ the life, and my belief was in Him.

When at any time my condition was veiled, my secret belief was stayed firm, and hope underneath held me, as an anchor in the bottom of the sea, and anchored my immortal soul to its Bishop, causing it to

swim above the sea, the world, where all the raging
waves, foul weather, tempests and temptations are.
But O! then did I see my troubles, trials, and temptations more clearly than ever I had done. As the
light appeared all appeared that is out of the light;
darkness, death, temptations, the unrighteous, the
ungodly; all was manifest and seen in the light.

I heard of a woman in Lancashire that had fasted
two and twenty days, and I travelled to see her; but
when I came to her I saw that she was under a temptation. When I had spoken to her what I had from
the Lord, I left her, her father being one high in profession.

Passing on, I went among the professors at
Duckingfield and Manchester, where I stayed awhile,
and declared truth among them. There were some
convinced who received the Lord's teaching, by which
they were confirmed and stood in the truth. But the
professors were in a rage, all pleading for sin and imperfection, and could not endure to hear talk of perfection, and of a holy and sinless life.[20] But the

---

[20] At the very beginning of his ministry in 1647
George Fox evidently preached the possibility of complete freedom from sin. But he was very careful to
avoid presenting the mere theory or "notion" of perfection, which was common among all the types of
"Ranters." He believed that Christ came to destroy
sin, and he stoutly held that when He ruled in a man
sin and the dominion of it were done away. Man
could come into "the condition Adam was in before he
fell," to use his own expression. One of his most frequent challenges was to demand that modern Chris-

Lord's power was over all, though they were chained under darkness and sin, which they pleaded for, and quenched the tender thing in them.

About this time there was a great meeting of the Baptists, at Broughton, in Leicestershire, with some that had separated from them, and people of other notions went thither, and I went also. Not many of the Baptists came, but many others were there. The Lord opened my mouth, and the everlasting truth was declared amongst them, and the power of the Lord was over them all. For in that day the Lord's power began to spring, and I had great openings in the Scriptures. Several were convinced in those parts and were turned from darkness to light, from the power of Satan unto God, and many were raised up to praise God. When I reasoned with professors and other people, some became convinced.

I went back into Nottinghamshire, and there the Lord showed me that the natures of those things, which were hurtful without, were within, in the hearts and minds of wicked men. The natures of dogs, swine, vipers, of Sodom and Egypt, Pharaoh, Cain, Ishmael, Esau, etc.; the natures of these I saw within, though people had been looking without. I cried to the Lord, saying, "Why should I be thus,*

* That is, why should I have suffered such troubles and temptations.

---

tians should come into "the same life and power which those were in who gave forth the Scriptures." But George Fox's test of holiness was the practical test of daily life. No man was to be accounted holy if he were not *in fact* holy.

seeing I was never addicted to commit those evils?" and the Lord answered, "That it was needful I should have a sense of all conditions, how else should I speak to all conditions!" and in this I saw the infinite love of God.

I saw, also, that there was an ocean of darkness and death; but an infinite ocean of light and love, which flowed over the ocean of darkness. In that also I saw the infinite love of God, and I had great openings.

Then came people from far and near to see me; but I was fearful of being drawn out by them; yet I was made to speak, and open things to them. There was one Brown, who had great prophecies and sights upon his death-bed of me. He spoke only of what I should be made instrumental by the Lord to bring forth. And of others he spoke, that they should come to nothing, which was fulfilled on some, who then were something in show.

When this man was buried a great work of the Lord fell upon me, to the admiration of many, who thought I had been dead, and many came to see me for about fourteen days. I was very much altered in countenance and person, as if my body had been new moulded or changed.[21]

---

[21] For those who are interested in the psychology of George Fox this is one of the most important passages in the Journal. These sweeping psychical and physical changes are most significant. On two other occasions of his life, which will be noted later, he underwent similar, though perhaps profounder, changes.

My sorrows and troubles began to wear off, and
tears of joy dropped from me, so that I could have
wept night and day with tears of joy to the Lord,
in humility and brokenness of heart.

I saw into that which was without end, things
which cannot be uttered, and of the greatness and in-
finitude of the love of God, which cannot be expressed by words. For I had been brought through
the very ocean of darkness and death, and through
and over the power of Satan, by the eternal, glorious
power of Christ; even through that darkness was I
brought, which covered over all the world, and which
chained down all and shut up all in death. The same
eternal power of God, which brought me through
these things, was that which afterwards shook the
nations, priests, professors and people.

Then could I say I had been in spiritual Baby-
lon, Sodom, Egypt, and the grave; but by the
eternal power of God I was come out of it,
and was brought over it, and the power of it, into the
power of Christ. I saw the harvest white, and the
seed of God lying thick in the ground, as ever did
wheat that was sown outwardly, and none to gather
it; for this I mourned with tears.

A report went abroad of me, that I was a young
man that had a discerning spirit; whereupon many

These passages in the Journal reveal, to those who are
familiar with such phenomena, the fact that George
Fox was subject to deep subliminal transformations.
The passage, too, throws much light back upon his long
travail through distress and darkness.

came to me, from far and near, professors, priests, and people. The Lord's power broke forth, and I had great openings and prophecies, and spoke unto them of the things of God, which they heard with attention and silence, and went away and spread the fame thereof.

Then came the tempter and set upon me again, charging me that I had sinned against the Holy Ghost; but I could not tell in what. Then Paul's condition came before me, how after he had been taken up into the third heaven, and seen things not lawful to be uttered, a messenger of Satan was sent to buffet him. Thus by the power of Christ I got over that temptation also.

CHAPTER II.

The First Years of Ministry

1648-1649.

After this* I went to Mansfield, where was a great meeting of professors and people. Here I was moved to pray; and the Lord's power was so great that the house seemed to be shaken. When I had done, some of the professors said it was now as in the days of the apostles, when the house was shaken where they were.[1] After I had prayed, one of the professors would pray, which brought deadness and a veil over them; and others of the professors were grieved at him and told him it was a temptation upon him. Then he came to me, and desired that I would pray again; but I could not pray in man's will.

Soon after there was another great meeting of professors, and a captain, whose name was Amor Stoddard, came in. They were discoursing of the blood of Christ; and as they were discoursing of it, I saw,

* In the year 1648.

---

[1] William Penn gives the following testimony to Fox's power in prayer:

"But above all he excelled in prayer. The inwardness and weight of his spirit, the reverence and solemnity of his address and behaviour, and the fewness and fulness of his words, have often struck, even strangers, with admiration, as they used to reach others

through the immediate opening of the invisible Spirit,
the blood of Christ. And I cried out among them,
and said, " Do ye not see the blood of Christ? See
it in your hearts, to sprinkle your hearts and consciences from dead works, to serve the living God";
for I saw it, the blood of the New Covenant, how it
came into the heart.[2]

This startled the professors, who would have the
blood only without them, and not in them. But
Captain Stoddard was reached, and said, " Let the
youth speak; hear the youth speak "; when he saw
they endeavoured to bear me down with many words.

There was also a company of priests, that were
looked upon to be tender; one of their names was
Kellett; and several people that were tender went to
hear them. I was moved to go after them, and bid
them mind the Lord's teaching in their inward parts.
That priest Kellett was against parsonages then; but
afterwards he got a great one, and turned a persecutor.

Now, after I had had some service in these parts,
I went through Derbyshire into my own county,

---

with consolation. The most awful, living, reverent
frame I ever felt or beheld, I must say, was his in
prayer. And truly it was a testimony he knew and
lived nearer to the Lord than other men."—Preface to
George Fox's " Journal."

[2] This is a characteristic illustration of the way Fox
passed beyond theories and doctrines, and demanded
practical *life-results.*

Leicestershire, again, and several tender people were convinced.

Passing thence, I met with a great company of professors in Warwickshire, who were praying, and expounding the Scriptures in the fields. They gave the Bible to me, and I opened it on the fifth of Matthew, where Christ expounded the law; and I opened the inward state to them, and the outward state; upon which they fell into a fierce contention, and so parted; but the Lord's power got ground.

Then I heard of a great meeting to be at Leicester, for a dispute, wherein Presbyterians, Independents, Baptists and Common-prayer-men * were said to be all concerned. The meeting was in a steeple-house; and thither I was moved by the Lord God to go, and be amongst them. I heard their discourse and reasonings, some being in pews, and the priest in the pulpit; abundance of people being gathered together.

At last one woman asked a question out of Peter, What that birth was, viz., a being born again of incorruptible seed, by the Word of God, that liveth and abideth for ever? And the priest said to her, " I permit not a woman to speak in the church "; though he had before given liberty for any to speak. Whereupon I was wrapped up, as in a rapture, in the Lord's power; and I stepped up and asked the priest, " Dost thou call this (the steeple-house) a church? Or dost thou call this mixed multitude a church?" For the woman asking a question, he ought to have answered it, having given liberty for any to speak.

But, instead of answering me, he asked me what a

* That is, members of the English or Episcopal Church.

church was? I told him the church was the pillar
and ground of truth, made up of living stones, living
members, a spiritual household, which Christ was the
head of; but he was not the head of a mixed multitude, or of an old house made up of lime, stones and
wood.[3]

This set them all on fire. The priest came down
from his pulpit, and others out of their pews,
and the dispute there was marred. I went to a great
inn, and there disputed the thing with the priests and
professors, who were all on fire. But I maintained
the true church, and the true head thereof, over their
heads, till they all gave out and fled away. One man
seemed loving, and appeared for a while to join with
me; but he soon turned against me, and joined with
a priest in pleading for infant-baptism, though himself had been a Baptist before; so he left me alone.
Howbeit, there were several convinced that day; the
woman that asked the question was convinced, and
her family; and the Lord's power and glory shone
over all.

After this I returned into Nottinghamshire again,
and went into the Vale of Beavor.[4] As I went, I

---

[3] The Friends from the time of Fox until the present
have been careful to use the word "church" only for
the community of spiritual believers. The cathedrals
and churches were called "steeple-houses," and their
own places of worship were called "meeting-houses."

[4] A beautiful valley southwest of Nottingham, near
the edge of the counties of Nottinghamshire and Leicestershire, just west of Bardon Hills.

preached repentance to the people. There were many
convinced in the Vale of Beavor, in many towns; for
I stayed some weeks amongst them.

One morning, as I was sitting by the fire,
a great cloud came over me, and a temptation
beset me; and I sat still. It was said, " All
things come by nature "; and the elements and
stars came over me, so that I was in a manner quite
clouded with it. But as I sat still and said nothing,
the people of the house perceived nothing. And as I
sat still under it and let it alone, a living hope and a
true voice arose in me, which said, " There is a living God who made all things." [5] Immediately the
cloud and temptation vanished away, and life rose
over it all; my heart was glad, and I praised the living God.

After some time I met with some people who
had a notion that there was no God, but that all
things come by nature. I had a great dispute with
them, and overturned them, and made some of them
confess that there is a living God. Then I saw that
it was good that I had gone through that exercise.*
We had great meetings in those parts; for the power
of the Lord broke through in that side of the country.

Returning into Nottinghamshire, I found there
a company of shattered Baptists, and others. The
Lord's power wrought mightily, and gathered many
of them. Afterwards I went to Mansfield and there-

* He means experience.

---

[5] See Whittier's poem, " Revelation."

away, where the Lord's power was wonderfully manifested both at Mansfield and other towns thereabouts.

In Derbyshire the mighty power of God wrought in a wonderful manner. At Eton, a town near Derby, there was a meeting of Friends,[c] where appeared such a mighty power of God that they were greatly shaken, and many mouths were opened in the power of the Lord God. Many were moved by the Lord to go to steeple-houses, to the priests and people, to declare the everlasting truth unto them.

At a certain time, when I was at Mansfield, there was a sitting of the justices about hiring of servants; and it was upon me from the Lord to go and speak to the justices, that they should not oppress the servants in their wages. So I walked towards the inn where they sat; but finding a company of fiddlers there, I did not go in, but thought to come in the morning, when I might have a more serious opportunity to discourse with them.

But when I came in the morning, they were gone, and I was struck even blind, that I could not see. I inquired of the innkeeper where the justices were to sit that day; and he told me, at a town eight miles off.

---

[c] There is no account of the origin of this meeting, which seems to have been in existence before Fox came to Eton. There seems to have been considerable definite work done which is not detailed in the " Journal." [See " Epistles," Vol. I., page 2, " Truth sprang up (to us as to be a people of the Lord) in Derbyshire in 1647."] Eton is in Derbyshire.

My sight began to come to me again; and I went and ran thitherward as fast as I could. When I was come to the house where they were, and many servants with them, I exhorted the justices not to oppress the servants in their wages, but to do that which was right and just to them; and I exhorted the servants to do their duties, and serve honestly.[7] They all received my exhortation kindly; for I was moved of the Lord therein.

Moreover, I was moved to go to several courts and steeple-houses at Mansfield, and other places, to warn them to leave off oppression and oaths, and to turn from deceit to the Lord, and to do justly. Particularly at Mansfield, after I had been at a court there, I was moved to go and speak to one of the most wicked men in the country, one who was a common drunkard, a noted whore-master, and a rhyme-maker; and I reproved him in the dread of the mighty God, for his evil courses.

When I had done speaking, and left him, he came after me, and told me that he was so smitten when I spoke to him, that he had scarcely any strength left in him. So this man was convinced, and turned from his wickedness, and remained an honest, sober man, to the astonishment of the people who had known him before.

Thus the work of the Lord went forward, and many were turned from the darkness to the light,

---

[7] This is an interesting illustration of Fox's sensitiveness to wrong social conditions and of the practical character of his religion.

within the compass of these three years, 1646, 1647 and 1648. Divers meetings of Friends, in several places, were then gathered to God's teaching, by his light, Spirit, and power; for the Lord's power broke forth more and more wonderfully.

Now I was come up in spirit through the flaming sword, into the paradise of God. All things were new; and all the creation gave unto me another smell than before, beyond what words can utter. I knew nothing but pureness, and innocency, and righteousness; being renewed into the image of God by Christ Jesus, to the state of Adam, which he was in before he fell. The creation was opened to me; and it was showed me how all things had their names given them according to their nature and virtue.

I was at a stand in my mind whether I should practise physic for the good of mankind, seeing the nature and virtues of things were so opened to me by the Lord. But I was immediately taken up in spirit to see into another or more steadfast state than Adam's innocency, even into a state in Christ Jesus that should never fall. And the Lord showed me that such as were faithful to Him, in the power and light of Christ, should come up into that state in which Adam was before he fell; in which the admirable works of the creation, and the virtues thereof, may be known, through the openings of that divine Word of wisdom and power by which they were made.

Great things did the Lord lead me into, and wonderful depths were opened unto me, beyond what can by words be declared; but as people come into subjection to the Spirit of God, and grow up in the image and power of the Almighty, they may receive the Word of wisdom that opens all things, and come to know the hidden unity in the Eternal Being.[8]

Thus I travelled on in the Lord's service, as He led me. When I came to Nottingham, the mighty power of God was there among Friends.[9] From thence I went to Clawson, in Leicestershire, in the Vale of Beavor; and the mighty power of God appeared there also, in several towns and villages where Friends were gathered.

While I was there the Lord opened to me three things relating to those three great professions in the world,—law, physic, and divinity (so called). He showed me that the physicians were out of the wisdom of God, by which the creatures were made; and

---

[8] This passage which records a striking personal experience is undated. It is strangely like an experience of the great German mystic, Jacob Boehme, whose works were published in England about the time Fox was beginning his missionary labors. He, too, had all nature opened to him, so that he says he saw the true significance and essence of things. See Jacob Boehme, " Signatura Rerum," which was published in English in 1649. Muggleton, in his " Looking Glass for G. Fox " (second edition, 1756, page 10), says that the writings of Boehme are the " chief books " bought by the followers of Fox.

[9] The name " Friends " is apparently used as formerly on page 77 to designate the gatherings of persons who sympathized with Fox's message and who *afterwards* were called " Friends."

knew not the virtues of the creatures, because they were out of the Word of wisdom, by which they were made. He showed me that the priests were out of the true faith, of which Christ is the author,—the faith which purifies, gives victory and brings people to have access to God, by which they please God; the mystery of which faith is held in a pure conscience. He showed me also that the lawyers were out of the equity, out of the true justice, and out of the law of God, which went over the first transgression, and over all sin, and answered the Spirit of God that was grieved and transgressed in man; and that these three,—the physicians, the priests, and the lawyers, —ruled the world out of the wisdom, out of the faith, and out of the equity and law of God; one pretending the cure of the body, another the cure of the soul, and the third the protection of the property of the people. But I saw they were all out of the wisdom, out of the faith, out of the equity and perfect law of God.

And as the Lord opened these things unto me I felt that His power went forth over all, by which all might be reformed if they would receive and bow unto it. The priests might be reformed and brought into the true faith, which is the gift of God. The lawyers might be reformed and brought into the law of God, which answers that [indwelling Spirit] of God [10] which is [in every one, is] transgressed in

---

[10] One could wish that this important account of Fox's practical mission to the world were more clearly expressed than is here done in his phraseology, which

every one, and.[which yet, if heeded] brings one to
love his neighbour as himself. This lets man see that
if he wrongs his neighbour, he wrongs himself; and
teaches him to do unto others as he would they
should do unto him. The physicians might be reformed and brought into the wisdom of God, by
which all things were made and created; that they
might receive a right knowledge of the creatures,
and understand their virtues, which the Word of
wisdom, by which they were made and are upheld,
hath given them.

Abundance was opened concerning these things;
how all lay out of the wisdom of God, and out of the
righteousness and holiness that man at the first was
made in. But as all believe in the Light, and walk
in the Light,—that Light with which Christ hath
enlightened every man that cometh into the world,—
and become children of the Light, and of the day of
Christ, all things, visible and invisible, are seen, by
the divine Light of Christ, the spiritual heavenly
man, by whom all things were created.

Moreover, when I was brought up into His image

needs translation into modern terms. There is, he
means to say, a universal Divine principle or law of
life which finds expression or voice in every soul.
"That of God" in the individual "answers" or cor-
responds with the universal Divine principle. But,
unfortunately, this Divine Light within is disobeyed,
and thus men are astray—out of their true life and
function. Fox's mission is to call all such to obedience
to "that of God" within them.

in righteousness and holiness, and into the paradise of God He let me see how Adam was made a living soul; and also the stature of Christ, the mystery that had been hid from ages and generations: which things are hard to be uttered, and cannot be borne by many. For of all the sects in Christendom (so called) that I discoursed with, I found none who could bear to be told that any should come to Adam's perfection,—into that image of God, that righteousness and holiness, that Adam was in before he fell; to be clean and pure, without sin, as he was. Therefore how shall they be able to bear being told that any shall grow up to the measure of the stature of the fulness of Christ, when they cannot bear to hear that any shall come, whilst upon earth, into the same power and Spirit that the prophets and apostles were in?—though it be a certain truth that none can understand their writings aright without the same Spirit by which they were written.

Now the Lord God opened to me by His invisible power that every man was enlightened by the divine Light of Christ,[11] and I saw it shine through all; and that they that believed in it came out of condemnation to the Light of life, and became the children of it; but they that hated it, and did not believe in it, were condemned by it, though they made a profession

---

[11] This is the central teaching of George Fox. Everything else comes out of this elemental truth. It is, as he says, clearly enough taught in the Scriptures, but he now saw the truth as an immediate revelation—as a primary fact of experience.

of Christ. This I saw in the pure openings of the Light without the help of any man; neither did I then know where to find it in the Scriptures; though afterwards, searching the Scriptures, I found it. For I saw, in that Light and Spirit which was before the Scriptures were given forth, and which led the holy men of God to give them forth, that all, if they would know God or Christ, or the Scriptures aright, must come to that Spirit by which they that gave them forth were led and taught.

On a certain time, as I was walking in the fields, the Lord said unto me, " Thy name is written in the Lamb's book of life, which was before the foundation of the world ": and as the Lord spoke it, I believed, and saw in it the new birth. Some time after the Lord commanded me to go abroad into the world, which was like a briery, thorny wilderness. When I came in the Lord's mighty power with the Word of life into the world, the world swelled, and made a noise like the great raging waves of the sea. Priests and professors, magistrates and people, were all like a sea when I came to proclaim the day of the Lord amongst them, and to preach repentance to them.

I was sent to turn people from darkness to the Light, that they might receive Christ Jesus; for to as many as should receive Him in His Light, I saw He would give power to become the sons of God; which power I had obtained by receiving Christ. I was to direct people to the Spirit that gave forth the Scriptures, by which they might be led into all truth, and up to Christ and God, as those had been who gave them forth.

Yet I had no slight esteem of the holy Scriptures. They were very precious to me; for I was in that Spirit by which they were given forth; and what the Lord opened in me I afterwards found was agreeable to them. I could speak much of these things, and many volumes might be written upon them; but all would prove too short to set forth the infinite love, wisdom, and power of God, in preparing, fitting, and furnishing me for the service to which He had appointed me; letting me see the depths of Satan on the one hand, and opening to me, on the other hand, the divine mysteries of His own everlasting kingdom.

When the Lord God and His Son Jesus Christ sent me forth into the world to preach His everlasting gospel and kingdom, I was glad that I was commanded to turn people to that inward Light, Spirit, and Grace, by which all might know their salvation and their way to God; even that Divine Spirit which would lead them into all truth, and which I infallibly knew would never deceive any.[12]

But with and by this divine power and Spirit of God, and the Light of Jesus, I was to bring people off

---

[12] The soul's own assurance of salvation was well proclaimed by Luther, but the high and joyous experience was well-nigh lost in Calvinistic England. Fox reaffirms the privilege of this experience. He proclaims no man's infallibility, but rather the infallibility of the Spirit, in union with which a man may know that he pleases God.

from all their own ways, to Christ, the new and living way; and from their churches, which men had made and gathered, to the Church in God, the general assembly written in heaven, of which Christ is the head. And I was to bring them off from the world's teachers, made by men, to learn of Christ, who is the Way, the Truth, and the Life, of whom the Father said, " This is my beloved Son, hear ye Him "; and off from all the world's worships, to know the Spirit of Truth in the inward parts, and to be led thereby; that in it they might worship the Father of spirits, who seeks such to worship Him. And I saw that they that worshipped not in the Spirit of Truth, knew not what they worshipped.

And I was to bring people off from all the world's religions, which are vain, that they might know the pure religion; might visit the fatherless, the widows, and the strangers, and keep themselves from the spots of the world. Then there would not be so many beggars, the sight of whom often grieved my heart, as it denoted so much hard-heartedness amongst them that professed the name of Christ.

I was to bring them off from all the world's fellowships, and prayings, and singings, which stood in forms without power; that their fellowship might be in the Holy Ghost, and in the Eternal Spirit of God; that they might pray in the Holy Ghost, and sing in the Spirit and with the grace that comes by Jesus; making melody in their hearts to the Lord, who hath sent His beloved Son to be their Saviour, and hath caused His heavenly sun to shine upon all the world, and His heavenly rain to fall upon the just and the unjust, as His outward rain doth fall, and His outward sun doth shine on all.

I was to bring people off from Jewish ceremonies, and from heathenish fables,[13] and from men's inventions and worldly doctrines, by which they blew the people about this way and the other, from sect to sect; and from all their beggarly rudiments, with their schools and colleges for making ministers of Christ,—who are indeed ministers of their own making, but not of Christ's; and from all their images, and crosses, and sprinkling of infants, with all their holy-days (so called), and all their vain traditions, which they had instituted since the Apostles' days, against all of which the Lord's power was set: in the dread and authority of which power I was moved to declare against them all, and against all that preached and not freely, as being such as had not received freely from Christ.

Moreover, when the Lord sent me forth into the world, He forbade me to put off my hat to any, high or low; and I was required to Thee and Thou all men and women, without any respect to rich or poor, great or small.[14] And as I travelled up and down I

---

[13] By a clear spiritual insight Fox saw how large a contribution both Judaism and Paganism had made to the historic church. He went to work to carry the reformation to its logical conclusion. To re-instate primitive Christianity was his aim.

[14] The real principles here involved were simplicity of life, equal respect for *all* men alike, and strict sincerity. It must be confessed that these principles

was not to bid people Good morrow, or Good evening; neither might I bow or scrape with my leg to
any one; and this made the sects and professions to
rage.   But the Lord's power carried me over all to
His glory, and many came to be turned to God in a
little time; for the heavenly day of the Lord sprung
from on high, and broke forth apace, by the light of
which many came to see where they were.

Oh, the blows, punchings, beatings, and imprisonments that we underwent for not putting off our hats
to men!   Some had their hats violently plucked off
and thrown away, so that they quite lost them.   The
bad language and evil usage we received on this
account are hard to be expressed, besides the danger
we were sometimes in of losing our lives for this matter; and that by the great professors of Christianity,
who thereby discovered they were not true believers.

And though it was but a small thing in the eye of
man, yet a wonderful confusion it brought among all
professors and priests; but, blessed be the Lord,
many came to see the vanity of that custom of putting off the hat to men, and felt the weight of Truth's
testimony* against it.

About this time I was sorely exercised in going to
their courts to cry for justice, in speaking and writing to judges and justices to do justly; in warning
such as kept public houses for entertainment that

---

* That is, the testimony of the Spirit.

---

have sometimes been lost sight of, and dress and language have sometimes become a form to those who
opposed all forms.

they should not let people have more drink than would do them good; in testifying against wakes, feasts, May-games, sports, plays, and shows, which trained up people to vanity and looseness, and led them from the fear of God; and the days set forth for holidays were usually the times wherein they most dishonoured God by these things.

In fairs, also, and in markets, I was made to declare against their deceitful merchandise, cheating, and cozening; warning all to deal justly, to speak the truth, to let their yea be yea, and their nay be nay, and to do unto others as they would have others do unto them; forewarning them of the great and terrible day of the Lord, which would come upon them all.

I was moved, also, to cry against all sorts of music, and against the mountebanks playing tricks on their stages; for they burthened the pure life, and stirred up people's minds to vanity. I was much exercised, too, with school-masters and school-mistresses, warning them to teach children sobriety in the fear of the Lord, that they might not be nursed and trained up in lightness, vanity, and wantonness. I was made to warn masters and mistresses, fathers and mothers in private families, to take care that their children and servants might be trained up in the fear of the Lord, and that themselves should be therein examples and patterns of sobriety and virtue to them.

The earthly spirit of the priests wounded my life; and when I heard the bell toll to call people together to the steeple-house, it struck at my life; for it was just like a market-bell, to gather people together, that the priest might set forth his ware for sale. Oh, the vast sums of money that are gotten by the trade they make of selling the Scriptures, and by their preaching, from the highest bishop to the lowest priest! What one trade else in the world is comparable to it? notwithstanding the Scriptures were given forth freely, and Christ commanded His ministers to preach freely, and the prophets and apostles denounced judgment against all covetous hirelings and diviners for money.

But in this free Spirit of the Lord Jesus was I sent forth to declare the Word of life and reconciliation freely, that all might come to Christ, who gives freely, and who renews up into the image of God, which man and woman were in before they fell, that they might sit down in heavenly places in Christ Jesus.

CHAPTER III

The Challenge and the First Taste of Prison
1648–1649.

Now, as I went towards Nottingham, on a First-day, in the morning, going with Friends to a meeting there, when I came on the top of a hill in sight of the town, I espied the great steeple-house. And the Lord said unto me, " Thou must go cry against yonder great idol, and against the worshippers therein."

I said nothing of this to the Friends that were with me, but went on with them to the meeting, where the mighty power of the Lord was amongst us; in which I left Friends sitting in the meeting, and went away to the steeple-house. When I came there, all the people looked like fallow ground; and the priest (like a great lump of earth) stood in his pulpit above.

He took for his text these words of Peter, " We have also a more sure Word of prophecy, whereunto ye do well that ye take heed, as unto a light that shineth in a dark place, until the day dawn, and the day-star arise in your hearts." And he told the people that this was the Scriptures, by which they were to try all doctrines, religions, and opinions.

Now the Lord's power was so mighty upon me, and so strong in me, that I could not hold, but was made to cry out and say, " Oh, no; it is not the Scriptures ! " and I told them what it was, namely, the Holy Spirit, by which the holy men of God gave forth the Scriptures, whereby opinions, religions, and judgments were to be tried; for it led into all truth, and so gave the knowledge of all truth. The Jews had the Scriptures, and yet resisted the Holy Ghost, and rejected Christ, the bright morning star. They persecuted Christ and His apostles, and took upon them to try their doctrines by the Scriptures; but they erred in judgment, and did not try them aright, because they tried without the Holy Ghost.

As I spoke thus amongst them, the officers came and took me away, and put me into a nasty, stinking prison; [1] the smell whereof got so into my nose and throat that it very much annoyed me.

But that day the Lord's power sounded so in their ears that they were amazed at the voice, and could not get it out of their ears for some time after, they were so reached by the Lord's power in the steeple-house. At night they took me before the mayor, aldermen, and sheriffs of the town; and when I was brought before them, the mayor was in a peevish, fretful temper, but the Lord's power allayed him. They examined me at large; and I told them how the Lord had moved me to come. After some discourse between them and me, they sent me back to prison again. Some time after, the head sheriff, whose

---

[1] This is one of the very few instances in his entire career when Fox interrupted a minister. It was neither illegal nor contrary to custom for any one to speak after the minister was done—a privilege which Fox often used. On this particular occasion, his feeling overmastered him, and he spoke before his time.

name was John Reckless, sent for me to his house. When I came in, his wife met me in the hall, and said, " Salvation is come to our house." She took me by the hand, and was much wrought upon by the power of the Lord God; and her husband, and children, and servants were much changed, for the power of the Lord wrought upon them.

I lodged at the sheriff's, and great meetings we had in his house. Some persons of considerable condition in the world came to them, and the Lord's power appeared eminently amongst them.

This sheriff sent for the other sheriff, and for a woman they had had dealings with in the way of trade; and he told her, before the other sheriff, that they had wronged her in their dealings with her (for the other sheriff and he were partners), and that they ought to make her restitution. This he spoke cheerfully; but the other sheriff denied it, and the woman said she knew nothing of it. But the friendly sheriff said it was so, and that the other knew it well enough; and having discovered the matter, and acknowledged the wrong done by them, he made restitution to the woman, and exhorted the other sheriff to do the like. The Lord's power was with this friendly sheriff, and wrought a mighty change in him; and great openings he had.

The next market-day, as he was walking with me in the chamber, he said, " I must go into the market, and preach repentance to the people." Accordingly he went in his slippers into the market, and into several streets, and preached repentance to the people. Several others also in the town were moved to speak to the mayor and magistrates, and to the people, exhorting them to repent. Hereupon the magistrates grew very angry, sent for me from the sheriff's house and committed me to the common prison.

When the assize came on, one person was moved to come and offer up himself for me, body for body, yea, life also; but when I should have been brought before the judge, the sheriff's man being somewhat long in bringing me to the sessions-house, the judge was risen before I came. At which I understood the judge was offended, and said, " I would have admonished the youth if he had been brought before me ": for I was then imprisoned by the name of a youth. So I was returned to prison again, and put into the common jail.

The Lord's power was great among Friends; but the people began to be very rude: wherefore the governor of the castle sent soldiers, and dispersed them. After that they were quiet. Both priests and people were astonished at the wonderful power that broke forth. Several of the priests were made tender, and some did confess to the power of the Lord.

After I was set at liberty from Nottingham jail, where I had been kept prisoner a pretty long time, I travelled as before, in the work of the Lord.

Coming to Mansfield-Woodhouse, I found there a distracted woman under a doctor's hand, with her hair loose about her ears. He was about to let her blood,[2] she being first bound, and many people about

---

[2] This gives a glimpse at the medical practice of the time. Fox frequently showed remarkable power in

her, holding her by violence; but he could get no blood from her.

I desired them to unbind her and let her alone, for they could not touch the spirit in her by which she was tormented. So they did unbind her; and I was moved to speak to her, and in the name of the Lord to bid her be quiet; and she was so. The Lord's power settled her mind, and she mended. Afterwards she received the truth, and continued in it to her death; and the Lord's name was honoured.

Many great and wonderful things were wrought by the heavenly power in those days; for the Lord made bare His omnipotent arm, and manifested His power, to the astonishment of many, by the healing virtue whereby many have been delivered from great infirmities. And the devils were made subject through His name; of which particular instances might be given, beyond what this unbelieving age is able to receive or bear.

Now while I was at Mansfield-Woodhouse, I was moved to go to the steeple-house there, and declare

---

dealing with cases of hysteria, such as the one here reported. He evidently did not understand the nature of the disease. But his commanding presence, his piercing eye (testified to by even his persecutors), and the absolute assurance which his voice gave that he was equal to the occasion, were worth a thousand doctors with their lancets. Those who understand the psychology of suggestion, and the effect of faith on certain diseases, will hardly question the simple accounts given here and elsewhere.

the truth to the priest and people; but the people
fell upon me in great rage, struck me down, and almost stifled and smothered me; and I was cruelly
beaten and bruised by them with their hands, and
with Bibles and sticks. Then they haled me out,
though I was hardly able to stand, and put me into
the stocks, where I sat some hours; and they brought
dog-whips and horse-whips, threatening to whip me.

After some time they had me before the magistrate, at a knight's house, where were many great
persons; who, seeing how evilly I had been used,
after much threatening, set me at liberty. But the
rude people stoned me out of the town, for preaching
the Word of life to them.

I was scarcely able to move or stand by reason of
the ill usage I had received; yet with considerable
effort I got about a mile from the town, and then I
met with some people who gave me something to
comfort me, because I was inwardly bruised; but the
Lord's power soon healed me again. That day some
people were convinced of the Lord's truth, and
turned to His teaching, at which I rejoiced.

Then I went into Leicestershire, several Friends
accompanying me. There were some Baptists in that
country, whom I desired to see and speak with, because they were separated from the public worship.
So one Oates, who was one of their chief teachers,
and others of the heads of them, with several others
of their company, came to meet us at Barrow; and
there we discoursed with them.

One of them said that what was not of faith was
sin, whereupon I asked them what faith was and how

it was wrought in man. But they turned off from that, and spoke of their baptism in water. Then I asked them whether their mountain of sin was brought down and laid low in them and their rough and crooked ways made smooth and straight in them, —for they looked upon the Scriptures as meaning outward mountains and ways.[3] But I told them they must find these things in their own hearts; at which they seemed to wonder.

We asked them who baptized John the Baptist, and who baptized Peter, John and the rest of the apostles, and put them to prove by Scripture that these were baptized in water; but they were silent. Then I asked them, " Seeing Judas, who betrayed Christ, and was called the son of perdition, had hanged himself, what son of perdition was that of which Paul spoke, that sat in the temple of God, exalted above all that is called God? and what temple of God was that in which this son of perdition sat?" And I 'asked them whether he that betrays Christ within himself be not one in nature with that Judas that betrayed Christ without. But they could not tell what to make of this, nor what to say to it. So, after some discourse, we parted; and some of them were loving to us.

On the First-day following we came to Bagworth, and went to a steeple-house, where some Friends

---

[3] As everywhere, he is interested in the state of the person himself, and in the real and vital things of religion. Many of Fox's followers came from the Baptists.

were got in, and the people locked them in, and themselves, too, with the priest. But, after the priest had done, they opened the door, and we went in also, and had service for the Lord amongst them. Afterwards we had a meeting in the town, amongst several that were in high notions.

Passing thence, I heard of a people in prison at Coventry for religion. As I walked towards the jail, the word of the Lord came to me, saying, " My love was always to thee, and thou art in my love." And I was ravished with the sense of the love of God, and greatly strengthened in my inward man. But when I came into the jail where those prisoners were, a great power of darkness struck at me; and I sat still, having my spirit gathered into the love of God.

At last these prisoners began to rant, vapour, and blaspheme; at which my soul was greatly grieved. They said that they were God; but we could not bear such things. When they were calm, I stood up and asked them whether they did such things by motion, or from Scripture. They said, " From Scripture." Then, a Bible lying by, I asked them for that Scripture; and they showed me that place where the sheet was let down to Peter; and it was said to him that what was sanctified he should not call common or unclean. When I had showed them that that Scripture made nothing for their purpose, they brought another, which spake of God's reconciling all things to Himself, things in heaven and things in earth. I told them I owned that Scripture also; but showed them that it likewise was nothing to their purpose.

Then, seeing they said that they were God, I asked them if they knew whether it would rain to-morrow. They said they could not tell. I told them God could tell. I asked them if they thought they should be always in that condition, or should change. They answered that they could not tell. " Then," said I, " God can tell, and He doth not change. You say you are God, and yet you cannot tell whether you shall change or no." So they were confounded, and quite brought down for the time.

After I had reproved them for their blasphemous expressions, I went away; for I perceived they were Ranters. I had met with none before; and I admired the goodness of the Lord in appearing so unto me before I went amongst them. Not long after this one of these Ranters, whose name was Joseph Salmon, published a recantation; upon which they were set at liberty.

CHAPTER IV.

A Year in Derby Jail

1650–1651.

As I travelled through markets, fairs, and divers
places, I saw death and darkness in all people where
the power of the Lord God had not shaken them.
As I was passing on in Leicestershire I came to Twy-
Cross, where there were excise-men. I was moved
of the Lord to go to them, and warn them to take
heed of oppressing the poor; and people were much
affected with it.

There was in that town a great man that had long
lain sick, and was given up by the physicians; and
some Friends in the town desired me to go to see
him. I went up to him in his chamber, and spoke
the Word of life to him, and was moved to pray by
him; and the Lord was entreated, and restored him
to health. But when I was come down stairs, into a
lower room, and was speaking to the servants, and to
some people that were there, a serving-man of his
came raving out of another room, with a naked
rapier in his hand, and set it just to my side. I
looked steadfastly on him, and said, " Alack for thee,
poor creature! what wilt thou do with thy carnal
weapon? It is no more to me than a straw." The
bystanders were much troubled, and he went away
in a rage and full of wrath. But when the news of
it came to his master, he turned him out of his service.

Thus the Lord's power preserved me and raised up the weak man, who afterwards was very loving to Friends; and when I came to that town again both he and his wife came to see me.

After this I was moved to go into Derbyshire, where the mighty power of God was among Friends. And I went to Chesterfield, where one Britland was priest. He saw beyond the common sort of priests, for he had been partly convinced, and had spoken much on behalf of Truth before he was priest there; but when the priest of that town died, he got the parsonage, and choked himself with it. I was moved to speak to him and the people in the great love of God, that they might come off from all men's teaching unto God's teaching; and he was not able to gainsay.

But they had me before the mayor, and threatened to send me, with some others, to the house of correction, and kept us in custody till it was late in the night. Then the officers, with the watchmen, put us out of the town, leaving us to shift as we could. So I bent my course towards Derby, having a friend or two with me. In our way we met with many professors; and at Kidsey Park many were convinced.

Then, coming to Derby, I lay at the house of a doctor, whose wife was convinced; and so were several more in the town. As I was walking in my chamber, the [steeple-house] bell rang, and it struck at my life at the very hearing of it; so I asked the woman of the house what the bell rang for. She said there was to be a great lecture there that day, and many of the officers of the army, and priests, and

preachers were to be there, and a colonel, that was a
preacher.

Then was I moved of the Lord to go up to them;
and when they had done I spoke to them what the
Lord commanded me, and they were pretty quiet.
But there came an officer and took me by the hand,
and said that I and the other two that were with me
must go before the magistrates. It was about the
first hour after noon that we came before them.

They asked me why we came thither. I said God
moved us so to do; and I told them, " God dwells
not in temples made with hands." I told them also
that all their preaching, baptism and sacrifices would
never sanctify them, and bade them look unto Christ
within them, and not unto men; for it is Christ that
sanctifies. Then they ran into many words; but I
told them they were not to dispute of God and
Christ, but to obey Him.[1]

The power of God thundered among them, and
they did fly like chaff before it. They put me in and
out of the room often, hurrying me backward and
forward, for they were from the first hour till the
ninth at night in examining me. Sometimes they
would tell me in a deriding manner that I was taken
up in raptures.

At last they asked me whether I was sanctified.
I answered, " Yes; for I am in the paradise of God."
Then they asked me if I had no sin. I answered,

---

[1] No single sentence better sums up George Fox's
whole theology than this: " I told them they were not
to dispute of God and Christ, *but to obey Him.*"

" Christ my Saviour has taken away my sin; and in Him there is no sin." They asked how we knew that Christ did abide in us. I said, " By His Spirit, that He hath given us." They temptingly asked if any of us were Christ. I answered, " Nay; we are nothing; Christ is all." They said, " If a man steal, is it no sin ? " I answered, " All unrighteousness is sin." [2]

When they had wearied themselves in examining me, they committed me and one other man to the house of correction in Derby for six months, as blasphemers,[3] as may appear by the mittimus, a copy whereof here followeth:

" To the master of the house of correction in Derby, greeting:

" We have sent you herewithal the bodies of George Fox, late of Mansfield, in the county of Nottingham, and John Fretwell, late of Staniesby, in

---

[2] These answers sufficiently differentiate George Fox from the " Ranters."

[3] Here begins Fox's first serious imprisonment. The charge was direct and distinct. He was committed as a blasphemer. Under the law passed by both Houses of Parliament, in 1648, Fox might easily have been condemned to suffer a death penalty. It was an offense, punishable by death, to deny that the Scriptures are the Word of God, or that the bodies of men shall rise after they are dead. It was blasphemy to say that the two sacraments of Baptism and the Lord's Supper are not commanded by God. It was also blasphemy to declare that man has by nature free will to turn to

the county of Derby, husbandman, brought before us this present day, and charged with the avowed uttering and broaching of divers blasphemous opinions, contrary to the late Act of Parliament; which, upon their examination before us, they have confessed. These are therefore to require you forthwith, upon sight hereof, to receive them, the said George Fox and John Fretwell, into your custody, and them therein safely to keep during the space of six months, without bail or mainprize, or until they shall find sufficient security to be of good behaviour, or be thence delivered by order from ourselves. Hereof you are not to fail. Given under our hands and seals this 30th day of October, 1650.

" GERVASE BENNET,
" NATH. BARTON."

While I was here in prison divers professors came to discourse with me. I had a sense, before they spoke, that they came to plead for sin and imperfection. I asked them whether they were believers and had faith. They said, " Yes." I asked them, " In whom?" They said, " In Christ." I replied. " If

---

God. It was, of course, not difficult to find a charge of the violation of this drag-net act.

From Derby prison he wrote many letters, to the magistrates, to the justices, to the " priests," to the court at Derby, to the mayor, to the individual justices, and to " the ringers of bells in steeple-houses." He calls them all to obedience to the light within them. " Mind that which is eternal and invisible." " Keep in the innocency and be obedient to the faith in Him."

ye are true believers in Christ, you are passed from
death to life; and if passed from death, then from
sin that bringeth death; and if your faith be true, it
will give you victory over sin and the devil, purify
your hearts and consciences (for the true faith is held
in a pure conscience), and bring you to please God,
and give you access to Him again."

But they could not endure to hear of purity, and
of victory over sin and the devil. They said they
could not believe any could be free from sin on this
side of the grave. I bade them give over babbling
about the Scriptures, which were holy men's words,
whilst they pleaded for unholiness.

At another time a company of professors came,
who also began to plead for sin. I asked them
whether they had hope. They said, " Yes: God forbid but we should have hope." I asked them,
" What hope is it that you have ? Is Christ in you the
hope of your glory ? Doth it purify you, as He is
pure ? " But they could not abide to hear of being
made pure here. Then I bade them forbear talking
of the Scriptures, which were the holy men's words;
" for," said I, " the holy men that wrote the Scriptures pleaded for holiness in heart, life, and conversation here; but since you plead for impurity and
sin, which is of the devil, what have you to do with
the holy men's words ? "

The keeper of the prison, being a high professor,
was greatly enraged against me, and spoke very wickedly of me; but it pleased the Lord one day to strike
him, so that he was in great trouble and under much
terror of mind. And, as I was walking in my cham-

ber I heard a doleful noise, and, standing still, I heard him say to his wife, " Wife, I have seen the day of judgment, and I saw George there; and I was afraid of him, because I had done him so much wrong, and spoken so much against him to the ministers and professors, and to the justices, and in taverns and alehouses."

After this, towards the evening, he came into my chamber, and said to me, " I have been as a lion against you; but now I come like a lamb, and like the jailer that came to Paul and Silas trembling." And he desired he might lodge with me. I told him I was in his power; he might do what he would; but he said, " Nay," that he would have my leave, and that he could desire to be always with me, but not to have me as a prisoner. He said he had been plagued, and his house had been plagued, for my sake. So I suffered him to lodge with me.

Then he told me all his heart, and said that he believed what I had said of the true faith and hope to be true; and he wondered that the other man, who was put in prison with me, did not stand it; and said, " That man was not right, but you are an honest man." He confessed also to me that at those times when I had asked him to let me go forth to speak the word of the Lord to the people, when he refused to let me go, and I laid the weight thereof upon him, he used to be under great trouble, amazed, and almost distracted for some time after, and in such a condition that he had little strength left him.

When the morning came he rose and went to the justices, and told them that he and his house had been plagued for my sake. One of the justices replied (as he reported to me) that the plagues were upon them, too, for keeping me. This was Justice Bennet, of Derby, who was the first that called us Quakers, because I bade them tremble at the word of the Lord.[4] This was in the year 1650.

After this the justices gave leave that I should have liberty to walk a mile. I perceived their end, and told the jailer, that if they would set down to me how far a mile was, I might take the liberty of walking it sometimes. For I had a sense that they thought I would go away. And the jailer confessed afterwards they did it with that intent, to have me go away, to ease them of their plague; but I told him I was not of that spirit.

While I was in the house of correction my relations came to see me; and, being troubled for my im-

---

[4] This is the whole of our data for the origin of the name " Quaker." Fox told the Justice to tremble at the word of the Lord, and the Justice thereupon fixed the name " quaker " upon him. There is probably, however, something back of this particular incident which helped give the name significance. The editors of the New English Dictionary (see the word Quaker) have discovered the fact that this name for a religious sect was not entirely new at this time. Letter No. 2,624 of the Clarendon collection, written in 1647, speaks of a sect from the continent possessed of a remarkable capacity for trembling or quaking: " I heare of a sect of woemen (they are at Southworke) come from beyond the Sea, called quakers, and these swell, shiver and shake, and when they come to themselves (for in all

prisonment, they went to the justices that cast me
into prison and desired to have me home with them,
offering to be bound in one hundred pounds, and
others of Derby in fifty pounds apiece with them,
that I should come no more thither to declare against
the priests.

So I was taken up before the justices; and because
I would not consent that they or any should be
bound for me (for I was innocent of any ill behaviour, and had spoken the Word of life and truth
unto them), Justice Bennet rose up in a rage; and, as
I was kneeling down to pray to the Lord to forgive
him, he ran upon me, and struck me with both his
hands, crying, " Away with him, jailer; take him
away, jailer." Whereupon I was taken again to
prison, and there kept till the time of my commitment for six months was expired.

But I had now the liberty of walking a mile by
myself, which I made use of as I felt freedom. Sometimes I went into the market and streets, and warned
the people to repent of their wickedness, and re-

---

this fitt Mahomett's holy-ghost hath bin conversing
with them) they begin to preach what hath been delivered to them by the Spirit." It seems probable that
Justice Bennet merely employed a term of reproach
already familiar. It is, further, evident that the
Friends themselves were sometimes given to trembling,
and that the name came into general use because it
fitted. (See Sewel's " History of the People Called
Quakers," Vol. I., p. 63. Philadelphia, 1823.) The
name first appears in the records of Parliament, in the
Journals of the House of Commons, in 1654.

turned to prison again. And there being persons of several sorts of religion in the prison, I sometimes visited them in their meetings on First-days.

While I was yet in the house of correction there came unto me a trooper, and said that as he was sitting in the steeple-house, hearing the priest, exceeding great trouble fell upon him; and the voice of the Lord came to him, saying, " Dost thou not know that my servant is in prison? Go to him for direction." So I spake to his condition, and his understanding was opened. I told him that that which showed him his sins, and troubled him for them, would show him his salvation; for He that shows a man his sin is the same that takes it away.

While I was speaking to him the Lord's power opened his mind, so that he began to have a good understanding in the Lord's truth, and to be sensible of God's mercies. He spoke boldly in his quarters amongst the soldiers, and to others, concerning truth (for the Scriptures were very much opened to him), insomuch that he said that his colonel was " as blind as Nebuchadnezzar, to cast the servant of the Lord into prison."

Upon this his colonel conceived a spite against him, and at Worcester fight, the year after, when the two armies lay near one another, and two came out from the king's army and challenged any two of the Parliament army to fight with them, his colonel made choice of him and another to answer the challenge. When in the encounter his companion was slain, he drove both his enemies within musket-shot of the town without firing a pistol at them. This, when he returned, he told me with his own mouth. But when the fight was over he saw the deceit and hypocrisy of the officers, and, being sensible how wonderfully the Lord had preserved him, and seeing also to the end of fighting, he laid down his arms.

The time of my commitment to the house of correction being very nearly ended, and there being many new soldiers raised, the commissioners would have made me captain over them; and the soldiers cried out that they would have none but me. So the keeper of the house of correction was commanded to bring me before the commissioners and soldiers in the market-place, where they offered me that preferment, as they called it, asking me if I would not take up arms for the Commonwealth against Charles Stuart. I told them I knew whence all wars arose, even from the lusts, according to James' doctrine; and that I lived in the virtue of that life and power that took away the occasion of all wars.[5]

Yet they courted me to accept of their offer, and thought I did but compliment them. But I told them I was come into the covenant of peace, which was before wars and strifes were. They said they offered it in love and kindness to me because of my virtue; and such-like flattering words they used. But I told them, if that was their love and kindness, I trampled it under my feet.

Then their rage got up, and they said, " Take him

---

[5] This is the true ground of opposition to war, namely, that a Christian is to live a life that does away with the *occasion* for war.

away, jailer, and put him into the prison amongst the rogues and felons." So I was put into a lousy, stinking place, without any bed, amongst thirty felons, where I was kept almost half a year; [6] yet at times they would let me walk to the garden, believing I would not go away.

When they had got me into Derby prison, it was the saying of people that I would never come out; but I had faith in God that I should be delivered in His time; for the Lord had given me to believe that I was not to be removed from that place yet, being set there for a service which He had for me to do.

While I was here in prison there was a young woman in the jail for robbing her master. When she was to be tried for her life I wrote to the judge and jury, showing them how contrary it was to the law of God in old time to put people to death for stealing, and moving them to show mercy. Yet she was condemned to die, and a grave was made for her, and at the time appointed she was carried forth to execution. Then I wrote a few words, warning all to beware of greediness or covetousness, for it leads from God; and that all should fear the Lord, avoid earthly lusts, and prize their time while they have it; this I gave to be read at the gallows. And, though they had her upon the ladder, with a cloth bound

---

[6] He was imprisoned on a definite charge for six months, and then, without any further trial, apparently because he would not join Cromwell's army, he was held in close confinement for nearly six months more.

over her face, ready to be turned off, yet they did
not put her to death, but brought her back to prison,
where she afterwards came to be convinced of God's
everlasting truth.

There was also in the jail, while I was there, a
wicked, ungodly man, who was reputed a conjurer.
He threatened that he would talk with me, and
boasted of what he would do; but he never had
power to open his mouth to me. And the jailer and
he falling out, he threatened to raise the devil and
break his house down; so that he made the jailer
afraid. I was moved of the Lord to go in His power
and rebuke him, and to say to him, " Come, let us
see what thou canst do; do thy worst." I told him
that the devil was raised high enough in him already;
but the power of God chained him down, so he slunk
away from me.

The time of Worcester fight coming on, Justice
Bennet sent constables to press me for a soldier, seeing I would not voluntarily accept of a command. I
told them that I was brought off from outward wars.
They came again to give me press-money; but I
would take none. Then I was brought up to Ser-
geant Holes, kept there awhile, and taken down
again. Afterwards the constables brought me a second time before the commissioners, who said I
should go for a soldier; but I told them I was dead
to it. They said I was alive. I told them that where
envy and hatred is there is confusion. They offered
me money twice, but I refused it. Being disappointed, they were angry, and committed me close
prisoner, without bail or mainprize.

Great was the exercise and travail in spirit that I underwent during my imprisonment here, because of the wickedness that was in this town; for though some were convinced, yet the generality were a hardened people. I saw the visitation of God's love pass away from them. I mourned over them.

There was a great judgment upon the town, and the magistrates were uneasy about me; but they could not agree what to do with me. One while they would have sent me up to the Parliament; another while they would have banished me to Ireland. At first they called me a deceiver, a seducer and a blasphemer. Afterwards, when God had brought his plagues upon them, they styled me an honest, virtuous man. But their good report and bad report were nothing to me; for the one did not lift me up, nor the other cast me down; praised be the Lord! At length they were made to turn me out of jail, about the beginning of winter, in the year 1651, after I had been a prisoner in Derby almost a year,—six months in the house of correction, and the rest of the time in the common jail.

CHAPTER V.

One Man May Shake the Country for Ten Miles
1651-1652.

Being again at liberty, I went on, as before, in the work of the Lord, passing through the country into Leicestershire, having meetings as I went; and the Lord's Spirit and power accompanied me.

As I was walking with several Friends, I lifted up my head and saw three steeple-house spires, and they struck at my life. I asked them what place that was. They said, "Lichfield." Immediately the Word of the Lord came to me that I must go thither. Being come to the house we were going to, I wished the Friends to walk into the house, saying nothing to them of whither I was to go. As soon as they were gone I stepped away, and went by my eye over hedge and ditch till I came within a mile of Lichfield, where, in a great field, shepherds were keeping their sheep.

Then was I commanded by the Lord to pull off my shoes. I stood still, for it was winter; and the Word of the Lord was like a fire in me. So I put off my shoes, and left them with the shepherds; and the poor shepherds trembled, and were astonished. Then I walked on about a mile, and as soon as I was got within the city, the Word of the Lord came to me again, saying, " Cry, ' Woe to the bloody city of Lichfield ! ' " So I went up and down the streets, crying with a loud voice, " Woe to the bloody city of Lichfield! " It being market-day, I went into the market-place, and to and fro in the several parts of it, and made stands, crying as before, " Woe to the bloody city of Lichfield! " And no one laid hands on me.

As I went thus crying through the streets, there seemed to me to be a channel of blood running down the streets, and the market-place appeared like a pool of blood.

When I had declared what was upon me, and felt myself clear, I went out of the town in peace, and, returning to the shepherds, I gave them some money, and took my shoes of them again. But the fire of the Lord was so in my feet, and all over me, that I did not matter to put on my shoes again, and was at a stand whether I should or no, till I felt freedom from the Lord so to do; then, after I had washed my feet, I put on my shoes again.

After this a deep consideration came upon me, for what reason I should be sent to cry against that city, and call it the bloody city! For, though the Parliament had had the minster one while, and the King another, and much blood had been shed in the town during the wars between them, yet that was no more than had befallen many other places. But afterwards I came to understand, that in the Emperor Diocletian's time a thousand Christians were martyred in Lichfield.[1]

---

[1] It must be remembered that this act of George Fox occurred at the close of a year of imprisonment,

Passing on, I was moved of the Lord to go to Beverley steeple-house, which was then a place of high profession; and being very wet with rain, I went first to an inn. As soon as I came to the door, a young woman of the house came to the door, and said, " What, is it you? come in," as if she had known me before; for the Lord's power bowed their hearts. So I refreshed myself and went to bed; and in the morning, my clothes being still wet, I got ready, and having paid for what I had had in the inn, I went up to the steeple-house, where was a man preaching. When he had done, I was moved to speak to him, and to the people, in the mighty power of God, and to turn them to their teacher, Christ Jesus. The power of the Lord was so strong, that it struck a mighty dread amongst the people. The mayor came and

---

a part of which had been in a horrible jail. He was throughout his life restless and active to an extreme degree. For an entire year, just as his work was getting well begun, he had been forced to live in this nut-shell of a prison—day after day inactive. Now he was free again, and the old restlessness to be doing something came upon him with irresistible force. He was in no condition to inhibit suggestions. It is quite possible that some subconscious memory here gave the suggestion. In 1612 one Wightman was burned at the stake in Lichfield, and the deed was fresh in the minds of men at this time. Then the name Lichfield means " field of dead bodies," a name which doubtless had its origin in some baptism of blood, and George in his boyhood may have heard some tale of those bloody times.

spoke a few words to me; but none of them had any power to meddle with me.

So I passed away out of the town, and in the afternoon went to another steeple-house about two miles off. When the priest had done, I was moved to speak to him, and to the people very largely, showing them the way of life and truth, and the ground of election and reprobation. The priest said he was but a child, and could not dispute with me. I told him I did not come to dispute, but to hold forth the Word of life and truth unto them, that they might all know the one Seed, to which the promise of God was given, both in the male and in the female. Here the people were very loving, and would have had me come again on a week-day, and preach among them; but I directed them to their teacher, Christ Jesus, and so passed away.

The next day I went to Cranswick, to Captain Pursloe's, who accompanied me to Justice Hotham's. This Justice Hotham was a tender man, one that had had some experience of God's workings in his heart. After some discourse with him of the things of God, he took me into his closet, where, sitting with me, he told me he had known that principle* these ten years, and was glad that the Lord did now publish it abroad to the people. After a while there came a priest to visit him, with whom also I had some discourse concerning the Truth. But his mouth was quickly stopped, for he was nothing but a notionist, and not in possession of what he talked of.

While I was here, there came a great woman of

* The light of Christ working on the heart.

Beverley to speak to Justice Hotham about some business; and in discourse she told him that the last Sabbath-day (as she called it) there came an angel or spirit into the church at Beverley, and spoke the wonderful things of God, to the astonishment of all that were there; and when it had done, it passed away, and they did not know whence it came, nor whither it went; but it astonished all,—priest, professors, and magistrates of the town. This relation Justice Hotham gave me afterwards, and then I gave him an account of how I had been that day at Beverley steeple-house, and had declared truth to the priest and people there.

I went to another steeple-house about three miles off, where preached a great high-priest, called a doctor, one of them whom Justice Hotham would have sent for to speak with me. I went into the steeple-house, and stayed till the priest had done. The words which he took for his text were these, " Ho, every one that thirsteth, come ye to the waters; and he that hath no money, come ye, buy and eat, yea come, buy wine and milk without money and without price."

Then was I moved of the Lord God to say unto him, " Come down, thou deceiver; dost thou bid people come freely, and take of the water of life freely, and yet thou takest three hundred pounds a year of them for preaching the Scriptures to them. Mayest thou not blush for shame? Did the prophet Isaiah, and Christ do so, who spoke the words, and gave them forth freely? Did not Christ say to His ministers, whom He sent to preach, ' Freely ye have received, freely give ' ? "

The priest, like a man amazed, hastened away. After he had left his flock, I had as much time as I could desire to speak to the people; and I directed them from the darkness to the Light, and to the grace of God, that would teach them, and bring them salvation; to the Spirit of God in their inward parts, which would be a free teacher unto them.

Having cleared myself amongst the people, I returned to Justice Hotham's house that night. When I came in he took me in his arms, and said his house was my house; for he was exceedingly glad of the work of the Lord, and that His power was revealed.

Thence I passed on through the country, and came at night to an inn where was a company of rude people. I bade the woman of the house, if she had any meat, to bring me some; but because I said Thee and Thou to her, she looked strangely on me. I asked her if she had any milk. She said, No. I was sensible she spake falsely; and, being willing to try her further, I asked her if she had any cream? She denied that she had any.

There stood a churn in the room, and a little boy, playing about, put his hands into it and pulled it down, and threw all the cream on the floor before my eyes. Thus was the woman manifested to be a liar. She was amazed, blessed herself, took up the child, and whipped it sorely: but I reproved her for her lying and deceit. After the Lord had thus discovered her deceit and perverseness, I walked out of the house, and went away till I came to a stack of hay, and lay in the hay-stack that night, in rain and

snow, it being but three days before the time called
Christmas.

The next day I came into York, where were several very tender people. Upon the First-day following, I was commanded of the Lord to go and speak
to priest Bowles and his hearers in their great cathe-
dral. Accordingly I went. When the priest had
done, I told them I had something from the Lord
God to speak to the priest and people. " Then say
on quickly," said a professor, for there was frost and
snow, and it was very cold weather. Then I told
them that this was the Word of the Lord God unto
them,—that they lived in words, but God Almighty
looked for fruits amongst them.

As soon as the words were out of my mouth, they
hurried me out, and threw me down the steps. But
I got up again without hurt, and went to my lodging,
and several were convinced there. For that which
arose from the weight and oppression that was upon
the Spirit of God in me, would open people, strike
them, and make them confess that the groans which
broke forth through me did reach them, for my
life was burthened with their profession without possession, and their words without fruit.

[After being thus violently tumbled down the steps
of the great minster, George Fox found his next few
days crowded with hot discussion. Papists and Ranters
and Scotch " priests " made him stand forth for the
hope that was in him. The Ranters, he says, " had
spent their portions, and not living in that which they
spake of, were now become dry. They had some kind
of meetings, but they took tobacco and drank ale in

their meetings and were grown light and loose." After
the narrative of an attempt to push him over the cliffs
the account continues.]

Another priest sent to have a dispute with me,
and Friends went with me to the house where he
was; but when he understood we were come, he
slipped out of the house, and hid himself under an
hedge. The people went and found him, but could
not get him to come to us.

Then I went to a steeple-house hard by, where the
priest and people were in a great rage. This priest
had threatened Friends what he would do; but when
I came he fled; for the Lord's power came over him
and them. Yea, the Lord's everlasting power was
over the world, and reached to the hearts of people, and made both priests and professors tremble.
It shook the earthly and airy spirit in which they
held their profession of religion and worship; so that
it was a dreadful thing to them when it was told
them, " The man in leathern breeches is come." [2]
At the hearing thereof the priests in many places got
out of the way, they were so struck with the dread

---

[2] This is the foundation for the famous passage on
George Fox, in Carlyle's " Sartor Resartus," Book III.,
Chap. 1. There is, however, no foundation for Carlyle's picture of Fox cutting and stitching his own
leather suit. Sewel distinctly says that these leather
breeches had no connection with " his former leather
work." Croese says that his entire suit was leather.
This form of dress was not very unusual at the time,
and was probably chosen for its durability.

of the eternal power of God; and fear surprised the hypocrites.

[At Pickering he stood in " the steeple-house yard " and told the people what his mission was, with as clear a claim to a divine commission as a Hebrew prophet would have made.]

I was sent of the Lord God of heaven and earth to preach freely, and to bring people off from these outward temples made with hands, which God dwelleth not in; that they might know their bodies to become the temples of God and of Christ; and to draw people off from all their superstitious ceremonies, Jewish and heathenish customs, traditions, and doctrines of men; and from all the world's hireling teachers, that take tithes and great wages, preaching for hire, and divining for money, whom God and Christ never sent, as themselves confess when they say that they never heard God's nor Christ's voice. I exhorted the people to come off from all these things, directing them to the Spirit and grace of God in themselves, and to the Light of Jesus in their own hearts; that they might come to know Christ, their free teacher, to bring them salvation, and to open the Scriptures to them.

Thus the Lord gave me a good opportunity to open things largely unto them. All was quiet, and many were convinced; blessed be the Lord.

I passed to another town, where was another great meeting, the old priest being with me; and there came professors of several sorts to it. I sat on a haystack, and spoke nothing for some hours; for I was to famish them from words. The professors would ever and anon be speaking to the old priest, and asking him when I would begin, and when I would speak? He bade them wait; and told them that the people waited upon Christ a long while before He spoke.

At last I was moved of the Lord to speak; and they were struck by the Lord's power. The Word of life reached to them, and there was a general convincement amongst them.

Now I came towards Cranswick, to Captain Pursloe's and Justice Hotham's, who received me kindly, being glad that the Lord's power had so appeared; that truth was spread, and so many had received it. Justice Hotham said that if God had not raised up this principle of Light and life which I preached, the nation would have been overrun with Ranterism,[3] and all the justices in the nation could not have stopped it with all their laws; "Because," said he, "they would have said as we said, and done as we commanded, and yet have kept their own principle still. But this principle of truth," said he, "overthrows their principle, and the root and ground thereof"; and therefore he was glad the Lord had raised up this principle of life and truth.

The next day Friends and friendly people having left me, I travelled alone, declaring the day of the Lord amongst people in the towns where I came, and warning them to repent. I came towards night into

---

[3] This remark of Justice Hotham is an observation of considerable historical significance.

a town called Patrington. As I walked along the
town, I warned both priest and people (for the priest
was in the street) to repent and turn to the Lord. It
grew dark before I came to the end of the town, and
a multitude of people gathered about me, to whom I
declared the Word of life.

When I had cleared myself I went to an inn, and
desired them to let me have a lodging; but they
would not. I desired a little meat or milk, and said
I would pay for it; but they refused. So I walked
out of the town, and a company of fellows followed,
and asked me, " What news? " I bade them repent,
and fear the Lord.

After I was gone a pretty way, I came to another
house, and desired the people to let me have a little
meat, drink, and lodging for my money; but they
denied me. I went to another house, and desired the
same; but they refused me also. By this time it was
grown so dark that I could not see the highway; but
I discerned a ditch, and got a little water, and
refreshed myself. Then I got over the ditch; and,
being weary with travelling, I sat down amongst the
furze bushes till it was day.

About break of day I got up, and passed on over
the fields. A man came after me with a great pike-
staff and went along with me to a town; and he
raised the town upon me, with the constable and
chief constable, before the sun was up. I declared
God's everlasting truth amongst them, warning them
of the day of the Lord, that was coming upon all sin
and wickedness; and exhorted them to repent. But
they seized me, and had me back to Patrington, about

three miles, guarding me with watch-bills, pikes, staves, and halberds.

When I was come to Patrington, all the town was in an uproar, and the priest and constables were consulting together; so I had another opportunity to declare the Word of life amongst them, and warn them to repent. At last a professor, a tender man, called me into his house, and there I took a little milk and bread, having not eaten for some days before. Then they guarded me about nine miles to a justice.

When I was come near his house, a man came riding after us, and asked me whether I was the man that was apprehended. I asked him wherefore he asked. He said, " For no hurt." I told him I was: so he rode away to the justice before us. The men that guarded me said it would be well if the justice were not drunk before we got to him; for he used to get drunk early.

When I was brought in before him, because I did not put off my hat, and because I said Thou to him, he asked the man that rode thither before me whether I was not mazed or fond.* The man told him, No; it was my principle.

I warned him to repent, and come to the Light with which Christ had enlightened him; that by it he might see all his evil words and actions, and turn to Christ Jesus whilst he had time; and that whilst he had time he should prize it. " Ay, ay," said he, " the Light that is spoken of in the third of John." I desired he would mind it, and obey it.

* Foolish.

As I admonished him, I laid my hand upon him, and he was brought down by the power of the Lord; and all the watchmen stood amazed. Then he took me into a little parlour with the other man, and desired to see what I had in my pockets of letters or intelligence. I plucked out my linen, and showed him I had no letters. He said, " He is not a vagrant, by his linen "; then he set me at liberty.

I went back to Patrington with the man that had rode before me to the justice: for he lived at Patrington. When I came there, he would have had me have a meeting at the Cross; but I said it was no matter; his house would serve. He desired me to go to bed, or lie down upon a bed; which he did, that they might say they had seen me in a bed, or upon a bed; for a report had been raised that I would not lie on any bed, because at that time I lay many times out of doors.[4] Now when the First-day of the week was come, I went to the steeple-house, and declared the truth to the priest and people; and the people did not molest me, for the power of God was come over them. Presently after I had a great meeting at the man's house where I lay, and many were convinced

---

[4] Fox's power of endurance will be noticed in every part of this autobiography. He sleeps under hedges, fences or haystacks. He goes days without suitable food. He speaks in difficult places as often as occasion presents, and goes through the attacks of hostile crowds with an endurance which is astonishing. This iron constitution carried him through the long imprisonments which thinned the ranks of his co-laborers.

of the Lord's everlasting truth, who stand faithful witnesses of it to this day. They were exceedingly grieved that they had not received me, nor given me lodging, when I was there before.

Thence I travelled through the country, even to the furthest part thereof, warning people, in towns and villages, to repent, and directing them to Christ Jesus, their teacher.

On the First-day of the week I came to one Colonel Overton's house, and had a great meeting of the prime of the people of that country; where many things were opened out of the Scriptures which they had never heard before. Many were convinced, and received the Word of life, and were settled in the truth of God.

Then I returned to Patrington again, and visited those Friends that were convinced there; by whom I understood that a tailor, and some wild blades in that town, had occasioned my being carried before the justice. The tailor came to ask my forgiveness, fearing I would complain of him. The constables also were afraid, lest I should trouble them. But I forgave them all, and warned them to turn to the Lord, and to amend their lives.

Now that which made them the more afraid was this: when I was in the steeple-house at Oram, not long before, there came a professor, who gave me a push on the breast in the steeple-house, and bade me get out of the church. " Alas, poor man ! " said I, " dost thou call the steeple-house the Church? The Church is the people, whom God hath purchased with His blood, and not the house." It happened that

Justice Hotham came to hear of this man's abuse, sent his warrant for him, and bound him over to the sessions; so affected was he with the Truth and so zealous to keep the peace. And indeed this Justice Hotham had asked me before whether any people had meddled with me, or abused me; but I was not at liberty to tell him anything of that kind, but was to forgive all.

The next First-day I went to Tickhill, whither the Friends of that side gathered together, and a mighty brokenness by the power of God there was amongst the people. I went out of the meeting, being moved of God to go to the steeple-house. When I came there, I found the priest and most of the chief of the parish together in the chancel.

I went up to them, and began to speak; but they immediately fell upon me; the clerk up with his Bible, as I was speaking, and struck me on the face with it, so that my face gushed out with blood; and I bled exceedingly in the steeple-house. The people cried, " Let us have him out of the church." When they had got me out, they beat me exceedingly, threw me down, and turned me over a hedge. They afterwards dragged me through a house into the street, stoning and beating me as they dragged me along; so that I was all over besmeared with blood and dirt. They got my hat from me, which I never had again. Yet when I was got upon my legs, I declared the Word of life, showed them the fruits of their teacher, and how they dishonored Christianity.

After awhile I got into the meeting again amongst Friends, and the priest and people coming by the house, I went with Friends into the yard, and there spoke to the priest and people. The priest scoffed at us, and called us Quakers. But the Lord's power was so over them, and the Word of life was declared in such authority and dread to them, that the priest fell a-trembling himself; and one of the people said, "Look how the priest trembles and shakes; he is turned a Quaker also."

When the meeting was over, Friends departed; and I went without my hat to Balby, about seven or eight miles. Friends were much abused that day by the priest and his people: insomuch that some moderate justices hearing of it, two or three of them came and sat at the town to examine the business. He that had shed my blood was afraid of having his hand cut off for striking me in the church, as they called it; but I forgave him, and would not appear against him.

Thence I went to Wakefield; and on the First-day after, I went to a steeple-house where James Nayler[5] had been a member of an Independent church; but upon his receiving truth, he was excommunicated. When I came in, and the priest had done, the people called upon me to come up to the priest, which I did; but when I began to declare the Word of life to them, and to lay open the deceit of the priest, they

---

[5] This James Nayler, who left his Independent church to become a Quaker had a future history of pathetic interest. He was a powerful minister, and his very success led to his downfall, which will be recorded in the proper place later on.

rushed upon me suddenly, thrust me out at the other door, punching and beating me, and cried, " Let us have him to the stocks." But the Lord's power restrained them, that they were not suffered to put me in.

So I passed away to the meeting, where were a great many professors and friendly people gathered, and a great convincement there was that day; for the people were mightily satisfied that they were directed to the Lord's teaching *in themselves.* Here we got some lodging; for four of us had lain under a hedge the night before, there being then few Friends in that place.

The priest of that church, of which James Nayler had been a member, whose name was Marshall, raised many wicked slanders about me, as that I carried bottles with me, and made people drink of them, which made them follow me; and that I rode upon a great black horse, and was seen in one country upon it in one hour, and at the same hour in another country threescore miles off; and that I would give a fellow money to follow me, when I was on my black horse. With these lies he fed his people, to make them think evil of the truth which I had declared amongst them. But by these lies he preached many of his hearers away from him; for I was then travelling on foot, and had no horse at that time; which the people generally knew.

As we travelled through the country, preaching repentance to the people, we came into a market-town, where a lecture was held that day. I went into the steeple-house, where many priests, professors and people were. The priest that preached took for his text those words of Jeremiah 5: 31, " My people love to have it so ": leaving out the foregoing words, viz.: " The prophets prophesy falsely, and the priests bear rule by their means." I showed the people his deceit; and directed them to Christ, the true teacher within; declaring that God was come to teach His people himself, and to bring them off from all the world's teachers and hirelings; that they might come to receive freely from Him. Then, warning them of the day of the Lord that was coming upon all flesh, I passed thence without much opposition.

At night we came to a country place, where there was no public house near. The people desired us to stay all night; which we did, and had good service for the Lord, declaring His truth amongst them.

The Lord had said unto me that if but one man or woman were raised by His power to stand and live in the same Spirit that the prophets and apostles were in who gave forth the Scriptures, that man or woman should shake all the country in their profession* for ten miles round. For people had the Scriptures, but were not in the same Light, power, and Spirit which those were in who gave forth the Scriptures; so they neither knew God, Christ, nor the Scriptures aright; nor had they unity one with another, being out of the power and Spirit of God. Therefore we warned all, wherever we met them, of the day of the Lord that was coming upon them.

* "All the country in their profession" means "all the people throughout the country who are mere nominal Christians."

CHAPTER VI.

𝕬 𝕹𝖊𝖜 𝕰𝖗𝖆 𝕭𝖊𝖌𝖎𝖓𝖘

1652.

As we travelled we came near a very great hill, called Pendle Hill, and I was moved of the Lord to go up to the top of it; which I did with difficulty, it was so very steep and high. When I was come to the top, I saw the sea bordering upon Lancashire. From the top of this hill the Lord let me see in what places he had a great people to be gathered. As I went down, I found a spring of water in the side of the hill, with which I refreshed myself, having eaten or drunk but little for several days before.[1]

At night we came to an inn, and declared truth to the man of the house, and wrote a paper to the priests and professors, declaring the day of the Lord, and that Christ was come to teach people Himself, by His power and Spirit in their hearts, and to bring people off from all the world's ways and teachers, to His own free teaching, who had bought them, and was the Saviour of all them that believed in Him. The man of the house spread the paper abroad, and was mightily affected with the truth. Here the Lord opened unto me, and let me see a great people in white raiment by a river side, coming to the Lord;

---

[1] This spring is still called " George Fox's well."

and the place that I saw them in was about Wensleydale and Sedbergh.[2]

The next day we travelled on, and at night got a
little fern or bracken to put under us, and lay upon
a common. Next morning we reached a town, where
Richard Farnsworth[3] parted from me; and then I
travelled alone again. I came up Wensleydale, and
at the market-town in that Dale, there was a lecture
on the market-day. I went into the steeple-house;
and after the priest had done I proclaimed the day
of the Lord to the priest and people, warning them
to turn from darkness to the Light, and from the
power of Satan unto God, that they might come to
know God and Christ aright, and to receive His
teaching, who teacheth freely. Largely and freely
did I declare the Word of life unto them, and had
not much persecution there.

Afterwards I passed up the Dales, warning people

---

[2] No part of Fox's life is more remarkable than these
few months of service that follow in Westmoreland—
" in and about Wensleydale and Sedbergh." Here he
gathers about himself a band of preachers only slightly
less gifted than himself. He wins the support of the
Fells of Swarthmore Hall, which becomes henceforth
a sort of headquarters to the movement, and he gains
the incalculable assistance of Margaret Fell,—for
many years a wise and faithful friend, and finally his
wife.

[3] Richard Farnsworth was " convinced " at Balby in
1651, and became one of George Fox's most valuable
helpers.

to fear God, and preaching the everlasting gospel to them. In my way I came to a great house, where was a schoolmaster; and they got me into the house. I asked them questions about their religion and worship; and afterwards I declared the truth to them. They had me into a parlour, and locked me in, pretending that I was a young man that was mad, and had run away from my relations; and that they would keep me till they could send to them. But I soon convinced them of their mistake, and they let me forth, and would have had me to stay; but I was not to stay there.

Then having exhorted them to repentance, and directed them to the Light of Christ Jesus, that through it they might come unto Him and be saved, I passed from them, and came in the night to a little ale-house on a common, where there was a company of rude fellows drinking. Because I would not drink with them, they struck me with their clubs; but I reproved them, and brought them to be somewhat cooler; and then I walked out of the house upon the common in the night.

After some time one of these drunken fellows came out, and would have come close up to me, pretending to whisper to me; but I perceived he had a knife; and therefore I kept off him, and bade him repent, and fear God. So the Lord by His power preserved me from this wicked man; and he went into the house again. The next morning I went on through other Dales, warning and exhorting people everywhere as I passed, to repent and turn to the Lord: and several were convinced. At one house

that I came to, the man of the house (whom I afterwards found to be a kinsman of John Blakelin's)
would have given me money, but I would not receive
it.

The next day I went to a meeting at Justice Benson's, where I met a people that were separated from
the public worship. This was the place I had seen,
where a people came forth in white raiment. A large
meeting it was, and the people were generally convinced; and they continue still a large meeting of
Friends near Sedbergh; which was then first gathered through my ministry in the name of Jesus.

In the same week there was a great fair, at which
servants used to be hired; and I declared the day of
the Lord through the fair. After I had done so, I
went into the steeple-house yard, and many of the
people of the fair came thither to me, and abundance
of priests and professors. There I declared the everlasting truth of the Lord and the Word of life for
several hours, showing that the Lord was come to
teach His people Himself, and to bring them off
from all the world's ways and teachers, to Christ, the
true teacher, and the true way to God. I laid open
their teachers, showing that they were like them that
were of old condemned by the prophets, and by
Christ, and by the apostles. I exhorted the people to
come off from the temples made with hands; and
wait to receive the Spirit of the Lord, that they
might know themselves to be the temples of God.

Not one of the priests had power to open his
mouth against what I declared: but at last a captain
said, " Why will you not go into the church? this is

not a fit place to preach in." I told him I denied
their church. Then stood up Francis Howgill, who
was preacher to a congregation. He had not seen me
before; yet he undertook to answer that captain; and
he soon put him to silence. Then said Francis Howgill of me, " This man speaks with authority, and not
as the scribes."

After this, I opened to the people that that ground
and house were no holier than another place; and
that the house is not the Church, but the people, of
whom Christ is the head. After awhile the priests
came up to me, and I warned them to repent. One
of them said I was mad; so they turned away. But
many were convinced there that day, who were glad
to hear the truth declared, and received it with joy.
Amongst these was Captain Ward, who received the
truth in the love of it, and lived and died in it.

The next First-day I came to Firbank chapel in
Westmoreland, where Francis Howgill and John
Audland [4] had been preaching in the morning. The
chapel was full of people, so that many could not get
in. Francis said he thought I looked into the chapel,
and his spirit was ready to fail, the Lord's power did
so surprise him: but I did not look in. They made
haste, and had quickly done, and they and some of
the people went to dinner; but abundance stayed till
they came again. John Blakelin and others came to
me, and desired me not to reprove them publicly; for

---

[4] Howgill and Audland became two of the little
band of powerful ministers who gave their lives to the
proclamation of the truth as Fox interpreted it.

they were not parish-teachers, but pretty tender men.
I could not tell them whether I should or no, though
I had not at that time any drawings to declare publicly against them; but I said they must leave me to
the Lord's movings.

While others were gone to dinner, I went to a
brook, got a little water, and then came and sat down
on the top of a rock hard by the chapel. In the afternoon the people gathered about me, with several of
their preachers. It was judged there were above a
thousand people; to whom I declared God's everlasting truth and Word of life freely and largely for
about the space of three hours. I directed all to the
Spirit of God in themselves; that they might be
turned from darkness to Light, and believe in it; that
they might become the children of it, and might be
turned from the power of Satan unto God; and by
the Spirit of truth might be led into all truth, and
sensibly understand the words of the prophets, of
Christ, and of the apostles; and might all come to
know Christ to be their teacher to instruct them,
their counsellor to direct them, their shepherd to
feed them, their bishop to oversee them, and their
prophet to open divine mysteries to them; and might
know their bodies to be prepared, sanctified, and
made fit temples for God and Christ to dwell in. In
the openings of heavenly life I explained unto them
the prophets, and the figures and shadows, and
directed them to Christ, the substance. Then I
opened the parables and sayings of Christ, and things
that had been long hid.

Now there were many old people who went into

the chapel and looked out at the windows, thinking
it a strange thing to see a man preach on a hill, and
not in their church, as they called it; whereupon I
was moved to open to the people that the steeple-
house, and the ground whereon it stood were no more
holy than that mountain; and that those temples,
which they called the dreadful houses of God were
not set up by the command of God and of Christ;
nor their priests called, as Aaron's priesthood was;
nor their tithes appointed by God, as those amongst
the Jews were; but that Christ was come, who ended
both the temple and its worship, and the priests and
their tithes; and that all should now hearken unto
Him; for He said, " Learn of me "; and God said of
Him, " This is my beloved Son, in whom I am well
pleased; hear ye Him."

I declared unto them that the Lord God had sent
me to preach the everlasting gospel and Word of life
amongst them, and to bring them off from all these
temples, tithes, priests, and rudiments of the world,
which had been instituted since the apostles' days,
and had been set up by such as had erred from the
Spirit and power the apostles were in. Very largely
was I opened at this meeting, and the Lord's convincing power accompanied my ministry, and reached the
hearts of the people, whereby many were convinced;
and all the teachers of that congregation (who were
many) were convinced of God's everlasting truth.

At Kendal a meeting was held in the Town-hall.
Several were convinced and many were loving. One
whose name was Cock met me in the street and would
have given me a roll of tobacco, for people were then

much given to smoking. I accepted his love, but did
not receive his tobacco.

Thence I went to Underbarrow, and several people
going along with me, great reasonings I had with
them, especially with Edward Burrough.[5]

At night the priest and many professors came to
the house; and a great deal of disputing I had with
them. Supper being provided for the priest and the
rest of the company, I had not freedom to eat with
them; but told them that if they would appoint a
meeting for the next day at the steeple-house, and
acquaint the people with it, I might meet them.
They had a great deal of reasoning about it; some
being for, and some against it.

In the morning, after I had spoken to them again
concerning the meeting, as I walked upon a bank by
the house, there came several poor travellers, asking
relief, who I saw were in necessity; and they gave
them nothing, but said they were cheats. It grieved
me to see such hard-heartedness amongst professors;
whereupon, when they were gone in to their breakfast, I ran after the poor people about a quarter of a
mile, and gave them some money.

---

[5] Edward Burrough has been called the Whitefield
of Quakerism. He possessed a trained mind and
unusual original power. He was a vigorous writer, and
his ministry was remarkably effective. " Son of thun-
der and consolation," he was named. He was one of
the early martyrs to the truth, dying in a London prison
in 1662. Just before his death he said: " Now my soul
and spirit is entered into its own being with God, and
this form of person must return whence it was taken."

Meanwhile some that were in the house, coming out, and seeing me a quarter of a mile off, said I could not have gone so far in such an instant, if I had not had wings. Hereupon the meeting was like to have been put by; for they were filled with such strange thoughts concerning me that many of them were against having a meeting with me.*

I told them that I had run after those poor people to give them some money; being grieved at the hardheartedness of those who gave them nothing.

Then came Miles and Stephen Hubbersty, who, being more simple-hearted men, would have the meeting held. So to the chapel I went, and the priest came.

A great meeting there was, and the way of life and salvation was opened; and after awhile the priest fled away. Many of Crook and Underbarrow were convinced that day, received the Word of life, and stood fast in it under the teaching of Christ Jesus.

After I had declared the truth to them for some hours, and the meeting was ended, the chief constable and some other professors fell to reasoning with me in the chapel yard. Whereupon I took a Bible and opened the Scriptures, and dealt tenderly with them, as one would do with a child. They that were in the Light of Christ and Spirit of God knew when I spake Scripture, though I did not mention chapter and verse, after the priest's form, to them.

Then I went to an ale-house, to which many resorted betwixt the time of their morning and after-

* The superstitions everywhere existent among the people should be noted.

noon preaching, and had a great deal of reasoning with the people, declaring to them that God was come to teach His people, and to bring them off from the false teachers, such as the prophets, Christ, and the apostles cried against. Many received the Word of life at that time, and abode in it.

Thence I went to Ulverstone, and so to Swarthmore * to Judge Fell's; whither came up one Lampitt, a priest, who was a high notionist. With him I had much reasoning; for he talked of high notions and perfection, and thereby deceived the people. He would have owned me, but I could not own nor join with him, he was so full of filth.[6] He said he was above John; and made as though he knew all things. But I told him that death reigned from Adam to Moses; that he was under death, and knew not Moses, for Moses saw the paradise of God; but he knew neither Moses nor the prophets nor John; for that crooked and rough nature stood in him, and the mountain of sin and corruption; and the way was not prepared in him for the Lord.

He confessed he had been under a cross in things; but now he could sing psalms, and do anything. I told him that now he could see a thief, and join hand in hand with him; but he could not preach Moses, nor

* In the Furness district.

---

[6] Of no other minister has Fox spoken so harshly as of this man Lampitt. There is every reason for believing that the picture which he gives of Lampitt is correct, though in Calamy's "Ejected Ministers" he is spoken of as " a warm and lively preacher."

the prophets, nor John, nor Christ, except he were in the same Spirit that they were in.

Margaret Fell had been absent in the day-time; and at night her children told her that priest Lampitt and I had disagreed, which somewhat troubled her, because she was in profession with him; but he hid his dirty actions from them. At night we had much reasoning, and I declared the truth to her and her family. The next day Lampitt came again, and I had much discourse with him before Margaret Fell, who then clearly discerned the priest. A convincement of the Lord's truth came upon her and her family.

Soon after a day was to be observed for a humiliation, and Margaret Fell asked me to go with her to the steeple-house at Ulverstone, for she was not wholly come off from them. I replied, " I must do as I am ordered by the Lord." So I left her, and walked into the fields; and the Word of the Lord came to me, saying, " Go to the steeple-house after them."

When I came, Lampitt was singing with his people; but his spirit was so foul, and the matter they sung so unsuitable to their states, that after they had done singing, I was moved of the Lord to speak to him and the people. The word of the Lord to them was, " He is not a Jew that is one outwardly, but he is a Jew that is one inwardly, whose praise is not of man, but of God."

As the Lord opened further, I showed them that God was come to teach His people by His Spirit, and to bring them off from all their old ways, religions, churches, and worships; for all their religions, worships, and ways were but talking with other men's words; but they were out of the life and Spirit which they were in who gave them forth.

Then cried out one, called Justice Sawrey, "Take him away"; but Judge Fell's wife said to the officers, "Let him alone; why may not he speak as well as any other?"[7] Lampitt also, the priest, in deceit said, "Let him speak." So at length, when I had declared some time, Justice Sawrey caused the constable to put me out; and then I spoke to the people in the graveyard.

From thence I went into the island of Walney; and after the priest had done I spoke to him, but he got away. Then I declared the truth to the people, but they were something rude. I went to speak with the priest at his house, but he would not be seen. The people said he went to hide himself in the haymow; and they looked for him there, but could not find him. Then they said he was gone to hide himself in the standing corn, but they could not find him there either. I went to James Lancaster's, in the

----

[7] During the Commonwealth period it was no violation of law or custom for a person in the congregation to stand up and speak or object after the minister had finished his sermon. In most cases, where Fox spoke in the churches, he was exercising a right which was well-established. Occasionally he interrupted, which was contrary to good order, but he justified it by an appeal to the call of the Spirit, which he could not resist. (See page 110.) Justices of the Peace had authority to forbid any person to speak.

island, who was convinced, and from thence returned
to Swarthmore, where the Lord's power seized upon
Margaret Fell, her daughter Sarah, and several
others.

Then I went to Baycliff, where Leonard Fell was
convinced, and became a minister of the everlasting
gospel.   Several others were convinced there, and
came into obedience to the truth.   Here the people
said they could not dispute; and would fain have put
some other to hold talk with me; but I bade them
fear the Lord, and not in a light way hold a talk of
the Lord's words, but put the things in practice.[8]

I directed them to the Divine Light of Christ, and
His Spirit in their hearts, which would let them see
all the evil thoughts, words, and actions that they
had thought, spoken, and acted; by which Light they
might see their sin, and also their Saviour Christ
Jesus to save them from their sins.   This I told them
was their first step to peace, even to stand still in the
Light that showed them their sins and transgressions; by which they might come to see they were in
the fall of old Adam, in darkness and death, strangers to the covenant of promise, and without God in
the world; and by the same Light they might see
Christ that died for them to be their Redeemer and
Saviour, and their way to God.

Soon after, Judge Fell being come home, Margaret
Fell, his wife, sent to me, desiring me to return

---

[8] Most wholesome words these, for that period of
endless dispute, when religion too often meant the
acceptance of some verbal statement.

thither; and feeling freedom from the Lord so to do, I went back to Swarthmore. I found the priests and professors, and that envious Justice Sawrey, had much incensed Judge Fell and Captain Sands against the truth by their lies; but when I came to speak with him I answered all his objections, and so thoroughly satisfied him by the Scriptures that he was convinced in his judgment. He asked me if I was that George Fox of whom Justice Robinson spoke so much in commendation amongst many of the Parliament men? I told him I had been with Justice Robinson, and with Justice Hotham in Yorkshire, who were very civil and loving to me; and that they were convinced in their judgment by the Spirit of God that the principle to which I bore testimony was the truth; and they saw over and beyond the priests of the nation, so that they, and many others, were now come to be wiser than their teachers.

After we had discoursed some time together, Judge Fell himself was satisfied also, and came to see, by the openings of the Spirit of God in his heart, over all the priests and teachers of the world, and did not go to hear them for some years before he died; for he knew it was the truth that I declared, and that Christ was the teacher of His people, and their Saviour. He sometimes wished that I were a while with Judge Bradshaw to discourse with him.

There came to Judge Fell's Captain Sands beforementioned, endeavouring to incense the Judge against me, for he was an evil-minded man, and full of envy against me; and yet he could speak high things, and use the Scripture words, and say, " Behold, I make all things new." But I told him, then he must have a new God, for his God was his belly. Besides him came also that envious justice, John Sawrey. I told him his heart was rotten, and he was full of hypocrisy to the brim. Several other people also came, of whose states the Lord gave me a discerning; and I spoke to their conditions.* While I was in those parts, Richard Farnsworth and James Nayler came to see me and the family; and Judge Fell, being satisfied that it was the way of truth, notwithstanding all their opposition, suffered the meeting to be kept at his house. A great meeting was settled there in the Lord's power, which continued near forty years, until the year 1690, when a new meeting-house was erected near it.[9]

On the market-day I went to Lancaster, and spoke through the market in the dreadful power of God, declaring the day of the Lord to the people, and crying out against all their deceitful merchandise. I preached righteousness and truth unto them, which

---

* "Speaking to their conditions" meant describing their inward state.

---

[9] Justice Fell never became an avowed Friend. He, however, had much sympathy with the movement, and used his influence and authority to protect the Friends. He put no hindrance in the way of his wife, who did join them. Swarthmore Hall was always open to travelling ministers, and there is good reason to believe that substantial assistance went from Swarthmore Hall to those who were labouring throughout the kingdom. Margaret Fell was a great-granddaughter of Anne

all should follow after, walk and live in, directing them how and where they might find and receive the Spirit of God to guide them thereinto.

After I had cleared myself in the market, I went to my lodging, whither several people came; and many were convinced who have since stood faithful to the truth.

The First-day following, in the forenoon, I had a great meeting in the street at Lancaster, amongst the soldiers and people, to whom I declared the Word of life, and the everlasting truth. I opened unto them that all the traditions they had lived in, all their worships and religions, and the profession they made of the Scriptures, were good for nothing while they lived out of the life and power which those were in who gave forth the Scriptures. I directed them to the Light of Christ, the heavenly man, and to the Spirit of God in their own hearts, that they might come to be acquainted with God and Christ, receive Him for their teacher, and know His kingdom set up in them.

In the afternoon I went to the steeple-house at Lancaster, and declared the truth to the priest and people, laying open before them the deceit they lived in, and directing them to the power and Spirit of God which they wanted. But they haled me out, and

---

Askew, who was burned at the stake in 1545. Judge Fell was member for Parliament in 1645.

This meeting-house, erected near Swarthmore Hall in 1690, the gift of George Fox, is still standing, and contains many objects of interest.

stoned me along the street till I came to John Lawson's house.

Another First-day I went to a steeple-house by the water-side, where one Whitehead was priest. To him and to the people I declared the truth in the dreadful power of God. There came a doctor so full of envy that he said he could find it in his heart to run me through with his rapier, though he were hanged for it the next day; yet this man came afterwards to be convinced of the truth so far as to be loving to Friends. Some were convinced thereabouts who willingly sat down under the ministry of Christ, their teacher; and a meeting was settled there in the power of God, which has continued to this day.

After this I returned into Westmoreland, and spoke through Kendal on a market-day. So dreadful was the power of God upon me, that people flew like chaff before me into their houses. I warned them of the mighty day of the Lord, and exhorted them to hearken to the voice of God in their own hearts, who was now come to teach His people Himself. When some opposed, many others took my part. At last some fell to fighting about me; but I went and spoke to them, and they parted again. Several were convinced.

After I had travelled up and down in those countries, and had had great meetings, I came to Swarthmore again. And when I had visited Friends in those parts, I heard of a great meeting the priests were to have at Ulverstone, on a lecture-day. I went to it, and into the steeple-house in the dread and power of the Lord. When the priest had done, I

spoke among them the Word of the Lord, which was
as a hammer, and as a fire amongst them. And though
Lampitt, the priest of the place, had been at variance
with most of the priests before, yet against the truth
they all joined together. But the mighty power of
the Lord was over all; and so wonderful was the
appearance thereof, that priest Bennett said the
church shook, insomuch that he was afraid and trembled. And when he had spoken a few confused
words he hastened out for fear it should fall on his
head. Many priests got together there; but they had
no power as yet to persecute.

When I had cleared my conscience towards them,
I went up to Swarthmore again, whither came four
or five of the priests. Coming to discourse, I asked
them whether any one of them could say he had ever
had the word of the Lord to go and speak to such or
such a people. None of them durst say he had; but
one of them burst out into a passion and said that he
could speak his experiences as well as I.

I told him experience was one thing; but to receive
and go with a message, and to have a Word from the
Lord, as the prophets and apostles had had and done,
and as I had done to them, this was another thing.
And therefore I put it to them again, " Can any of
you say you have ever had a command or word from
the Lord immediately at any time ? " but none of
them could say so.

Then I told them that the false prophets, the false
apostles, and the antichrists, could use the words of
the true prophets, the true apostles, and of Christ,
and would speak of other men's experiences, though

they themselves never knew or heard the voice of
God or Christ; and that such as they might obtain
the good words and experiences of others. This puz-
zled them much, and laid them open.

At another time, when I was discoursing with
several priests at Judge Fell's house, and he was by,
I asked them the same question,—whether any of
them had ever heard the voice of God or Christ, to
bid him go to such and such a people, to declare His
word or message unto them. Any one, I told them,
that could but read, might declare the experiences of
the prophets and apostles, which were recorded in the
Scriptures. Thereupon Thomas Taylor,[10] an ancient
priest, did ingenuously confess before Judge Fell
that he had never heard the voice of God, nor of
Christ, to send him to any people; but that he spoke
his experiences, and the experiences of the saints in
former ages, and that he preached. This very much
confirmed Judge Fell in the persuasion he had that
the priests were wrong; for he had thought formerly,
as the generality of people then did, that they were
sent from God.

Now began the priests to rage more and more, and
as much as they could to stir up persecution. James
Nayler and Francis Howgill were cast into prison in
Appleby jail, at the instigation of the malicious
priests, some of whom prophesied that within a

---

[10] This Thomas Taylor was educated at Oxford, and
was a man of profound insight. He became a valiant
supporter of Fox and a convincing minister.

month we should be all scattered again, and come to nothing. But, blessed for ever be the worthy name of the Lord, His work went on and prospered; for about this time John Audland, Francis Howgill, John Camm, Edward Burrough, Richard Hubberthorn, Miles Hubbersty, and Miles Halhead, with several others, being endued with power from on high, came forth in the work of the ministry, and approved themselves faithful labourers therein, travelling up and down, and preaching the gospel freely; by means whereof multitudes were convinced, and many effectually turned to the Lord.

On a lecture-day I was moved to go to the steeple-house at Ulverstone, where were abundance of professors, priests, and people. I went near to priest Lampitt, who was blustering on in his preaching. After the Lord had opened my mouth to speak, John Sawrey, the justice, came to me and said that if I would speak according to the Scriptures, I should speak. I admired him for speaking so to me, and told him I would speak according to the Scriptures, and bring the Scriptures to prove what I had to say; for I had something to speak to Lampitt and to them. Then he said I should not speak, contradicting himself, for he had said just before that I should speak if I would speak according to the Scriptures. The people were quiet, and heard me gladly, till this Justice Sawrey (who was the first stirrer-up of cruel persecution in the north) incensed them against me, and set them on to hale, beat, and bruise me. But now on a sudden the people were in a rage, and fell upon me in the steeple-house before his face, knocked me

down, kicked me, and trampled upon me. So great
was the uproar, that some tumbled over their seats
for fear.

At last he came and took me from the people, led
me out of the steeple-house, and put me into the
hands of the constables and other officers, bidding
them whip me, and put me out of the town. They
led me about a quarter of a mile, some taking hold
by my collar, some by my arms and shoulders; and
they shook and dragged me along.

Many friendly people being come to the market,
and some to the steeple-house to hear me, divers of
these they knocked down also, and broke their heads,
so that the blood ran down from several; and Judge
Fell's son running after to see what they would do
with me, they threw him into a ditch of water, some
of them crying, " Knock the teeth out of his head."

When they had haled me to the common moss-
side, a multitude following, the constables and other
officers gave me some blows over my back with their
willow rods, and thrust me among the rude multitude, who, having furnished themselves with staves,
hedge-stakes, holm or holly bushes, fell upon me,
and beat me on my head, arms, and shoulders, till
they had deprived me of sense; so that I fell down
upon the wet common.

When I recovered again, and saw myself lying in
a watery common, and the people standing about me,
I lay still a little while, and the power of the Lord
sprang through me, and the eternal refreshings
revived me; so that I stood up again in the strengthening power of the eternal God, and stretching out

my arms toward them, I said, with a loud voice,
" Strike again; here are my arms, my head, and my
cheeks."

There was in the company a mason, a professor,
but a rude fellow, who with his walking rule-staff
gave me a blow with all his might just over the back
of my hand, as it was stretched out; with which blow
my hand was so bruised, and my arm so benumbed,
that I could not draw it to me again. Some of the
people cried, " He hath spoiled his hand for ever
having the use of it any more." But I looked at it in
the love of God (for I was in the love of God to all
that persecuted me), and after awhile the Lord's
power sprang through me again, and through my
hand and arm, so that in a moment I recovered
strength in my hand and arm in the sight of them
all.

Then they began to fall out among themselves.
Some of them came to me, and said that if I would
give them money they would secure me from the
rest. But I was moved of the Lord to declare the
Word of life, and showed them their false Christianity, and the fruits of their priest's ministry, telling them that they were more like heathens and
Jews than true Christians.

Then was I moved of the Lord to come up again
through the midst of the people, and go into Ulverstone market. As I went, there met me a soldier,
with his sword by his side. " Sir," said he to me, " I
see you are a man, and I am ashamed and grieved
that you should be thus abused "; and he offered to
assist me in what he could. I told him that the Lord's

power was over all; and I walked through the people in the market, none of whom had power to touch me then. But some of the market people abusing some Friends in the market, I turned about, and saw this soldier among them with his naked rapier; whereupon I ran, and, catching hold of the hand his rapier was in, bid him put up his sword again if he would go along with me.

About two weeks after this I went into Walney island, and James Nayler went with me. We stayed one night at a little town on this side, called Cockan, and had a meeting there, where one was convinced.

After a while there came a man with a pistol, whereupon the people ran out of doors. He called for me; and when I came out to him he snapped his pistol at me, but it would not go off. This caused the people to make a great bustle about him; and some of them took hold of him, to prevent his doing mischief. But I was moved in the Lord's power to speak to him; and he was so struck by the power of the Lord that he trembled for fear, and went and hid himself. Thus the Lord's power came over them all, though there was a great rage in the country.

Next morning I went over in a boat to James Lancaster's. As soon as I came to land there rushed out about forty men with staves, clubs, and fishing-poles, who fell upon me, beating and punching me, and endeavouring to thrust me backward into the sea. When they had thrust me almost into the sea, and I saw they would knock me down in it, I went up into the midst of them; but they laid at me again, and knocked me down, and stunned me.

When I came to myself, I looked up and saw James Lancaster's wife throwing stones at my face, and her husband, James Lancaster, was lying over me, to keep the blows and the stones off me. For the people had persuaded James Lancaster's wife that I had bewitched her husband, and had promised her that if she would let them know when I came thither they would be my death. And having got knowledge of my coming, many of the town rose up in this manner with clubs and staves to kill me; but the Lord's power preserved me, that they could not take away my life.

At length I got up on my feet, but they beat me down again into the boat; which James Lancaster observing, he presently came into it, and set me over the water from them; but while we were on the water within their reach they struck at us with long poles, and threw stones after us. By the time we were come to the other side, we saw them beating James Nayler; for whilst they had been beating me, he walked up into a field, and they never minded him till I was gone; then they fell upon him, and all their cry was, " Kill him, kill him."

When I was come over to the town again, on the other side of the water, the townsmen rose up with pitchforks, flails, and staves, to keep me out of the town, crying, " Kill him, knock him on the head, bring the cart, and carry him away to the church-yard." So after they had abused me, they drove me some distance out of the town, and there left me.

Then James Lancaster went back to look after James Nayler; and I being now left alone, went to a

ditch of water, and having washed myself (for they
had besmeared my face, hands, and clothes with miry
dirt), I walked about three miles to Thomas Hutton's
house, where lodged Thomas Lawson, the priest that
was convinced.

When I came in I could hardly speak to them, I
was so bruised; only I told them where I left James
Nayler. So they took each of them a horse, and went
and brought him thither that night. The next day
Margaret Fell hearing of it, sent a horse for me; but
I was so sore with bruises, I was not able to bear the
shaking of the horse without much pain.

When I was come to Swarthmore, Justice Sawrey
and one Justice Thompson, of Lancaster, granted a
warrant against me; but Judge Fell coming home, it
was not served upon me; for he was out of the country all this time that I was thus cruelly abused.
When he came home he sent forth warrants into the
isle of Walney, to apprehend all those riotous persons; whereupon some of them fled the country.

James Lancaster's wife was afterwards convinced
of the truth, and repented of the evils she had done
me; and so did others of those bitter persecutors
also; but the judgments of God fell upon some of
them, and destruction is come upon many of them
since. Judge Fell asked me to give him a relation of
my persecution; but I told him they could do no
otherwise in the spirit wherein they were, and that
they manifested the fruits of their priest's ministry,
and their profession and religion to be wrong. So
he told his wife I made light of it, and that I spoke

of it as a man that had not been concerned; for, indeed, the Lord's power healed me again.

The time for the sessions at Lancaster being come, I went thither with Judge Fell, who on the way told me he had never had such a matter brought before him before, and he could not well tell what to do in the business. I told him, when Paul was brought before the rulers, and the Jews and priests came down to accuse him, and laid many false things to his charge, Paul stood still all that while. And when they had done, Festus, the governor, and king Agrippa, beckoned to him to speak for himself; which Paul did, and cleared himself of all those false accusations; so he might do with me.

Being come to Lancaster, Justice Sawrey and Justice Thompson having granted a warrant to apprehend me, though I was not apprehended by it, yet hearing of it, I appeared at the sessions, where there appeared against me about forty priests. These had chosen one Marshall, priest of Lancaster, to be their orator; and had provided one young priest, and two priests' sons, to bear witness against me, who had sworn beforehand that I had spoken blasphemy.

When the justices were sat, they heard all that the priests and their witnesses could say and charge against me, their orator Marshall sitting by, and explaining their sayings for them. But the witnesses were so confounded that they discovered themselves to be false witnesses; for when the court had examined one of them upon oath, and then began to examine another, he was at such loss he could not answer directly, but said the other could say it. Which made the justices say to him, "Have you sworn it, and given it in already upon your oath, and now say that he can say it? It seems you did not hear those words spoken yourself, though you have sworn it."

There were then in court several who had been at that meeting, wherein the witnesses swore I spoke those blasphemous words which the priests accused me of; and these, being men of integrity and reputation in the country, did declare and affirm in court that the oath which the witnesses had taken against me was altogether false; and that no such words as they had sworn against me were spoken by me at that meeting. Indeed, most of the serious men of that side of the country, then at the sessions, had been at that meeting; and had heard me both at that and at other meetings also.

This was taken notice of by Colonel West, who, being a justice of the peace, was then upon the bench; and having long been weak in body, blessed the Lord and said that He had healed him that day; adding that he never saw so many sober people and good faces together in all his life. Then, turning himself to me, he said in the open sessions, "George, if thou hast anything to say to the people, thou mayest freely declare it."

I was moved of the Lord to speak; and as soon as I began, priest Marshall, the orator for the rest of the priests, went his way. That which I was moved to declare was this: that the holy Scriptures were given forth by the Spirit of God; and that all people must come to the Spirit of God in themselves in order to know God and Christ, of whom the prophets and apostles learnt: and that by the same Spirit all men might know the holy Scriptures. For as the Spirit of God was in them that gave forth the Scriptures, so the same Spirit must be in all them that come to understand the Scriptures. By this Spirit they might have fellowship with the Father, with the Son, with the Scriptures, and with one another: and without this Spirit they can know neither God, Christ, nor the Scriptures, nor have a right fellowship one with another.

I had no sooner spoken these words than about half a dozen priests, that stood behind me, burst into a passion. One of them, whose name was Jackus, amongst other things that he spake against the Truth, said that the Spirit and the letter were inseparable. I replied, " Then every one that hath the letter hath the Spirit; and they might buy the Spirit with the letter of the Scriptures."

This plain discovery of darkness in the priest moved Judge Fell and Colonel West to reprove them openly, and tell them that according to that position they might carry the Spirit in their pockets as they did the Scriptures. Upon this the priests, being confounded and put to silence, rushed out in a rage against the justices, because they could not have their bloody ends upon me. The justices, seeing the witnesses did not agree, and perceiving that they were brought to answer the priests' envy, and finding that all their evidences were not sufficient in law to make good their charge against me, discharged me.

After Judge Fell had spoken to Justice Sawrey and Justice Thompson concerning the warrant they

had given forth against me, and showing them the
errors thereof, he and Colonel West granted a super-
sedeas* to stop the execution of it. Thus I was
cleared in open sessions of those lying accusations
which the malicious priests had laid to my charge:
and multitudes of people praised God that day, for
it was a joyful day to many. Justice Benson, of
Westmoreland, was convinced; and Major Ripan,
mayor of the town of Lancaster, also.

It was a day of everlasting salvation to hundreds
of people: for the Lord Jesus Christ, the way to the
Father, the free Teacher, was exalted and set up; His
everlasting gospel was preached, and the Word of
eternal life was declared over the heads of the
priests, and all such lucrative preachers. For the
Lord opened many mouths that day to speak His
Word to the priests, and several friendly people and
professors reproved them in their inns, and in the
streets, so that they fell, like an old rotten house: and
the cry was among the people that the Quakers had
got the day, and the priests were fallen.

* A writ or order from the Court setting aside or staying the
execution of the original writ.

CHAPTER VII.

In Prison Again

1653.

About the beginning of the year 1653 I returned to Swarthmore, and going to a meeting at Gleaston, a professor challenged to dispute with me. I went to the house where he was, and called him to come forth; but the Lord's power was over him, so that he durst not meddle.

I departed thence, visited the meetings of Friends in Lancashire, and came back to Swarthmore. Great openings I had from the Lord, not only of divine and spiritual matters, but also of outward things relating to the civil government.

Being one day in Swarthmore Hall, when Judge Fell and Justice Benson were talking of the news, and of the Parliament then sitting (called the Long Parliament), I was moved to tell them that before that day two weeks the Parliament should be broken up, and the Speaker plucked out of his chair. That day two weeks Justice Benson told Judge Fell that now he saw George was a true prophet; for Oliver had broken up the Parliament.[1]

---

[1] Cromwell ejected the "Rump" Parliament April 20th, 1653. There is no contemporary authentification of this prophecy, but there is no reason to doubt the correctness of this account. Such cases of specific fore-

About this time I was in a fast for about ten days, my spirit being greatly exercised on Truth's behalf: for James Milner and Richard Myer went out into imaginations, and a company followed them. This James Milner and some of his company had true openings at the first; but getting up into pride and exaltation of spirit, they ran out from Truth. I was sent for to them, and was moved of the Lord to go and show them their outgoings. They were brought to see their folly, and condemned it; and came into the way of Truth again.

After some time I went to a meeting at Arnside, where was Richard Myer, who had been long lame of one of his arms. I was moved of the Lord to say unto him amongst all the people, " Stand up upon thy legs," for he was sitting down. And he stood up, and stretched out his arm that had been lame a long time, and said, " Be it known unto you, all people, that this day I am healed." [2] Yet his parents could hardly believe it; but after the meeting was done, they had him aside, took off his doublet, and then saw it was true.

---

seeing have been common throughout the entire history of Friends. They have received some slight investigation by the London branch of the Society for Psychical Research, though they have never received the careful investigation which they deserve.

[2] This case of healing belongs in the inexhaustible list of cases of healing by faith. There are many forms of mental healing and of faith healing, and the researches of modern psychology have given us a princi-

He came soon after to Swarthmore meeting, and there declared how the Lord had healed him. Yet after this the Lord commanded him to go to York with a message from Him, which he disobeyed; and the Lord struck him again, so that he died about three-quarters of a year after.

Now were great threatenings given forth in Cumberland that if ever I came there they would take away my life. When I heard it I was drawn to go into Cumberland; and went to Miles Wennington's, in the same parish from which those threatenings came: but they had not power to touch me.

On a First-day I went into the steeple-house at Bootle; * and when the priest had done, I began to speak. But the people were exceeding rude, and struck and beat me in the yard; one gave me a very great blow over my wrist, so that the people thought he had broken my hand to pieces. The constable was very desirous to keep the peace, and would have set some of them that struck me by the heels, if I would have given way to it. After my service amongst them was over, I went to Joseph Nicholson's house, and the constable went a little way with us, to keep off the rude multitude.

In the afternoon I went again. The priest had got

* In Cumberland.

---

ple of explanation for all cures of this sort. All such remarkable events seemed to George Fox to partake of the miraculous and most naturally gave him the impression that he was a peculiarly-chosen instrument of the Lord.

to help him another priest, that came from London, and was highly accounted of. Before I went into the steeple-house, I sat a little upon the cross, and Friends with me; but the Friends were moved to go into the steeple-house, and I went in after them.

The London priest was preaching. He gathered up all the Scriptures he could think of that spoke of false prophets, and antichrists, and deceivers, and threw them upon us; but when he had done I recollected all those Scriptures, and brought them back upon himself. Then the people fell upon me in a rude manner; but the constable charged them to keep the peace, and so made them quiet again. Then the priest began to rage, and said I must not speak there. I told him he had his hour-glass, by which he had preached; and he having done, the time was free for me, as well as for him, for he was but a stranger there himself.[3]

So I opened the Scriptures to them, and let them see that those Scriptures that spoke of the false prophets, and antichrists, and deceivers, described them and their generation; and belonged to them who were found walking in their steps, and bringing forth their fruits; and not unto us, who were not guilty of such things. I manifested to them that they were out of the steps of the true prophets and apos-

---

[3] This passage throws interesting light on the church customs of the time. After the minister has preached his hour by the hour glass there is then liberty for any one to speak. George Fox himself evidently did not observe the hour glass.

tles; and showed them clearly, by the fruits and marks, that it was they of whom those Scriptures spoke, and not we. And I declared the Truth, and the Word of life to the people; and directed them to Christ their teacher.

When I came down again to Joseph Nicholson's house, I saw a great hole in my coat, which was cut with a knife; but it was not cut through my doublet, for the Lord had prevented their mischief. The next day there was a rude, wicked man who would have done violence to a Friend, but the Lord's power stopped him.

Now was I moved to send James Lancaster to appoint a meeting at the steeple-house of John Wilkinson, near Cockermouth,—a preacher in great repute, who had three parishes under him. I stayed at Milholm, in Bootle, till James Lancaster came back again. In the meantime some of the gentry of the country had formed a plot against me, and had given a little boy a rapier, with which to do me mischief. They came with the boy to Joseph Nicholson's to seek me; but the Lord had so ordered it that I was gone into the fields. They met with James Lancaster, but did not much abuse him; and not finding me in the house, they went away again. So I walked up and down in the fields that night, as very often I used to do, and did not go to bed.

We came the next day to the steeple-house where James Lancaster had appointed the meeting. There were at this meeting twelve soldiers and their wives, from Carlisle; and the country people came in, as if it were to a fair. I lay at a house somewhat short of

the place, so that many Friends got thither before
me. When I came I found James Lancaster speaking under a yew tree which was so full of people that
I feared they would break it down.

I looked about for a place to stand upon, to speak
unto the people, for they lay all up and down, like
people at a leaguer.* After I was discovered, a professor asked if I would not go into the church? I,
seeing no place abroad convenient to speak to the
people from, told him, Yes; whereupon the people
rushed in, so that when I came the house and pulpit
were so full I had much ado to get in. Those that
could not get in stood abroad about the walls.

When the people were settled I stood up on a seat,
and the Lord opened my mouth to declare His everlasting Truth and His everlasting day. When I had
largely declared the Word of life unto them for
about the space of three hours, I walked forth
amongst the people, who passed away well satisfied.
Among the rest a professor followed me, praising
and commending me; but his words were like a this-
tle to me. Many hundreds were convinced that day,
and received the Lord Jesus Christ and His free
teaching, with gladness; of whom some have died in
the Truth, and many stand faithful witnesses thereof. The soldiers also were convinced, and their wives.

After this I went to a village, and many people
accompanied me. As I was sitting in a house full of
people, declaring the Word of life unto them, I cast
mine eye upon a woman, and discerned an unclean

* This indicates that he had seen besieging armies during the
Civil War.

spirit in her. And I was moved of the Lord to speak sharply to her, and told her she was under the influence of an unclean spirit;[4] whereupon she went out of the room. Now, I being a stranger there, and knowing nothing of the woman outwardly, the people wondered at it, and told me afterwards that I had discovered a great thing; for all the country looked upon her to be a wicked person.

The Lord had given me a spirit of discerning, by which I many times saw the states and conditions of people, and could try their spirits. For not long before, as I was going to a meeting, I saw some women in a field, and I discerned an evil spirit in them; and I was moved to go out of my way into the field to them, and declare unto them their conditions. At another time there came one into Swarthmore Hall in the meeting time, and I was moved to speak sharply to her, and told her she was under the power of an evil spirit; and the people said afterwards she was generally accounted so. There came also at another time another woman, and stood at a distance from me, and I cast mine eye upon her, and said, " Thou hast been an harlot "; for I perfectly saw the condition and life of the woman. The woman answered and said that many could tell her of her outward sins, but none could tell her of her inward. Then I told her her heart was not right before the Lord, and that from the inward came the outward.

---

[4] It must be remembered that Fox uses here the language and the popular ideas of the time, as we should expect him to do.

This woman came afterwards to be convinced of God's truth, and became a Friend.

Thence we travelled to Carlisle. The pastor of the Baptists, with most of his hearers, came to the abbey, where I had a meeting; and I declared the Word of life amongst them. Many of the Baptists and of the soldiers were convinced. After the meeting the pastor of the Baptists, an high notionist and a flashy man, asked me what must be damned. I was moved immediately to tell him that that which spoke in him was to be damned. This stopped his mouth; and the witness of God was raised up in him. I opened to him the states of election and reprobation; so that he said he never heard the like in his life. He came afterwards to be convinced.

Then I went to the castle among the soldiers, who beat a drum and called the garrison together. I preached the Truth amongst them, directing them to the Lord Jesus Christ to be their teacher, and to the measure of His Spirit in themselves, by which they might be turned from darkness to light, and from the power of Satan unto God. I warned them all that they should do no violence to any man, but should show forth a Christian life: telling them that He who was to be their Teacher would be their condemner if they were disobedient to Him. So I left them, having no opposition from any of them, except the sergeants, who afterwards came to be convinced.

On the market-day I went up into the market, to the market-cross. The magistrates had both threatened, and sent their sergeants; and the magistrates' wives had said that if I came there they would pluck the hair off my head; and the sergeants should take me up. Nevertheless I obeyed the Lord God, went up on the cross, and declared unto them that the day of the Lord was coming upon all their deceitful ways and doings, and deceitful merchandise; that they should put away all cozening and cheating, and keep to Yea and Nay, and speak the truth one to another. So the Truth and the power of God was set over them.

After I had declared the Word of life to the people, the throng being so great that the sergeants could not reach me, nor the magistrates' wives come at me, I passed away quietly. Many people and soldiers came to me, and some Baptists, that were bitter contenders; amongst whom one of their deacons, an envious man, finding that the Lord's power was over them, cried out for very anger. Whereupon I set my eyes upon him, and spoke sharply to him in the power of the Lord: and he cried, " Do not pierce me so with thy eyes; keep thy eyes off me." [5]

The First-day following I went into the steeple-house: and after the priest had done, I preached the Truth to the people, and declared the Word of life amongst them. The priest got away; and the magistrates desired me to go out of the steeple-house. But I still declared the way of the Lord unto them, and

---

[5] This is an interesting testimony to the power of George Fox's eyes. The same remark is made on several occasions during his life. This power of the eye undoubtedly was a considerable element in his commanding influence over others.

told them I came to speak the Word of life and **salvation** from the Lord amongst them. The power of the Lord was dreadful amongst them, so that the people trembled and shook, and they thought the steeple-house shook; some of them feared it would have fallen down on their heads. The magistrates' wives were in a rage, and strove mightily to get at me: but the soldiers and friendly people stood thick about me.

At length the rude people of the city rose, and came with staves and stones into the steeple-house, crying, " Down with these round-headed rogues "; and they threw stones. Whereupon the governor sent a file or two of musketeers into the steeple-house to appease the tumult, and commanded all the other soldiers out. So those soldiers took me by the hand in a friendly manner, and said they would have me along with them.

When we came into the street the city was in an uproar. The governor came down; and some of the soldiers were put in prison for standing by me against the townspeople.

A lieutenant, who had been convinced, came and brought me to his house, where there was a Baptist meeting, and thither came Friends also. We had a very quiet meeting; they heard the Word of life gladly, and many received it.

The next day, the justices and magistrates of the town being gathered together in the town-hall, they granted a warrant against me, and sent for me before them. I was then gone to a Baptist's; but hearing of it, I went up to the hall, where many rude people were, some of whom had sworn false things against me. I had a great deal of discourse with the magistrates, wherein I laid open the fruits of their priests' preaching, showed them how they were void of Christianity, and that, though they were such great professors (for they were Independents and Presbyterians) they were without the possession of that which they professed. After a large examination, they committed me to prison as a blasphemer, a heretic, and a seducer,[6] though they could not justly charge any such thing against me.

The jail at Carlisle had two jailers, an upper and an under, who looked like two great bear-wards. When I was brought in the upper jailer took me up into a great chamber, and told me I should have what I would in that room. But I told him he should not expect any money from me, for I would neither lie in any of his beds, nor eat any of his victuals. Then he put me into another room, where after awhile I got something to lie upon.

There I lay till the assizes came, and then all the talk was that I was to be hanged. The high sheriff, Wilfred Lawson, stirred them much up to take away my life, and said he would guard me to my execution himself. They were in a rage, and set three musketeers for guard upon me, one at my chamber-door, another at the stairs-foot, and a third at the street-

---

[6] As in Derby, the charge is blasphemy, under the Act of 1648. The report, spoken of later, that he would be put to death, was not mere rumor, for it was a real possibility under this Act.

door; and they would let none come at me, except
one sometimes, to bring me some necessary things.

At night, sometimes as late as the tenth hour, they
would bring up priests to me, who were exceeding
rude and devilish. There were a company of bitter
Scotch priests, Presbyterians, made up of envy and
malice, who were not fit to speak of the things of
God, they were so foul-mouthed. But the Lord, by
His power, gave me dominion over them all, and I
let them see both their fruits and their spirits. Great
ladies also (as they were called) came to see the man
that they said was to die. While the judge, justices,
and sheriff were contriving together how they might
put me to death, the Lord disappointed their design
by an unexpected way.[7]

The next day, after the judges were gone out of
town, an order was sent to the jailer to put me down
into the prison amongst the moss-troopers,* thieves,
and murderers; which accordingly he did. A filthy,
nasty place it was, where men and women were put
together in a very uncivil manner, and never a house
of office to it; and the prisoners were so lousy that
one woman was almost eaten to death with lice. Yet

* A kind of freebooter.

---

[7] Justice Anthony Pearson pointed out to the
judges of the Carlisle courts that there was no evidence
to support the charges against the prisoner, and that
he was illegally held. He was finally dismissed without
formal trial. The release of Fox was, however, hastened by an urgent letter from Parliament (the famous
Barebones Parliament), requesting that he be set free.

bad as the place was, the prisoners were all made very loving and subject to me, and some of them were convinced of the Truth, as the publicans and harlots were of old; so that they were able to confound any priest that might come to the grates to dispute.

But the jailer was cruel, and the under-jailer very ·abusive both to me and to Friends that came to see me; for he would beat with a great cudgel Friends who did but come to the window to look in upon me. I could get up to the grate, where sometimes I took in my meat; at which the jailer was often offended. Once he came in a great rage and beat me with his cudgel, though I was not at the grate at that time; and as he beat me, he cried, " Come out of the window," though I was then far from it. While he struck me, I was moved in the Lord's power to sing, which made him rage the more. Then he fetched a fiddler, and set him to play, thinking to vex me. But while he played, I was moved in the everlasting power of the Lord God to sing; and my voice drowned the noise of the fiddle, struck and confounded them, and made them give over fiddling and go their way.

Whilst I was in prison at Carlisle, James Parnell, a little lad about sixteen years of age, came to see me, and was convinced. The Lord quickly made him a powerful minister of the Word of life, and many were turned to Christ by him, though he lived not long. For, travelling into Essex in the work of the ministry, in the year 1655, he was committed to Colchester castle, where he endured very great hardships and sufferings. He was put by the cruel jailer into a hole in the castle wall, called the oven, so high from the ground that he went up to it by a ladder, which being six feet too short, he was obliged to climb from the ladder to the hole by a rope that was fastened above. When Friends would have given him a cord and a basket in which to draw up his victuals, the inhuman jailer would not suffer them, but forced him to go down and up by that short ladder and rope to fetch his victuals, which for a long time he did, or else he might have famished in the hole.

At length his limbs became much benumbed with lying in that place; yet being still obliged to go down to take up some victuals, as he came up the ladder again with his victuals in one hand, and caught at the rope with the other, he missed the rope, and fell down from a very great height upon the stones; by which fall he was so wounded in the head, arms, and body, that he died a short time after.[8]

While I thus lay in the dungeon at Carlisle, the report raised at the time of the assize that I should be put to death was gone far and near; insomuch that the Parliament then sitting, which, I think, was called the Little Parliament, hearing that a young

---

[8] This is one of the saddest stories in the annals of Quaker martyrology. James Parnell was well trained mentally, and held successful discussions with the Cambridge students. The dungeon in Colchester Castle, where this brief holy life came to an end, is still visited by tourists.

man at Carlisle was to die for religion, caused a letter
to be sent the sheriff and magistrates concerning me.

Not long after this the Lord's power came over
the justices, and they were made to set me at liberty.
But some time previous the governor and Anthony
Pearson came down into the dungeon, to see the
place where I was kept and understand what usage I
had had. They found the place so bad and the savour
so ill, that they cried shame on the magistrates for
suffering the jailer to do such things. They called
for the jailers into the dungeon, and required them
to find sureties for their good behaviour; and the
under-jailer, who had been such a cruel fellow, they
put into the dungeon with me, amongst the moss-
troopers.

Now I went into the country, and had mighty
great meetings. The everlasting gospel and Word
of life flourished, and thousands were turned to the
Lord Jesus Christ, and to His teaching.

The priests and magistrates were in a great rage
against me in Westmoreland, and had a warrant to
apprehend me, which they renewed from time to
time, for a long time; yet the Lord did not suffer
them to serve it upon me. I travelled on amongst
Friends, visiting the meetings till I came to Swarthmore, where I heard that the Baptists and professors
in Scotland had sent to have a dispute with me. I
sent them word that I would meet them in Cumberland, at Thomas Bewley's house, whither accordingly
I went, but none of them came.

Some dangers at this time I underwent in my
travels; for at one time, as we were passing from a

meeting, and going through Wigton on a market-day, the people of the town had set a guard with pitch-forks; and although some of their own neighbours were with us, they kept us out of the town, and would not let us pass through it, under the pretence of preventing the sickness; though there was no occasion for any such thing. However, they fell upon us, and had like to have spoiled us and our horses; but the Lord restrained them, that they did not much hurt; and we passed away.

Another time, as I was passing between two Friends' houses, some rude fellows lay in wait in a lane, and exceedingly stoned and abused us; but at last, through the Lord's assistance, we got through them, and had not much hurt. But this showed the fruits of the priest's teaching, which shamed their profession of Christianity.

After I had visited Friends in that county, I went through the county into Durham, having large meetings by the way. A very large one I had at Anthony Pearson's, where many were convinced. From thence I passed through Northumberland to Derwentwater, where there were great meetings; and the priests threatened that they would come, but none came. The everlasting Word of life was freely preached, and freely received; and many hundreds were turned to Christ, their teacher.

In Northumberland many came to dispute, of whom some pleaded against perfection. Unto these I declared that Adam and Eve were perfect before they fell; that all that God made was perfect; that the imperfection came by the devil, and the fall; but that Christ, who came to destroy the devil, said, "Be ye perfect."

One of the professors alleged that Job said, "Shall mortal man be more pure than his Maker? The heavens are not clean in His sight. God charged His angels with folly." But I showed him his mistake, and let him see that it was not Job that said so, but one of those that contended against Job; for Job stood for perfection, and held his integrity; and they were called miserable comforters.

Then these professors said that the outward body was the body of death and sin. I showed them their mistake in that also; for Adam and Eve had each of them an outward body, before the body of death and sin got into them; and that man and woman will have bodies when the body of sin and death is put off again; when they are renewed again into the image of God by Christ Jesus, in which they were before they fell. So they ceased at that time from opposing further; and glorious meetings we had in the Lord's power.

Then passed we to Hexam, where we had a great meeting on top of a hill. The priest threatened that he would come and oppose us, but he came not; so all was quiet. And the everlasting day and renowned Truth of the everliving God was sounded over those dark countries, and His Son exalted over all. It was proclaimed amongst the people that the day was now come wherein all that made a profession of the Son of God might receive Him; and that to as many as would receive Him He would give power to become the sons of God, as He had done to me.

It was further declared that he who had the Son of God, had life eternal; but he that had not the Son of God, though he professed all the Scriptures from the first of Genesis to the last of the Revelation, had no life.

So after all were directed to the light of Christ, by which they might see Him, receive Him, and know where their true teacher was, and the everlasting Truth had been largely declared amongst them, we passed through Hexam peaceably, and came into Gilsland, a country noted for thieving.

The next day we came into Cumberland again, where we had a general meeting of thousands of people on top of an hill near Langlands. A glorious and heavenly meeting it was; for the glory of the Lord did shine over all; and there were as many as one could well speak over,* the multitude was so great. Their eyes were turned to Christ, their teacher; and they came to sit under their own vine; insomuch that Francis Howgill, coming afterwards to visit them, found they had no need of words; for they were sitting under their teacher Christ Jesus; in the sense whereof He sat down amongst them, without speaking anything.

A great convincement there was in Cumberland, Bishoprick, Northumberland, Westmoreland, Lancashire, and Yorkshire; and the plants of God grew and flourished, the heavenly rain descending, and God's glory shining upon them. Many mouths were opened by the Lord to His praise; yea, to babes and sucklings he ordained strength.

* That is, reach with the voice.

CHAPTER VIII.

𝔄 𝔙𝔦𝔰𝔦𝔱 𝔱𝔬 𝔒𝔩𝔦𝔳𝔢𝔯 ℭ𝔯𝔬𝔪𝔴𝔢𝔩𝔩

1653–1654.

About this time the priests and professors fell to prophesying against us afresh. They had said long before that we should be destroyed within a month; and after that, they prolonged the time to half a year. But that time being long expired, and we mightily increased in number, they now gave forth that we would eat out one another. For often after meetings many tender people, having a great way to go, tarried at Friends' houses by the way, and sometimes more than there were beds to lodge in; so that some lay on the hay-mows. Hereupon Cain's fear possessed the professors and world's people; for they were afraid that when we had eaten one another out, we should all come to be maintained by the parishes, and be chargeable to them.

But after awhile, when they saw that the Lord blessed and increased Friends, as he did Abraham, both in the field and in the basket, at their goings forth and their comings in, at their risings up and their lyings down, and that all things prospered with them; then they saw the falseness of all their prophecies against us, and that it was in vain to curse whom God had blessed.

At the first convincement, when Friends could not put off their hats to people, or say You to a single person, but Thou and Thee;—when they could not bow, or use flattering words in salutation, or adopt the fashions and customs of the world, many Friends, that were tradesmen of several sorts, lost their customers at first, for the people were shy of them, and would not trade with them; so that for a time some Friends could hardly get money enough to buy bread.

But afterwards, when people came to have experience of Friends' honesty and faithfulness, and found that their yea was yea, and their nay was nay; that they kept to a word in their dealings, and would not cozen and cheat, but that if a child were sent to their shops for anything, he was as well used as his parents would have been;—then the lives and conversation of Friends did preach, and reached to the witness of God in the people.

Then things altered so, that all the inquiry was, " Where is there a draper, or shop-keeper, or tailor, or shoemaker, or any other tradesman, that is a Quaker?" Insomuch that Friends had more trade than many of their neighbours, and if there was any trading, they had a great part of it. Then the envious professors altered their note, and began to cry out, " If we let these Quakers alone, they will take the trade of the nation out of our hands." [1]

---

[1] This record of the effect of Quaker honesty is supported by impartial contemporary testimony. A curious confirmation of the business successes of the Quaker traders is found in a satiric ballad of the times, called " Wickham Wakened; or, the Quakers Madrigall

This has been the Lord's doing to and for His people! which my desire is that all who profess His holy
truth may be kept truly sensible of, and that all may
be preserved in and by His power and Spirit, faithful to God and man. Faithful first to God, in obeying Him in all things; and next in doing unto all
men that which is just and righteous in all things,
that the Lord God may be glorified in their prac-
tising truth, holiness, godliness, and righteousness
amongst people in all their lives and conversation.

While Friends abode in the northern parts, a priest
of Wrexham, in Wales, named Morgan Floyd, having heard reports concerning us, sent two of his congregation into the north to inquire concerning us, to
try us, and bring him an account of us. When these
triers came amongst us, the power of the Lord seized
on them, and they were both convinced of the truth.
So they stayed some time with us, and then returned
to Wales; where afterwards one of them departed
from his convincement; but the other, named John-
ap-John, abode in the truth, and received a part in
the ministry, in which he continued faithful.[2]

---

in Rime Dogerell," published in Ebsworth's "Choyce
Drollery." The Rhymster tells how the Quaker is settling down to "great thrift," his period of "tipling
being done," i.e., his days of ranting being over, and
those who come into competition with him wish him
back in the ranting stage.

> "O be drunk again, Quaker,
>   Take thy canniken and shake her,
>   For thou art the worse for thy mending."

[2] This was the beginning of the movement in Wales.

About this time the oath or engagement to Oliver Cromwell was tendered to the soldiers, many of whom were disbanded because, in obedience to Christ, they could not swear.[3] John Stubbs, for one, who was convinced when I was in Carlisle prison, became a good soldier in the Lamb's war, and a faithful minister of Christ Jesus; travelling much in the service of the Lord in Holland, Ireland, Scotland, Italy, Egypt, and America. And the Lord's power preserved him from the hands of the papists, though many times he was in great danger of the Inquisition. But some of the soldiers, who had been convinced in their judgment, but had not come into obedience to the Truth, took Oliver Cromwell's oath; and, going afterwards into Scotland, and coming before a garrison there, the garrison, thinking they had been enemies, fired at them, and killed divers of them, which was a sad event.

When the churches were settled in the north, and Friends were established under Christ's teaching, and the glory of the Lord shined over them, I passed from Swarthmore to Lancaster about the beginning of the year 1654, visiting Friends, till I came to Synder-hill green, where a meeting had been appointed three weeks before. We passed through Halifax, a rude town of professors, and came to Thomas Taylor's, who had been a captain, where we

---

In 1657, George Fox travelled and laboured extensively in Wales, where many followers were gathered.

[3] Nothing caused Friends so much trouble as their absolute refusal to take any kind of an oath.

met with some janglers;* but the Lord's power was over all; for I travelled in the motion of God's power.

When I came to Synder-hill green, there was a mighty meeting. Some thousands of people, as it was judged, were there, and many persons of note, captains and other officers. There was a general convincement; for the Lord's power and Truth was set over all, and there was no opposition.

About this time did the Lord move upon the spirits of many whom He had raised up and sent forth to labour in His vineyard, to travel southwards, and spread themselves in the service of the gospel to the eastern, southern, and western parts of the nation. Francis Howgill and Edward Burrough went to London; John Camm and John Audland to Bristol; Richard Hubberthorn and George Whitehead towards Norwich; Thomas Holmes into Wales; and many others different ways: for above sixty ministers had the Lord raised up, and did now send abroad out of the north country. The sense of their service was very weighty upon me.[4]

About this time Rice Jones, of Nottingham, (who had been a Baptist, and was turned Ranter), and his

* Ranters.

---

[4] At the end of six years of ministry these sixty ministers had been gathered to the work which now absorbed George Fox. It was a remarkable group of men,—young, vigorous, ready speakers, eager for the hard service, welcoming persecution and undaunted by any dangers or difficulties. They so completely caught

company, began to prophesy against me; giving out
that I was then at the highest, and that after that
time I should fall down as fast. He sent a bundle of
railing papers from Nottingham to Mansfield, Clawson, and the towns thereabouts, judging Friends for
declaring the Truth in the markets and in steeple-
houses; which papers I answered. But his and his
company's prophecies came upon themselves; for
soon after they fell to pieces, and many of his followers became Friends, and continued so.

And through the Lord's blessed power, Truth and
Friends have increased, and do increase in the increase of God: and I, by the same power, have been
and am preserved, and kept in the everlasting Seed,
that never fell, nor changes. But Rice Jones took
the oaths that were put to him, and so disobeyed the
command of Christ.

Many such false prophets have risen up against
me, but the Lord hath blasted them, and will blast all

---

the idea of Fox that they practically all spoke the same
religious language.

To them George Fox addressed a quaint, but strikingly spiritual, epistle of advice as they went out to
begin their labours. Here are a few sentences from it:

" All Friends everywhere, Know the Seed of God,
which bruiseth the seed of the serpent, and is atop of
the seed of the serpent: which Seed sins not, but bruiseth the serpent's head that doth sin, and that tempts to
sin: to which Seed is God's promise and blessing; and
which Seed is one in the male and in the female. . .

" This is the Word of the Lord to you all: Every one

who rise against the blessed Seed, and me in that. My confidence is in the Lord; for I saw their end, and how the Lord would confound them, before He sent me forth.

I travelled up and down in Yorkshire, as far as Holderness, and to the land's end that way, visiting Friends and the churches of Christ; which were finely settled under Christ's teaching. At length I came to Captain Bradford's house, whither came many Ranters from York to wrangle; but they were confounded and stopped. Thither came also she who was called the Lady Montague, who was then convinced, and lived and died in the Truth.

Thence I went to Drayton in Leicestershire to visit my relations. As soon as I was come in, Nathaniel Stephens, the priest, having got another priest, and given notice to the country, sent to me to come to them, for they could not do anything till I came. Having been three years away from my rela-

---

in the measure of life wait, that with it all your minds may be guided up to the Father of life, the Father of spirits: to receive power from Him, and wisdom, that with it you may be ordered to His glory: to whom be all glory forever! All keep in the Light and Life, that judgeth down that which is contrary to the Light and Life. So the Lord God Almighty be with you all. . . .

"All Friends that speak in public, see that it be in the life of God; for that begets to God; the fruits of that shall never wither. This sows to the Spirit which is in prison, and of the Spirit reaps life; and the other sows to the flesh, and of the flesh reaps corruption

tions, I knew nothing of their design. But at last I went into the steeple-house yard, where the two priests were; and they had gathered abundance of people.

When I came there, they would have had me go into the steeple-house. I asked them what I should do there; and they said that Mr. Stephens could not bear the cold. I told him he might bear it as well as I. At last we went into a great hall, Richard Farnsworth being with me; and a great dispute we had with these priests concerning their practices, how contrary they were to Christ and His apostles.

The priests would know where tithes were forbidden or ended. I showed them out of the seventh chapter to the Hebrews that not only tithes, but the priesthood that took tithes, was ended; and the law by which the priesthood was made, and tithes were commanded to be paid, was ended and annulled. Then the priests stirred up the people to some lightness and rudeness.

This you may see all the world over amongst these seeds-men,—that which may be reaped in the field, that is the world. Therefore wait in the Spirit of the Lord, which cuts down and casts out all this, the root and branches of it. So in that wait to receive power, and the Lord God Almighty preserve you in it; whereby you may come to feel the Light, that comprehends time and the world, and fathoms it: which, believed in, gives you victory over the world. Here the power of the Lord is received, which subdues all the contrary, and puts off the garments that will stain and pollute."

I had known Stephens from a child, therefore I
laid open his condition, and the manner of his preaching; and how he, like the rest of the priests, did
apply the promises to the first birth, which must die.
But I showed that the promises were to the Seed,
not to many seeds, but to one Seed, Christ; who was
one in male and female; for all were to be born again
before they could enter into the kingdom of God.

Then he said, I must not judge so; but I told him
that He that was spiritual judged all things. Then
he confessed that that was a full Scripture; " but,
neighbours," said he, " this is the business; George
Fox is come to the light of the sun, and now he thinks
to put out my star-light."

I told him that I would not quench the least measure of God in any, much less put out his star-light, if
it were true star-light—light from the Morning Star.
But, I told him, if he had anything from Christ or
God, he ought to speak it freely, and not take tithes
from the people for preaching, seeing that Christ
commanded His ministers to give freely, as they had
received freely. So I charged him to preach no more
for tithes or any hire. But he said he would not
yield to that.

After a while the people began to be vain and
rude, so we broke up; yet some were made loving to
the Truth that day. Before we parted I told them
that if the Lord would, I intended to be at the town
again that day week. In the interim I went into the
country, and had meetings, and came thither again
that day week.

Against that time this priest had got seven priests

to help him; for priest Stephens had given notice at
a lecture on a market-day at Adderston, that such a
day there would be a meeting and a dispute with me.
I knew nothing of it; but had only said I should be
in town that day week again.   These eight priests
had gathered several hundreds of people, even most
of the country thereabouts, and they would have had
me go into the steeple-house; but I would not go in,
but got on a hill, and there spoke to them and the
people.

There were with me Thomas Taylor, who had been
a priest, James Parnell, and several other Friends.
The priests thought that day to trample down Truth;
but the Truth overcame them. Then they grew light,
and the people rude; and the priests would not stand
trial with me; but would be contending here a little
and there a little, with one Friend or another. At
last one of the priests brought his son to dispute with
me; but his mouth was soon stopped. When he could
not tell how to answer, he would ask his father;
and his father was confounded also, when he came to
answer for his son.

So, after they had toiled themselves, they went
away in a rage to priest Stephens's house to drink.
As they went away, I said, " I never came to a place
where so many priests together would not stand the
trial with me." Thereupon they and some of their
wives came about me, laid hold of me, and fawningly
said, " What might you not have been, if it had not
been for the Quakers! "

Then they began to push Friends to and fro, to
thrust them from me, and to pluck me to themselves.

After a while several lusty fellows came, took me up in their arms, and carried me into the steeple-house porch, intending to carry me into the steeple-house by force; but the door being locked they fell down in a heap, having me under them. As soon as I could, I got up from under them, and went to the hill again. Then they took me from that place to the steeple-house wall, and set me on something like a stool; and all the priests being come back, stood under with the people.

The priests cried, " Come, to argument, to argument." I said that I denied all their voices, for they were the voices of hirelings and strangers. They cried, " Prove it, prove it." Then I directed them to the tenth of John, where they might see what Christ said of such. He declared that He was the true Shepherd that laid down His life for His sheep, and His sheep heard His voice and followed Him; but the hireling would fly when the wolf came, because he was a hireling. I offered to prove that they were such hirelings. Then the priests plucked me off the stool again; and they themselves got all upon stools under the steeple-house wall.

Then I felt the mighty power of God arise over all, and I told them that if they would but give audience, and hear me quietly, I would show them by the Scriptures why I denied those eight priests, or teachers, that stood before me, and all the hireling teachers of the world whatsoever; and I would give them Scriptures for what I said. Whereupon both priests and people consented. Then I showed them out of the prophets Isaiah, Jeremiah, Ezekiel, Micah,

Malachi, and others, that they were in the steps of
such as God sent His true prophets to cry against.

When I appealed to that of God in their consciences, the Light of Christ Jesus in them, they
could not abide to hear it. They had been all quiet
before; but then a professor said, "George, what!
wilt thou never have done?" I told him I should
have done shortly. I went on a little longer, and
cleared myself of them in the Lord's power. When
I had done, all the priests and people stood silent for
a time.

At last one of the priests said that they would read
the Scriptures I had quoted. I told them I desired
them to do so with all my heart. They began to read
the twenty-third of Jeremiah, where they saw the
marks of the false prophets that he cried against.
When they had read a verse or two I said, "Take
notice, people"; but the priests said, "Hold thy
tongue, George." I bade them read the whole chapter, for it was all against them. Then they stopped,
and would read no further.

My father, though a hearer and follower of the
priest, was so well satisfied that he struck his cane
upon the ground, and said, "Truly, I see that he that
will but stand to the truth, it will bear him out." [5]

After this I went into the country, had several
meetings, and came to Swannington, where the sol-

---

[5] This is the only indication of the extent of "Righteous Christer's" sympathy with his son's somewhat
revolutionary message.

diers came; but the meeting was quiet, the Lord's power was over all, and the soldiers did not meddle.

Then I went to Leicester; and from Leicester to Whetstone. There came about seventeen troopers of Colonel Hacker's regiment, with his marshal, and took me up before the meeting, though Friends were beginning to gather together; for there were several Friends from divers parts.[6] I told the marshal he might let all the Friends go; that I would answer for them all. Thereupon he took me, and let all the Friends go; only Alexander Parker went along with me.

At night they had me before Colonel Hacker, his major, and captains, a great company of them; and a great deal of discourse we had about the priests, and about meetings; for at this time there was a noise of a plot against Oliver Cromwell. Much reasoning I had with them about the Light of Christ, which enlighteneth every man that cometh into the world. Colonel Hacker asked whether it was not this Light of Christ that made Judas betray his Master, and afterwards led him to hang himself? I told him, "No; that was the spirit of darkness, which hated Christ and His Light."

---

[6] Colonel Hacker and his regiment superintended the execution of Charles I., and held back the threatening crowd of London citizens. He apparently now suspected that Fox and the Quakers in a plot to bring in Charles II. Cromwell had for about six months been Lord Protector. Gerard and Vowel's plot was discovered about this time.

Then Colonel Hacker said I might go home, and keep at home, and not go abroad to meetings. I told him I was an innocent man, free from plots, and denied all such work. His son Needham said, "Father, this man hath reigned too long; it is time to have him cut off." I asked him, "For what? What have I done? Whom have I wronged? I was bred and born in this country, and who can accuse me of any evil, from childhood up?" Colonel Hacker asked me again if I would go home, and stay at home. I told him that if I should promise him this, it would manifest that I was guilty of something, to make my home a prison; and if I went to meetings they would say I broke their order. Therefore I told them I should go to meetings as the Lord should order me, and could not submit to their requirings; but I said we were a peaceable people.

"Well, then," said Colonel Hacker, "I will send you to-morrow morning by six o'clock to my Lord Protector, by Captain Drury, one of his life-guard."

That night I was kept prisoner at the Marshalsea; and the next morning by the sixth hour I was delivered to Captain Drury. I desired that he would let me speak with Colonel Hacker before I went; and he took me to his bedside. Colonel Hacker again admonished me to go home, and keep no more meetings. I told him I could not submit to that; but must have my liberty to serve God, and to go to meetings. "Then," said he, "you must go before the Protector." Thereupon I kneeled at his bedside, and besought the Lord to forgive him; for he was as Pilate, though he would wash his hands; and I bade him

remember, when the day of his misery and trial
should come upon him, what I had said to him. But
he was stirred up and set on by Stephens,[7] and the
other priests and professors, wherein their envy and
baseness was manifest. When they could not overcome me by disputes and arguments, nor resist the
Spirit of the Lord that was in me, they got soldiers
to take me up.

Afterwards, when Colonel Hacker was imprisoned
in London, a day or two before his execution, he was
put in mind of what he had done against the innocent; and he remembered it, and confessed it to Margaret Fell, saying he knew well whom she meant; and
he had trouble upon him for it.

Now I was carried up a prisoner by Captain Drury
from Leicester; and when we came to Harborough
he asked me if I would go home and stay a fortnight?
I should have my liberty, he said, if I would not go
to, nor keep meetings. I told him I could not promise any such thing. Several times upon the road did
he ask and try me after the same manner, and still I
gave him the same answers. So he brought me to
London, and lodged me at the Mermaid* over against
the Mews at Charing-Cross.

As we travelled I was moved of the Lord to warn
people at the inns and places where I came of the

* This was not the famous " Mermaid " of Shakespeare and Ben
Jonson.

---

[7] This is the minister of Drayton, who said " there
was never such a plant bred in England " as George
Fox.

day of the Lord that was coming upon them. William Dewsbury and Marmaduke Storr being in prison at Northampton, Captain Drury let me go and visit them.

After Captain Drury had lodged me at the Mermaid, he left me there, and went to give the Protector an account of me. When he came to me again, he told me that the Protector required that I should promise not to take up a carnal sword or weapon against him or the government, as it then was, and that I should write it in what words I saw good, and set my hand to it. I said little in reply to Captain Drury.

The next morning I was moved of the Lord to write a paper to the Protector, Oliver Cromwell; wherein I did, in the presence of the Lord God, declare that I denied the wearing or drawing of a carnal sword, or any other outward weapon, against him or any man; and that I was sent of God to stand a witness against all violence, and against the works of darkness; and to turn people from darkness to light; and to bring them from the causes of war and fighting, to the peaceable gospel. When I had written what the Lord had given me to write, I set my name to it, and gave it to Captain Drury to hand to Oliver Cromwell, which he did.

After some time Captain Drury brought me before the Protector himself at Whitehall.[8] It was in a

---

[8] Cromwell and Fox were at this period the two most striking men in England. Cromwell's greatest work was already done; Fox, now thirty years old, was only

morning, before he was dressed, and one Harvey, who had come a little among Friends, but was disobedient, waited upon him. When I came in I was moved to say, " Peace be in this house "; and I exhorted him to keep in the fear of God, that he might receive wisdom from Him, that by it he might be directed, and order all things under his hand to God's glory.

---

getting well under way with his earthly mission. He never comprehended the greatness of Cromwell's work, nor did he appreciate the complex tangle which the Protector had to unravel. He was so sun-clear and ingenuous himself that he could not fathom a man who skillfully zigzagged toward the ends which he could not reach by perfectly direct steps. Carlyle gives a happy paraphrase of this passage in the Journal: " ' I exhorted him,' writes George, ' to keep in the fear of God,' whereby he might ' receive Wisdom from God,' which would be a useful guidance for any sovereign person. In fact, I had ' much discourse ' with him; explaining what I and Friends had been led to think ' Concerning Christ and His Apostles ' of old time, and His Priests and Ministers of new; concerning Life and concerning Death; concerning the Unfathomable Universe in general, and the Light in it from Above and the Darkness in it that is from Below: to all which the Protector ' carried himself with much moderation.' Yes, George; this Protector has a sympathy with the Perennial; and feels it across the Temporary: no hulls, leathern or other, can entirely hide it from the sense of him." Carlyle's " Oliver Cromwell's Letters and Speeches." (Centenary Edition.) Vol. III., p. 225.

I spoke much to him of Truth, and much discourse I had with him about religion; wherein he carried himself very moderately. But he said we quarrelled with priests, whom he called ministers. I told him I did not quarrel with them, but that they quarrelled with me and my friends. " But," said I, " if we own the prophets, Christ, and the apostles, we cannot hold up such teachers, prophets, and shepherds, as the prophets, Christ, and the apostles declared against; but we must declare against them by the same power and Spirit."

Then I showed him that the prophets, Christ, and the apostles declared freely, and against them that did not declare freely; such as preached for filthy lucre, and divined for money, and preached for hire, and were covetous and greedy, that could never have enough; and that they that have the same spirit that Christ, and the prophets, and the apostles had, could not but declare against all such now, as they did then. As I spoke, he several times said, it was very good, and it was truth. I told him that all Christendom (so called) had the Scriptures, but they wanted the power and Spirit that those had who gave forth the Scriptures; and that was the reason they were not in fellowship with the Son, nor with the Father, nor with the Scriptures, nor one with another.

Many more words I had with him; but people coming in, I drew a little back. As I was turning, he caught me by the hand, and with tears in his eyes said, " Come again to my house; for if thou and I were but an hour of a day together, we should be nearer one to the other "; adding that he wished me no more ill than he did to his own soul. I told him if he did he wronged his own soul; and admonished him to hearken to God's voice, that he might stand in his counsel, and obey it; and if he did so, that would keep him from hardness of heart; but if he did not hear God's voice, his heart would be hardened. He said it was true.

Then I went out; and when Captain Drury came out after me he told me the Lord Protector had said I was at liberty, and might go whither I would.

Then I was brought into a great hall, where the Protector's gentlemen were to dine. I asked them what they brought me thither for. They said it was by the Protector's order, that I might dine with them. I bid them let the Protector know that I would not eat of his bread, nor drink of his drink. When he heard this he said, " Now I see there is a people risen that I cannot win with gifts or honours, offices or places; but all other sects and people I can." It was told him again that we had forsaken our own possessions; and were not like to look for such things from him.

Being set at liberty, I went to the inn where Captain Drury at first lodged me. This captain, though he sometimes carried it fairly, was an enemy to me and to Truth, and opposed it. When professors came to me, while I was under his custody, and he was by, he would scoff at trembling, and call us Quakers, as the Independents and Presbyterians had nicknamed us before.[9] But afterwards he came and told me that, as he was lying on his bed to rest himself in the daytime, a sudden trembling seized on him; that his joints knocked together, and his body shook so that he could not rise from his bed. He was so shaken that he had not strength enough left to rise. But he felt the power of the Lord was upon him; and he tumbled off his bed, and cried to the Lord, and said he would never speak more against the Quakers, such as trembled at the word of God.

During the time I was prisoner at Charing-Cross, there came abundance to see me, almost of all sorts, priests, professors, officers of the army, etc. Once a company of officers, being with me, desired me to pray with them. I sat still, with my mind retired to the Lord. At last I felt the power and Spirit of God move in me; and the Lord's power did so shake and shatter them that they wondered, though they did not live in it.

Among those that came was Colonel Packer, with several of his officers. While they were with me, there came in one Cob, and a great company of Ranters with him. The Ranters began to call for drink and tobacco; but I desired them to forbear it in my room, telling them if they had such a mind to it, they might go into another room. One of them cried, " All is ours "; and another of them said, " All is well." I replied, " How is all well, while thou art so peevish, envious, and crabbed?" for I saw he was of

---

[9] This implies that the nickname was given because the Friends trembled when they spoke.

a peevish nature. I spake to their conditions, and they were sensible of it, and looked one upon another, wondering.

Then Colonel Packer began to talk with a light, chaffy mind, concerning God, and Christ, and the Scriptures. It was a great grief to my soul and spirit when I heard him talk so lightly; so that I told him he was too light to talk of the things of God, for he did not know the solidity of a man. Thereupon the officers raged, and were wroth that I should speak so of their colonel.

This Packer was a Baptist, and he and the Ranters bowed and scraped to one another very much; for it was the manner of the Ranters to be exceedingly complimentary (as they call it), so that Packer bade them give over their compliments. But I told them they were fit to go together, for they were both of one spirit.

This Colonel Packer lived at Theobald's, near Waltham, and was made a justice of the peace. He set up a great meeting of the Baptists at Theobald's Park; for he and some other officers had purchased it. They were exceedingly high, and railed against Friends and Truth, and threatened to apprehend me with their warrants if ever I came there.

Yet after I was set at liberty, I was moved of the Lord God to go down to Theobald's, and appoint a meeting hard by them; to which many of his people came, and divers of his hearers were convinced of the way of Truth, and received Christ, the free teacher, and came off from the Baptist; and that made him rage the more. But the Lord's power came over him, so that he had not power to meddle with me.

Then I went to Waltham, close by him, and had a meeting there; but the people were very rude, and gathered about the house and broke the windows. Thereupon I went out to them, with the Bible in my hand, and desired them to come in; and told them that I would show them Scripture both for our principles and practices. When I had done so, I showed them also that their teachers were in the steps of such as the prophets, and Christ, and the apostles testified against. Then I directed them to the Light of Christ and Spirit of God in their own hearts, that by it they might come to know their free teacher, the Lord Jesus Christ.

The meeting being ended, they went away quieted and satisfied, and a meeting hath since been settled in that town. But this was some time after I was set at liberty by Oliver Cromwell.

When I came from Whitehall to the Mermaid at Charing-Cross, I stayed not long there, but went into the city of London, where we had great and powerful meetings. So great were the throngs of people that I could hardly get to and from the meetings for the crowds; and the Truth spread exceedingly. Thomas Aldam, and Robert Craven, who had been sheriff of London, and many Friends, came up to London after me; but Alexander Parker abode with me.[10]

---

[10] During this same year, 1654, a remarkable work was done in London by Edward Burrough and Francis

After a while I went to Whitehall again, and was moved to declare the day of the Lord amongst them, and that the Lord was come to teach His people Himself. So I preached Truth, both to the officers, and to them that were called Oliver's gentlemen, who were of his guard. But a priest opposed while I was declaring the Word of the Lord amongst them; for Oliver had several priests about him, of which this was his newsmonger, an envious priest, and a light, scornful, chaffy man. I bade him repent, and he put it in his newspaper the next week that I had been at Whitehall and had bidden a godly minister there to repent.

When I went thither again I met with him; and abundance of people gathered about me. I manifested the priest to be a liar in several things that he had affirmed; and he was put to silence. He put in the news that I wore silver buttons; which was false, for they were but alchemy.[11] Afterwards he put in the news that I hung ribands on people's arms, which made them follow me. This was another of his lies, for I never used nor wore ribands in my life.

Three Friends went to examine this priest, that gave forth this false intelligence, and to know of him where he had had that information. He said it was a woman that told him so, and that if they

---

Howgill. It is estimated that not less than 10,000 adherents were gathered in the city during these early years of Friends' ministry.

[11] A cheap metal made to imitate gold.

would come again he would tell them the woman's name. When they came again he said it was a man, but would not tell them his name then, but said that if they would come again he would tell them his name and where he lived.

They went the third time; and then he would not say who told him; but offered, if I would give it under my hand that there was no such thing he would put that into the news. Thereupon the Friends carried it to him under my hand; but when they came he broke his promise, and would not put it in: but was in a rage, and threatened them with the constable.

This was the deceitful doing of this forger of lies; and these lies he spread over the nation in the news, to render Truth odious and to put evil into people's minds against Friends and Truth; of which a more large account may be seen in a book printed soon after this time, for the clearing of Friends and Truth from the slanders and false reports raised and cast upon them.

These priests, the newsmongers, were of the Independent sect, like them in Leicester; but the Lord's power came over all their lies, and swept them away; and many came to see the naughtiness of these priests. The God of heaven carried me over all in His power, and His blessed power went over the nation; insomuch that many Friends about this time were moved to go up and down to sound forth the everlasting gospel in most parts of this nation, and also in Scotland; and the glory of the Lord was felt over all, to His everlasting praise.

A great convincement there was in London; some in the Protector's house and family. I went to see him again, but could not get to him, the officers were grown so rude.

CHAPTER IX.

𝔄 𝔙isit to t𝔥e 𝔖out𝔥ern ℭounties 𝔚𝔥ic𝔥 𝔈nds in 𝔏aunceston 𝔍ail

1655–1656.

It came upon me about this time from the Lord to write a short paper and send it forth as an exhortation and warning to the Pope, and to all kings and rulers in Europe.

Besides this I was moved to write a letter to the Protector (so called) to warn him of the mighty work the Lord hath to do in the nations, and the shaking of them; and to beware of his own wit, craft, subtilty, and policy, and of seeking any by-ends to himself.[1]

---

[1] This paper to the Protector was published in 1656. The paper mentioned just before was " A Warning from the Lord to the Pope and to all his Train of Idolatries." Published " at the Black-Spread Eagle " in 1656. He wrote many more letters at this period. Among them was a long letter to all professors of Christianity. Here is a characteristic passage from it:

" Let us be glad, and rejoice for ever! Singleness of heart is come; pureness of heart is come; joy and gladness is come. The glorious God is exalting Himself; Truth hath been talked of, but now it is possessed. Christ hath been talked of; but now He is come and possessed. The glory hath been talked of; but now it is possessed, and the glory of man is defacing. The Son of God hath been talked of; but now He is come,

I travelled till I came to Reading, where I found a few that were convinced of the way of the Lord. I stayed till the First-day, and had a meeting in George Lamboll's orchard; and a great part of the town came to it. A glorious meeting it proved; great convincement there was, and the people were mightily satisfied. Thither came two of Judge Fell's daughters to me, and George Bishop, of Bristol, with his sword by his side, for he was a captain.

After the meeting many Baptists and Ranters came privately, reasoning and discoursing; but the Lord's power came over them. The Ranters pleaded that God made the devil. I denied it, and told them I was come into the power of God, the seed Christ, which was before the devil was, and bruised his head; and he became a devil by going out of truth; and so became a murderer and a destroyer. I showed them that God did not make him a devil; for God is a God of truth, and made all things good, and blessed them; but God did not bless the devil. And the devil is bad, and was a liar and a murderer from the beginning, and spoke of himself, and not from God.

So the Truth stopped and bound them, and came over all the highest notions in the nation, and confounded them. For by the power of the Lord I was manifest, and sought to be made manifest to the Spirit of God in all, that by it they might be turned to God; as many were turned to the Lord Jesus

---

and hath given us an understanding. Unity hath been talked of; but now it is come. Virgins have been talked of; but now they are come with oil in their lamps."

Christ by the Holy Spirit, and were come to sit under His teaching.

After this I passed to London, where I stayed awhile, and had large meetings; then went into Essex, and came to Cogshall, where was a meeting of about two thousand people, as it was judged, which lasted several hours, and a glorious meeting it was. The Word of life was freely declared, and people were turned to the Lord Jesus Christ their Teacher and Saviour, the Way, the Truth, and the Life.

On the Sixth-day I had a large meeting near Colchester, to which many professors and the Independent teachers came. After I had done speaking, and was stepped down from the place on which I stood, one of the Independent teachers began to make a jangling; which Amor Stoddart perceiving, said, "Stand up again, George"; for I was going away, and did not at first hear them. But when I heard the Independent, I stood up again, and after awhile the Lord's power came over him and his company; they were confounded and the Lord's Truth went over all. A great flock of sheep hath the Lord in that country, that feed in His pastures of life.

On the First-day following we had a very large meeting not far from Colchester, wherein the Lord's power was eminently manifested, and the people were very well satisfied; for, being turned to the Lord Jesus Christ's free teaching, they received it gladly. Many of these people were of the stock of the martyrs.

As I passed through Colchester, I went to visit James Parnell in prison; but the jailer would hardly

let us come in or stay with him. Very cruel they
were to him. The jailer's wife threatened to have his
blood; and in that jail they did destroy him, as the
reader may see in a book printed soon after his death,
giving an account of his life and death; and also in
an epistle printed with his collected books and writings.

We came to Yarmouth, where there was a Friend,
Thomas Bond, in prison for the Truth of Christ, and
there stayed a while. There we had some service;
and some were turned to the Lord in that town.

Thence we rode to another town, about twenty
miles off, where were many tender people; and I was
moved of the Lord to speak to them, as I sat on my
horse, in several places as I passed along. We went
to another town about five miles beyond, and put up
our horses at an inn, Richard Hubberthorn and I
having travelled five and forty miles that day. There
were some Friendly people in the town; and we had
a tender, broken meeting amongst them, in the Lord's
power.

We bade the hostler have our horses ready by
three in the morning; for we intended to ride to
Lynn, about three and thirty miles, next morning.
But when we were in bed at our inn, about eleven at
night, the constable and officers came, with a great
rabble of people, into the inn. They said they were
come with a hue-and-cry from a justice of the peace
that lived near the town, about five miles off, where
I had spoken to the people in the streets, as I rode
along. They had been told to search for two horse-
men, that rode upon gray horses, and in gray clothes;

a house having been broken into the Seventh-day before at night. We told them we were honest, innocent men, and abhorred such things; yet they apprehended us, and set a guard with halberts and pikes upon us that night, calling upon some of those Friendly people, with others, to watch us.

Next morning we were up betimes, and the constable, with his guard, carried us before a justice of the peace about five miles off. We took with us two or three of the sufficient men of the town, who had been with us at the great meeting at Captain Lawrence's, and could testify that we lay both the Seventh-day night and the First-day night at Captain Lawrence's; and it was on the Seventh-day night that they said the house was broken into.

During the time that I was a prisoner at the Mermaid at Charing-Cross, this Captain Lawrence brought several Independent justices to see me there, with whom I had much discourse, at which they took offence. For they pleaded for imperfection, and to sin as long as they lived; but did not like to hear of Christ teaching His people Himself, and making people as clear, whilst here upon the earth, as Adam and Eve were before they fell. These justices had plotted together this mischief against me in the country, pretending that a house was broken into, that they might send their hue-and-cry after me. They were vexed, also, and troubled, to hear of the great meeting at John Lawrence's aforesaid; for a colonel was there convinced that day who lived and died in the Truth.

But Providence so ordered that the constable carried us to a justice about five miles onward in our way towards Lynn, who was not an Independent, as the rest were. When we were brought before him he began to be angry because we did not put off our hats to him. I told him I had been before the Protector, and he was not offended at my hat; and why should he be offended at it, who was but one of his servants? Then he read the hue-and-cry; and I told him that that night wherein the house was said to have been broken into, we were at Captain Lawrence's house and that we had several men present who could testify the truth thereof.

Thereupon the justice, having examined us and them, said he believed we were not the men that had broken into the house; but he was sorry, he said, that he had no more against us. We told him he ought not to be sorry for not having evil against us, but ought rather to be glad; for to rejoice when he got evil against people, as for housebreaking or the like, was not a good mind in him.

It was a good while, however, before he could resolve whether to let us go or send us to prison, and the wicked constable stirred him up against us, telling him we had good horses and that if it pleased him he would carry us to Norwich jail. But we took hold of the justice's confession that he believed we were not the men that had broken into the house; and, after we had admonished him to fear the Lord in his day, the Lord's power came over him, so that he let us go; so their snare was broken.

A great people was afterwards gathered to the Lord in that town, where I was moved to speak to them in the street, and whence the hue-and-cry came.

Being set at liberty, we passed on to Cambridge. When I came into the town the scholars, hearing of me, were up, and were exceeding rude. I kept on my horse's back, and rode through them in the Lord's power; but they unhorsed Amor Stoddart before he could get to the inn. When we were in the inn they were so rude in the courts and in the streets that the miners, colliers and carters could not be ruder. The people of the house asked us what we would have for supper. "Supper!" said I, "were it not that the Lord's power is over them, these rude scholars look as if they would pluck us in pieces and make a supper of us." They knew I was so against the trade of preaching, which they were there as apprentices to learn, that they raged as greatly as ever Diana's craftsmen did against Paul.

At this place John Crook met us.[2] When it was night the mayor of the town being friendly, came and fetched me to his house;[3] and as we walked through the streets there was a bustle in the town;

---

[2] John Crook was Justice of the Peace in Bedford County. He became an eminent minister among the Friends and suffered many imprisonments.

[3] The wife of this mayor of Cambridge had been to a great meeting which Fox held the day before near the Isle of Ely. James Parnell had already labored in Cambridge before this visit of George Fox. One gets here an interesting glimpse at the students of two hundred and fifty years ago. It is an interesting fact that they failed to unhorse Fox. The struggle between Fox and the students is the subject of one of Robert Spence's etchings.

but they did not know me, it being darkish. They were in a rage, not only against me, but against the mayor also; so that he was almost afraid to walk the streets with me for the tumult. We sent for the Friendly people, and had a fine meeting in the power of God; and I stayed there all night.

Next morning, having ordered our horses to be ready by the sixth hour, we passed peaceably out of town. The destroyers were disappointed: for they thought I would have stayed longer in the town, and intended to have done us mischief; but our passing away early in the morning frustrated their evil purposes against us.

At Evesham I heard that the magistrates had cast several Friends into divers prisons, and that, hearing of my coming, they made a pair of high stocks. I sent for Edward Pittaway, a Friend that lived near Evesham, and asked him the truth of the thing. He said it was so. I went that night with him to Evesham; and in the evening we had a large, precious meeting, wherein Friends and people were refreshed with the Word of life, the power of the Lord.

Next morning I rode to one of the prisons, and visited Friends there, and encouraged them. Then I rode to the other prison, where were several prisoners. Amongst them was Humphry Smith, who had been a priest, but was now become a free minister of Christ. When I had visited Friends at both prisons, and was turned to go out of the town, I espied the magistrates coming up the town, intending to seize me in prison. But the Lord frustrated their intent, the innocent escaped their snare, and God's blessed power came over them all. But exceeding rude and envious were the priests and professors about this time in these parts.

I went from Evesham to Worcester, and had a quiet and a precious meeting there. From Worcester we went to Tewkesbury, where in the evening we had a great meeting, to which came the priest of the town with a great rabble of rude people.

Leaving Tewkesbury, we passed to Warwick, where in the evening we had a meeting with many sober people at a widow-woman's house. A precious meeting we had in the Lord's power; several were convinced and turned to the Lord. After the meeting a Baptist in the company began to jangle; and the bailiff of the town, with his officers, came in and said, " What do these people here at this time of night ? " So he secured John Crook, Amor Stoddart, Gerrard Roberts and me; but we had leave to go to our inn, and to be forthcoming in the morning.

The next morning many rude people came into the inn, and into our chambers, desperate fellows; but the Lord's power gave us dominion over them. Gerrard Roberts and John Crook went to the bailiff to know what he had to say to us. He said we might go our ways, for he had little to say to us. As we rode out of town it lay upon me to ride to his house to let him know that, the Protector having given forth an instrument of government in which liberty of conscience was granted, it was very strange that, contrary to that instrument of government, he would trouble peaceable people that feared God.

The Friends went with me, but the rude people

gathered about us with stones. One of them took hold of my horse's bridle and broke it; but the horse, drawing back, threw him under him. Though the bailiff saw this, yet he did not stop, nor so much as rebuke the rude multitude; so that it was strange we were not slain or hurt in the streets; for the people threw stones and struck at us as we rode along the town.

When we were quite out of the town I told Friends that it was upon me from the Lord that I must go back into the town again; and if any one of them felt anything upon him from the Lord he might follow me; the rest, that did not, might go on to Dun-Cow. So I passed through the market in the dreadful power of God, declaring the Word of life to them; and John Crook followed me. Some struck at me; but the Lord's power was over them, and gave me dominion over all. I showed them their unworthiness to claim the name of Christians, and the unworthiness of their teachers, that had not brought them into more sobriety; and what a shame they were to Christianity.

Having cleared myself, I turned out of the town again, and passed to Coventry, where we found the people closed up with darkness. I went to the house of a professor, where I had formerly been, and he was drunk; which grieved my soul so that I did not go into any house in the town; but rode into some of the streets, and into the market-place. I felt that the power of the Lord was over the town.

Then I went on to Dun-Cow, and had a meeting in the evening, and some were turned to the Lord by

His Spirit, as some also were at Warwick and at Tewkesbury. We lay at Dun-Cow that night; we met with John Camm, a faithful minister of the ever-lasting gospel. In the morning there gathered a rude company of priests and people who behaved more like beasts than men, for some of them came riding on horseback into the room where we were; but the Lord gave us dominion over them.

Thence we passed into Leicestershire, and after that to Baddesley in Warwickshire. Here William Edmundson, who lived in Ireland, having some draw-ings upon his spirit to come into England to see me, met with me; by whom I wrote a few lines to Friends then convinced in the north of Ireland.[4]

Friends:

In that which convinced you, wait; that you may have that removed you are convinced of. And all my dear Friends, dwell in the life, and love, and power, and wisdom of God, in unity one with another, and with God; and the peace and wisdom of God fill all your hearts that nothing may rule in you but the life which stands in the Lord God.   G. F.

---

[4] This William Edmundson was one of the first per-sons to espouse and proclaim the principles of the Quakers in Ireland. He had been a soldier in Crom-well's army, and he carried the spirit and courage of an Ironside into the new service. He had strange and un-speakably difficult experiences to endure in those try-ing days of unsettlement in Ireland, but he was enabled to do a great work for the cause which he served. He also had large and valuable service in America.

When these few lines were read amongst the Friends in Ireland at their meeting, the power of the Lord came upon all in the room.

From Baddesley we passed to Swannington and Higham, and so into Northamptonshire and Bedfordshire, having great meetings; and many were turned to the Lord by His power and Spirit.

When we came to Baldock in Hertfordshire, I asked if there was nothing in that town, no profession; and it was answered me that there were some Baptists, and a Baptist woman who was sick. John Rush, of Bedfordshire, went with me to visit her. When we came in there were many tender people about her. They told me she was not a woman for this world, but if I had anything that would comfort her concerning the world to come, I might speak to her. I was moved of the Lord God to speak to her; and the Lord raised her up again, to the astonishment of the town and country. This Baptist woman and her husband, whose name was Baldock, came to be convinced, and many hundreds of people have met at their house since. Great meetings and convincements were in those parts afterwards; many received the Word of life, and sat down under the teaching of Christ, their Saviour.

When we had visited this sick woman we returned to our inn, where were two desperate fellows fighting so furiously that none durst come nigh to part them. But I was moved, in the Lord's power, to go to them; and when I had loosed their hands, I held one of them by one hand and the other by the other, showed them the evil of their doings, and reconciled them one to the other; and they were so loving and thankful to me that people marveled at it.[5]

Now, after I had tarried some time in London, and had visited Friends in their meetings, I went out of town, leaving James Nayler in the city. As I passed from him I cast my eyes upon him, and a fear struck me concerning him; but I went away and rode down to Ryegate, in Surrey, where I had a little meeting.[6] There the Friends told me of one Thomas Moore, a justice of the peace, that lived not far from Ryegate, a Friendly, moderate man. I went to visit him at his house, and he came to be a serviceable man in Truth.

Thence we went to Dorchester, and alighted at an inn, a Baptist's house. We sent into the town to the Baptists, to ask them to let us have their meeting-house to assemble in, and to invite the sober people to the meeting; but they denied it us. We sent to them again, to know why they would deny us their meeting-house, so the thing was noised about in the town. Then we sent them word that if they would not let us come to their house, they, or any people that feared God, might come to our inn, if they pleased; but they were in a great rage. Their teacher and many of them came up, and slapped their Bibles on the table.

I asked them why they were so angry,—" Were

---

[5] These cases are further illustration of Fox's power to deal with sickness and with desperate persons. He always *felt* himself equal to any emergency which confronted him.

[6] James Nayler's fall, which is here felt in dim forecast, became very soon only too sadly real.

they angry with the Bible?" But they fell into a discourse about their water-baptism. I asked them whether they could say they were sent of God to baptize people, as John was, and whether they had the same Spirit and power that the apostles had? They said they had not.

Then I asked them how many powers there are,—whether there are any more than the power of God and the power of the devil. They said there was not any other power than those two. Then said I, " If you have not the power of God that the apostles had, you act by the power of the devil." Many sober people were present, who said they have thrown themselves on their backs. Many substantial people were convinced that night; a precious service we had there for the Lord, and His power came over all.

Next morning, as we were passing away, the Baptists, being in a rage, began to shake the dust off their feet after us. " What," said I, " in the power of darkness! We, who are in the power of God, shake off the dust of our feet against you."

Leaving Dorchester, we came to Weymouth; where also we inquired after sober people; and about fourscore of them gathered together at a priest's house. Most of them received the Word of life and were turned to their teacher, Christ Jesus, who had enlightened them with His divine Light, by which they might see their sins, and Him who saveth from sin. A blessed meeting we had with them, and they received the Truth in the love of it, with gladness of heart.

The meeting held several hours. The state of

their teachers, and their apostasy was opened to
them; and the state of the apostles, and of the Church
in their days; and the state of the law and of the
prophets before Christ, and how Christ came to fulfill
them; that He was their teacher in the apostles' days;
and that He was come now to teach His people Himself by His power and spirit. All was quiet, the
meeting broke up peaceably, the people were very
loving; and a meeting is continued in that town to
this day. Many are added to them; and some who
had been Ranters came to own the Truth, and to live
very soberly.

There was a captain of horse in the town, who
sent to me, and would fain have had me stay longer;
but I was not to stay. He and his man rode out of
town with me about seven miles; Edward Pyot also
being with me. This captain was the fattest, merriest,
cheerfullest man, and the most given to laughter,
that ever I met with: insomuch that I was several
times moved to speak in the dreadful power of the
Lord to him; yet it was become so customary to him
that he would presently laugh at anything he saw.
But I still admonished him to come to sobriety, and
the fear of the Lord and sincerity.

We lay at an inn that night, and the next morning
I was moved to speak to him again, when he parted
from us. The next time I saw him he told me that
when I spoke to him at parting, the power of the
Lord so struck him that before he got home he was
serious enough, and discontinued his laughing. He
afterwards was convinced, and became a serious and
good man, and died in the Truth.

After this we passed to Totness, a dark town. We lodged there at an inn; and that night Edward Pyot was sick, but the Lord's power healed him, so that the next day we got to Kingsbridge, and at our inn inquired for the sober people of the town. They directed us to Nicholas Tripe and his wife; and we went to their house. They sent for the priest, with whom we had some discourse; but he, being confounded, quickly left us. Nicholas Tripe and his wife were convinced; and since that time there has been a good meeting of Friends in that country.

In the evening we returned to our inn. There being many people drinking in the house, I was moved of the Lord to go amongst them, and to direct them to the Light with which Christ, the heavenly man, had enlightened them; by which they might see all their evil ways, words, and deeds, and by the same Light might also see Christ Jesus their Saviour.

The innkeeper stood uneasy, seeing it hindered his guests from drinking; and as soon as the last words were out of my mouth he snatched up the candle, and said, " Come, here is a light for you to go into your chamber." Next morning, when he was cool, I represented to him what an uncivil thing it was for him so to do; then, warning him of the day of the Lord, we got ready and passed away.

We came next day to Plymouth, refreshed ourselves at our inn, and went to Robert Cary's, where we had a very precious meeting. At this meeting was Elizabeth Trelawny, daughter to a baronet. She being somewhat thick of hearing, came close up to me, and clapped her ear very nigh me while I spake;

and she was convinced. After this meeting came in some jangling Baptists; but the Lord's power came over them, and Elizabeth Trelawny gave testimony thereto. A fine meeting was settled there in the Lord's power, which hath continued ever since, where many faithful Friends have been convinced.

Thence we passed into Cornwall, and came to an inn in the parish of Menheriot. At night we had a meeting at Edward Hancock's, to which came Thomas Mounce and a priest, with many people. We brought the priest to confess that he was a minister made by the state, and maintained by the state; and he was confounded and went his way; but many of the people stayed.

I directed them to the Light of Christ, by which they might see their sins; and their Saviour Christ Jesus, the way to God, their Mediator, to make peace betwixt God and them; their Shepherd to feed them, and their Prophet to teach them. I directed them to the Spirit of God in themselves, by which they might know the Scriptures, and be led into all Truth; and by the Spirit might know God, and in it have unity one with another. Many were convinced at that time, and came under Christ's teaching; and there are fine gatherings in the name of Jesus in those parts at this day.

When we came to Ives, Edward Pyot's horse having cast a shoe, we stayed to have it set; and while he was getting his horse shod, I walked down to the seaside. When I returned I found the town in an uproar. They were haling Edward Pyot and the other Friend before Major Peter Ceely, a major in the army and a justice of the peace. I followed them into the justice's house, though they did not lay hands upon me.

When we came in, the house was full of rude people; whereupon I asked if there were not an officer among them to keep the people civil. Major Ceely said that he was a magistrate. I told him that he should then show forth gravity and sobriety, and use his authority to keep the people civil; for I never saw any people ruder; the Indians were more like Christians than they.

After a while they brought forth a paper, and asked whether I would own it.* I said, Yes. Then he tendered the oath of abjuration to us; whereupon I put my hand in my pocket and drew forth the answer to it which I had given to the Protector. After I had given him that, he examined us severally, one by one. He had with him a silly young priest, who asked us many frivolous questions; and amongst the rest he desired to cut my hair, which was then pretty long; but I was not to cut it, though many times many were offended at it. I told them I had no pride in it, and it was not of my own putting on.

At length the justice put us under a guard of soldiers, who were hard and wild, like the justice himself; nevertheless we warned the people of the day of the Lord, and declared the Truth to them. The next day he sent us, guarded by a party of horse with swords and pistols, to Redruth. On First-day the sol-

* A paper which George Fox had written to the seven parishes of Land's End.

diers would have taken us away; but we told them it
was their Sabbath, and it was not usual to travel on
that day.

Several of the townspeople gathered about us, and
whilst I held the soldiers in discourse, Edward Pyot
spoke to the people; and afterwards he held the soldiers in discourse, whilst I spoke to the people.   In
the meantime the other Friend got out the back way,
and went to the steeple-house to speak to the priest
and people.   The people were exceedingly desperate, in a mighty rage against him, and they sorely
abused him.   The soldiers also, missing him, were in
a great rage, ready to kill us; but I declared the day
of the Lord and the Word of eternal life to the people that gathered about us.

In the afternoon the soldiers were resolved to take
us away, so we took horse.   When we were come to
the town's end I was moved of the Lord to go back
again, to speak to the old man of the house.   The
soldiers drew out their pistols, and swore I should
not go back.   I heeded them not, but rode back, and
they rode after me.   I cleared myself to the old man
and the people, and then returned with them, and reproved them for being so rude and violent.

At night we were brought to a town then called
Smethick, but since known as Falmouth.   It being
the evening of the First-day, there came to our inn
the chief constable of the place, and many sober people, some of whom began to inquire concerning us.
We told them we were prisoners for Truth's sake;
and much discourse we had with them concerning the
things of God.   They were very sober and loving to

us. Some were convinced, and stood faithful ever after.

When the constable and these people were gone, others came in, who were also very civil, and went away very loving. When all were gone, we went to our chamber to go to bed; and about the eleventh hour Edward Pyot said, "I will shut the door; it may be some may come to do us mischief." Afterwards we understood that Captain Keat, who commanded the party, had intended to do us some injury that night; but the door being bolted, he missed his design.

Next morning Captain Keat brought a kinsman of his, a rude, wicked man, and put him into the room; himself standing without. This evil-minded man walked huffing up and down the room; I bade him fear the Lord. Thereupon he ran upon me, struck me with both his hands, and, clapping his leg behind me, would have thrown me down if he could; but he was not able, for I stood stiff and still, and let him strike.

As I looked towards the door, I saw Captain Keat look on, and see his kinsman thus beat and abuse me. I said to him, "Keat, dost thou allow this?" He said he did. "Is this manly or civil," said I, "to have us under a guard, and then put a man to abuse and beat us? Is this manly, civil, or Christian?" I desired one of our friends to send for the constables, and they came.

Then I desired the Captain to let the constables see his warrant or order, by which he was to carry us; which he did. His warrant was to conduct us safe to Captain Fox, governor of Pendennis Castle; and if the governor should not be at home, he was to convey us to Launceston jail. I told him he had broken his order concerning us; for we, who were his prisoners, were to be safely conducted; but he had brought a man to beat and abuse us; so he having broken his order, I wished the constable to keep the warrant. Accordingly he did, and told the soldiers they might go their ways, for he would take charge of the prisoners; and if it cost twenty shillings in charges to carry us up, they should not have the warrant again. I showed the soldiers the baseness of their carriage towards us; and they walked up and down the house, pitifully blank and down.

The constables went to the castle, and told the officers what they had done. The officers showed great dislike of Captain Keat's base carriage towards us; and told the constables that Major-General Desborough was coming to Bodmin, and that we should meet him; and it was likely he would free us. Meanwhile our old guard of soldiers came by way of entreaty to us, and promised that they would be civil to us if we would go with them.

Thus the morning was spent till about the eleventh hour; and then, upon the soldiers' entreaty, and their promise to be more civil, the constables gave them the order again; and we went with them.

Great was the civility and courtesy of the constables and people of that town towards us. They kindly entertained us, and the Lord rewarded them with His truth; for many of them have since been convinced thereof, and are gathered into the name of Jesus, and sit under Christ, their Teacher and Saviour.

Captain Keat, who commanded our guard, understanding that Captain Fox, who was governor of Pendennis Castle, was gone to meet Major-General Desborough,[7] did not carry us thither; but took us directly to Bodmin, in the way to Launceston. We met Major-General Desborough on the way. The captain of his troop, who rode before him, knew me, and said, " Oh, Mr. Fox, what do you here? " I replied, " I am a prisoner." " Alack," he said, " for what? " I told him I was taken up as I was travelling. " Then," said he, " I will speak to my lord, and he will set you at liberty."

So he came from the head of his troop, and rode up to the coach, and spoke to the Major-General. We also gave him an account of how we were taken. He began to speak against the Light of Christ; against which I exhorted him. Then he told the soldiers that they might carry us to Launceston; for he could not stay to talk with us, lest his horses should take cold.

To Bodmin we were taken that night; and when we came to our inn Captain Keat, who was in before us, put me into a room and went his way. When I

---

[7] Major-General Desborough was one of Cromwell's favorite generals, who received many places of honour from the Protector. In 1655 he received his commission as major-general, in charge of Wiltshire, Somersetshire, Devonshire and Cornwall, and in the main he proved an able administrator in this office.

was come in, there stood a man with a naked rapier in his hand. Whereupon I turned out again, called for Captain Keat, and said, " What now, Keat; what trick hast thou played now, to put me into a room where there is a man with his naked rapier? What is thy end in this?" "Oh," said he, "pray hold your tongue; for if you speak to this man, we cannot rule him, he is so devilish." "Then," said I, " dost thou put me into a room where there is such a man with a naked rapier that thou sayest you cannot rule him? What an unworthy, base trick is this? and to put me single into this room, away from my friends that were fellow-prisoners with me?" Thus his plot was discovered and the mischief they intended was prevented.

Afterward we got another room, where we were together all night; and in the evening we declared the Truth to the people; but they were dark and hardened. The soldiers, notwithstanding their fair promises, were very rude and wicked to us again, and sat up drinking and roaring all night.

Next day we were brought to Launceston, where Captain Keat delivered us to the jailer. Now was there no Friend, nor Friendly people, near us; and the people of the town were a dark, hardened people. The jailer required us to pay seven shillings a week for our horse-meat,* and seven shillings a week apiece for our diet. After some time several sober persons came to see us, and some people of the town were convinced, and many friendly people out of

* Provender for their horses.

several parts of the country came to visit us, and were convinced.

Then got up a great rage among the professors and priests against us. They said, " This people ' Thou ' and ' Thee ' all men without respect and will not put off their hats, nor bow the knee to any man; but we shall see, when the assize comes, whether they will dare to ' Thou ' and ' Thee ' the judge, and keep on their hats before him." They expected we should be hanged at the assize.

But all this was little to us; for we saw how God would stain the world's honour and glory; and were commanded not to seek that honour, nor give it; but knew the honour that cometh from God only, and sought that.

It was nine weeks from the time of our commitment to the time of the assizes, to which abundance of people came from far and near to hear the trial of the Quakers. Captain Bradden lay there with his troop of horse. His soldiers and the sheriff's men guarded us to the court through the multitude that filled the streets; and much ado they had to get us through. Besides, the doors and windows were filled with people looking upon us.

When we were brought into the court, we stood a while with our hats on, and all was quiet. I was moved to say, " Peace be amongst you."

Judge Glynne, a Welshman, then Chief-Justice of England, said to the jailer, " What be these you have brought here into the court?" " Prisoners, my lord," said he.

" Why do you not put off your hats ? " said the Judge to us. We said nothing.

" Put off your hats," said the Judge again. Still we said nothing. Then said the Judge, " The Court commands you to put off your hats."

Then I spoke, and said, " Where did ever any magistrate, king, or judge, from Moses to Daniel, command any to put off their hats, when they came before him in his court, either amongst the Jews, the people of God, or amongst the heathen ? [8] and if the law of England doth command any such thing, show me that law either written or printed."

Then the Judge grew very angry, and said, " I do not carry my law-books on my back." " But," said I, " tell me where it is printed in any statute-book, that I may read it."

Then said the Judge, " Take him away, prevaricator! I'll *ferk* him." So they took us away, and put us among the thieves.

Presently after he calls to the jailer, " Bring them up again." " Come," said he, " where had they hats, from Moses to Daniel; come, answer me: I have you fast now."

I replied, " Thou mayest read in the third of Daniel, that the three children were cast into the fiery furnace by Nebuchadnezzar's command, with their coats, their hose, and their hats on."

This plain instance stopped him: so that, not hav-

---

[8] This was Puritan England, and an appeal to Old Testament precedents was not out of place.

ing anything else to say to the point, he cried again, " Take them away, jailer."

Accordingly we were taken away, and thrust in among the thieves, where we were kept a great while; and then, without being called again, the sheriff's men and the troopers made way for us (but we were almost spent) to get through the crowd of people, and guarded us to the prison again, a multitude of people following us, with whom we had much discourse and reasoning at the jail.

We had some good books to set forth our principles, and to inform people of the Truth. The Judge and justices hearing of this, they sent Captain Bradden for them. He came into the jail to us, and violently took our books from us, some out of Edward Pyot's hands, and carried them away; so we never got them again.

[While in the jail Fox addressed a paper " against swearing " to the grand and petty juries.]

This paper passing among them from the jury to the justices, they presented it to the Judge; so that when we were called before the Judge, he bade the clerk give me that paper, and then asked me whether that seditious paper was mine. I said to him, " If they will read it out in open court, that I may hear it, if it is mine I will own it, and stand by it." He would have had me take it and look upon it in my own hand; but I again desired that it might be read, that all the country might hear it, and judge whether there was any sedition in it or not; for if there were, I was willing to suffer for it.

At last the clerk of the assize read it, with an audible voice, that all the people might hear it. When he had done I told them it was my paper; that I would own it, and so might they too, unless they would deny the Scripture: for was not this Scripture language, and the words and commands of Christ, and the Apostle, which all true Christians ought to obey?

Then they let fall that subject; and the Judge fell upon us about our hats again, bidding the jailer take them off; which he did, and gave them to us; and we put them on again. Then we asked the Judge and the justices, for what cause we had lain in prison these nine weeks, seeing they now objected to nothing but our hats. And as for putting off our hats, I told them that that was the honour which God would lay in the dust, though they made so much ado about it; the honour which is of men, and which men seek one of another, and is a mark of unbelievers. For " How can ye believe," saith Christ, " who receive honour one of another, and seek not the honour that cometh from God only?" Christ saith, " I receive not honour from men "; and all true Christians should be of His mind.

Then the Judge began to make a pompous speech, how he represented the Lord Protector's person, who made him Lord Chief-Justice of England, and sent him to come that circuit, etc. We desired him, then, that he would do us justice for our false imprisonment which we had suffered nine weeks wrongfully. But instead of that, they brought an indictment framed against us; so full of lies that I thought it had been against some of the thieves,—"that we came by force and arms, and in a hostile manner, into the court"; who were brought as aforesaid. I told them it was all false; and still we cried for justice for our false imprisonment, being taken up in our journey without cause by Major Ceely.

Then Peter Ceely said to the Judge, "May it please you, my lord, this man (pointing to me) went aside with me, and told me how serviceable I might be for his design; that he could raise forty thousand men at an hour's warning, involve the nation in blood, and so bring in King Charles. I would have aided him out of the country, but he would not go. If it please you, my lord, I have a witness to swear it."

So he called upon his witness; but the Judge not being forward to examine the witness, I desired that he would be pleased to let my mittimus be read in the face of the court and the country, in which the crime was signified for which I was sent to prison. The Judge said it should not be read. I said, "It ought to be, seeing it concerned my liberty and my life." The Judge said again, "It shall not be read." I said, "It ought to be read; for if I have done anything worthy of death, or of bonds, let all the country know it."

Then seeing they would not read it, I spoke to one of my fellow-prisoners: "Thou hast a copy of it; read it up." "It shall not be read," said the Judge; "jailer, take him away. I'll see whether he or I shall be master."

So I was taken away, and awhile after called for

again. I still called to have the mittimus read; for
that signified the cause of my commitment. I again
spoke to the Friend, my fellow-prisoner, to read it
up; which he did. The Judge, justices, and the whole
court were silent; for the people were eager to hear
it. It was as followeth:

" Peter Ceely, one of the justices of the peace of this
county, to the keeper of His Highness's jail at
Launceston, or his lawful deputy in that behalf,
greeting:

" I send you here withal by the bearers hereof,
the bodies of Edward Pyot, of Bristol, and George
Fox, of Drayton-in-the-Clay, in Leicestershire, and
William Salt, of London, which they pretend to be
the places of their habitations, who go under the
notion of Quakers, and acknowledge themselves to be
such; who have spread several papers tending to the
disturbance of the public peace, and cannot render
any lawful cause of coming into those parts, being
persons altogether unknown, having no pass for
travelling up and down the country, and refusing to
give sureties for their good behaviour, according to
the law in that behalf provided; and refuse to take
oath of abjuration, etc. These are, therefore, in the
name of his highness the Lord Protector, to will and
command you, that when the bodies of the said Edward Pyot, George Fox, and William Salt, shall be
unto you brought, you them receive, and in His
Highness's prison aforesaid you safely keep them,
until by due course of law they shall be delivered.

Hereof fail you not, as you will answer the contrary at your perils. Given under my hand and seal, at St. Ives, the 18th day of January, 1655.

" P. CEELY."

When it was read I spoke thus to the Judge and justices:

" Thou that sayest thou art Chief-Justice of England, and you justices, know that, if I had put in sureties, I might have gone whither I pleased, and have carried on the design (if I had had one) with which Major Ceely hath charged me. And if I had spoken those words to him, which he hath here declared, judge ye whether bail or mainprize could have been taken in that case."

Then, turning my speech to Major Ceely, I said:

" When or where did I take thee aside? Was not thy house full of rude people, and thou as rude as any of them, at our examination; so that I asked for a constable or some other officer, to keep the people civil? But if thou art my accuser, why sittest thou on the bench? It is not the place of accusers to sit with the judge. Thou oughtest to come down and stand by me, and look me in the face.

" Besides, I would ask the Judge and justices whether Major Ceely is not guilty of this treason, which he charges against me, in concealing it so long as he hath done? Does he understand his place, either as a soldier or a justice of the peace? For he tells you here that I went aside with him, and told him what a design I had in hand, and how serviceable he might be for my design: that I could raise **forty**

thousand men in an hour's time, bring in King
Charles, and involve the nation in blood. He saith,
moreover, that he would have aided me out of the
country, but I would not go; and therefore he committed me to prison for want of sureties for the good
behaviour, as the mittimus declares.

"Now, do you not see plainly that Major Ceely
is guilty of this plot and treason he talks of, and hath
made himself a party to it by desiring me to go out
of the country, demanding bail of me, and not charging me with this pretended treason till now, nor dis-
covering it? But I deny and abhor his words, and
am innocent of his devilish design."

So that business was let fall; for the Judge saw
clearly enough that instead of ensnaring me, Major
Ceely had ensnared himself.

Major Ceely got up again, and said, "If it please
you, my lord, to hear me: this man struck me, and
gave me such a blow as I never had in my life." At
this I smiled in my heart, and said, "Major Ceely,
art thou a justice of the peace, and a major of a troop
of horse, and tellest the Judge, in the face of the
court and country, that I, a prisoner, struck thee
and gave thee such a blow as thou never hadst the
like in thy life? What! art thou not ashamed?
Prithee, Major Ceely," said I, "where did I strike
thee? and who is thy witness for that? who was
by?"

He said it was in the Castle-Green, and Captain
Bradden was standing by when I struck him. I desired the Judge to let him produce his witness for
that; and called again upon Major Ceely to come

down from the bench, telling him that it was not fit
that the accuser should sit as judge over the accused.
When I called again for his witness he said that Cap·
tain Bradden was his witness.

Then I said, " Speak, Captain Bradden, didst thou
see me give him such a blow, and strike him as he
saith ? " Captain Bradden made no answer; but
bowed his head towards me. I desired him to speak
up, if he knew any such thing; but he only bowed
his head again. " Nay," said I, " speak up, and let
the court and country hear, and let not bowing of
the head serve the turn. If I have done so, let the
law be inflicted on me; I fear not sufferings, nor
death itself, for I am an innocent man concerning all
this charge."

But Captain Bradden never testified to it; and the
Judge, finding those snares would not hold, cried,
" Take him away, jailer; " and then, when we were
taken away, he fined us twenty marks apiece for not
putting off our hats; and sentenced us to be kept in
prison till we paid it; so he sent us back to the jail.

At night Captain Bradden came to see us, and
seven or eight justices with him, who were very civil
to us, and told us they believed neither the Judge
nor any in the court gave credit to the charges which
Major Ceely had brought forward against me in the
face of the country. And Captain Bradden said that
Major Ceely had an intent to take away my life if
he could have got another witness.

" But," said I, " Captain Bradden, why didst not
thou witness for me, or against me, seeing Major
Ceely produced thee for a witness, that thou saw me

strike him? and when I desired thee to speak either for me or against me, according to what thou saw or knew, thou wouldst not speak."

" Why," said he, " when Major Ceely and I came by you, as you were walking in the Castle-Green, he put off his hat to you, and said, ' How do you do, Mr. Fox? Your servant, Sir.' Then you said to him, ' Major Ceely, take heed of hypocrisy, and of a rotten heart: for when came I to be thy master, and thou my servant? Do servants cast their masters into prison?' This was the great blow he meant you gave him."

Then I called to mind that they walked by us, and that he spoke so to me, and I to him; which hypocrisy and rotten-heartedness he manifested openly, when he complained of this to the Judge in open court, and in the face of the country; and would have made them all believe that I struck him outwardly with my hand.

There came also to see us one Colonel Rouse a justice of the peace, and a great company with him. He was as full of words and talk as ever I heard any man in my life, so that there was no speaking to him. At length I asked him whether he had ever been at school, and knew what belonged to questions and answers; (this I said to stop him).

" At school!" said he, " Yes."

" At school!" said the soldiers; " doth he say so to our colonel, that is a scholar?"

" Then," said I, " if he be so, let him be still and receive answers to what he hath said."

Then I was moved to speak the Word of life to

him in God's dreadful power; which came so over him that he could not open his mouth. His face swelled, and was red like a turkey; his lips moved, and he mumbled something; but the people thought he would have fallen down. I stepped up to him, and he said he was never so in his life before: for the Lord's power stopped the evil power in him; so that he was almost choked.

The man was ever after very loving to Friends, and not so full of airy words to us; though he was full of pride; but the Lord's power came over him, and the rest that were with him.

Another time there came an officer of the army, a very malicious, bitter professor whom I had known in London. He was full of his airy talk also, and spoke slightingly of the Light of Christ, and against the Truth, and against the Spirit of God being in men, as it was in the apostles' days; till the power of God, that bound the evil in him, had almost choked him as it did Colonel Rouse: for he was so full of evil that he could not speak, but blubbered and stuttered. But from the time that the Lord's power struck him and came over him, he was ever after more loving to us.

The assizes being over, and we settled in prison upon such a commitment that we were not likely to be soon released, we broke off from giving the jailer seven shillings a week apiece for our horses, and seven shillings a week for ourselves, and sent our horses into the country. Upon which he grew very wicked and devilish, and put us down into Doomsdale, a nasty, stinking place, where they used to put **mur**-derers after they were condemned.[11]

The place was so noisome that it was observed few that went in did ever come out again in health. There was no house of office in it; and the excrement of the prisoners that from time to time had been put there had not been carried out (as we were told) for many years. So that it was all like mire, and in some places to the tops of the shoes in water and urine; and he would not let us cleanse it, nor suffer us to have beds or straw to lie on.

At night some friendly people of the town brought us a candle and a little straw; and we burned a little of our straw to take away the stink. The thieves lay over our heads, and the head jailer in a room by them, over our heads also. It seems the smoke went up into the room where the jailer lay; which put him into such a rage that he took the pots of excrement from the thieves and poured them through a hole upon our heads in Doomsdale, till we were so bespattered that we could not touch ourselves nor one another. And the stink increased upon us; so that what with stink, and what with smoke, we were almost choked and smothered. We had the stink under our feet before, but now we had it on our heads and backs also; and he having quenched our straw

---

[11] This description of Doomsdale is far from pleasant reading, but it is a true and faithful picture of a dungeon in the seventeenth century, and because of its historic importance it is left exactly as it was written. It is no wonder the Quakers became prison reformers.

with the filth he poured down, had made a great
smother in the place. Moreover, he railed at us most
hideously, calling us hatchet-faced dogs, and such
strange names as we had never heard of. In this
manner we were obliged to stand all night, for we
could not sit down, the place was so full of filthy
excrement.

A great while he kept us after this manner before
he would let us cleanse it, or suffer us to have any
victuals brought in but what we got through the
grate. One time a girl brought us a little meat; and
he arrested her for breaking his house, and sued her
in the town-court for breaking the prison. A great
deal of trouble he put the young woman to; whereby
others were so discouraged that we had much ado to
get water, drink, or victuals. Near this time we sent
for a young woman, Ann Downer, from London, who
could write and take things well in short-hand, to
buy and dress our meat for us; which she was very
willing to do, it being also upon her spirit to come to
us in the love of God; and she was very serviceable
to us.

The head-jailer, we were informed, had been a
thief, and was burnt both in the hand and in the
shoulder; his wife, too, had been burnt in the hand.
The under-jailer had been burnt both in the hand
and in the shoulder: his wife had been burnt in the
hand also. Colonel Bennet, a Baptist teacher, having purchased the jail and lands belonging to the castle, had placed this head-jailer there. The prisoners
and some wild people would be talking of spirits that
haunted Doomsdale, and how many had died in it,

thinking perhaps to terrify us therewith. But I told them that if all the spirits and devils in hell were there, I was over them in the power of God, and feared no such thing; for Christ, our Priest, would sanctify the walls of the house to us, He who had bruised the head of the devil.[12] The priest was to cleanse the plague out of the walls of the house under the law, which had been ended by Christ, our Priest, who sanctifies both inwardly and outwardly the walls of the house, the walls of the heart, and all things to his people.

By this time the general quarter-sessions drew nigh; and the jailer still carrying himself basely and wickedly towards us, we drew up our suffering case, and sent it to the sessions at Bodmin. On the reading thereof, the justices gave order that Doomsdale door should be opened, and that we should have liberty to cleanse it, and to buy our meat in the town. We also sent a copy of our sufferings to the Protector, setting forth how we had been taken and committed by Major Ceely; and abused by Captain Keat as aforesaid, and the rest in order. The Protector sent down an order to Captain Fox, governor of Pendennis Castle, to examine the matter about the soldiers abusing us, and striking me.

There were at that time many of the gentry of the country at the Castle; and Captain Keat's kinsman, that struck me, was sent for before them, and much threatened. They told him that if I should change my principles, I might take the extremity of the

---

[12] This has the ring of one of Luther's utterances.

law against him, and might recover sound damages
of him. Captain Keat also was checked, for suffering the prisoners under his charge to be abused.

This was of great service in the country; for afterwards Friends might speak in any market or steeple-house thereabouts, and none would meddle with
them. I understood that Hugh Peters, one of the
Protector's chaplains, told him they could not do
George Fox a greater service for the spreading of his
principles in Cornwall, than to imprison him there.

And indeed my imprisonment there was of the
Lord, and for His service in those parts; for after the
assizes were over, and it was known that we were
likely to continue prisoners, several Friends from
most parts of the nation came in to the country to
visit us. Those parts of the west were very dark
countries at that time, but the Lord's light and truth
broke forth, shone over all, and many were turned
from darkness to light, and from Satan's power unto
God. Many were moved to go to the steeple-houses;
and several were sent to prison to us; and a great
convincement began in the country. For now we
had liberty to come out, and to walk in the Castle-
Green; and many came to us on First-days, to whom
we declared the Word of life.

Great service we had among them, and many were
turned to God, up and down the country; but great
rage possessed the priests and professors against
the Truth and us. One of the envious professors had collected many Scripture sentences to
prove that we ought to put off our hats to
the people; and he invited the town of Launces-

ton to come into the castle-yard to hear him
read them. Amongst other instances that he there
brought, one was that Saul bowed to the witch of
Endor. When he had done, we got a little liberty to
speak; and we showed both him and the people that
Saul was gone from God, and had disobeyed God
when he went to the witch of Endor: that neither the
prophets, nor Christ, nor the apostles ever taught
people to bow to a witch.

Another time, about eleven at night, the jailer,
being half drunk, came and told me that he had got
a man now to dispute with me: (this was when we
had leave to go a little into the town). As soon as
he spoke these words I felt there was mischief intended to my body. All that night and the next day
I lay down on a grass-plot to slumber, and felt something still about my body: I started up, and struck
at it in the power of the Lord, and still it was about
my body.

Then I rose and walked into the Castle-Green, and
the under-keeper came and told me that there was a
maid would speak with me in the prison. I felt a
snare in his words, too, therefore I went not into the
prison, but to the grate; and looking in, I saw a man
that was lately brought to prison for being a conjurer, who had a naked knife in his hand. I spoke to
him, and he threatened to cut my chaps; but, being
within the jail he could not come at me. This was
the jailer's great disputant.

I went soon after into the jailer's house, and found
him at breakfast; he had then got his conjurer out

with him. I told the jailer his plot was discovered. Then he got up from the table, and cast his napkin away in a rage; and I left them, and went to my chamber; for at this time we were out of Doomsdale.

At the time the jailer had said the dispute should be, I went down and walked in the court (the place appointed) till about the eleventh hour; but nobody came. Then I went up to my chamber again; and after awhile heard one call for me. I stepped to the stairshead, where I saw the jailer's wife upon the stairs, and the conjurer at the bottom of the stairs, holding his hand behind his back, and in a great rage.

I asked him, "Man, what hast thou in thy hand behind thy back? Pluck thy hand before thee," said I; "let's see thy hand, and what thou hast in it."

Then he angrily plucked forth his hand, with a naked knife in it. I showed the jailer's wife their wicked design against me; for this was the man they brought to dispute of the things of God. But the Lord discovered their plot, and prevented their evil design; and they both raged, and the conjurer threatened.

Then I was moved of the Lord to speak sharply to him in the dreadful power of the Lord; and the Lord's power came over him, and bound him down; so that he never after durst appear before me, to speak to me. I saw it was the Lord alone that had preserved me out of their bloody hands; for the devil had a great enmity to me, and stirred up his instruments to seek my hurt. But the Lord prevented them; and my heart was filled with thanksgivings and praises to him.[13]

In Cornwall, Devonshire, Dorsetshire, and Somersetshire, Truth began mightily to spread. Many were turned to Christ Jesus and His free teaching: for many Friends that came to visit us were drawn to declare the Truth in those counties. This made the priests and professors rage, and they stirred up the magistrates to ensnare Friends. ·They set up watches in the streets and highways, on pretence of taking up suspicious persons, under which colour they stopped and took up Friends coming to visit us in prison; which was done that these Friends might not pass up and down in the Lord's service.

But that by which they thought to have stopped the Truth was the means of spreading it so much the more; for then Friends were frequently moved to speak to one constable and to another officer, and to the justices before whom they were brought; which caused the Truth to spread the more in all their parishes. And when Friends were got among the

---

[13] The 14th of May, 1656, Edward Pyot, Fox's fellow prisoner, wrote a long letter to John Glyn, Chief Justice of England, in which he showed that they were suffering contrary to law. George Fox himself, as his custom was, spent much of his time of imprisonment writing letters and religious epistles. Here is a sound word of advice from his Epistle to "Friends": "Be patterns, be examples in all countries, places, islands, nations, wherever you come, that your life and conduct may preach among all sorts of people and to them."

watches, it would be a fortnight or three weeks before they could get out of them again; for no sooner had one constable taken and carried them before the justices, and these had discharged them, but another would take them up and carry them before other justices: which put the country to a great deal of needless trouble and charges.

As Thomas Rawlinson was coming out of the north to visit us, a constable in Devonshire took him up, and at night took twenty shillings out of his pocket: and after being thus robbed he was cast into Exeter jail. They cast into prison in Devonshire, under pretence of his being a Jesuit, Henry Pollexfen, who had been a justice of the peace for almost forty years. Many Friends were cruelly beaten by them; nay, some clothiers that were but going to mill with their cloth, and others about their outward occasions, they took up and whipped; though men of about eighty or an hundred pounds by the year, and not above four or five miles from their families.

The mayor of Launceston took up all he could, and cast them into prison. He would search substantial, grave women, their petticoats and their head-cloths. A young man coming to see us, I drew up all the gross, inhuman, and unchristian actions of the mayor, gave it him, and bade him seal it up, and go out again the back way; and then come into the town through the gates. He did so, and the watch took him up and carried him before the mayor; who presently searched his pockets and found the letter. Therein he saw all his actions characterized; which shamed him so that from that time he meddled little with the Lord's servants.

While I was in prison here, the Baptists and Fifth-monarchy men prophesied that this year Christ should come, and reign upon earth a thousand years. And they looked upon this reign to be outward: when He was come inwardly in the hearts of His people, to reign and rule; where these professors would not receive Him. So they failed in their prophecy and expectation, and had not the possession of Him. But Christ is come, and doth dwell and reign in the hearts of His people.[14] Thousands, at the door of whose hearts He hath been knocking, have opened to Him, and He is come in, and doth sup with them, and they with Him; the heavenly supper with the heavenly and spiritual man. So many of these Baptists and Monarchy-people turned the greatest enemies to the followers of Christ; but He reigns in the hearts of His saints over all their envy.

At the assize divers justices came to us, and were pretty civil, and reasoned of the things of God soberly; expressing a pity to us. Captain Fox, gov-

---

[14] It will be found interesting to compare this brief comment on the views of the " Fifth-monarchy men " with Cromwell's treatment of them. See Speech II., in First Parliament. Carlyle's " Oliver Cromwell," Centenary Edition, Vol. III., p. 113. The modern reader will also find it interesting to compare this passage with the present-day teachings of the " Second Coming."

ernor of Pendennis Castle, came and looked me in the face, and said never a word; but went to his company and told them he never saw a simpler man in his life. I called after him, and said, " Stay, man; we will see who is the simpler man." But he went his way. A light, chaffy person.

Thomas Lower[15] also came to visit us, and offered us money, which we refused; accepting nevertheless of his love. He asked us many questions concerning our denying the Scriptures to be the Word of God; concerning the sacraments, and such like: to all which he received satisfaction. I spoke particularly to him; and he afterwards said my words were as a flash of lightning, they ran so through him. He said he had never met with such men in his life, for they knew the thoughts of his heart; and were as the wise master-builders of the assemblies that fastened their words like nails. He came to be convinced of the truth, and remains a Friend to this day.

When he came home to his aunt Hambley's, where he then lived, and made report to her concerning us, she, with her sister Grace Billing, hearing the report of Truth, came to visit us in prison, and was convinced also. Great sufferings and spoiling of goods both he and his aunt have undergone for the Truth's sake.

After the assizes, the sheriff, with some soldiers, came to guard to execution a woman that was sentenced to die; and we had much discourse with them.

---

[15] This Thomas Lower married Judge Fell's daughter, Mary.

One of them wickedly said, " Christ was as passionate a man as any that lived upon the earth;" for
which we rebuked him. Another time we asked the
jailer what doings there were at the sessions; and
he said, " Small matters; only about thirty for bas-
tardy." We thought it very strange that they who
professed themselves Christians should make small
matters of such things.

But this jailer was very bad himself; I often admonished him to sobriety; but he abused people that
came to visit us. Edward Pyot had a cheese sent
him from Bristol by his wife; and the jailer took it
from him, and carried it to the mayor, to search it
for treasonable letters, as he said; and though they
found no treason in the cheese, they kept it from
us.[16] This jailer might have been rich—if he had
carried himself civilly; but he sought his own ruin,
which soon after came upon him.

The next year he was turned out of his place, and

---

[16] This, however, was not the last of the cheese. After
their release they revisited Launceston, as this extract
will show:

" From Thomas Mounce's we passed to Launceston
again, and visited that little remnant of Friends that
had been raised up there while we were in prison. The
Lord's plants grew finely, and were established on
Christ, their rock and foundation. As we were going
out of town again, the constable of Launceston came
running to us with the cheese that had been taken from
Edward Pyot; which they had kept from us all this
while, and were tormented with it. But being now set
at liberty, we would not receive it."

for some wickedness cast into the jail himself; and there begged of our Friends. And for some unruliness in his conduct he was, by the succeeding jailer, put into Doomsdale, locked in irons, and beaten, and bidden to remember how he had abused those good men whom he had wickedly, without any cause, cast into that nasty dungeon; and told that now he deservedly should suffer for his wickedness; and the same measure he had meted to others, should be meted out to himself. He became very poor, and died in prison; and his wife and family came to misery.

While I was in prison in Launceston, a Friend went to Oliver Cromwell, and offered himself, body for body, to lie in Doomsdale in my stead; if he would take him, and let me have liberty. Which thing so struck him, that he said to his great men and council, " Which of you would do as much for me if I were in the same condition ? " And though he did not accept of the Friend's offer, but said he could not do it, for that it was contrary to law, yet the Truth thereby came mightily over him. A good while after this he sent down Major-General Desborough, pretending to set us at liberty. When he came, he offered us our liberty if we would say we would go home and preach no more; but we could not promise him. Then he urged that we should promise to go home, if the Lord permitted.

After this [17] Major-General Desborough came to

---

[17] Both Edward Pyot and George Fox had written letters to Major-General Desborough, showing that

the Castle-Green, and played at bowls with the justices and others. Several Friends were moved to go
and admonish them not to spend their time so vainly,
desiring them to consider, that though they professed
themselves to be Christians, yet they gave themselves
up to their pleasures, and kept the servants of God
meanwhile in prison; and telling them that the Lord
would plead with them and visit them for such
things. But notwithstanding what was written or
said to him, he went away, and left us in prison.

We understood afterwards that he left the business
to Colonel Bennet, who had the command of the jail.
For some time after Bennet would have set us at
liberty if we would have paid his jailer's fees. But
we told him we could give the jailer no fees, for we
were innocent sufferers; and how could they expect
fees of us, who had suffered so long wrongfully?
After a while Colonel Bennet coming to town, sent
for us to an inn, and insisted again upon fees, which
we refused. At last the power of the Lord came so
over him, that he freely set us at liberty on the 13th
day of the Seventh month, 1656. We had been prisoners nine weeks at the first assize, called the Lent-
assize, which was in the spring of the year.

---

they were innocent, law-abiding men, doing the Lord's
work in the world, and that they could not promise to
go home, it being the free right of an Englishman to go
where his duty or his business carried him.

CHAPTER X.

Planting the Seed in Wales.

1656-1657.

Being released from our imprisonment, we got horses, rode towards Humphrey Lower's, and met him upon the road. He told us he was much troubled in his mind concerning us, and could not rest at home, but was going to Colonel Bennet to seek our liberty. When we told him we were set at liberty, and were going to his house, he was exceeding glad. To his house we went, and had a fine, precious meeting; many were convinced, and turned by the Spirit of the Lord to the Lord Jesus Christ's teaching.

Soon after we came to Exeter, where many Friends were in prison; and amongst the rest James Nayler. For a little before we were set at liberty, James had run out into imaginations, and a company with him, who raised a great darkness in the nation. He came to Bristol, and made a disturbance there.[1]

---

[1] Poor James Nayler proved unable to stand the strain of this strenuous work. A fanatical group got about him and in a period of evident aberration he allowed these flattering followers to give him a Triumphal Entry into Bristol, as Christ, returned in the flesh. Here is Carlyle's account: "In the month of October, 1655, there was seen a strange sight at Bristol

From thence he was coming to Launceston to see me; but was stopped by the way, and imprisoned at Exeter; as were several others, one of whom, an honest, tender man, died in prison there. His blood lieth on the heads of his persecutors.

The night that we came to Exeter I spoke with James Nayler: for I saw he was out, and wrong, and so was his company. The next day, being First-day, we went to visit the prisoners, and had a meeting with them in the prison; but James Nayler, and some of them, could not stay the meeting. There came a corporal of horse into the meeting, who was convinced, and remained a very good Friend.

---

in the West. A procession of eight persons: one a man on horseback, riding single; the others, men and women, partly riding double, partly on foot, in the muddiest highway, in the wettest weather; singing, all but the single-rider, at whose bridle splash and walk two women: ' Hosannah! Holy, holy! Lord God of Sabaoth!' . . . The single-rider is a raw-boned male figure, ' with lank hair reaching below his cheeks'; hat drawn close over his brows; of abstruse ' down look' and large, dangerous jaws, strictly closed; he sings not; sits there covered, and is sung to by the others, bare. Amid pouring deluges and mud knee-deep: ' so that the rain ran in at their necks, and they vented it at their hose and breeches,' a spectacle to the west of England and posterity! Singing as above; answering no questions except in song. At the High Cross, they are laid hold of by the Authorities; turn out to be James Nayler and Company." (Carlyle's " Oliver Cromwell's Letters and Speeches." Vol. III., pp. 223, 224.) What he

The next day I spoke to James Nayler again; and he slighted what I said, was dark, and much out; yet he would have come and kissed me. But I said that since he had turned against the power of God, I could not receive his show of kindness. The Lord moved me to slight him, and to set the power of God over him. So after I had been warring with the world, there was now a wicked spirit risen amongst Friends to war against. I admonished him and his company.

When he was come to London, his resisting the power of God in me, and the Truth that was declared to him by me, became one of his greatest burdens. But he came to see his out-going, and to condemn it; and after some time he returned to Truth

---

needed was mental treatment. What he received was the harshest punishment Parliament could devise. He missed the death penalty by a vote of 82 to 96. His sentence, passed by Parliament December 16th, 1656, was to be pilloried for two hours, to be whipped by the hangman through the streets from Westminster to the Old Exchange in the city, to be pilloried again after two days for two hours more, to have his tongue bored through with a red-hot iron, and to be branded in the forehead with the letter B, to be again flogged through the streets of Bristol, and then to be committed to prison with solitary confinement and hard labor during the pleasure of Parliament. Poor James Nayler! His fall did the Quakers almost irreparable injury in public estimation. Fox had already had an intimation of this trouble. As he left James Nayler in London he wrote: "As I passed him I cast my eye upon him and a fear struck me concerning him."

again;[2] as in the printed relation of his repentance, condemnation, and recovery may be more fully seen.

On First-day morning I went to the meeting in Broadmead at Bristol, which was large and quiet. Notice was given of a meeting to be in the afternoon in the orchard.

There was at Bristol a rude Baptist, named Paul Gwin, who had before made great disturbance in our meetings, being encouraged and set on by the mayor, who, it was reported, would sometimes give him his dinner to encourage him. Such multitudes of rude people he gathered after him, that it was thought there had been sometimes ten thousand people at our meeting in the orchard.

As I was going into the orchard, the people told me that Paul Gwin was going to the meeting. I bade them never heed, for it was nothing to me who went to it.

---

[2] His death came not long after his awful punishment, and just before the end of life he wrote these words:

" There is a spirit which I feel, which delights to do no evil, nor to revenge any wrong; but delights to endure all things, in hope to enjoy its own in the end. Its hope is to outlive all wrath and contention, and to weary out all exaltation and cruelty, or whatever is of a nature contrary to itself. It sees to the end of all temptations; as it bears no evil in itself, so it conceives none in thought to any other. If it be betrayed, it bears it; for its ground and spring is the mercy and forgiveness of God. Its crown is meekness; its life is everlasting love unfeigned. It takes its kingdom with entreaty,

When I was come into the orchard, I stood upon the stone that Friends used to stand on when they spoke; and I was moved of the Lord to put off my hat, and to stand a while, and let the people look at me; for some thousands of people were there. While I thus stood silent, this rude Baptist began to find fault with my hair; but I said nothing to him. Then he ran on into words; and at last, " Ye wise men of Bristol," said he, " I marvel at you, that you will stand here, and hear a man speak and affirm that which he cannot make good."

Then the Lord opened my mouth (for as yet I had not spoken a word), and I asked the people whether they had ever heard me speak, or had ever seen me before; and I bade them take notice what kind of man this was amongst them that should so impudently say that I spoke and affirmed that which I

---

and not with contention, and keeps it by lowliness of mind. In God alone it can rejoice, though none else regard it, or can own its life. It is conceived in sorrow, and brought forth without any to pity it; nor doth it murmur at grief and oppression. It never rejoiceth, but through sufferings; for with the world's joy it is murdered. I found it alone; being forsaken. I have fellowship therein, with those who lived in dens and desolate places in the earth; who through death obtained this resurrection, and eternal, holy life! "

See also " James Nayler's answer to the Fanatick History as far as it relates to him."

The wild extreme to which Nayler went had a very sobering effect on the Friends themselves.

could not make good; and yet neither he nor they had ever heard me or seen me before. Therefore that was a lying, envious, malicious spirit that spoke in him; and it was of the devil, and not of God. I charged him in the dread and power of the Lord to be silent: and the mighty power of God came over him, and all his company.

Then a glorious, peaceable meeting we had, and the Word of life was divided amongst them; and they were turned from darkness to the Light,—to Jesus their Saviour. The Scriptures were largely opened to them; and the traditions, rudiments, ways, and doctrines of men were laid open before the people; and they were turned to the Light of Christ, that with it they might see these things, and see Him to lead them out of them.

I opened also to them the types, figures, and shadows of Christ in the time of the law; and showed them that Christ was come, and had ended the types, shadows, tithes, and oaths, and put down swearing; and had set up yea and nay instead of it, and a free ministry. For He was now come to teach the people Himself, and His heavenly day was springing from on high.

For many hours did I declare the Word of life amongst them in the eternal power of God, that by Him they might come up into the beginning, and be reconciled to Him. And having turned them to the Spirit of God in themselves, that would lead into all Truth, I was moved to pray in the mighty power of God; and the Lord's power came over all. When I had done, this fellow began to babble again; and John

Audland was moved to bid him repent, and fear God. So his own people and followers being ashamed of him, he passed away, and never came again to disturb the meeting. The meeting broke up quietly, and the Lord's power and glory shone over all: a blessed day it was, and the Lord had the praise. After a while this Paul Gwin went beyond the seas; and many years after I met him in Barbadoes.

Soon after we rode to London. When we came near Hyde Park we saw a great concourse of people, and, looking towards them, espied the Protector coming in his coach. Whereupon I rode to his coach side. Some of his life-guard would have put me away; but he forbade them. So I rode by his coach side with him, declaring what the Lord gave me to say to him, of his condition, and of the sufferings of Friends in the nation, showing him how contrary this persecution was to the words of Christ and His apostles, and to Christianity.

When we were come to James's Park Gate, I left him; and at parting he desired me to come to his house. The next day one of his wife's maids, whose name was Mary Sanders, came to me at my lodging, and told me that her master came to her, and said he would tell her some good news. When she asked him what it was, he told her, " George Fox is come to town." She replied " That is good news indeed " (for she had received Truth), but she said she could hardly believe him till he told her how I met him, and rode from Hyde Park to James's Park with him.

After a little time Edward Pyot and I went to

Whitehall to see Oliver Cromwell; and when we came before him, Dr. Owen, vice-chancellor of Oxford, was with him. We were moved to speak to him concerning the sufferings of Friends, and laid them before him: and we directed him to the Light of Christ, who had enlightened every man that cometh into the world. He said it was a natural light; but we showed him the contrary; and proved that it was divine and spiritual, proceeding from Christ the spiritual and heavenly man; and that that which was called the life in Christ the Word, was called the Light in us.

The power of the Lord God arose in me, and I was moved in it to bid him lay down his crown at the feet of Jesus. Several times I spoke to him to the same effect. I was standing by the table, and he came and sat upon the table's side by me, saying he would be as high as I was. So he continued speaking against the Light of Christ Jesus; and went his way in a light manner. But the Lord's power came over him so that when he came to his wife and other company, he said, "I never parted so from them before"; for he was judged in himself.

After this I travelled into Yorkshire, and returned out of Holderness, over Humber, visiting Friends; and then returning into Leicestershire, Staffordshire, Worcestershire, and Warwickshire, among Friends, I had a meeting at Edge-Hill. There came to it Ranters, Baptists, and several sorts of rude people; for I had sent word about three weeks before to have a meeting there, so that hundreds of people were gathered thither, and many Friends came to it from afar. The Lord's everlasting Truth and Word of life reached over all; the rude and unruly spirits were chained down; and many that day were turned to the Lord Jesus Christ, by His power and Spirit, and came to sit under His blessed, free teaching, and to be fed with His eternal, heavenly food. All was peaceable; the people passed quietly away, and some of them said it was a mighty, powerful meeting; for the presence of the Lord was felt, and His power and Spirit was amongst them.

Thence I passed to Warwick and to Bagley, having precious meetings; and then into Gloucestershire, and so to Oxford, where the scholars were very rude; but the Lord's power came over them. Great meetings we had as we travelled up and down.

Thus having travelled over most of the nation, I returned to London again, having cleared myself of that which lay upon me from the Lord. For after I was released out of Launceston jail, I was moved of the Lord to travel over the nation, the Truth being now spread in most places, that I might answer, and remove out of the minds of the people, some objections which the envious priests and professors had raised and spread abroad concerning us.

In this year the Lord's Truth was finely planted over the nation, and many thousands were turned to the Lord; insomuch that there were seldom fewer than one thousand in prison in this nation for Truth's testimony; some for tithes, some for going to the steeple-houses, some for contempts (as they called them), some for not swearing, and others for not putting off their hats.

Having stayed some time in London, and visited the meetings of Friends in and about the city, and cleared myself of what services the Lord had at that time laid upon me there, I left the town and travelled into Kent, Sussex, and Surrey, visiting Friends. I had great meetings, and often met with opposition from Baptists and other jangling professors; but the Lord's power went over them.

We lay one night at Farnham, where we had a little meeting. The people were exceeding rude; but at last the Lord's power came over them. After meeting we went to our inn, and gave notice that any who feared God might come to our inn to us. There came abundance of rude people, the magistrates of the town, and some professors. I declared the Truth to them; and those people that behaved themselves rudely, the magistrates put out of the room.

When they were gone, another rude company of professors came up, and some of the chief of the town. They called for faggots and drink, though we forbade them, and were as rude a people as ever I met. The Lord's power chained them, that they had not power to do us any mischief; but when they went away they left all the faggots and beer, for which they had called, in the room, for us to pay for in the morning. We showed the innkeeper what an unworthy thing it was; but he told us we must pay it; and pay it we did.

Before we left the town I wrote to the magistrates and heads of the town, and to the priest, showing them how he had taught his people, and laying before them their rude and uncivil carriage to strangers that sought their good.

Leaving that place we came to Basingstoke, a very rude town; where they had formerly very much abused Friends. There I had a meeting in the evening, which was quiet; for the Lord's power chained the unruly. At the close of the meeting I was moved to put off my hat and to pray to the Lord to open their understandings; upon which they raised a report that I put off my hat to them and bade them good night, which was never in my heart.

After the meeting, when we came to our inn, I sent for the innkeeper, as I was used to do; and he came into the room to us, and showed himself a very rude man. I admonished him to be sober, and fear the Lord; but he called for faggots and a pint of wine, and drank it off himself; then called for another, and called up half a dozen men into our chamber. Thereupon I bade him go out of the chamber, and told him he should not drink there; for we called him up to speak to him concerning his eternal good.

He was exceeding mad, rude, and drunk. When he continued his rudeness and would not be gone, I told him that the chamber was mine for the time I lodged in it; and called for the key. Then he went away in a rage. In the morning he would not be seen; but I told his wife of his unchristian carriage towards us.

We then travelled to Exeter; and at the sign of the Seven Stars, an inn at the bridge foot, had a general meeting of Friends out of Cornwall and Devonshire; to which came Humphrey Lower, Thomas Lower,

and John Ellis from the Land's End; Henry Pollexfen, and Friends from Plymouth; Elizabeth Trelawny, and divers other Friends. A blessed heavenly
meeting we had, and the Lord's everlasting power
came over all, in which I saw and said that the Lord's
power had surrounded this nation round about as
with a wall and bulwark, and His seed reached from
sea to sea. Friends were established in the everlasting Seed of life, Christ Jesus, their Life, Rock,
Teacher, and Shepherd.

Next morning Major Blackmore sent soldiers to
apprehend me; but I was gone before they came. As
I was riding up the street I saw the officers going
down; so the Lord crossed them in their design, and
Friends passed away peaceably and quietly. The soldiers examined some Friends after I was gone, asking
them what they did there; but when they told them
that they were in their inn, and had business in the
city, they went away without meddling any further
with them.

We passed through the countries,* having meetings, and gathering people in the name of Christ,
their heavenly teacher, till we came to Brecknock,
where we put up our horses at an inn. There went
with me Thomas Holmes and John ap-John, who was
moved of the Lord to speak in the streets. I walked
out but a little into the fields; and when I returned
the town was in an uproar. When I came into the
chamber in the inn, it was full of people, and they
were speaking in Welsh. I desired them to speak in

* In Wales.

English, which they did; and much discourse we had. After a while they went away.

Towards night the magistrates gathered in the streets with a multitude of people, and they bade them shout, and gathered up the town; so that, for about two hours together, there was a noise the like of which we had not heard; and the magistrates set them on to shout again when they had given over. We thought it looked like the uproar amongst Diana's craftsmen. This tumult continued till night, and if the Lord's power had not limited them, they would likely have pulled down the house, and torn us to pieces.

At night the woman of the house would have had us go to supper in another room; but we, discerning her plot, refused. Then she would have had half a dozen men come into the room to us, under the pretence of discoursing with us. We told her, " No person shall come into our room this night, neither will we go to them." Then she said we should sup in another room; but we told her we would have no supper if we had it not in our own room. At length, when she saw she could not get us out, she brought up our supper.

So she and they were crossed in their design; for they had an intent to do us mischief, but the Lord prevented them. Next morning I wrote a paper to the town concerning their unchristian carriage, showing the fruits of their priests and magistrates; and as I passed out of town I spoke to the people, and told them they were a shame to Christianity and religion.

After this we returned to England, and came to

Shrewsbury, where we had a great meeting, and visited Friends all over the countries in their meetings, till we came to William Gandy's, in Cheshire, where we had a meeting of between two and three thousand people, as it was thought; and the everlasting Word of life was held forth, and received that day. A blessed meeting it was, for Friends were settled by the power of God upon Christ Jesus, the Rock and Foundation.

At this time there was a great drought; and after this general meeting was ended, there fell so great a rain that Friends 'said they thought we could not travel, the waters would be so risen. But I believed the rain had not extended as far as they had come that day to the meeting. Next day, in the afternoon, when we turned back into some parts of Wales again, the roads were dusty, and no rain had fallen there.

When Oliver Cromwell sent forth a proclamation for a fast throughout the nation, for rain, when there was a very great drought, it was observed that as far as Truth had spread in the north, there were pleasant showers and rain enough, while in the south, in many places, the fields were almost spoiled for want of rain. At that time I was moved to write an answer to the Protector's proclamation, wherein I told him that if he had come to own God's Truth, he should have had rain; and that the drought was a sign unto them of their barrenness, and their want of the water of life.

We passed through Montgomeryshire into Wales, and so into Radnorshire, where there was a meeting

like a leaguer,* for multitudes. I walked a little aside
whilst the people were gathering: and there came to
me John ap-John, a Welshman, whom I asked to go
to the people; and if he had anything upon him from
the Lord to them, he might speak in Welsh, and
thereby gather more together. Then came Morgan
Watkins to me, who was become loving to Friends,
and said, " The people lie like a leaguer, and the gentry of the country are come in." I bade him go up
also, and leave me; for I had a great travail upon me
for the salvation of the people.

When they were well gathered, I went into the
meeting, and stood upon a chair about three hours. I
stood a pretty while before I began to speak. After
some time I felt the power of the Lord over the
whole assembly: and His everlasting life and Truth
shone over all. The Scriptures were opened to them,
and the objections they had in their minds answered.
They were directed to the Light of Christ, the heavenly man; that by it they might see their sins, and
Christ Jesus to be their Saviour, their Redeemer,
their Mediator; and come to feed upon Him, the
bread of life from heaven.

Many were turned to the Lord Jesus Christ, and to
His free teaching that day; and all were bowed down
under the power of God; so that though the multitude was so great that many sat on horseback to hear,
there was no opposition. A priest sat with his wife
on horseback, heard attentively, and made no objection.

The people parted peaceably, with great satisfac-

* A besieging army.

tion; many of them saying they had never heard such a sermon before, nor the Scriptures so opened. For the new covenant was opened, and the old, and the nature and terms of each; and the parables were explained. The state of the Church in the apostles' days was set forth, and the apostasy since was laid open; the free teaching of Christ and the apostles was set atop of all the hireling teachers; and the Lord had the praise of all, for many were turned to Him that day.[3]

I went thence to Leominster, where was a great meeting in a close, many hundreds of people being gathered together. There were about six congregational preachers and priests amongst the people; and Thomas Taylor, who had been a priest, but was now become a minister of Christ Jesus, was with me. I stood up and declared about three hours; and none of the priests were able to open their mouths in opposition; the Lord's power and Truth so reached and bound them.

At length one priest went off about a bow-shot from me, drew several of the people after him, and began to preach to them. So I kept our meeting, and he kept his. After awhile Thomas Taylor was moved to go and speak to him, upon which he gave over: and he, with the people he had drawn off, came to us again; and the Lord's power went over all.

---

[3] Great numbers of these Welsh Friends migrated to Pennsylvania and settled Montgomery County. Haverford, Bryn Mawr, Merion and Radnor are some of the historic townships whose names were transferred to the new world by these followers of Fox.

From this place I travelled on in Wales, having several meetings, till I came to Tenby, where, as I rode up the street, a justice of the peace came out to me, asked me to alight, and desired that I would stay at his house, which I did. On First-day the mayor, with his wife, and several others of the chief people of the town, came in about the tenth hour, and stayed all the time of the meeting. A glorious meeting it was.

John ap-John being then with me, left the meeting, and went to the steeple-house; and the governor cast him into prison. On Second-day morning the governor sent one of his officers to the justice's to fetch me; which grieved the mayor and the justice; for they were both with me in the justice's house when the officer came. The mayor and the justice went to the governor before me; and awhile after I went with the officer. When I came in I said, "Peace be unto this house," and before the governor could examine me I asked him why he cast my friend into prison. He said, "For standing with his hat on in the church."

I said, "Had not the priest two caps on his head, a black one and a white one? Cut off the brims of the hat, and then my friend would have but one: and the brims of the hat were but to defend him from weather."

"These are frivolous things," said the governor.

"Why, then," said I, "dost thou cast my friend into prison for such frivolous things?"

He asked me whether I owned election and repro-

bation. " Yes," said I, " and thou art in the reprobation."

At that he was in a rage and said he would send
me to prison till I proved it. I told him I would
prove that quickly if he would confess Truth. I
asked him whether wrath, fury, rage and persecution were not marks of reprobation; for he that was
born of the flesh persecuted him that was born of the
Spirit; but Christ and His disciples never persecuted
nor imprisoned any.

He fairly confessed that he had too much wrath,
haste and passion in him. I told him that Esau was
up in him, the first birth; not Jacob, the second birth.
The Lord's power so reached the man and came over
him that he confessed to Truth; and the other justice
came and shook me kindly by the hand.

As I was passing away I was moved to speak to the
governor again; and he invited me to dinner with
him, and set my friend at liberty. I went back to
the other justice's house; and after some time the
mayor and his wife, and the justice and his wife, and
divers other Friends of the town, went about half a
mile out of town with us, to the water-side, when
we went away; and there, when we parted from them,
I was moved of the Lord to kneel down with them,
and pray to the Lord to preserve them. So, after I
had recommended them to the Lord Jesus Christ,
their Saviour and free Teacher, we passed away in the
Lord's power; and He had the glory.

We travelled to Pembrokeshire, and in Pembroke
had some service for the Lord. Thence we passed
to Haverford West, where we had a great meeting,

and all was quiet. The Lord's power came over all, and many were settled in the new covenant, Christ Jesus, and built upon Him, their Rock and Foundation; and they stand a precious meeting to this day. Next day, being their fair-day, we passed through it, and sounded the day of the Lord, and His everlasting Truth, amongst them.

After this we passed into another county, and at noon came into a great market-town, and went into several inns before we could get any meat for our horses. At last we came to one where we got some. Then John ap-John being with me, went and spoke through the town, declaring the Truth to the people; and when he came to me again, he said he thought all the town were as people asleep. After awhile he was moved to go and declare Truth in the streets again; then the town was all in an uproar, and they cast him into prison.

Presently after several of the chief people of the town came, with others, to the inn where I was, and said, " They have cast your man into prison."

" For what ? " said I.

" He preached in our streets," said they.

Then I asked them, " What did he say ? Had he reproved some of the drunkards and swearers, and warned them to repent, and leave off their evil doings, and turn to the Lord ? " I asked them who cast him into prison. They said, the high-sheriff and justices, and the mayor. I asked their names, and whether they understood themselves; and whether that was their conduct to travellers that passed through their town, and strangers that admonished

and exhorted them to fear the Lord, and reproved
sin in their gates.

These went back, and told the officers what I had
said; and after awhile they brought down John ap-
John, guarded with halberts, in order to put him out
of the town. Being at the inn door, I bade the officers take their hands off him. They said that the
mayor and justices had commanded them to put him
out of town. I told them I would talk with their
mayor and justices concerning their uncivil and unchristian carriage towards him.

So I spoke to John to go look after the horses, and
get them ready, and charged the officers not to touch
him. After I had declared the Truth to them, and
showed them the fruits of their priests, and their in-
civility and unchristian carriage, they left us. They
were a kind of Independents; a very wicked town,
and false. We bade the innkeeper give our horses
a peck of oats; and no sooner had we turned our
backs than the oats were stolen from our horses.

After we had refreshed ourselves a little, and were
ready, we took horse, and rode up to the inn, where
the mayor, sheriff, and justices were. I called to
speak with them, and asked them why they had imprisoned John ap-John, and kept him in prison two or
three hours. But they would not answer me a word;
they only looked out at the windows upon me. So
I showed them how unchristian was their carriage
to strangers and travellers, and how it manifested the
fruits of their teachers; and I declared the truth unto
them, and warned them of the day of the Lord, that
was coming upon all evil-doers; and the Lord's power

came over them, that they looked ashamed; but not
a word could I get from them in answer.

So when I had warned them to repent, and turn to
the Lord, we passed away. At night we came to a
little inn, very poor, but very cheap; for our own
provision and that for our two horses cost but eight-
pence; but the horses would not eat their oats. We
declared the Truth to the people of the place, and
sounded the day of the Lord through the countries.*

Passing thence we came to a great town, and went
to an inn. Edward Edwards went into the market,
and declared the Truth amongst the people; and they
followed him to the inn, and filled the yard, and were
exceedingly rude. Yet good service we had for the
Lord amongst them; for the life of Christianity and
the power of it tormented their chaffy spirits, and
came over them, so that some were reached and convinced; and the Lord's power came over all. The
magistrates were bound; they had no power to meddle with us.

After this we came to another great town on a
market-day; and John ap-John declared the everlasting Truth through the streets, and proclaimed the
day of the Lord amongst them. In the evening many
people gathered about the inn; and some of them,
being drunk, would fain have had us come into the
street again. But seeing their design, I told them
that if there were any that feared God and desired
to hear the Truth, they might come into our inn; or
else we might have a meeting with them next morning.

* Counties.

Some service for the Lord we had amongst them, both over night and in the morning; and though the people were slow to receive the Truth, yet the seed was sown; and thereabouts the Lord hath a people gathered to Himself.

In that inn, also, I but turned my back to the man that was giving oats to my horse, and, looking round again, I observed he was filling his pockets with the provender. A wicked, thievish people, to rob the poor, dumb creature of his food. I would rather they had robbed me.

Thence we went to Beaumaris, a town wherein John ap-John had formerly been a preacher. After we had put up our horses at an inn, John went and spoke through the street; and there being a garrison in the town, they took him and put him into prison. The innkeeper's wife came and told me that the governor and magistrates were sending for me, to commit me to prison also. I told her that they had done more than they could answer already; and had acted contrary to Christianity in imprisoning him for reproving sin in their streets and gates, and for declaring the Truth. Soon after came other friendly people, and told me that if I went into the street, the governor and magistrates would imprison me also; therefore they desired me to keep within the inn.

Upon this I was moved to go and walk up and down in the streets.[4] And I told the people what an uncivil, unchristian thing they had done in casting my friend into prison. And they being high professors, I asked them if this was the entertainment

---

[4] This was very characteristic of the man.

they had for strangers; if they would willingly be so served themselves; and whether they, who looked upon the Scriptures to be their rule, had any example in the Scriptures from Christ or His apostles, for what they had done. So after awhile they set John ap-John at liberty.

Next day, being market-day, we were to cross a great water;[5] and not far from the place where we were to take boat, many of the market-people drew to us. Amongst these we had good service for the Lord, declaring the Word of Life and everlasting Truth unto them, proclaiming amongst them the day of the Lord, which was coming upon all wickedness; and directing them to the Light of Christ, with which He, the heavenly man, had enlightened them; by which they might see all their sins, and all their false ways, religions, worships and teachers; and by the same Light might see Christ Jesus, who was come to save them, and lead them to God.

After the Truth had been declared to them in the power of God, and Christ the free teacher set over all the hireling teachers, I made John ap-John get his horse into the boat, which was then ready. But there being a company of wild "gentlemen," as they were called, gotten into it (whom we found very rude, and far from gentleness), they, with others, kept his horse out of the boat. I rode to the boat's side, and spoke to them, showing them what an unmanly and unchristian carriage it was; and told them

---

[5] Beaumaris is in Anglesey, so that they were to cross Beaumaris Bay to the mainland.

that they showed an unworthy spirit, below Christianity or humanity.

As I spoke, I leaped my horse into the boat amongst them, thinking John's horse would follow when he had seen mine go in before him. But the water being pretty deep, John could not get his horse into the boat. Therefore I leaped out again on horseback into the water, and stayed with John on that side till the boat returned.

There we tarried, from the eleventh hour of the forenoon to the second in the afternoon, before the boat came to fetch us; and then had forty-two miles to ride that evening; and by the time we had paid for our passage, we had but one groat left between us in money.

We rode about sixteen miles, and then got a little hay for our horses. Setting forward again, we came in the night to a little ale-house, where we thought to have stayed and baited. But, finding we could have neither oats nor hay there, we travelled all night; and about the fifth hour in the morning got to a place within six miles of Wrexham, where that day we met with many Friends, and had a glorious meeting. The Lord's everlasting power and Truth was over all; and a meeting is continued there to this day.

Next day we passed thence into Flintshire, sounding the day of the Lord through the towns; and came into Wrexham at night. Here many of Floyd's people came to us; but very rude, wild, and airy they were, and little sense of truth they had; yet some were convinced in that town. Next morning one called a lady sent for me, who kept a preacher in her house. I went, but found both her and her preacher very light and airy; too light to receive the weighty things of God. In her lightness she came and asked me if she should cut my hair; but I was moved to reprove her, and bade her cut down the corruptions in herself with the sword of the Spirit of God. So after I had admonished her to be more grave and sober, we passed away; and afterwards, in her frothy mind, she made her boast that she came behind me and cut off the curl of my hair; [6] but she spoke falsely.

From Wrexham we came to Chester; and it being the fair time, we stayed a while, and visited Friends. For I had travelled through every county in Wales, preaching the everlasting gospel of Christ; and a brave people there is now, who have received it, and sit under Christ's teaching. But before I left Wales I wrote to the magistrates of Beaumaris concerning the imprisoning of John ap-John; letting them see their conditions, and the fruits of their Christianity, and of their teachers. Afterwards I met with some of them near London; but, oh, how ashamed they were of their action!

Soon we came to Manchester, and the sessions being there that day many rude people were come out of the country. In the meeting they threw at me coals, clods, stones, and water; yet the Lord's power bore me up over them that they could not strike me

---

[6] This "curl" is two or three times mentioned. He always wore his hair long and apparently had a long curling lock behind.

down. At last, when they saw they could not prevail by throwing water, stones, and dirt at me, they went and informed the justices in the sessions, who thereupon sent officers to fetch me before them.

The officers came in while I was declaring the Word of life to the people, plucked me down, and haled me into their court. When I came there all the court was in a disorder and a noise. I asked, "Where are the magistrates that they do not keep the people civil?" Some of the justices said that they were magistrates. I asked them why, then, they did not appease the people, and keep them sober, for one cried, "I'll swear," and another cried, "I'll swear."

I declared to the justices how we were abused in our meeting by the rude people, who threw stones, clods, dirt, and water; and how I was haled out of the meeting and brought thither, contrary to the instrument of government, which said that none should be molested in their meetings that professed God, and owned the Lord Jesus Christ; which I did. The Truth so came over them that when one of the rude followers cried, "I'll swear," one of the justices checked him, saying "What will you swear? hold your tongue."

At last they bade the constable take me to my lodging, and there secure me till they sent for me again to-morrow morning. So the constable took me to my lodging.

As we went the people were exceedingly rude; but I let them see the fruits of their teachers, how they shamed Christianity, and dishonored the name of Jesus which they professed.

At night we went to see a justice in the town who was pretty moderate, and I had a great deal of discourse with him. Next morning we sent to the constable to know if he had anything more to say to us. He sent us word that he had nothing to say to us; we might go whither we would.

The Lord hath since raised up a people to stand for His name and Truth in that town over those chaffy professors.

We passed from Manchester, having many precious meetings in several places, till we came to Preston. Between Preston and Lancaster I had a general meeting, from which I went to Lancaster. There at our inn I met with Colonel West, who was very glad to see me, and meeting with Judge Fell he told him that I was mightily grown in the Truth; when, indeed, he was come nearer to the Truth, and so could better discern it.

We came from Lancaster to Robert Widders's. On the First-day after I had a general meeting of Friends of Westmoreland and Lancashire near Sandside, when the Lord's everlasting power was over all. In this meeting the Word of eternal life was declared, and Friends were settled upon the foundation Christ Jesus, under His free teaching; and many were convinced, and turned to the Lord.

Next day I came over the Sands to Swarthmore, where Friends were glad to see me. I stayed there two First-days, visiting Friends in their meetings thereabouts. They rejoiced with me in the goodness of the Lord, who by His eternal power had carried me through and over many difficulties and dangers in His service; to Him be the praise for ever!

CHAPTER XI.

In the Home of the Covenanters.

1657.

After I had tarried two First-days at Swarth-more,[1] and had visited Friends in their meetings thereabouts, I passed into Westmoreland, in the same work, till I came to John Audland's, where there was a general meeting.

The night before I had had a vision of a desperate creature that was coming to destroy me, but I got victory over it. And next day in meeting-time came one Otway, with some rude fellows. He rode round about the meeting with his sword or rapier, and would fain have got in through the Friends to me; but the meeting being great, the Friends stood close, so that he could not easily come at me. When he had ridden about several times raging, and found he could not get in, being limited by the Lord's power, he went away.

---

[1] While waiting at Swarthmore, between the labors in Wales and the visit to Scotland, George Fox wrote several epistles. Here is a beautiful little Postscript to his epistle " to Friends ":

" Postscript—And, Friends, be careful how ye set your feet among the tender plants, that are springing up out of God's earth; lest ye tread upon them, hurt, bruise, or crush them in God's vineyard."

It was a glorious meeting, ended peaceably, and the Lord's everlasting power came over all. This wild man went home, became distracted, and not long after died. I sent a paper to John Blakelin to read to him, while he lay ill, showing him his wickedness, and he acknowledged something of it.

I had for some time felt drawings on my spirit to go into Scotland, and had sent to Colonel William Osburn of Scotland, desiring him to meet me; and he, with some others, came out of Scotland to this meeting.[2] After it was over (which, he said, was the most glorious meeting that ever he saw in his life), I passed with him and his company into Scotland, having with me Robert Widders, a thundering man against hypocrisy, deceit, and the rottenness of the priests.

The first night we came into Scotland we lodged at an inn. The innkeeper told us an earl lived about a quarter of a mile off, who had a desire to see me; and had left word at the inn that if ever I came into Scotland, he should be told of it. The innkeeper told us there were three drawbridges to the earl's house; and that it would be nine o'clock before the third bridge was drawn.

Finding we had time in the evening, we walked to his house. He received us very lovingly, and said he would have gone with us on our journey, but that he was before engaged to go to a funeral. After we had spent some time with him, we parted very friendly,

---

[2] This was a great general meeting at Langlands, in Cumberland.

and returned to our inn. Next morning we travelled on, and passing through Dumfries, came to Douglas, where we met with some Friends. Thence we passed to the Heads, where we had a blessed meeting in the name of Jesus, and felt Him in the midst.

Leaving Heads, we went to Badcow, and had a meeting there, to which abundance of people came, and many were convinced. Amongst them was one called a lady. From thence we passed towards the Highlands to William Osburn's, where we gathered up the sufferings of Friends, and the principles of the Scotch priests, which may be seen in a book called "The Scotch Priests' Principles."

Afterwards we returned to Heads, Badcow, and Garshore, where the said lady, Margaret Hambleton, was convinced; who afterwards went to warn Oliver Cromwell and Charles Fleetwood of the day of the Lord that was coming upon them.

On First-day we had a great meeting, and several professors came to it. Now, the priests had frightened the people with the doctrine of election and reprobation, telling them that God had ordained the greatest part of men and women for hell; and that, let them pray, or preach, or sing, or do what they would, it was all to no purpose, if they were ordained for hell. Also that God had a certain number elected for heaven, let them do what they would; as David was an adulterer, and Paul a persecutor, yet still they were elected vessels for heaven. So the priests said the fault was not at all in the creature, less or more, but that God had ordained it so.

I was led to open to the people the falseness and

folly of their priests' doctrines, and showed how they,
the priests, had abused those Scriptures they quoted.
Now all that believe in the Light of Christ, as He
commands, are in the election, and sit under the
teaching of the grace of God, which brings their salvation. But such as turn this grace into wantonness,
are in the reprobation; and such as hate the Light,
are in the condemnation.

So I exhorted all the people to believe in the Light,
as Christ commands, and to own the grace of God,
their free teacher; and it would assuredly bring them
their salvation; for it is sufficient. Many Scriptures
were opened concerning reprobation,[3] and the eyes
of the people were opened; and a spring of life rose
up among them.

These things soon came to the priest's ears; for the
people that sat under their dark teachings began to
see light, and to come into the covenant of light.
The noise was spread over Scotland, amongst the
priests, that I was come thither; and a great cry
went up among them that all would be spoiled; for,
they said, I had spoiled all the honest men and
women in England already; so, according to their
own account, the worst were left to them.

Upon this they gathered great assemblies of priests
together, and drew up a number of curses to be read
in their several steeple-houses, that all the people
might say " Amen " to them. Some few of these I

---

[3] In this discussion the Scripture arguments were
gone over, and George Fox offset the proof-texts on
election with passages showing man's responsibility.

will here set down; the rest may be read in the book before mentioned, of "The Scotch Priests' Principles."

The first was, "Cursed is he that saith, Every man hath a light within him sufficient to lead him to salvation; and let all the people say, Amen."

The second, "Cursed is he that saith, Faith is without sin; and let all the people say, Amen."

The third, "Cursed is he that denieth the Sabbath-day; and let all the people say, Amen."

In this last they make the people curse themselves; for on the Sabbath-day (which is the seventh day of the week, which the Jews kept by the command of God to them) they kept markets and fairs, and so brought the curse upon their own heads.[4]

Now were the priests in such a rage that they posted to Edinburgh to Oliver Cromwell's Council there, with petitions against me. The noise was that "all was gone"; for several Friends were come out of England and spread over Scotland, sounding the day of the Lord, preaching the everlasting gospel of salvation, and turning people to Christ Jesus, who died for them, that they might receive His free teaching.

After I had gathered the principles of the Scotch priests, and the sufferings of Friends, and had seen the Friends, in that part of Scotland settled by the

---

[4] The Friends always refused to keep the First Day as though it were a continuation of the Jewish Sabbath. For them it was a day set apart for man's high spiritual use.

Lord's power, upon Christ their foundation, I went to Edinburgh, and in the way came to Linlithgow, where lodging at an inn, the innkeeper's wife, who was blind, received the Word of life, and came under the teaching of Christ Jesus, her Saviour.

At night there came in abundance of soldiers and some officers, with whom we had much discourse; and some were rude. One of the officers said he would obey the Turk's or Pilate's command, if they should command him to guard Christ to crucify Him. So far was he from all tenderness, or sense of the Spirit of Christ, that he would rather crucify the just than suffer for or with them; whereas many officers and magistrates have lost their places before they would turn against the Lord and His Just One.

When I had stayed a while at Edinburgh, I went to Leith, where many officers of the army came in with their wives, and many were convinced. Among these Edward Billings's wife was one. She brought a great deal of coral in her hand, and threw it on the table before me, to see whether I would speak against it or not. I took no notice of it, but declared the Truth to her, and she was reached. There came in many Baptists, who were very rude; but the Lord's power came over them, so that they went away confounded.

Then there came in another sort, and one of them said he would dispute with me; and for argument's sake would deny there was a God. I told him he might be one of those fools that said in his heart, "There is no God," but he would know Him in the day of His judgment. So he went his way.

A precious time we had afterwards with several

people of account; and the Lord's power came over all. William Osburn was with me. Colonel Lidcot's wife, and William Welch's wife, and several of the officers themselves, were convinced. Edward Billings and his wife at that time lived apart; and she being reached by Truth, and become loving to Friends, we sent for her husband, who came. The Lord's power reached unto them both, and they joined in it, and agreed to live together in love and unity as man and wife.

After this we returned to Edinburgh where many thousands were gathered together, with abundance of priests among them, about burning a witch, and I was moved to declare the day of the Lord amongst them. When I had done, I went thence to our meeting, whither came many rude people and Baptists.

The Baptists began to vaunt with their logic and syllogisms; but I was moved in the Lord's power to thresh their chaffy, light minds. I showed the people that, after that fallacious way of discoursing, they might make white seem black, and black seem white; as, that because a cock had two legs, and each of them had two legs, therefore they were all cocks.[5] Thus they might turn anything into lightness and vanity; but it was not the way of Christ, or His apostles, to teach, speak, or reason after that manner.

Hereupon those Baptists went their way; and after they were gone we had a blessed meeting in the Lord's power, which was over all.

---

[5] The reference is to the logical definition of man as " an unfeathered biped," which is as old as Plato.

I mentioned before that many of the Scotch priests, being greatly disturbed at the spreading of Truth, and the loss of their hearers thereby, were gone to Edinburgh to petition the Council against me. When I came from the meeting to the inn where I lodged, an officer belonging to the Council brought me the following order:

" Thursday, the 8th of October, 1657, at his Highness' Council in Scotland:

" Ordered, That George Fox do appear before the Council on Tuesday, the 13th of October next, in the forenoon.

" E. Downing, Clerk of the Council."

When he had delivered me the order, he asked me whether I would appear or not. I did not tell him; but asked him if he had not forged the order. He said " No "; that it was a real order from the Council, and he was sent as their messenger with it.

When the time came I appeared, and was taken into a great room, where many persons came and looked at me. After awhile the doorkeeper took me into the council-chamber; and as I was going he took off my hat. I asked him why he did so, and who was there that I might not go in with my hat on. I told him I had been before the Protector with my hat on. But he hung up my hat and took me in before them.

When I had stood awhile, and they said nothing to me, I was moved of the Lord to say, " Peace be amongst you. Wait in the fear of God, that ye may receive His wisdom from above, by which all things were made and created; that by it ye may all be ordered, and may order all things under your hands to God's glory."

They asked me what was the occasion of my coming into that nation. I told them I came to visit the Seed of God, which had long lain in bondage under corruption, so that all in the nation who professed the Scriptures, the words of Christ, of the prophets and apostles, might come to the Light, Spirit and power, which they were in who gave them forth. I told them that in and by the Spirit they might understand the Scriptures, and know Christ and God aright, and might have fellowship with them, and one with another.

They asked me whether I had any outward business there. I said, "Nay." Then they asked me how long I intended to stay in that country. I told them I should say little to that; my time was not to be long; yet in my freedom in the Lord I stood, in the will of Him that sent me.

Then they bade me withdraw, and the doorkeeper took me by the hand and led me forth. In a little time they sent for me again, and told me that I must depart the nation of Scotland by that day sevennight. I asked them, "Why? What have I done? What is my transgression that you pass such a sentence upon me to depart out of the nation?" They told me they would not dispute with me. I desired them to hear what I had to say to them. They said they would not hear me. I told them, "Pharaoh heard Moses and Aaron, yet he was an heathen; and Herod heard John the Baptist; and you should not be worse than these." But they cried, "Withdraw, withdraw." Thereupon the doorkeeper took me again by the hand and led me out.

I returned to my inn, and continued still in Edinburgh; visiting Friends there and thereabouts, and strengthening them in the Lord. After a little time I wrote a letter to the Council to lay before them their unchristian dealings in banishing me, an innocent man, that sought their salvation and eternal good.

After I had spent some time among Friends at Edinburgh and thereabouts, I passed thence to Heads again, where Friends had been in great sufferings. For the Presbyterian priests had excommunicated them, and given charge that none should buy or sell or eat or drink with them. So they could neither sell their commodities nor buy what they wanted; which made it go very hard with some of them; for if they had bought bread or other victuals of any of their neighbors, the priests threatened them so with curses that they would run and fetch it from them again. But Colonel Ashfield, being a justice of the peace in that country, put a stop to the priests' proceedings. This Colonel Ashfield was afterwards convinced himself, had a meeting settled at his house, declared the Truth, and lived and died in it.

After I had visited Friends at and about Heads, and encouraged them in the Lord, I went to Glasgow, where a meeting was appointed; but not one of the town came to it. As I went into the city, the guard at the gates took me before the governor, who was a moderate man. A great deal of discourse I had with him. He was too light to receive the Truth; yet he set me at liberty; so I passed to the meeting.

Seeing none of the town's people came to the meeting, we declared Truth through the town; then passed away, visited Friends' meetings thereabouts, and returned towards Badcow. Several Friends declared Truth in the steeple-houses and the Lord's power was with them.

Once as I was going with William Osburn to his house there lay a company of rude fellows by the wayside, hid under the hedges and in bushes. Seeing them, I asked him what they were. "Oh," said he, "they are thieves." Robert Widders, being moved to go and speak to a priest, was left behind, intending to come after. So I said to William Osburn, "I will stay here in this valley, and do thou go and look after Robert Widders"; but he was unwilling to go, being afraid to leave me there alone, because of those fellows, till I told him I feared them not.

Then I called to them, asking them what they lay .lurking there for, and I bade them come to me; but they were loath to come. I charged them to come up to me, or else it might be worse with them; then they came trembling, for the dread of the Lord had struck them. I admonished them to be honest, and directed them to the Light of Christ in their hearts, that by it they might see what an evil it was to follow after theft and robbery; and the power of the Lord came over them.

I stayed there till William Osburn and Robert Widders came up, then we passed on together. But it is likely that, if we two had gone away before, they would have robbed Robert Widders when he had come after alone, there being three or four of them.

We went to William Osburn's house, where we had a good opportunity to declare the Truth to several people that came in. Then we went among the Highlanders, who were so devilish they were like to have spoiled us and our horses; for they ran at us with pitchforks. But through the Lord's goodness we escaped them, being preserved by His power.

Thence we passed to Stirling, where the soldiers took us up, and had us to the main guard. After a few words with the officers, the Lord's power coming over them, we were set at liberty; but no meeting could we get amongst them in the town, they were so closed up in darkness. Next morning there came a man with a horse that was to run a race, and most of the townspeople and officers went to see it. As they came back from the race, I had a brave opportunity to declare the day of the Lord and His Word of life amongst them. Some confessed to it, and some opposed; but the Lord's truth and power came over them all.

Leaving Stirling, we came to Burntisland, where I had two meetings at one Captain Pool's house; one in the morning, the other in the afternoon. Whilst they went to dine I walked to the seaside, not having freedom to eat with them. Both he and his wife were convinced, and became good Friends afterward; and several officers of the army came in and received the Truth.

We passed thence through several other places, till we came to Johnstons, where were several Baptists that were very bitter, and came in a rage to dispute with us. Vain janglers and disputers indeed they were. When they could not prevail by disputing they went and informed the governor against us; and next morning he raised a whole company of foot, and banished me and Alexander Parker, also James Lancaster and Robert Widders, out of the town.

As they guarded us through the town, James Lancaster was moved to sing with a melodious sound in the power of God; and I was moved to proclaim the day of the Lord, and preach the everlasting gospel to the people. For the people generally came forth, so that the streets were filled with them, and the soldiers were so ashamed that they said they would rather have gone to Jamaica than guarded us so.

But we were put into a boat with our horses, carried over the water, and there left. The Baptists, who were the cause of our being thus put out of this town, were themselves, not long after, turned out of the army; and he that was then governor was discarded also when the king came in.

Being thus thrust out of Johnstons, we went to another market-town, where Edward Billings and many soldiers were quartered. We went to an inn, and desired to have a meeting in the town, that we might preach the everlasting gospel amongst them. The officers and soldiers said we should have it in the town-hall; but the Scotch magistrates in spite appointed a meeting there that day for the business of the town.

When the officers of the soldiery understood this, and perceived that it was done in malice, they would

have had us go into the town-hall nevertheless. But
we told them, "No; by no means; for then the magistrates might inform the governor against us and
say, 'They took the town-hall from us by force, when
we were to do our town-business therein.'" We told
them we would go to the market-place. They said it
was market-day. We replied, "It is so much the better; for we would have all people to hear the Truth
and know our principles."

Alexander Parker went and stood upon the market-cross, with a Bible in his hand, and declared the
Truth amongst the soldiers and market-people;
but the Scots, being a dark, carnal people, gave little
heed, and hardly took notice what was said. After
awhile I was moved of the Lord to stand up at the
cross, and to declare with a loud voice the everlasting Truth, and the day of the Lord that was coming
upon all sin and wickedness. Thereupon the people
came running out of the town-hall and gathered so
together that at last we had a large meeting; for they
only sat in the court for a colour to hinder us from
having the hall to meet in.

When the people were come away the magistrates
followed them. Some walked by, but some stayed
and heard; and the Lord's power came over all and
kept all quiet. The people were turned to the Lord
Jesus Christ, who died for them, and had enlightened
them, that with His Light they might see their evil
deeds, be saved from their sins by Him, and might
come to know Him to be their teacher. But if they
would not receive Christ, and own Him, it was told

them that this Light which came from Him would be their condemnation.

We travelled from this town to Leith, warning and exhorting people, as we went, to turn to the Lord. At Leith the innkeeper told me that the Council had granted warrants to apprehend me, because I was not gone out of the nation after the seven days were expired that they had ordered me to depart in. Several friendly people also came and told me the same; to whom I said, " Why do ye tell me of their warrants against me? If there were a cart-load of them I would not heed them, for the Lord's power is over them all." [6]

I went from Leith to Edinburgh again, where they said the warrants from the Council were out against me. I went to the inn where I had lodged before, and no man offered to meddle with me. After I had visited Friends in the city, I desired those that travelled with me to get ready their horses in the morning, and we rode out of town together. There were with me at that time Thomas Rawlinson, Alexander Parker, and Robert Widders.

When we were out of town they asked me whither I would go. I told them it was upon me from the Lord to go back again to Johnstons (the town out of which we had been lately thrust), to set the power of God and His Truth over them also. Alexander Parker said he would go along with me; and I wished

---

[6] Here is more of the Luther spirit. He is reported to have said: " I would go to Leipsic if it rained Duke Georges nine days running."

the other two to stay at a town about three miles from Edinburgh till we returned.

Then Alexander and I got over the water, about three miles across, and rode through the country; but in the afternoon, his horse being weak and not able to hold up with mine, I rode on ahead and got into Johnstons just as they were drawing up the bridges, the officers and soldiers never questioning me. I rode up the street to Captain Davenport's house, from which we had been banished. There were many officers with him; and when I came amongst them they lifted up their hands, wondering that I should come again. But I told them the Lord God had sent me amongst them again; so they went their way.

The Baptists sent me a letter, by way of challenge, to discourse with me next day. I sent them word that I would meet them at such a house, about half a mile out of the town, at such an hour. For I considered that if I should stay in town to discourse with them they might, under pretence of discoursing with me, raise men to put me out of the town again, as they had done before.

At the time appointed I went to the place, Captain Davenport and his son accompanying me. There I stayed some hours, but not one of them came. While I stayed there waiting for them, I saw Alexander Parker coming. Not being able to reach the town, he had lain out the night before; and I was exceedingly glad that we were met again.

This Captain Davenport was then loving to Friends; and afterwards, coming more into obedience to Truth, he was turned out of his place for not putting off his hat, and for saying Thou and Thee to them.

When we had waited beyond reasonable ground to expect any of them coming, we departed; and Alexander Parker being moved to go again to the town, where we had the meeting at the market-cross, I passed alone to Lieutenant Foster's quarters, where I found several officers that were convinced. Thence I went up to the town, where I had left the other two Friends, and we went back to Edinburgh together.

When we were come to the city, I bade Robert Widders follow me; and in the dread and power of the Lord we came up to the two first sentries. The Lord's power came so over them that we passed by them without any examination. Then we rode up the street to the market-place and by the main-guard, out at the gate by the third sentry, and so clear out into the suburbs; and there we came to an inn and put up our horses, it being Seventh-day. I saw and felt that we had ridden as it were against the cannon's mouth or the sword's point; but the Lord's power and immediate hand carried us over the heads of them all.

Next day I went to the meeting in the city, Friends having had notice that I would attend it. There came many officers and soldiers to it, and a glorious meeting it was; the everlasting power of God was set over the nation, and His Son reigned in His glorious power. All was quiet, and no man offered to meddle with me.

When the meeting was ended, and I had visited

Friends, I came out of the city to my inn again. The next day, being Second-day, we set forward towards the borders of England.

As we travelled along the country I espied a steeple-house, and it struck at my life. I asked what steeple-house it was, and was told that it was Dunbar. When I came thither, and had put up at an inn, I walked to the steeple-house, having a Friend or two with me.

When we came to the steeple-house yard, one of the chief men of the town was walking there. I asked one of the Friends that was with me to go to him and tell him that about the ninth hour next morning there would be a meeting there of the people of God called Quakers; of which we desired he would give notice to the people of the town. He sent me word that they were to have a lecture there by the ninth hour; but that we might have our meeting there by the eighth hour, if we would. We concluded to do so, and desired him to give notice of it.

Accordingly, in the morning both poor and rich came; and there being a captain of horse quartered in the town, he and his troopers came also, so that we had a large concourse; and a glorious meeting it was, the Lord's power being over all. After some time the priest came, and went into the steeple-house; but we being in the yard, most of the people stayed with us. Friends were so full and their voices so high in the power of God, that the priest could do little in the house, but quickly came out again, stood awhile, and then went his way.

I opened to the people where they might find

Christ Jesus, and turned them to the Light with which He had enlightened them, that in the Light they might see Christ who died for them, turn to Him, and know him to be their Saviour and Teacher. I let them see that the teachers they had hitherto followed were hirelings, who made the gospel chargeable; showed them the wrong ways they had walked in in the night of apostasy; directed them to Christ, the new and living way to God, and manifested unto them how they had lost the religion and worship which Christ set up in spirit and truth, and had hitherto been in the religions and worships of men's making and setting up.

After I had turned the people to the Spirit of God which led the holy men of God to give forth the Scriptures, and showed them that they must also come to receive and be led by the same Spirit in themselves (a measure of which was given unto every one of them) if ever they would come to know God and Christ and the Scriptures aright, perceiving the other Friends to be full of power and the Word of the Lord, I stepped down, giving way for them to declare what they had from the Lord to the people.

Towards the latter end of the meeting some professors began to jangle, whereupon I stood up again, and answered their questions, so that they seemed to be satisfied, and our meeting ended in the Lord's power, quiet and peaceable.

This was the last meeting I had in Scotland; the Truth and the power of God was set over that nation, and many, by the power and Spirit of God, were turned to the Lord Jesus Christ, their Saviour and

Teacher, whose blood was shed for them; and there is since a great increase and great there will be in Scotland. For when first I set my horse's feet upon Scottish ground I felt the Seed of God to sparkle about me, like innumerable sparks of fire.

Not but that there is abundance of the thick, cloddy earth of hypocrisy and falseness above, and a briery, brambly nature, which is to be burnt up with God's Word, and ploughed up with His spiritual plough, before God's Seed brings forth heavenly and spiritual fruit to His glory. But the husbandman is to wait in patience.[7]

---

[7] This passage has suggested the idea which finds beautiful expression in the closing stanzas of Whittier's "Barclay of Ury":

> "Knowing this, that never yet
> Share of truth was vainly set
>   In the world's wide fallow;
> After hands shall sow the seed,
> After hands from mill and mead
>   Reap the harvests yellow.

> "Thus with somewhat of the seer
> Must the moral pioneer
>   From the future borrow;
> Clothe the waste with dreams of grain,
> And, on midnight's sky of rain
>   Paint the golden morrow."

CHAPTER XII.

𝕲𝖗𝖊𝖆𝖙 𝕰𝖛𝖊𝖓𝖙𝖘 𝖎𝖓 𝕷𝖔𝖓𝖉𝖔𝖓.

1658-1659.

We came into Bedfordshire, where we had large
gatherings in the name of Jesus.[1] After some time
we came to John Crook's, where a general yearly
meeting for the whole nation was appointed to be
held.[2] This meeting lasted three days, and many
Friends from most parts of the nation came to it;
so that the inns and towns round thereabouts were
filled, for many thousands of people were at it. And
although there was some disturbance by some rude
people that had run out from Truth, yet the Lord's

---

[1] There were few novel experiences on the way from
Scotland to Bedfordshire. At Nottingham he had a
controversy with Rice Jones, an opposer of the earlier
visit. He pointed out that many of Rice Jones's followers " were become the greatest foot-ball players and
wrestlers in the whole country," which is an interesting comment on the ministry of Rice Jones!

[2] " John Crook's House " was at Luton, in Bedfordshire. This is among the first of the great national general meetings out of which came in course of development the present London Yearly Meeting of Friends.
The first general meeting was held at Swannington in
Leicestershire in 1654. Isaac Penington was convinced at this meeting. He tells us that he " felt the
healings drop upon his soul from under His wings."

power came over all, and a glorious meeting it was.
The everlasting gospel was preached, and many received it, which gospel brought life and immortality
to light in them, and shined over all.

Now these things were upon me to open unto all,
that they might mind and see what it is they sit down
in.*

" First, They that sit down in Adam in the fall, sit
down in misery, in death, in darkness and corruption.

" Secondly, They that sit down in the types, figures, and shadows, and under the first priesthood,
law, and covenant, sit down in that which must have
an end, and which made nothing perfect.

" Thirdly, They that sit down in the apostasy that
hath got up since the Apostles' days, sit down in spiritual Sodom and Egypt; and are drinking of the
whore's cup, under the beast's and dragon's power.

" Fourthly, They that sit down in the state in
which Adam was before he fell, sit down in that
which may be fallen from; for he fell from that state,
though it was perfect.

" Fifthly, They that sit down in the prophets, sit
down in that which must be fulfilled; and they that
sit down in the fellowship of water, bread, and wine,
these being temporal things, they sit down in that
which is short of Christ, and of His baptism.

" Sixthly, To sit down in a profession of all the
Scriptures, from Genesis to the Revelations, and not
be in the power and Spirit which those were in that
gave them forth;—that was to be turned away from

* The sentence means: " I felt called to set forth the significance of
various religious states and the things to which they lead."

by them that came into the power and Spirit which
those were in that gave forth the Scriptures.

" Seventhly, They that sit down in the heavenly
places in Christ Jesus, sit down in Him that never
fell, nor ever changed."

After this meeting was over, and most of the
Friends gone away, as I was walking in John Crook's
garden, there came a party of horse, with a constable, to seize me. I heard them ask, " Who is in the
house ? " Somebody made answer that I was there.
They said that I was the man they looked for; and
went forthwith into the house, where they had many
words with John Crook and some few Friends that
were with him. But the Lord's power so confounded
them that they came not into the garden to look for
me; but went their way in a rage.

When I came into the house, Friends were very
glad to see that I had escaped them. Next day I
passed thence; and, after I had visited Friends in
several places, came to London, the Lord's power
accompanying me, and bearing me up in His service.

During the time I was at London I had many services laid upon me, for it was a time of much suffering. I was moved to write to Oliver Cromwell, and
lay before him the sufferings of Friends both in this
nation and in Ireland. There was also a talk
about this time of making Cromwell king; whereupon I was moved to go to him and warn him against
accepting it; and of divers dangers which, if he did
not avoid them, would, I told him, bring shame and
ruin upon himself and his posterity. He seemed to
take well what I said to him, and thanked me; yet

afterwards I was moved to write to him more fully concerning that matter.

About this time the Lady Claypole (so called) was sick, and much troubled in mind, and could receive no comfort from any that came to her. When I heard of this I was moved to write to her.[8]

---

[8] Here is a long extract from the letter to Lady Claypole, Cromwell's daughter, who died soon after this time:

"Keep in the fear of the Lord God; that is the Word of the Lord unto thee. For all these things happen to thee for thy good, and for the good of those concerned for thee, to make you know yourselves and your own weakness, that ye may know the Lord's strength and power, and may trust in Him. Let the time past be sufficient to every one, who in any thing hath been lifted up in transgression out of the power of the Lord; for He can bring down and abase the mighty, and lay them in the dust of the earth. Therefore, all keep low in His fear, that thereby ye may receive the secrets of God and His wisdom, may know the shadow of the Almighty, and sit under it in all tempests, storms, and heats. For God is a God at hand, and the Most High rules in the children of men. This is the word of the Lord God unto you all; what the Light doth make manifest and discover, as temptations, distractions, confusions; do not look at these temptations, confusions, corruptions, but at the Light which discovers them and makes them manifest; and with the same Light you may feel over them, to receive power to stand against them. The same Light which lets you see sin and transgression, will let you see the covenant of God, which blots **out**

About this time came forth a declaration from Oliver Cromwell, the Protector, for a collection towards the relief of divers Protestant churches, driven out of Poland; and of twenty Protestant families, driven out of the confines of Bohemia. And there having been a like declaration published some time

---

your sin and transgression, which gives victory and dominion over it, and brings into covenant with God. For looking down at sin, corruption, and distraction, ye are swallowed up in it; but looking at the Light, which discovers them, ye will see over them. That will give victory, and ye will find grace and strength; there is the first step to peace. That will bring salvation; by it ye may see to the beginning, and the ' Glory that was with the Father before the world began '; and come to know the Seed of God, which is the heir of the promise of God, and of the world which hath no end; and which bruises the head of the serpent, who stops people from coming to God. That ye may feel the power of an endless life, the power of God which is immortal, which brings the immortal soul up to the immortal God, in whom it doth rejoice. So in the name and power of the Lord Jesus Christ, God Almighty strengthen thee.

" G. F."

This note follows the letter:

" When the foregoing paper was read to Lady Claypole, she said, it stayed her mind for the present. Afterwards many Friends got copies of it, both in England and Ireland, and read it to people that were troubled in mind; and it was made useful for the settling of the minds of several."

before, to invite the nation to a day of solemn fasting and humiliation, in order to a contribution being made for the suffering Protestants of the valleys of Lucerne, Angrona, etc., who were persecuted by the Duke of Savoy,[4] I was moved to write to the Protector and chief magistrates on this occasion, both to show them the nature of a true fast (such as God requires and accepts), and to make them sensible of their injustice and self-condemnation in blaming the Papists for persecuting the Protestants abroad, while they themselves, calling themselves Protestants, were at the same time persecuting their Protestant neighbours and friends at home.

Divers times, both in the time of the Long Parliament and of the Protector (so called) and of the Committee of Safety, when they proclaimed fasts, I was moved to write to them, and tell them their fasts were like unto Jezebel's; for commonly, when they proclaimed fasts, there was some mischief contrived against us. I knew their fasts were for strife and debate, to smite with the fist of wickedness; as the New England professors soon after did; who, before they put our Friends to death, proclaimed a fast also.

Now it was a time of great suffering; and many Friends being in prisons, many other Friends were moved to go to the Parliament, to offer themselves

---

[4] This was the persecution which called forth Milton's great sonnet:

" Avenge, O Lord ! thy slaughtered saints whose bones
Lie scattered on the Alpine mountains cold."

up to lie in the same prisons where their friends lay, that those in prison might go forth, and not perish in the stinking jails. This we did in love to God and our brethren, that they might not die in prison; and in love to those that cast them in, that they might not bring innocent blood upon their own heads, which we knew would cry to the Lord, and bring His wrath, vengeance, and plagues upon them.

But little favour could we find from those professing Parliaments; instead thereof, they would rage, and sometimes threaten Friends that attended them, to whip and send them home. Then commonly soon after the Lord would turn them out, and send them home; who had not an heart to do good in the day of their power. But they went not off without being forewarned; for I was moved to write to them, in their several turns, as I did to the Long Parliament, unto whom I declared, before they were broken up, "that thick darkness was coming over them all, even a day of darkness that should be felt."

And because the Parliament that now sat was made up mostly of high professors, who, pretending to be more religious than others, were indeed greater persecutors of those that were truly religious, I was moved to send them the following lines, as a reproof of their hypocrisy:[5]

"O friends, do not cloak and cover yourselves; there is a God that knoweth your hearts, and that will uncover you. He seeth your way. 'Wo be unto him that covereth, but not with my Spirit, saith the

---

[5] This was Cromwell's *Second Parliament.*

Lord.' Do ye act contrary to the law, and then put it from you! Mercy and true judgment ye neglect. Look, what was spoken against such. My Saviour spoke against such; ' I was sick, and ye visited me not; I was hungry, and ye fed me not; I was a stranger, and ye took me not in; I was in prison, and ye visited me not.' But they said, ' When saw we thee in prison, and did not come to thee?' ' Inasmuch as ye did it not unto one of these little ones, ye did it not unto me.' Friends, ye imprison them that are in the life and power of Truth, and yet profess to be the ministers of Christ; but if Christ had sent you, ye would bring out of prison, out of bondage, and receive strangers. Ye have lived in pleasure on the earth, and been wanton; ye have nourished your hearts, as in a day of slaughter; ye have condemned and killed the just, and he doth not resist you.   G. F."

After this, as I was going out of town, having two Friends with me, when we were little more than a mile out of the city, there met us two troopers belonging to Colonel Hacker's regiment, who took me, and the Friends that were with me, and brought us back to the Mews, and there kept us prisoners. But the Lord's power was so over them that they did not take us before any officer; but shortly after set us at liberty again.

The same day, taking boat, I went to Kingston, and thence to Hampton Court, to speak with the Protector about the sufferings of Friends. I met him riding in Hampton Court Park, and before I came to him, as he rode at the head of his life-guard, I saw and felt a waft [or apparition] of death go forth against him; and when I came to him he looked like a dead man.

After I had laid the sufferings of Friends before him, and had warned him, according as I was moved to speak to him, he bade me come to his house. So I returned to Kingston, and next day went to Hampton Court, to speak further with him. But when I came he was sick, and —— Harvey,* who was one that waited on him, told me the doctors were not willing I should speak with him. So I passed away, and never saw him more.[6]

From Kingston I went to Isaac Penington's,[7] in Buckinghamshire, where I had appointed a meeting, and the Lord's Truth and power were preciously

* Harvey was " groom of the bed chamber."

---

[6] This visit of Fox to Cromwell is treated in Carlyle's Oliver Cromwell, Vol IV., pp. 199, 200. Oliver Cromwell died September 3d, 1658. This " waft " or whiff of death which Fox felt was not the only forewarning of his end which came to Friends. A letter was delivered into Cromwell's hand a month before his death, which contained these words: " If thou continueth in thy oppression, the Lord will suddenly smite thee." See Burrough's " Good Counsel and Advice Rejected by Disobedient Men."

[7] Isaac Penington was one of the finest, richest spirits that came under the influence of Fox. He was highest in social rank of all the early Friends, and after Fox himself the best exponent of the fundamental Quaker idea.

manifested amongst us. After I had visited Friends in those parts, I returned to London, and soon after went into Essex, where I had not been long before I heard that the Protector was dead, and his son Richard made Protector in his room. Thereupon I came up to London again.

Before this time the church faith (so called) was given forth, which was said to have been made at the Savoy in eleven days' time.[8] I got a copy before it was published, and wrote an answer to it; and when their book of church faith was sold in the streets, my answer to it was sold also. This angered some of the Parliament men, so that one of them told me, " We must have you to Smithfield." I told him, " I am above your fires, and fear them not." And, reasoning with him, I wished him to consider, had all people been without a faith these sixteen hundred years, that now the priests must make them one? Did not the apostle say that Jesus was the author and finisher of their faith? And since Christ Jesus was the author of the Apostles' faith, of the Church's faith in primitive times, and of the martyrs' faith, should not

---

[8] This " Church-faith (so-called) " was a " Declaration of the Faith and Order owned and practiced in the Congregational Churches in England: Agreed upon and consented unto by their Elders and messengers in their meeting at the Savoy, October 12th, 1658." Fox's reply has the following title: " Something in Answer to that Book called, The Church-Faith: Set forth by Independants (sic) and others; agreed upon by Divine messengers at the Savoy in London."

all people look unto Him to be the author and finisher of their faith, and not to the priests? Much
work we had about the priest-made faith.

There was great persecution in many places, both
by imprisoning, and by breaking up of meetings. At
a meeting about seven miles from London, the rude
people usually came out of several parishes round
about, to abuse Friends, and often beat and bruised
them exceedingly. One day they abused about
eighty Friends that went to that meeting out of London, tearing their coats and cloaks from off their
backs, and throwing them into ditches and ponds;
and when they had besmeared them with dirt, they
said they looked like witches.

The next First-day I was moved of the Lord to go
to that meeting, though I was then very weak.
When I came there I bade Friends bring a table, and
set it in the close, where they used to meet, to stand
upon. According to their wonted course, the rude
people came; and I, having a Bible in my hand,
showed them theirs and their teachers' fruits; and
the people became ashamed, and were quiet.

But it was a time of great sufferings; for, besides
imprisonments, through which many died, our meetings were greatly disturbed. They have thrown rotten eggs and wild-fire into our meetings, and brought
in drums beating, and kettles to make noises with,
that the Truth might not be heard; and, among these,
the priests were as rude as any, as may be seen in the
book of the fighting priests, wherein a list is given
of some priests that had actually beaten and abused
Friends.

Many Friends were brought prisoners to London, to be tried before the Committee; where Henry Vane, being chairman, would not suffer Friends to come in, except they would put off their hats.[9]   But at last the Lord's power came over him, so that, through the mediation of others, they were admitted. Many of us having been imprisoned upon contempts (as they called them) for not putting off our hats, it was not a likely thing that Friends, who had suffered so long for it from others, should put off their hats to him.   But the Lord's power came over all, and wrought so that several were set at liberty by them.

I wrote to Oliver several times, and let him know that while he was persecuting God's people, they whom he accounted his enemies were preparing to come upon him.   When some forward spirits that came amongst us would have bought Somerset-House, that we might have meetings in it, I forbade them to do so: for I then foresaw the King's coming in again.   Besides, there came a woman to me in the Strand, who had a prophecy concerning King Charles's coming in, three years before he came: and

---

[9] From being Cromwell's most intimate friend Sir Harry Vane had become his most fearless opposer, and an advocate of extreme republicanism. After the downfall of Richard Cromwell, Vane had a brief return to influence and power. In September, 1659, he was made President of the Council, and was in this position the executive head of the nation in civil affairs. This episode must, therefore, be dated in the autumn of 1659.

she told me she must go to him to declare it. I advised her to wait upon the Lord, and keep it to herself; for if it should be known that she went on such a message, they would look upon it to be treason: but she said she must go, and tell him that he should be brought into England again.

I saw her prophecy was true, and that a great stroke must come upon them in power; for they that had then got possession were so exceeding high, and such great persecution was acted by them, who called themselves saints, that they would take from Friends their copyhold lands, because they could not swear in their courts.

Sometimes when we laid these sufferings before Oliver Cromwell, he would not believe it. Therefore Thomas Aldam and Anthony Pearson were moved to go through all the jails in England, and to get copies of Friends' commitments under the jailer's hands, that they might lay the weight of their sufferings upon Oliver Cromwell. And when he would not give order for the releasing of them, Thomas Aldam was moved to take his cap from off his head, and to rend it in pieces before him, and to say unto him, "So shall thy government be rent from thee and thy house."

Another Friend also, a woman, was moved to go to the Parliament (that was envious against Friends) with a pitcher in her hand, which she broke into pieces before them, and told them that so should they be broken to pieces: which came to pass shortly after.

In my great suffering and travail of spirit for the

nation, being grievously burdened with their hypocrisy, treachery, and falsehood, I saw God would
bring that over them which they had been above;
and that all must be brought down to that which convinced them, before they could get over that bad
spirit within and without: for it is the pure, invisible
Spirit, that doth and only can work down all deceit
in people.

Now was there a great pother made about the
image or effigy of Oliver Cromwell lying in state;
men standing and sounding with trumpets over his
image, after he was dead. At this my spirit was
greatly grieved, and the Lord, I found, was highly
offended.

About this time great stirs were in the nation, the
minds of people being unsettled. Much plotting and
contriving there was by the several factions, to carry
on their several interests. And a great care being
upon me, lest any young or ignorant people,
that might sometimes come amongst us, should be
drawn into that snare, I was moved to give forth an
epistle [10] as a warning unto all such.

---

[10] This epistle begins: " All Friends everywhere keep
out of plots and bustling and the arm of flesh." A
little later he writes again:

" Stand in the fear and dread of the Lord God; His
power, life, light, seed and wisdom, by which ye may
take away the occasion of wars, and so know a kingdom
which hath no end, and fight for that with spiritual
weapons, which takes away the occasion of the carnal,
and there gather men to war, as many as ye can, and
set up as many as ye can with these weapons.   G. F."

CHAPTER XIII.

In the First Year of King Charles.

1660.

I entered Bristol on the Seventh day of the week.[1] The day before, the soldiers came with their muskets into the meeting, and were exceedingly rude, beating and striking Friends with them, and drove them out of the orchard in a great rage, threatening what they would do if Friends came there again. For the mayor and the commander of the soldiers had, it seems, combined together to make a disturbance amongst Friends.

When Friends told me what a rage there was in the town, how they were threatened by the mayor and soldiers, and how unruly the soldiers had been the day before, I sent for several Friends, as George Bishop, Thomas Gouldney, Thomas Speed, and Edward Pyot, and desired them to go to the mayor and aldermen, and request them, seeing he and they had broken up our meetings, to let Friends have the town-hall to meet in. For the use of it Friends would give them twenty pounds a-year, to be distributed amongst the poor and when the mayor and aldermen

---

[1] After leaving London, he had travelled extensively through the eastern and southern counties, revisiting Cornwall, where he had had such a long experience in Launceston jail in 1656.

had business to do in it, Friends would not meet in
it, but only on First-days.

These Friends were astonished at this, and said
the mayor and aldermen would think that they were
mad. I said, Nay; for this would be a considerable
benefit to the poor. And it was upon me from the
Lord to bid them go. At last they consented, and
went, though in the cross to their own wills.

When they had laid the thing before the mayor, he
said, " For my part I could consent to it, but I am
but one "; and he told Friends of another great hall
they might have; but that they did not accept, it
being inconvenient.

So Friends came away, leaving the mayor in a very
loving frame towards them; for they felt the Lord's
power had come over him. When they came back, I
spoke to them to go also to the colonel that commanded the soldiers, and lay before him the rude
conduct of his soldiers, how they came armed
amongst innocent people, who were waiting upon and
worshipping the Lord; but they were backward to go
to him.

Next morning, being First-day, we went to the
meeting in the orchard, where the soldiers had lately
been so rude. After I had declared the Truth some
time in the meeting, there came in many rude soldiers and people, some with drawn swords. The inn-
keepers had made some of them drunk; and one had
bound himself with an oath to cut down and kill the
man that spoke. He came pressing in, through all
the crowd of people, to within two yards of me, and
stopped at those four Friends before mentioned (who

should have gone to the colonel as I would have had them), and began jangling with them. Suddenly I saw his sword was put up and gone: for the Lord's power came over all, and chained him with the rest. We had a blessed meeting, and the Lord's everlasting power and presence were felt amongst us.

On the day following, the four Friends went and spoke with the colonel, and he sent for the soldiers, and cut and slashed some of them before the Friends' faces. When I heard of this I blamed the Friends for letting him do so, and also that they did not go on the Seventh-day, as I would have had them, which might have prevented this cutting of the soldiers, and the trouble they gave at our meeting. But thus the Lord's power came over all those persecuting, bloody minds, and the meeting there was held in peace for a good while after without disturbance.

I had then also a general meeting at Edward Pyot's, near Bristol, at which it was judged were several thousands of people:[2] for besides Friends from many parts thereabouts, some of the Baptists and Independents, with their teachers, came to it, and many of the sober people of Bristol; insomuch that the people who stayed behind said the city looked naked, so many were gone out of it to this meeting. It was very quiet, and many glorious truths were opened to the people.

As we had much work with priests and professors who pleaded for imperfection, I was opened to de-

---

[2] These great meetings were at this period held out of doors, in fields or orchards, or on some high hill.

clare and manifest to them that Adam and Eve were
perfect before they fell, and all that God made He
saw was good, and He blessed it; but the imperfection came in by the fall, through man's and woman's
hearkening to the devil who was out of Truth. And
though the law made nothing perfect, yet it made
way for the bringing in of the better hope, which
hope is Christ, who destroys the devil and his works,
which made man and woman imperfect.

Christ saith to His disciples, " Be ye perfect, even
as your heavenly Father is perfect ": and He, who
Himself was perfect, comes to make man and woman
perfect again, and brings them again to the state in
which God made them. So He is the maker-up of
the breach, and the peace betwixt God and man.

That this might the better be understood by the
lowest capacities, I used a comparison of two old
people who had their house broken down by an
enemy, so that they, with all their children, were
liable to all storms and tempests. And there came
to them some that pretended to be workmen, and
offered to build up their house again, if they would
give them so much a year; but when they had got
the money they left the house as they found it.

After this manner came a second, third, fourth,
fifth, and sixth, each with his several pretence to
build up the old house, and each got the people's
money, and then cried that they could not rear up
the house, the breach could not be made up; for
there is no perfection here. They tell the old people
that the house can never be perfectly built up again

in this life, though they have taken the people's money for doing it.

So all the sect-masters in Christendom (so called) have pretended to build up Adam's and Eve's fallen house; and when they have got the people's money, they tell them the work cannot be perfectly done here; so their house lies as it did. But I told the people Christ was come to do it freely, who by one offering hath perfected for ever all them that are sanctified, and renews them up into the image of God, which man and woman were in before they fell, and makes man's and woman's house as perfect again as God made them at the first; and this Christ, the heavenly Man, doth freely. Therefore all are to look unto Him, and all that have received Him are to walk in Him, the Life, the Substance, the First, and the Last, the Rock of Ages, the Foundation of many Generations.

About this time the soldiers under General Monk's command were rude and troublesome at Friends' meetings in many places, whereof complaint being made to him he gave forth the following order, which somewhat restrained them:

" St. James's, the 9th of March, 1659.

" I do require all officers and soldiers to forbear to disturb the peaceable meetings of the Quakers, they doing nothing prejudicial to the Parliament or Commonwealth of England. GEORGE MONK."

We passed thence to Tewkesbury and so to Worcester, visiting Friends in their meetings as we went.

And in all my time I never saw such drunkenness as in the towns, for they had been choosing Parliament men. At Worcester the Lord's Truth was set over all, people were finely settled therein, and Friends praised the Lord; nay, I saw the very earth rejoiced.

Yet great fears and troubles were in many people, and a looking for the King's coming in, and all things being altered. They would ask me what I thought of times and things. I told them the Lord's power was over all, and His light shone over all; that fear would take hold only on the hypocrites, such as had not been faithful to God, and on our persecutors.

In my travail and sufferings at Reading, when people were at a stand, and could not tell what might come in, and who might rule, I told them the Lord's power was over all (for I had travelled through in it), and His day shined, whosoever should come in; and whether the King came in or not, all would be well to them that loved the Lord, and were faithful to Him. Therefore I bade all Friends fear none but the Lord, and keep in His power.

From Worcester I visited Friends in their meetings, till I came to Badgley, and thence I went to Drayton, in Leicestershire, to visit my relations. While there, one Burton, a justice, hearing I had a good horse, sent a warrant to search for me and my horse; but I was gone before they came; and so he missed of his wicked end.

I passed on to Twy-Cross, Swannington, and Derby, where I visited Friends, and found amongst them my old jailer, who had formerly kept me in the house of correction there, now convinced of the Truth which I then suffered under him for.

Passing into Derbyshire and Nottinghamshire, I came to Synderhill-Green, visiting Friends through all those parts in their meetings, and so on to Balby in Yorkshire, where our Yearly Meeting at that time was held in a great orchard of John Killam's, where it was supposed some thousands of people and Friends were gathered together.

In the morning I heard that a troop of horse was sent from York to break up our meeting, and that the militia, newly raised, was to join them. I went into the meeting, and stood up on a great stool, and after I had spoken some time two trumpeters came up, sounding their trumpets near me, and the captain of the troop cried, " Divide to the right and left, and make way." Then they rode up to me.

I was declaring the everlasting Truth and Word of life in the mighty power of the Lord. The captain bade me come down, for he was come to disperse our meeting. After some time I told him they all knew we were a peaceable people, and used to have such great meetings; but if he apprehended that we met in a hostile way, I desired him to make search among us, and if he found either sword or pistol about any there, let such suffer.

He told me he must see us dispersed, for he came all night on purpose to disperse us. I asked him what honour it would be to him to ride with swords and pistols amongst so many unarmed men and women as there were. If he would be still and quiet our meeting probably might not continue above two or three hours; and when it was done, as we came peaceably together, so we should part; for he might perceive the meeting was so large, that all the country thereabouts could not entertain them, but that they intended to depart towards their homes at night.

He said he could not stay to see the meeting ended, but must disperse them before he went. I desired him, then, if he himself could not stay, that he would let a dozen of his soldiers stay, and see the order and peaceableness of our meeting. He said he would permit us an hour's time, and left half a dozen soldiers with us. Then he went away with his troop, and Friends of the house gave the soldiers that stayed, and their horses, some meat.

When the captain was gone the soldiers that were left told us we might stay till night if we would. But we stayed but about three hours after, and had a glorious, powerful meeting; for the presence of the living God was manifest amongst us, and the Seed, Christ, was set over all. Friends were built upon Him, the foundation, and settled under His glorious, heavenly teaching.

After the meeting Friends passed away in peace, greatly refreshed with the presence of the Lord, and filled with joy and gladness that the Lord's power had given them such dominion. Many of the militia-soldiers stayed also, much vexed that the captain and troopers had not broken up our meeting; and cursed the captain and his troopers. It was reported that they intended evil against us that day; but the troopers, instead of assisting them, were rather assistant to us, in not joining them as they expected, but preventing them from doing the mischief they designed.

This captain was a desperate man; for it was he that said to me in Scotland that he would obey his superior's commands; if it were to crucify Christ he would do it, or would execute the great Turk's commands against the Christians if he were under him. So that it was an eminent power of the Lord which chained both him and his troopers, and those envious militia-soldiers also, who went away, not having power to hurt any of us, nor to break up our meeting.

Next day we had an heavenly meeting at Warmsworth of Friends in the ministry, with several others; and then Friends parted. As they passed through the country several were taken up; for on the day on which our first meeting was held, Lambert was routed, and it made great confusion in the country; but Friends were not kept long in prison at that time.

As I went to this meeting there came to me several at Skegby, in Nottinghamshire, who were going to be soldiers under Lambert, and would have bought my horse of me. Because I would not sell him, they were in a great rage against me, using many threatening words: but I told them that God would confound and scatter them; and within two or three days after they were scattered indeed.

From Warmsworth I passed, in the Lord's power, to Barton Abbey, where I had a great meeting; thence to Thomas Taylor's; and so on to Skipton, where was a general meeting of men Friends out of many counties concerning the affairs of the Church.[3]

A Friend went naked through the town, declaring Truth, and was much beaten.[4] Some other Friends also came to me all bloody. As I walked in the street, a desperate fellow had an intent to do me mischief; but he was prevented, and our meeting was quiet.

To this meeting came many Friends out of most parts of the nation; for it was about business relating to the Church both in this nation and beyond the seas. Several years before, when I was in the north, I was moved to recommend to Friends the setting up of this meeting for that service; for many Friends had suffered in divers parts of the nation, their goods were taken from them contrary to law, and they understood not how to help themselves, or where to seek redress.[5] But after this meeting was set up, several Friends who had been magistrates, and others that understood something of the law, came thither,

---

[3] This meeting for the affairs of the Church, held at Skipton, in Yorkshire, in 1659, is generally considered to be the original yearly meeting.

[4] " Naked " means naked to the waist. There are a few other instances of similar actions in England and America.

[5] This is the beginning of what was later known as the " Meeting for Sufferings," which has been throughout its history a remarkable body. The minutes of the Meeting for Sufferings date from Fifth month 22d, 1675.

and were able to inform Friends, and to assist them in gathering up the sufferings, that they might be laid before the justices, judges, or Parliament.

This meeting had stood several years, and divers justices and captains had come to break it up, but when they understood the business Friends met about, and saw their books and accounts of collections for relief of the poor, how we took care one county to help another, and to help our Friends beyond the seas, and provide for our poor, that none of them should be chargeable to their parishes, etc., the justices and officers confessed we did their work, and passed away peaceably and lovingly, commending Friends' practice.

Sometimes there would come two hundred of the poor of other people, and wait there till the meeting was done (for all the country knew we met about the poor), and after the meeting Friends would send to the bakers for bread, and give every one of these poor people a loaf, how many soever there were of them; for we were taught to " do good unto all; though especially to the household of faith."

After this meeting I visited Friends in their meetings till I came to Lancaster; whence I went to Robert Widders's, and so on to Arnside, where I had a general meeting for all the Friends in Westmoreland, Cumberland, and Lancashire. It was quiet and peaceable, and the living presence of the Lord was amongst us. I went back with Robert Widders; and Friends all passed away, fresh in the life and power of Christ, in which they had dominion, being settled upon Him, the heavenly Rock and Foundation.

I went next day to Swarthmore, Francis Howgill and Thomas Curtis being with me. I had not been long there before Henry Porter, a justice, sent a warrant by the chief constable and three petty constables to apprehend me. I had a sense of this beforehand; and being in the parlor with Richard Richardson and Margaret Fell, her servants came and told her there were some come to search the house for arms; and they went up into the chambers under that pretence.

It came upon me to go out to them; and as I was going by some of them I spoke to them; whereupon they asked me my name. I readily told them my name; and then they laid hold on me, saying that I was the man they looked for, and led me away to Ulverstone.

They kept me all night at the constable's house, and set a guard of fifteen or sixteen men to watch me; some of whom sat in the chimney, for fear I should go up it; such dark imaginations possessed them. They were very rude and uncivil, and would neither suffer me to speak to Friends, nor suffer them to bring me necessaries; but with violence thrust them out, and kept a strong guard upon me. Very wicked and rude they were, and a great noise they made about me. One of the constables, whose name was Ashburnham, said he did not think a thousand men could have taken me. Another of the constables, whose name was Mount, a very wicked man, said he would have served Judge Fell himself so, if he had been alive, and he had had a warrant for him.

Next morning, about six, I was putting on my

boots and spurs to go with them before some justice; but they pulled off my spurs, took my knife out of my pocket, and hurried me away through the town, with a party of horse and abundance of people, not suffering me to stay till my own horse came down.

When I was gone about a quarter of a mile with them, some Friends, with Margaret Fell and her children, came towards me; and then a great party of horse gathered about me in a mad rage and fury, crying out, " Will they rescue him ? Will they rescue him ? " Thereupon I said unto them, " Here is my hair; here is my back; here are my cheeks; strike on ! " With these words their heat was a little assuaged.

Then they brought a little horse, and two of them took up one of my legs and put my foot in the stirrup, and two or three lifting over my other leg, set me upon it behind the saddle, and so led the horse by the halter; but I had nothing to hold by. When they were come some distance out of the town they beat the little horse, and made him kick and gallop. Thereupon I slipped off him. I told them they should not abuse the creature. They were much enraged at my getting off, and took me by the legs and feet, and set me upon the same horse, behind the saddle again; and so led it about two miles till they came to a great water called the Carter-Ford.

By this time my own horse was come to us, and the water being deep, and their little horse scarcely able to carry me through, they let me get upon my own, through the persuasion of some of their own company, leading him through the water. One wicked fellow kneeled down, and, lifting up his hands, blessed God that I was taken.

When I was come over the Sands, I told them that I heard I had liberty to choose what justice I would go before; but Mount and the other constables cried, " No, you shall not." Then they led me to Lancaster, about fourteen miles, and a great triumph they thought to have had; but as they led me I was moved to sing praises to the Lord, in His power triumphing over all.

When I was come to Lancaster, the spirits of the people being mightily up, I stood and looked earnestly upon them, and they cried, " Look at his eyes! " [6] After a while I spoke to them, and they were pretty sober. Then came a young man who took me to his house, and after a little time the officers took me to the house of Major Porter, the justice who had sent the warrant against me, and who had several others with him.

When I came in, I said, " Peace be amongst you." Porter asked me why I came into the country at that troublesome time.[7] I told him, " To visit my brethren." " But," said he, " you have great meetings up and down." I told him that though we had, our

---

[6] This is the second time the striking character of his eyes has been commented on.

[7] This was just at the troublous time when Charles II. was coming to the throne, and the kingdom was being reorganized. Every traveller was suspected, and every gathering of people was watched.

meetings were known throughout the nation to be peaceable, and we were a peaceable people.

He said that we saw the devil in people's faces. I told him that if I saw a drunkard, or a swearer, or a peevish heady man, I could not say I saw the Spirit of God in him. And I asked him if he could see the Spirit of God. He said we cried against their ministers. I told him that while we were as Saul, sitting under the priests, and running up and down with their packets of letters, we were never called pestilent fellows nor makers of sects; but when we were come to exercise our consciences towards God and man, we were called pestilent fellows, as Paul was.

He said we could express ourselves well enough, and he would not dispute with me; but he would restrain me. I desired to know for what, and by whose order he had sent his warrant for me; and I complained to him of the abuse of the constables and other officers after they had taken me, and in their bringing me thither. He would not take notice of that, but told me he had an order, but would not let me see it; for he would not reveal the King's secrets; and besides, " A prisoner," he said, " is not to see for what he is committed." I told him that was not reason; for how, then, should he make his defence? I said I ought to have a copy of it. But he said there was a judge once that fined one for letting a prisoner have a copy of his mittimus; " and," said he, " I have an old clerk, though I am a young justice."

Then he called to his clerk, saying, " Is it not ready yet? Bring it "; meaning the mittimus. But

it not being ready, he told me I was a disturber of
the nation. I told him I had been a blessing to the
nation, in and through the Lord's power and Truth;
and that the Spirit of God in all consciences would
answer it. Then he charged me as an enemy to the
King, that I endeavoured to raise a new war, and
imbrue the nation in blood again. I told him I had
never learned the postures of war, but was clear and
innocent as a child concerning those things; and
therefore was bold.

Then came the clerk with the mittimus, and the
jailer was sent for and commanded to take me, put
me into the Dark-house, and let none come at me,
but to keep me there close prisoner till I should be
delivered by the King or Parliament. Then the justice asked the constables where my horse was.
" For I hear," said he, " he hath a good horse; have
ye brought his horse?" I told him where my horse
was, but he did not meddle with him.

As they had me to the jail the constable gave me
my knife again, and then asked me to give it to him.
I told him, Nay; he had not been so civil to me. So
they put me into the jail, and the under-jailer, one
Hardy, a very wicked man, was exceeding rude and
cruel, and many times would not let me have meat
brought in but as I could get it under the door.
Many came to look at me, some in a rage, and very
uncivil and rude.

Being now a close prisoner in the common jail at
Lancaster, I desired Thomas Cummins and Thomas
Green to go to the jailer, and desire of him a copy
of my mittimus, that I might know what I stood com-

mitted for. They went and the jailer answered that
he could not give a copy of it, for another had
been fined for so doing; but he gave them liberty to
read it over. To the best of their remembrance the
matters therein charged against me were that I was
a person generally suspected to be a common disturber of the peace of the nation, an enemy to the
King, and a chief upholder of the Quakers' sect; and
that, together with others of my fanatic opinion, I
had of late endeavoured to raise insurrections in these
parts of the country, and to embroil the whole kingdom in blood. Wherefore the jailer was commanded
to keep me in safe custody until I should be released
by order of the King and Parliament.

When I had thus got the heads of the charge contained in the mittimus, I wrote a plain answer in vin-
dication of my innocency in each particular; as follows:

"I am a prisoner at Lancaster, committed by Justice Porter. A copy of the mittimus I cannot get,
but such expressions I am told are in it as are very
untrue; as that I am generally suspected to be a common disturber of the nation's peace, an enemy to the
King, and that I, with others, endeavour to raise insurrections to embroil the nation in blood; all of
which is utterly false, and I do, in every part thereof,
deny it.

"For I am not a person generally suspected to be
a disturber of the nation's peace, nor have I given
any cause for such suspicion; for through the nation
I have been tried for these things formerly. In the

days of Oliver I was taken up on pretence of raising
arms against him, which was also false; for I meddled not with raising arms at all.   Yet I was
then carried up a prisoner to London, and brought
before him; when I cleared myself, and denied the
drawing of a carnal weapon against him, or any man
upon the earth; for my weapons are spiritual, which
take away the occasion of war, and lead into peace.
Upon my declaring this to Oliver, I was set at liberty by him.

" After this I was taken and sent to prison by Major Ceely in Cornwall, who, when I was brought before the judge, informed against me that I took him
aside, and told him that I could raise forty thousand
men in an hour's time, to involve the nation in blood,
and bring in King Charles.   This also was utterly
false, and a lie of his own inventing, as was then
proved upon him for I never spoke any such word
to him.

" I never was found in any plot; I never took any
engagement or oath; nor have I ever learned war-postures.   As those were false charges against me then,
so are these now which come from Major Porter, who
is lately appointed to be justice, but formerly wanted
power to exercise his cruelty against us; which is but
the wickedness of the old enemy.   The peace of the
nation I am not a disturber of, nor ever was; but I
seek the peace of it, and of all men, and stand for all
nations' peace, and all men's peace upon the earth,
and wish all knew my innocency in these things.

" And whereas Major Porter saith I am an enemy
to the King, this is false; for my love is to him and

to all men, even though they be enemies to God, to themselves, and to me. And I can say it is of the Lord that the King is come in, to bring down many unrighteously set up; of which I had a sight three years before he came in. It is much Major Porter should say I am an enemy to the King; for I have no reason so to be, he having done nothing against me.

" But I have been often imprisoned and perse-cuted these eleven or twelve years by those that have been both against the King and his father, even the party by whom Porter was made a major and for whom he bore arms; but not by them that were for the King. I was never an enemy to the King, nor to any man's person upon the earth. I am in the love that fulfils the law, which thinks no evil, but loves even enemies; and would have the King saved, and come to the knowledge of the Truth, and be brought into the fear of the Lord, to receive His wisdom from above, by which all things were made and created; that with that wisdom he may order all things to the glory of God.

" Whereas he calleth me ' A chief upholder of the Quakers' sect,' I answer: The Quakers are not a sect,[8] but are in the power of God, which was before

---

[8] George Fox never admitted that the Quakers were a sect, nor did any Friend of the first fifty years. There was but one Church, composed of those who obeyed the Light and in whom Christ dwelt, and of this Church Fox and his followers claimed to be members. This position has been ably put in Thomas Hancock's " Peculium "—a Prize Essay.

sects were, and witness the election before the world began, and are come to live in the life in which the prophets and apostles lived, who gave forth the Scriptures; therefore are we hated by envious, wrathful, wicked, persecuting men. But God is the upholder of us all by His mighty power, and preserves us from the wrath of the wicked that would swallow us up.

"And whereas he saith that I, together with others of my fanatic opinion, as he calls it, have of late endeavoured to raise insurrections, and to embroil the whole kingdom in blood, I answer, This is altogether false. To these things I am as a child; I know nothing of them. The postures of war I never learned; my weapons are spiritual and not carnal, for with carnal weapons I do not fight. I am a follower of Him who said, ' My kingdom is not of this world,' and though these lies and slanders are raised upon me, I deny drawing any carnal weapon against the King or Parliament, or any man upon the earth. For I am come to the end of the Law, but am in that which saves men's lives. A witness I am against all murderers, plotters, and all such as would imbrue the nation in blood; for it is not in my heart to have any man's life destroyed.

" And as for the word fanatic, which signifies furious, foolish, mad, etc., he might have considered himself before he had used that word, and have learned the humility which goes before honour. We are not furious, foolish, or mad; but through patience and meekness have borne lies, slanders and persecutions many years, and have undergone great sufferings. The spiritual man, that wrestles not with flesh and blood, and the Spirit that reproves sin in the gate, which is the Spirit of Truth, wisdom, and sound judgment, is not mad, foolish, furious, which fanatic signifies; but all are of a mad, furious, foolish spirit that in their furiousness, foolishness and rage wrestle with flesh and blood, with carnal weapons. This is not the Spirit of God, but of error, that persecutes in a mad, blind zeal, like Nebuchadnezzar and Saul.

" Inasmuch as I am ordered to be kept prisoner till I be delivered by order from the King or Parliament, therefore I have written these things to be laid before you, the King and Parliament, that ye may consider of them before ye act anything therein; that ye may weigh, in the wisdom of God, the intent and end of men's spirits, lest ye act the thing that will bring the hand of the Lord upon you and against you, as many who have been in authority have done before you, whom God hath overthrown. In Him we trust whom we fear and cry unto day and night, who hath heard us, doth hear us, and will hear us, and avenge our cause. Much innocent blood hath been shed. Many have been persecuted to death by such as were in authority before you, whom God hath vomited out because they turned against the just. Therefore consider your standing now that ye have the day, and receive this as a warning of love to you.

" From an innocent sufferer in bonds, and close prisoner in Lancaster Castle, called

" GEORGE FOX."

After this Margaret Fell determined to go to London, to speak with the King about my being taken,

and to show him the manner of it, and the unjust
dealing and evil usage I had received.[9]   When Justice Porter heard of this, he vapoured that he would
go and meet her in the gap.   But when he came before the King, having been a zealous man for the
Parliament against the King, several of the courtiers
spoke to him concerning his plundering their houses;
so that he quickly had enough of the court, and soon
returned into the country.

Meanwhile the jailer seemed very fearful, and said
he was afraid Major Porter would hang him because
he had not put me in the dark-house.   But when the
jailer waited on him after his return from London,
he was very blank and down, and asked how I did,
pretending he would find a way to set me at liberty.
But having overshot himself in his mittimus by ordering me "to be kept a prisoner till I should be
delivered by the King or Parliament," he had put
it out of his power to release me if he would.

He was the more down also upon reading a letter
which I sent him; for when he was in the height of
his rage and threats against me, and thought to ingratiate himself into the King's favour by imprisoning me, I was moved to write to him and put him
in mind how fierce he had been against the King and

---

[9] Margaret Fell was now the head of Swarthmore
Hall, Judge Fell having died in 1658.   As the arrest
was made from her house she felt herself implicated in
the false charge.   She wrote a vigorous letter about the
case to the proper magistrates.

his party, though now he would be thought zealous
for the King.

Among other things in my letter I called to his
remembrance that when he held Lancaster Castle for
the Parliament against the King, he was so rough
and fierce against those that favoured the King that
he said he would leave them neither dog nor cat, if
they did not bring him provision to the Castle.
I asked him also whose great buck's horns
were those that were in his house; and whence
he had both them and the wainscot with which he
ceiled his house; had he them not from Hornby
Castle?

About this time Ann Curtis, of Reading, came to
see me; and understanding how I stood committed, it
was upon her also to go to the King about it. Her
father, who had been sheriff of Bristol, was hanged
near his own door for endeavouring to bring the
King in; upon which consideration she had some
hopes the King might hear her on my behalf. Accordingly, when she returned to London, she and
Margaret Fell went to the King together; who, when
he understood whose daughter she was, received her
kindly. Her request to him being to send for me up,
and hear the cause himself, he promised her he
would; and he commanded his secretary to send an
order for bringing me up.

But when they came to the secretary for the order
he said it was not in his power; he must go according
to law; and I must be brought up by a writ of habeas
corpus before the judges. So he wrote to the Judge
of the King's Bench, signifying that it was the King's

pleasure I should be sent up by a writ of habeas corpus. Accordingly a writ was sent and delivered to the sheriff; but because it was directed to the chancellor of Lancaster the sheriff put it off to him; on the other hand, the chancellor would not make the warrant upon it, but said the sheriff must do that.

At length both chancellor and sheriff were got together; but being both enemies to Truth, they sought occasion for delay, and found an error in the writ, which was that, being directed to the chancellor, it said, " George Fox in prison under *your* custody," whereas the prison I was in was not in the chancellor's custody, but the sheriff's; so the word *your* should have been *his*. Upon this they returned the writ to London again, only to have that one word altered.

When it was altered and brought down again, the sheriff refused to carry me up unless I would seal a writing to him and become bound to pay for the sealing and the charge of carrying me up: which I denied, telling them I would not seal anything.

I was moved also to write to the King to exhort him to exercise mercy and forgiveness towards his enemies and to warn him to restrain the profaneness and looseness that was risen up in the nation upon his return.

" TO THE KING.

" KING CHARLES:

" Thou camest not into this nation by sword, nor by victory of war, but by the power of the Lord. Now, if thou dost not live in this power, thou wilt not prosper.

" If the Lord hath showed thee mercy and forgiven thee, and thou dost not show mercy and forgive, God will not hear thy prayers, nor them that pray for thee. If thou dost not stop persecution and persecutors, and take away all laws that hold up persecution about religion; if thou persist in them, and uphold persecution, that will make thee as blind as those that have gone before thee: for persecution hath always blinded those that have gone into it. Such God by his power overthrows, doeth His valiant acts upon, and bringeth salvation to His oppressed ones.

" If thou bear the sword in vain, and let drunkenness, oaths, plays, May-games, as setting up of Maypoles, with the image of the crown atop of them, with such like abominations and vanities, be encouraged or go unpunished, the nation will quickly turn like Sodom and Gomorrah, and be as bad as those men of the old world, who grieved the Lord till He overthrew them. So He will overthrow you if these things be not suppressed.

" Hardly ever before has there been so much wickedness at liberty as there is at this day, as though there were no terror nor sword of magistracy. Such looseness doth not grace a government, nor please them that do well. Our prayers are for them that are in authority, that under them we may live a godly life in peace, and that we may not be brought into ungodliness by them. Hear and consider, and do good in thy time, whilst thou hast power; be merciful and forgive; that is the way to overcome and obtain the kingdom of Christ.　　　　G. F."

It was long before the sheriff would yield to remove me to London unless I would seal a bond to
him, and bear the charges; which I still refused to
do. Then they consulted how to convey me up, and
first concluded to send up a party of horse with me. I
told them, " If I were such a man as you have represented me to be, you would have need to send a troop
or two of horse to guard me."

When they considered what a charge it would
be to them to send up a party of horse with me, they
altered their purpose, and concluded to send me up
guarded only by the jailer and some bailiffs. But
upon farther consideration they found that this
also would be a great charge to them, and therefore
they sent for me to the jailer's house, and told me
that if I would put in bail that I would be in London
on such a day of the term, I should have leave to
go up with some of my own friends.

I told them I would neither put in bail, nor give
one piece of silver to the jailer; for I was an innocent man,—that they had imprisoned me wrongfully,
and laid a false charge upon me. Nevertheless, I
said, if they would let me go up with one or two of
my friends to bear me company, I might go up and
be in London on such a day, if the Lord should permit; and if they desired it, I or any of my friends
that went with me would carry up their charge
against myself.

When they saw they could do no otherwise with
me, the sheriff consented that I should come up with
some of my friends, without any other engagement

than my word, to appear before the judges at London such a day of the term, if the Lord should permit.

Thereupon I was let out of prison, and went to Swarthmore, where I stayed two or three days; and thence went to Lancaster, and so to Preston, having meetings amongst Friends till I came into Cheshire, to William Gandy's, where was a large meeting without doors, the house not being sufficient to contain it. That day the Lord's everlasting Seed, which is the heir of the promise, was set over all, and Friends were turned to it.

Thence I came into Staffordshire and Warwickshire, to Anthony Bickliff's, and at Nuneaton,* at a priest's widow's house, we had a blessed meeting, wherein the everlasting Word of life was powerfully declared, and many were settled in it. Then, travelling on, visiting Friends' meetings, in about three weeks' time from my coming out of prison I reached London, Richard Hubberthorn and Robert Withers being with me.

When we came to Charing-Cross, multitudes of people were gathered together to see the burning of the bowels of some of the old King's judges, who had been hanged, drawn and quartered.

We went next morning to Judge Mallet's chamber. He was putting on his red gown to sit in judgment upon some more of the King's judges. He was then very peevish and froward, and said I might come another time.

We went again to his chamber when there was

* Nuneaton was only two miles from his home at Drayton, but he seems not to have stopped for a visit.

with him Judge Foster, who was called the Lord
Chief-Justice of England. With me was one called
Esquire Marsh, who was one of the bedchamber to
the King. When we had delivered to the judges the
charge that was against me, and they had read to
those words, " that I and my friends were embroiling the nation in blood," etc., they struck their hands
on the table. Whereupon I told them that I was the
man whom that charge was against, but I was as innocent of any such thing as a new-born child, and had
brought it up myself; and some of my friends came
up with me, without any guard.

As yet they had not minded my hat, but now seeing it on, they said, " What, do you stand with your
hat on ! " I told them I did not so in any contempt
of them. Then they commanded it to be taken off;
and when they called for the marshal of the King's
Bench, they said to him, " You must take this man
and secure him; but let him have a chamber, and not
be put amongst the prisoners."

" My lord," said the marshal, " I have no chamber
to put him into; my house is so full I cannot tell
where to provide a room for him but amongst the
prisoners."

" Nay," said the judge, " you must not put him
amongst the prisoners."

But when the marshal still answered that he had
no other place wherein to put me, Judge Foster said
to me, " Will you appear to-morrow about ten o'clock
at the King's Bench bar in Westminster-Hall ? "

I said, " Yes, if the Lord gives me strength."

Then said Judge Foster to the other judge, " If he

says Yes, and promises it, you may take his word;" so I was dismissed.

Next day I appeared at the King's Bench bar at the hour appointed, Robert Widders, Richard Hubberthorn, and Esquire Marsh going with me. I was brought into the middle of the court; and as soon as I came in, was moved to look round, and, turning to the people, say, "Peace be among you." The power of the Lord spread over the court.

The charge against me was read openly. The people were moderate, and the judges cool and loving; and the Lord's mercy was to them. But when they came to that part which said that I and my friends were embroiling the nation in blood, and raising a new war, and that I was an enemy to the King, etc., they lifted up their hands.

Then, stretching out my arms, I said, "I am the man whom that charge is against; but I am as innocent as a child concerning the charge, and have never learned any war-postures. And," said I, "do ye think that, if I and my friends had been such men as the charge declares, I would have brought it up myself against myself? Or that I should have been suffered to come up with only one or two of my friends with me? Had I been such a man as this charge sets forth, I had need to be guarded with a troop or two of horse. But the sheriff and magistrates of Lancashire thought fit to let me and my friends come up with it ourselves, nearly two hundred miles, without any guard at all; which, ye may be sure, they would not have done, had they looked upon me to be such a man."

Then the Judge asked me whether it should be filed, or what I would do with it. I answered, " Ye are judges, and able, I hope, to judge in this matter; therefore, do with it what ye will; for I am the man these charges are against, and here ye see I have brought them up myself. Do ye what ye will with them; I leave it to you."

Then, Judge Twisden beginning to speak some angry words, I appealed to Judge Foster and Judge Mallet, who had heard me over-night. Thereupon they said they did not accuse me, for they had nothing against me. Then stood up Esquire Marsh, who was of the King's bedchamber, and told the judges it was the King's pleasure that I should be set at liberty, seeing no accuser came up against me. They asked me whether I would put it to the King and Council. I said, " Yes, with a good will."

Thereupon they sent the sheriff's return, which he had made to the writ of habeas corpus, containing the matter charged against me in the mittimus, to the King, that he might see for what I was committed. The return of the sheriff of Lancaster was as follows:

" By virtue of His Majesty's writ, to me directed, and hereunto annexed, I certify that before the receipt of the said writ George Fox, in the said writ mentioned, was committed to His Majesty's jail at the Castle of Lancaster, in my custody, by a warrant from Henry Porter, Esq., one of His Majesty's justices of peace within the county palatine aforesaid, bearing date the fifth of June now last past; for that he, the said George Fox, was generally suspected to be a common disturber of the peace of this nation, an enemy of our sovereign lord the King, and a chief upholder of the Quakers' sect; and that he, together with others of his fanatic opinion, have of late endeavoured to make insurrections in these parts of the country, and to embroil the whole kingdom in blood. And this is the cause of his taking and detaining. Nevertheless, the body of the said George Fox I have ready before Thomas Mallet, knight, one of His Majesty's justices, assigned to hold pleas before His Majesty, at his chamber in Sergeants' Inn, in Fleet Street, to do and receive those things which his Majesty's said justice shall determine concerning him in this behalf, as by the aforesaid writ is required.

"GEORGE CHETHAM, ESQ., Sheriff."

On perusal of this, and consideration of the whole matter, the King, being satisfied of my innocency, commanded his secretary to send an order to Judge Mallet for my release, which he did thus:

"It is his Majesty's pleasure that you give order for releasing, and setting at full liberty the person of George Fox, late a prisoner in Lancaster jail, and commanded hither by an habeas corpus. And this signification of his Majesty's pleasure shall be your sufficient warrant. Dated at Whitehall, the 24th of October, 1660. EDWARD NICHOLAS."

"For Sir Thomas Mallet, knight, one of the justices of the King's Bench."

When this order was delivered to Judge Mallet, he forthwith sent his warrant to the marshal of the King's Bench for my release; which warrant was thus worded:

" By virtue of a warrant which this morning I have received from the Right Honorable Sir Edward Nicholas, knight, one of his Majesty's principal secretaries, for the releasing and setting at liberty of George Fox, late a prisoner in Lancaster jail, and thence brought hither by habeas corpus, and yesterday committed unto your custody; I do hereby require you accordingly to release and set the said prisoner George Fox at liberty: for which this shall be your warrant and discharge. Given under my hand the 25th day of October, in the year of our Lord God 1660.   THOMAS MALLET."

" To Sir John Lenthal, knight,
        marshal of the King's Bench,
            or his deputy."

Thus, after I had been a prisoner somewhat more than twenty weeks, I was freely set at liberty by the King's command, the Lord's power having wonderfully wrought for the clearing of my innocency, and Porter, who committed me, not daring to appear to make good the charge he had falsely suggested against me. But, after it was known I was discharged, a company of envious, wicked spirits were troubled, and terror took hold of Justice Porter; for he was afraid I would take the advantage of the law against him for my wrong imprisonment, and thereby undo him, his wife and children. And indeed I was pressed by some in authority to make him and the rest examples; but I said I should leave them to the Lord; if the Lord forgave them I should not trouble myself with them.

CHAPTER XIV.

𝕷𝖆𝖇𝖔𝖗𝖘, 𝕯𝖆𝖓𝖌𝖊𝖗𝖘 𝖆𝖓𝖉 𝕾𝖚𝖋𝖋𝖊𝖗𝖎𝖓𝖌𝖘.

1661-1662.

Now did I see the end of the travail which I had in my sore exercise at Reading;[1] for the everlasting power of the Lord was over all, and His blessed Truth, life, and light shined over the nation. Great and glorious meetings we had, and very quiet; and many flocked unto the Truth. Richard Hubberthorn had been with the King, who said that none should molest us so long as we lived peaceably, and promised this upon the word of a king; telling Richard that we might make use of his promise.[2]

Some Friends were also admitted in the House of Lords, to declare their reasons why they could not pay tithes, swear, go to the steeple-house worship, or join with others in worship; and the Lords heard them moderately. There being about seven hundred

---

[1] In 1658 Fox had written: " I went to Reading, where I was under great exercises and sufferings, and in great travail of spirit for about ten weeks." This was apparently over the disturbed political situation, and he tells us that at this time he " had a sight and sense of the king's return."

[2] Poor George little realized how futile this promise was to prove, or how soon the whips of Oliver were to become scorpions under the new order of affairs.

Friends in prison, who had been committed under Oliver's and Richard's government, upon contempts (so called) when the King came in, he set them all at liberty.

There seemed at that time an inclination and intention in the government to grant Friends liberty, because those in authority were sensible that we had suffered as well as they under the former powers. But still, when anything was going forward in order thereto, some dirty spirits or other,[3] that would seem to be for us, threw something in the way to stop it. It was said there was an instrument drawn up for confirming our liberty, and that it only wanted signing; when suddenly that wicked attempt of the Fifth-monarchy people broke out, and put the city and nation in an uproar. This was on a First-day night, and very glorious meetings we had had that day, wherein the Lord's Truth shone over all, and His power was exalted above all; but about midnight, or soon after, the drums beat, and the cry was, " Arm, Arm! "

I got up out of bed, and in the morning took boat, and, landing at Whitehall-stairs, walked through Whitehall. The people there looked strangely at me, but I passed through them, and went to Pall-Mall, where divers Friends came to me, though it had now become dangerous to pass through the streets; for by this time the city and suburbs were up in arms. Exceedingly rude the people and soldiers were. Henry

---

[3] In this instance Fifth-monarchy men, whose insurrection brought on the new persecution.

Fell, going to a Friend's house, was knocked down by the soldiers, and he would have been killed had not the Duke of York come by.

Great mischief was done in the city this week; and when the next First-day came, as Friends went to their meetings, many were taken prisoners. I stayed at Pall-Mall, intending to be at the meeting there; but on Seventh-day night a company of troopers came and knocked at the door. The servant let them in. They rushed into the house, and laid hold of me; and, there being amongst them one that had served under the Parliament, he put his hand to my pocket and asked whether I had any pistol. I told him, " You know I do not carry pistols; why, therefore, ask such a question of me, whom you know to be a peaceable man? "

Others of the soldiers ran into the chambers, and there found in bed Esquire Marsh, who, though he was one of the King's bedchamber, out of his love to me came and lodged where I did. When they came down again they said, " Why should we take this man away with us. We will let him alone."

" Oh," said the Parliament soldier, " he is one of the heads, and a chief ringleader."

Upon this the soldiers were taking me away, but Esquire Marsh, hearing of it, sent for him that commanded the party, and desired him to let me alone, for he would see me forthcoming in the morning.

In the morning, before they could fetch me, and before the meeting was gathered, there came a company of foot soldiers to the house, and one of them, drawing his sword, held it over my head. I asked

him why he drew his sword at an unarmed man, at
which his fellows, being ashamed, bade him put up his
sword.

These foot soldiers took me away to Whitehall
before the troopers came for me.

As I was going out several Friends were coming in
to the meeting. I commended their boldness and
cheerfulness, and encouraged them to persevere
therein.

When I was brought to Whitehall, the soldiers
and people were exceedingly rude, yet I declared
Truth to them. But some great persons came by,
who were very full of envy. " Why," said they, " do
ye let him preach ? Put him into a place where he
may not stir."

So into such a place they put me, and the soldiers
watched over me. I told them that, though they
could confine my body and shut that up, yet they
could not stop the Word of life. Some came and
asked me what I was. I told them, " A preacher of
righteousness."

After I had been kept there two or three hours,
Esquire Marsh spoke to Lord Gerrard, and he came
and bade them set me at liberty. The marshal, when
I was discharged, demanded fees. I told him I could
not give him any, neither was it our practice; and I
asked him how he could demand fees of me, who was
innocent.

Then I went through the guards, the Lord's power
being over them; and, after I had declared Truth to
the soldiers, I went up the streets with two Irish
colonels that came from Whitehall to an inn where

many Friends were at that time prisoners under a guard. I desired these colonels to speak to the guard to let me go in to visit my friends that were prisoners there; but they would not. Then I stepped up to the sentry, and desired him to let me go up; and he did so.

While I was there the soldiers went again to Pall-Mall to search for me; but not finding me they turned towards the inn, and bade all come out that were not prisoners; so they went out. But I asked the soldiers that were within whether I might not stay there a while with my friends. They said, " Yes." I stayed, and so escaped their hands again. Towards night I went to Pall-Mall, to see how it was with the Friends there; and, after I had stayed a while, I went up into the city.

Great rifling of houses there was at this time to search for people. I went to a private Friend's house, and Richard Hubberthorn was with me. There we drew up a declaration against plots and fightings, to be presented to the King and Council; but when finished, and sent to print, it was taken in the press.

On this insurrection of the Fifth-monarchy men, great havoc was made both in city and country, so that it was dangerous for sober people to stir abroad for several weeks after. Men or women could hardly go up and down the streets to buy provisions for their families without being abused. In the country they dragged men and women out of their houses, and some sick men out of their beds by the legs. Nay, one man in a fever, the soldiers dragged out of bed to prison, and when he was brought there he died. His name was Thomas Pachyn.

Margaret Fell went to the King and told him what sad work there was in the city and nation, and showed him we were an innocent, peaceable people, and that we must keep our meetings as heretofore, whatever we suffered; but that it concerned him to see that peace was kept, that no innocent blood might be shed.

The prisons were now everywhere filled with Friends and others, in the city and country, and the posts were so laid for the searching of letters that none could pass unsearched. We heard of several thousands of our Friends that were cast into prison in several parts of the nation, and Margaret Fell carried an account of them to the King and Council. The next week we had an account of several thousands more that were cast into prison, and she went and laid them also before the King and Council. They wondered how we could have such intelligence, seeing they had given such strict charge for the intercepting of all letters; but the Lord did so order it that we had an account notwithstanding all their stoppings.[4]

Soon after the King gave forth a proclamation that no soldiers should search any house without a constable. But the jails were still full, many thousands of Friends being in prison; which mischief was occasioned by the wicked rising of the Fifth-mon-

---

[4] Fox wrote a tender letter to the sufferers in prison, and " a Declaration from the harmless, innocent people of God called Quakers " was sent to the King.

archy men. But when those that were taken came to be executed, they did us the justice to clear us openly from having any hand in or knowledge of their plot.

After that, the King being continually importuned thereunto, issued a declaration that Friends should be set at liberty without paying fees. But great labour, travail, and pains were taken before this was obtained; for Thomas Moore and Margaret Fell went often to the King about it.

Much blood was shed this year, many of the old King's judges being hung, drawn and quartered. Amongst them that so suffered, Colonel Hacker was one. He had sent me prisoner from Leicester to London in Oliver's time, of which an account is given before. A sad day it was, and a repaying of blood with blood. For in the time of Oliver Cromwell, when several men were put to death by him, being hung, drawn and quartered for pretended treasons, I felt from the Lord God that their blood would be required; and I said as much then to several.

And now, upon the King's return, several that had been against him were put to death, as the others that were for him had been before by Oliver. This was sad work, destroying people; contrary to the nature of Christians, who have the nature of lambs and sheep. But there was a secret hand in bringing this day upon that hypocritical generation of professors, who, being got into power, grew proud, haughty, and cruel beyond others, and persecuted the people of God without pity.

When Friends were under cruel persecutions and

sufferings in the Commonwealth's time, I was moved of the Lord to write to Friends to draw up accounts of their sufferings, and lay them before the justices at their sessions; and if they would not do justice, then to lay them before the judges at the assize; and if they would not do justice, then to lay them before the Parliament, the Protector and his Council, that they might all see what was done under their government; and if they would not do justice, then to lay it before the Lord, who would hear the cries of the oppressed, and of the widows and fatherless whom they had made so.

For that for which we suffered, and for which our goods were spoiled, was our obedience to the Lord in His Power and His Spirit. He was able to help and to succour, and we had no helper in the earth but Him. And He heard the cries of His people, and brought an overflowing scourge over the heads of all our persecutors, which brought a dread and a fear amongst and on them all. So that those who had nicknamed us (who are the children of Light) and in scorn called us Quakers, the Lord made to quake; and many of them would have been glad to hide themselves amongst us; and some of them, through the distress that came upon them, did at length come to confess to the Truth.

Many ways were these professors warned, by word, by writing, and by signs; but they would believe none till it was too late. William Sympson was moved of the Lord to go at several times for three years naked and barefooted before them, as a sign to them, in markets, courts, towns, cities, to priests' houses, and to great men's houses, telling them, " So shall ye be stripped naked as I am stripped naked ! "   And sometimes he was moved to put on hair-sackcloth, and to besmear his face, and to tell them, " So will the Lord God besmear all your religion as I am besmeared."

Great sufferings did that poor man undergo, sore whippings with horse-whips and coach-whips on his bare body, grievous stoning and imprisonments, in three years' time, before the King came in, that they might have taken warning; but they would not, and rewarded his love with cruel usage.   Only the mayor of Cambridge did nobly to him, for he put his gown about him and took him into his house.

Another Friend, Robert Huntingdon, was moved of the Lord to go into Carlisle steeple-house with a white sheet about him, amongst the great Presbyterians and Independents there, to show them that the surplice was coming up again; and he put an halter about his neck to show them that an halter was coming upon them; which was fulfilled upon some of our persecutors not long after.

Another, Richard Sale, living near Westchester, being constable of the place where he lived, had sent to him with a pass a Friend whom those wicked professors had taken up for a vagabond, because he travelled up and down in the work of the ministry.   This constable, being convinced by the Friend thus brought to him, gave him his pass and liberty, and was afterwards himself cast into prison.

After this, on a lecture-day, Richard Sale was moved to go to the steeple-house in the time of their worship, and to carry those persecuting priests and

people a lantern and candle, as a figure of their darkness. But they cruelly abused him, and like dark
professors as they were put him into their prison
called Little Ease, and so squeezed his body therein
that not long after he died.[5]

Although those Friends that had been imprisoned
on the rising of the Fifth-monarchy men were set at
liberty, meetings were much disturbed, and great sufferings Friends underwent. For besides what was
done by officers and soldiers, many wild fellows and
rude people often came in.

One time when I was at Pall-Mall there came an
ambassador with a company of Irishmen and rude fellows. The meeting was over before they came, and I
was gone into a chamber, where I heard one of them
say that he would kill all the Quakers. I went down
to him, and was moved in the power of the Lord to
speak to him. I told him, " The law said, ' An eye
for an eye, and a tooth for a tooth '; but thou threat-
eneth to kill all the Quakers, though they have done

---

[5] These Friends, in their use of signs and striking
symbolisms, were undoubtedly following in the steps of
the Hebrew prophets. Both William Sympson and
Richard Sale were squeezed in Little Ease, the latter,
being very stout, came to his death as a result. " Little Ease " was a hole hewed out of a rock; the breadth
across seventeen inches; from the back to the inside of
the great door at the top seven inches; at the shoulders,
eight inches; at the breast, nine and a half inches; from
the top to the bottom, one yard and a half, with a de-
vice to lessen the height for purposes of torture.

thee no hurt. But," said I, " here is gospel for thee: here is my hair, here is my cheek, and here is my shoulder," turning it to him.

This so overcame him that he and his companions stood as men amazed, and said that if that was our principle, and if we were as we said, they never saw the like in their lives. I told them that what I was in words, I also was in my life. Then the ambassador, who stood without, came in; for he said that this Irish colonel was a desperate man that he durst not come in with him for fear he should do us some mischief. But Truth came over the Irish colonel, and he carried himself lovingly towards us; as also did the ambassador; for the Lord's power was over them all.

At Mile-End Friends were kept out of their meeting-place by soldiers, but they stood nobly in the Truth, valiant for the Lord's name; and at last the Truth gave them dominion.

About this time we had an account that John Love, a Friend that was moved to go and bear testimony against the idolatry of the Papists, was dead in prison at Rome; it was suspected he was privately put to death. Also before this time we received account from New England that the government there had made a law to banish the Quakers out of their colonies, upon pain of death in case they returned; that several of our Friends, having been so banished and returning, were thereupon taken and actually hanged, and that divers more were in prison, in danger of the like sentence being executed upon them. When those were put to death I was in prison at Lancaster, and had a perfect sense of their sufferings as though it had been myself, and as though the halter had been put about my own neck, though we had not at that time heard of it.[6]

As soon as we heard of it, Edward Burrough went to the King and told him that there was a vein of innocent blood opened in his dominions which, if it were not stopped, would overrun all. To this the King replied, " But I will stop that vein." Edward Burrough said, " Then do it speedily, for we know not how many may soon be put to death." The King answered, " As speedily as ye will. Call," (said he to some present) " the secretary, and I will do it presently."

The secretary being called, a mandamus was forthwith granted. A day or two after, Edward Burrough going again to the King to desire the matter might be expedited, the King said he had no occasion at present to send a ship thither, but if we would send one we might do it as soon as we would. Edward then asked the King if it would please him to grant his deputation to one called a Quaker to carry the mandamus to New England. He said, " Yes, to whom ye will."

Whereupon Edward Burrough named Samuel Shattuck, who, being an inhabitant of New England, was banished by their law, to be hanged if he came again; and to him the deputation was granted. Then he sent for Ralph Goldsmith, an honest Friend, who was master of a good ship, and agreed with him for three hundred pounds (goods or no goods) to sail in

---

[6] We have already seen how frequently George Fox had what nowadays are called telepathic experiences.

ten days. He forthwith prepared to set sail, and with a prosperous gale, in about six weeks' time, arrived before the town of Boston in New England, upon a First-day morning.

With him went many passengers, both of New and Old England, Friends, whom the Lord moved to go to bear their testimony against those bloody persecutors, who had exceeded all the world in that age in their bloody persecutions.

The townsmen at Boston, seeing a ship come into the bay with English colours, soon came on board and asked for the captain. Ralph Goldsmith told them he was the commander. They asked him if he had any letters. He said, " Yes." They asked if he would deliver them. He said, " No; not to-day."

So they went ashore and reported that there was a ship full of Quakers, and that Samuel Shattuck, who they knew was by their law to be put to death if he came again after banishment, was among them, but they knew not his errand nor his authority.

So all were kept close that day, and none of the ship's company suffered to go on shore. Next morning Samuel Shattuck, the King's deputy, and Ralph Goldsmith, went on shore, and, sending back to the ship the men that landed them, they two went through the town to Governor John Endicott's door, and knocked. He sent out a man to know their business. They sent him word that their business was from the King of England, and that they would deliver their message to no one but the Governor himself.

Thereupon they were admitted, and the Governor

came to them; and having received the deputation and the mandamus, he put off his hat and looked upon them. Then, going out, he bade the Friends follow him. He went to the deputy-governor, and after a short consultation came out to the Friends, and said, " We shall obey his majesty's commands."

After this the master gave liberty to the passengers to come on shore, and presently the noise of the business flew about the town; and the Friends of the town and the passengers of the ship met together to offer up their praises and thanksgivings to God, who had so wonderfully delivered them from the teeth of the devourer.

While they were thus met, in came a poor Friend, who, being sentenced by their bloody law to die, had lain some time in irons expecting execution. This added to their joy, and caused them to lift up their hearts in high praise to God, who is worthy for ever to have the praise, the glory, and the honour; for He only is able to deliver, to save, and support all that sincerely put their trust in Him. Here follows a copy of the mandamus.

" CHARLES R.

" Trusty and well-beloved, We greet you well. Having been informed that several of our subjects amongst you, called Quakers, have been and are imprisoned by you, whereof some have been executed, and others (as hath been represented unto us) are in danger to undergo the like, we have thought fit to signify our pleasure in that behalf for the future; and do hereby require that if there be any of those people called Quakers amongst you, now already condemned to suffer death or other corporal punishment, or that are imprisoned and obnoxious to the like condemnation, you are to forbear to proceed any further therein; but that you forthwith send the said persons (whether condemned or imprisoned) over into this our kingdom of England, together with the respective crimes or offences laid to their charge, to the end that such course may be taken with them here as shall be agreeable to our laws and their demerits. And for so doing, these our letters shall be your sufficient warrant and discharge. Given at our court at Whitehall the ninth day of September, 1661, in the 13th year of our reign."

Subscribed: "To our trusty and well-beloved John Endicott, Esquire, and to all and every other the Governor or governors of our plantations of New England, and of all the colonies thereunto belonging, that now are or hereafter shall be, and to all and every the ministers and officers of our plantations and colonies whatsoever within the continent of New England.   "By his majesty's command,

"WILLIAM MORRIS." [7]

---

[7] Whittier has beautifully told the story of Samuel Shattuck's mission in his poem, "The King's Missive." Longfellow has made the sufferings of the Quakers the subject of his dramatic poem, "New England Tragedies." The story of Quaker sufferings is told in George Bishop's "New England Judged." The best modern book on the subject is Hallowell's "Quaker Invasion of Massachusetts." Four Friends were executed—William Robinson, Marmaduke Stevenson, William Ledra and Mary Dyer.

Some time after this several New England magistrates came over, with one of their priests. We had several discourses with them concerning their murdering our Friends, the servants of the Lord; but they were ashamed to stand to their bloody actions.

On one of these occasions I asked Simon Broadstreet, one of the New England magistrates, whether he had not had a hand in putting to death those four servants of God, whom they hung only for being Quakers, as they had nicknamed them. He confessed that he had. I then asked him and the rest of his associates that were present whether they would acknowledge themselves to be subject to the laws of England; and if they did, by what laws they had put our Friends to death. They said they were subject to the laws of England, and had put our Friends to death by the same law that the Jesuits were put to death in England.

I asked them then whether they believed those Friends of ours whom they had put to death were Jesuits or jesuitically affected. They said, "Nay." "Then," said I, "ye have murdered them, if ye have put them to death by the law by which Jesuits are put to death here in England, and yet confess they were no Jesuits. By this it plainly appears ye have put them to death in your own wills, without any law."

Then Simon Broadstreet, finding himself and his company ensnared by their own words, asked if we came to catch them. I told them they had caught themselves, and might justly be questioned for their lives; and if the father of William Robinson, one of

them that were put to death, were in town, it was
probable he would question them, and bring their
lives into jeopardy.

Here they began to excuse themselves, saying,
" There is no persecution now amongst us." But
next morning we had letters from New England telling us that our Friends were persecuted there afresh.
We went again and showed them our letters, which
put them both to silence and to shame; and in great
fear they seemed to be lest some one should call
them to account and prosecute them for their lives.
Especially was Simon Broadstreet fearful; for he had
before so many witnesses confessed that he had a
hand in putting our Friends to death, that he could
not get off from it; though he afterwards through
fear shuffled, and would have unsaid it again. After
this, he and the rest soon returned to New England
again.

I went also to Governor Winthrop, and discoursed
with him on these matters. He assured me that he
had no hand in putting our Friends to death, or in
any way persecuting them; but was one of them that
protested against it.

About this time I lost a very good book, being
taken in the printer's hands; it was a useful teaching
work, containing the signification and explanation of
names, parables, types, and figures in the Scriptures.
They who took it were so affected with it, that they
were loth to destroy it; but thinking to make a great
advantage of it, they would have let us have it again,
if we would have given them a great sum of money
for it; which we were not free to do.

Before this, while I was prisoner in Lancaster Castle, the book called the " Battledore " was published,
which was written to show that in all languages Thou
and Thee is the proper and usual form of speech to a
single person; and You to more than one. This was
set forth in examples or instances taken from the
Scriptures, and books of teaching, in about thirty
languages. J. Stubbs and Benjamin Furly took great
pains in compiling it, which I set them upon; and
some things I added to it.[8]

---

[8] Here is the title page to this curious old book
which is now very rare, and is much valued by collec-
tors:

" A Battle-Door for Teachers & Professors to learn
Singular and Plural; You to Many, and Thou to One:
Singular One, Thou; Plural Many, You, Wherein is
shewed forth by Grammar, or Scripture Examples, how
several Nations and People have made a distinction
between Singular and Plural, And First. In the former
part of this Book, Called the English Battle-Door, may
be seen how several People have spoken Singular and
Plural, As the Apharsathkites, The Tarpelites, The
Apharsites, The Archevites, The Babylonians, The
Susanchites, The Dehavites, The Elamites, The
Temanites, The Naomites, The Shuites, The
Buzites, The Moabites, The Hevites, The Edom-
ites, The Philistines, The Amalekites, The Sod-
omites, The Hittites, The Midianites, &c. Also,
in this Book is set forth Examples of the Singular and Plural About Thou, and You in several
Languages divided into distinct Battle-Doors, or Forms,
or Examples; English, Latine, Italian, Greek, Hebrew,

When it was finished, copies were presented to the King and his Council, to the Bishops of Canterbury and London, and to the two universities one each; and many purchased them. The King said it was the proper language of all nations; and the Bishop of Canterbury, being asked what he thought of it, was at a stand, and could not tell what to say to it. For it did so inform and convince people, that few afterwards were so rugged toward us for saying Thou and Thee to a single person, for which before they were exceedingly fierce against us.

Thou and Thee was a sore cut to proud flesh, and them that sought self-honour, who, though they

---

Caldec, Syriack, Arabick, Persiack, Ethiopick, Samaritan, Coptick or Egyptick, Armenian, Saxon, Welch, Mence, Cornish, French, Spanish, Portugal, High-Dutch, Low Dutch, Danish, Bohemian, Slavonian, and how Emperors and others have used the Singular Word to One; and how the Word You (to one) came first from the Pope. Likewise some examples, in the Polonian, Lithvanian, Irish and East-Indian, Together with the Singular and Plural Words thou and you, in Swedish, Turkish, Muscovian and Curlandian tongues,—In the latter part of this Book are contained several bad unsavoury words gathered first for certain School Books, which have been taught Boyes in England, which is a Rod and a Whip to the School Masters in England and elsewhere who teach such Books. Geo. Fox, Jno. Stubbs, Benjamin Furley.

" London: Printed for Robt. Wilson, and are to be sold at his Shop at the Signe of the Black-Spread-Eagle and Wind-Mil in Martins le Grand 1660."

would say it to God and Christ, could not endure to have it said to themselves. So that we were often beaten and abused, and sometimes in danger of our lives, for using those words to some proud men, who would say, " What! you ill-bred clown, do you Thou me ?" as though Christian breeding consisted in saying You to one; which is contrary to all their grammars and teaching books, by which they instructed their youth.

About this time many Papists and Jesuits began to fawn upon Friends, and talked up and down where they came, that of all the sects the Quakers were the best and most self-denying people; and they said it was great pity that they did not return to the Holy Mother Church. Thus they made a buzz among the people, and said they would willingly discourse with Friends. But Friends were loth to meddle with them, because they were Jesuits, looking upon it to be both dangerous and scandalous.

But when I understood it, I said to Friends, " Let us discourse with them, be they what they will." So a time being appointed at Gerrard Roberts's, there came two of them like courtiers. They asked our names, which we told them; but we did not ask their names, for we understood they were called Papists, and they knew we were called Quakers.

I asked them the same question that I had formerly asked a Jesuit, namely, whether the Church of Rome was not degenerated from the Church in the primitive times, from the Spirit, power, and practice that they were in in the Apostles' times ? He to whom I put this question, being subtle, said he would not answer it. I asked him why. But he would show no reason. His companion said he would answer me; and said that they were not degenerated from the Church in the primitive times. I asked the other whether he was of the same mind. He said, " Yes."

Then I replied that, for the better understanding one of another, and that there might be no mistake, I would repeat my question over again after this manner: "Is the Church of Rome now in the same purity, practice, power, and Spirit that the Church in the Apostles' time was in?" When they saw we would be exact with them, they flew off and denied that, saying it was presumption in any to say they had the same power and Spirit which the Apostles had.

I told them it was presumption in them to meddle with the words of Christ and His Apostles, and make people believe they succeeded the Apostles, yet be forced to confess they were not in the same power and Spirit that the Apostles were in. " This," said I, " is a spirit of presumption, and rebuked by the Apostles' spirit."

I showed them how different their fruits and practices were from the fruits and practices of the Apostles.

Then got up one of them, and said, " Ye are a company of dreamers." " Nay," said I, " ye are the filthy dreamers, who dream ye are the Apostles' successors, and yet confess ye have not the same power and Spirit which the Apostles were in. And are not they defilers of the flesh who say it is presumption for any to say they have the same power and Spirit

which the Apostles had? Now," said I, " if ye have
not the same power and Spirit which the Apostles
had, then it is manifest that ye are led by another
power and spirit than that by which the Apostles
and Church in the primitive times were led."

Then I began to tell them how that evil spirit by
which they were led had led them to pray by beads
and to images, and to set up nunneries, friaries, and
monasteries, and to put people to death for religion;
which practices I showed them were below the law,
and far short of the gospel, in which is liberty.

They were soon weary of this discourse, and went
their way, and gave a charge, as we heard, to the
Papists, that they should not dispute with us, nor
read any of our books.

So we were rid of them; but we had reasonings
with all the other sects, Presbyterians, Independents,
Seekers, Baptists, Episcopal men, Socinians, Brown-
ists, Lutherans, Calvinists, Arminians, Fifth-monarchy men, Familists, Muggletonians, and Ranters;
none of which would affirm that they had the same
power and Spirit that the Apostles had and were in;
so in that power and Spirit the Lord gave us
dominion over them all.

As for the Fifth-monarchy men I was moved to
give forth a paper, to manifest their error to them;
for they looked for Christ's personal coming in an
outward form and manner, and fixed the time to the
year 1666; at which time some of them prepared
themselves when it thundered and rained, thinking
Christ was then come to set up His kingdom, and

they imagined they were to kill the whore without them.

But I told them that the whore was alive in them, and was not burned with God's fire, nor judged in them with the same power and Spirit the Apostles were in; and that their looking for Christ's coming outwardly to set up His kingdom was like the Pharisees' "Lo here," and "Lo there." But Christ was come, and had set up His kingdom above sixteen hundred years ago, according to Nebuchadnezzar's dream and Daniel's prophecy, and He had dashed to pieces the four monarchies, the great image, with its head of gold, breast and arms of silver, belly and thighs of brass, legs of iron, and its feet part of iron part of clay; and they were all blown away with God's wind, as the chaff in the summer threshing-floor.

And I told them that when Christ was on earth, He said His kingdom was not of this world; if it had been, His servants would have fought; but it was not, therefore His servants did not fight. Therefore all the Fifth-monarchy men that are fighters with carnal weapons are none of Christ's servants, but the beast's and the whore's. Christ said, "All power in heaven and in earth is given to me"; so then His kingdom was set up above sixteen hundred years ago, and He reigns. "And we see Jesus Christ reign," said the Apostle, "and He shall reign till all things be put under His feet"; though all things are not yet put under His feet, nor subdued.

This year several Friends were moved to go beyond the seas, to publish Truth in foreign countries. John Stubbs, and Henry Fell, and Richard

Costrop were moved to go towards China and Prester
John's country; but no masters of ships would carry
them.[9] With much ado they got a warrant from the
King; but the East India Company found ways to
avoid it, and the masters of their ships would not
carry them.

Then they went into Holland, hoping to get passage there, but none could they get there either. Then
John Stubbs and Henry Fell took shipping for Alexandria, in Egypt, intending to go thence by the cara-
vans. Meanwhile Daniel Baker, being moved to
go to Smyrna, drew Richard Costrop, contrary to
his own freedom, to go along with him; and in the
passage, Richard falling sick, Daniel Baker left him
so in the ship, where he died; but that hard-hearted
man afterwards lost his own condition.

John Stubbs and Henry Fell reached Alexandria;
but they had not been long there before the English
consul banished them; yet before they came away,
they dispersed many books and papers for opening

---

[9] These Friends undoubtedly believed that the principles of truth which they had discovered would ultimately prevail over the entire globe.

" Prester John's Country " was Abyssinia. Prester
John was a legendary Christian priest, who was believed in the early Middle Ages to reign over this Eastern country. About this time Catherine Evans and
Sarah Chevers, in their travels, were put in the inqui-
sition-prison at Malta, from which Fox secured their
release, through the influence of Lord D'Aubeny, a
Roman Catholic.

the principles and way of Truth to the Turks and Grecians. They gave the book called, "The Pope's Strength Broken," to an old friar, for him to give or send to the Pope. When the friar had perused it he placed his hand on his breast and confessed, "What is written therein is truth; but," said he, "if I should confess it openly, they would burn me."

John Stubbs and Henry Fell, not being suffered to go further, returned to England, and came to London again. John had a vision that the English and Dutch, who had joined together not to carry them, would fall out one with the other; and so it came to pass.

Among the exercises and troubles that Friends had from without, one was concerning Friends' marriages, which sometimes were called in question.[10] In this year there happened to be a cause tried at the assize at Nottingham concerning a Friend's marriage.

The case was thus: Some years before two Friends were joined together in marriage amongst Friends, and lived together as man and wife about two years. Then the man died, leaving his wife with child, and leaving an estate in lands of copyhold. When the woman was delivered, the jury presented the child heir to its father's lands, and accordingly the child was admitted; afterwards another Friend married the widow. After that a person near of kin to her former

---

[10] Friends are married without clergyman or magistrate. The bridal couple stand up in a religious assembly, and, taking each other by the hand, promise to be husband and wife till death.

husband brought his action against the Friend who had last married her, endeavoring to dispossess them, and deprive the child of the inheritance, and to possess himself thereof as next heir to the woman's first husband. To effect this he endeavoured to prove the child illegitimate, alleging that the marriage was not according to law.

In opening the cause the plaintiff's counsel used unseemly words concerning Friends, saying that "they went together like brute beasts," with other ill expressions. After the counsel on both sides had pleaded, the Judge (viz., Judge Archer) took the matter in hand, and opened it to them, telling them, "There was a marriage in paradise when Adam took Eve and Eve took Adam, and it was the consent of the parties that made a marriage." And for the Quakers, he said, he did not know their opinions; but he did not believe they went together as brute beasts, as had been said of them, but as Christians; and therefore he did believe the marriage was lawful, and the child lawful heir.

The better to satisfy the jury he brought them a case to this purpose: "A man that was weak of body, and kept his bed, had a desire in that condition to marry, and did declare before witnesses that he did take such a woman to be his wife, and the woman declared that she took that man to be her husband. This marriage was afterwards called in question, and all the bishops did conclude it to be a lawful marriage."

Hereupon the jury gave in their verdict for the

Friend's child against the man that would have deprived it of its inheritance.

Now, there being very many Friends in prison in the nation,[11] Richard Hubberthorn and I drew up a paper concerning them, and got it delivered to the King, that he might understand how we were dealt with by his officers. It was directed thus:

" FOR THE KING:

" FRIEND, Who art the chief ruler of these dominions, here is a list of some of the sufferings of the people of God, in scorn called Quakers, that have suffered under the changeable powers before thee, by whom there have been imprisoned, and under whom there have suffered for good conscience' sake, and for bearing testimony to the truth as it is in Jesus, three thousand one hundred and seventy-three persons; and there lie yet in prison, in the name of the Commonwealth, seventy-three persons, that we know of. And there died in prison in the time of the Commonwealth, and of Oliver and Richard the Protectors, through cruel and hard imprisonments, upon nasty straw and in dungeons, thirty-two persons. There have been also imprisoned in thy name, since thy arrival, by such as thought to ingratiate themselves thereby with thee, three thousand sixty and eight persons. Besides this our meetings are daily

---

[11] It is estimated that at this time there were not less than 4,500 Friends in the prisons of England and Wales. This letter to the King is strikingly direct and straightforward.

broken up by men with clubs and arms, though we meet peaceably, according to the practice of God's people in the primitive times, and our Friends are thrown into waters, and trodden upon, till the very blood gushes out of them; the number of which abuses can hardly be uttered.

" Now this we would have of thee, to set them at liberty that lie in prison in the names of the Commonwealth, and of the two Protectors, and them that lie in thy own name, for speaking the truth, and for good conscience' sake, who have not lifted up a hand against thee or any man; and that the meetings of our Friends, who meet peaceably together in the fear of God, to worship Him, may not be broken up by rude people with their clubs, swords, and staves. One of the greatest things that we have suffered for formerly was, because we could not swear to the Protectors and all the changeable governments; and now we are imprisoned because we cannot take the oath of allegiance. Now, if our yea be not yea, and nay, nay, to thee, and to all men upon the earth, let us suffer as much for breaking that, as others do for breaking an oath. We have suffered these many years, both in lives and estates, under these changeable governments, because we cannot swear, but obey Christ's doctrine, who commands we should not ' swear at all,' and this we seal with our lives and estates, with our yea and nay, according to the doctrine of Christ.

" Hearken to these things, and so consider them in the wisdom of thy God that by it such actions may be stopped; thou that hast the government, and mayst do it. We desire all that are in prison may be set at liberty, and that for the time to come they may not be imprisoned for conscience' and for the Truth's sake. If thou question the innocency of their sufferings, let them and their accusers be brought before thee, and we shall produce a more particular and full account of their sufferings, if required."

CHAPTER XV.

In Prison for not Swearing.

1662-1665.

After I had made some stay in London, and had cleared myself of those services that at that time lay upon me there, I went into the country, having with me Alexander Parker and John Stubbs. We travelled through the country, visiting Friends' meetings, till we came to Bristol.

There we understood the officers were likely to come and break up the meeting; yet on First-day we went to the meeting at Broadmead, and Alexander Parker standing up first, while he was speaking the officers came and took him away. After he was gone, I stood up and declared the everlasting Truth of the Lord God in His eternal power, which came over all; the meeting was quiet the rest of the time, and broke up peaceably. I tarried till the First-day following, visiting Friends, and being visited by them.

On First-day morning several Friends came to Edward Pyot's house (where I lay the night before), and used great endeavours to persuade me not to go to the meeting that day, for the magistrates, they said, had threatened to take me, and had raised the trained bands. I wished them to go to the meeting, not telling them what I intended to do; but I told Edward Pyot I intended to go, and he sent his son to show me the way from his house by the fields.

As I went I met divers Friends who were coming to me to prevent my going, and who did what they could to stop me. " What! " said one, " wilt thou go into the mouth of the beast? " " Wilt thou go into the mouth of the dragon? " said another. I put them by and went on.

When I came to the meeting Margaret Thomas was speaking; and when she had done I stood up. I saw a concern and fear upon Friends for me; but the power of the Lord, in which I declared, soon struck the fear out of them; life sprang, and a glorious heavenly meeting we had.

After I had cleared myself of what was upon me from the Lord to the meeting, I was moved to pray; and after that to stand up again, and tell Friends how they might see there was a God in Israel that could deliver.

A very large meeting this was, and very hot; but Truth was over all, the life was exalted, which carried through all, and the meeting broke up in peace. The officers and soldiers had been breaking up another meeting, which had taken up their time, so that our meeting was ended before they came. But I understood afterwards they were in great rage because they had missed me; for they were heard to say one to another before, " I'll warrant we shall have him; " but the Lord prevented them.

I went from the meeting to Joan Hily's, where many Friends came to see me, rejoicing and blessing God for our deliverance. In the evening I had a fine fresh meeting among Friends at a Friend's house over the water, where we were much refreshed in the Lord.

From Barnet Hills we came to Swannington, in Leicestershire, where William Smith and some other Friends visited me; but they went away towards night, leaving me at a Friend's house in Swannington.

At night, as I was sitting in the hall speaking to a widow woman and her daughter, Lord Beaumont came with a company of soldiers, who, slapping their swords on the door, rushed into the house with swords and pistols in their hands, crying, " Put out the candles and make fast the doors." Then they seized upon the Friends in the house, and asked if there were no more about the house. The Friends told them there was one man more in the hall.

There being some Friends out of Derbyshire, one of whom was named Thomas Fauks, Lord Beaumont, after he had asked all their names, bid his man set down that man's name as Thomas Fox. The Friend said, Nay; that his name was not Fox, but Fauks. In the mean time some of the soldiers came, and fetched me out of the hall to him. He asked my name. I told him my name was George Fox, and that I was well known by that name. " Aye," said he, " you are known all the world over." I said, I was known for no hurt, but for good.

Then he put his hands into my pockets to search them, and plucked out my comb-case, and afterwards commanded one of his officers to search further for letters. I told him I was no letter-carrier, and asked him why he came amongst a peaceable people with

swords and pistols without a constable, contrary to
the king's proclamation and to the late act. For he
could not say there was a meeting, I being only talking with a poor widow-woman and her daughter.

By reasoning thus with him, he came somewhat
down; yet, sending for the constables, he gave them
charge of us that night, and told them to bring us
before him next morning. Accordingly the constables set a watch of the townspeople upon us that
night, and had us next morning to his house, about
a mile from Swannington.

When we came before him, he told us that we had
met " contrary to the Act." [1] I desired him to show
us the Act. " Why," says he, " you have it in your
pocket." I told him he did not find us in a meeting.
Then he asked whether we would take the oaths of
allegiance and supremacy. I told him I never took
any oath in my life, nor engagement, nor the covenant. Yet still he would force the oath upon us.
I desired him to show us the oath, that we might see
whether we were the persons it was to be tendered

---

[1] This was an act passed in 1662, " for preventing
mischiefs and dangers that may arise by certain persons
called Quakers, and others refusing to take oaths."
The act declared it " altogether unlawful and contrary
to the word of God " to refuse to take an oath, or to
persuade another person to refuse to do so. It further
made it an offense for more than five persons, " commonly called Quakers," " to assemble in any place
under pretense of joining in a religious worship not
authorized by the laws of this realm."

to, and whether it was not for the discovery of popish recusants. At length he brought a little book, but we called for the statute-book. He would not show us that, but caused a mittimus to be made, which mentioned that we " were to have had a meeting." With this mittimus he delivered us to the constables to convey us to Leicester jail.

But when the constables had brought us back to Swannington, it being harvest-time, it was hard to get anybody to go with us. The people were loth to take their neighbors to prison, especially in such a busy time. They would have given us our mittimus to carry ourselves to the jail; for it had been usual for constables to give Friends their own mittimuses, and they have gone themselves with them to the jailer. But we told them that, though our Friends had sometimes done so, we would not take this mittimus; but some of them should go with us to the jail.

At last they hired a poor labouring man, who was loth to go, though hired. So we rode to Leicester, being five in number; some carried their Bibles open in their hands, declaring Truth to the people as we rode in the fields and through the towns, and telling them we were prisoners of the Lord Jesus Christ, going to suffer bonds for His name and Truth. One woman Friend carried her wheel on her lap to spin on·in prison; and the people were mightily affected.

At Leicester we went to an inn. The master of the house seemed troubled that we should go to the prison; and being himself in commission, he sent for **lawyers** in the town to advise with, and would **have** taken up the mittimus, kept us in his own house, and not have let us go into the jail.

But I told Friends it would be a great charge to lie at an inn; and many Friends and people would be coming to visit us, and it might be hard for him to bear our having meetings in his house. Besides, we had many Friends in the prison already, and we had rather be with them. So we let the man know that we were sensible of his kindness, and to prison we went; the poor man that brought us thither delivering both the mittimus and us to the jailer.

This jailer had been a very wicked, cruel man. Six or seven Friends being in prison before we came, he had taken some occasion to quarrel with them, and had thrust them into the dungeon amongst the felons, where there was hardly room for them to lie down. We stayed all that day in the prison-yard, and desired the jailer to let us have some straw. He surlily answered, " You do not look like men that would lie on straw."

After a while William Smith, a Friend, came to me, and he being acquainted in the house, I asked him what rooms there were in it, and what rooms Friends had usually been put into before they were put into the dungeon. I asked him also whether the jailer or his wife was the master. He said that the wife was master; and that, though she was lame, and sat mostly in her chair, being only able to go on crutches, yet she would beat her husband when he came within her reach if he did not do as she would have him.

I considered that probably many Friends might

come to visit us, and that if we had a room to ourselves, it would be better for them to speak to me, and me to them, as there should be occasion. Wherefore I desired William Smith to go speak with the woman, and acquaint her that if she would let us have a room, suffer our Friends to come out of the dungeon, and leave it to us to give her what we would, it might be better for her.

He went, and after some reasoning with her, she consented; and we were put into a room. Then we were told that the jailer would not suffer us to have any drink out of the town brought into the prison, but that what beer we drank we must take of him. I told them I would remedy that, for we would get a pail of water and a little wormwood once a day, and that might serve us; so we should have none of his beer, and the water he could not deny us.

Before we came, when the few Friends that were prisoners there met together on First-days, if any of them was moved to pray to the Lord, the jailer would come up with his quarter-staff in his hand, and his mastiff dog at his heels, and pluck them down by the hair of the head, and strike them with his staff; but when he struck Friends, the mastiff dog, instead of falling upon them, would take the staff out of his hand.

When the First-day came, I spoke to one of my fellow-prisoners, to carry a stool and set it in the yard, and give notice to the debtors and felons that there would be a meeting in the yard, and they that would hear the Word of the Lord declared might come thither. So the debtors and prisoners gathered in the yard, and we went down, and had a very precious meeting, the jailer not meddling.

Thus every First-day we had a meeting as long as we stayed in prison; and several came in out of the town and country. Many were convinced, and some there received the Lord's Truth who have stood faithful witnesses for it ever since.

When the sessions came we were brought before the justices, with many more Friends, sent to prison whilst we were there, to the number of about twenty. The jailer put us into the place where the thieves were put, and then some of the justices began to tender the oaths of allegiance and supremacy to us. I told them I never took any oath in my life; and they knew we could not swear, because Christ and His Apostle forbade it; therefore they but put it as a snare to us. We told them that if they could prove that, after Christ and the Apostle had forbidden swearing, they did ever command Christians to swear, then we would take these oaths; otherwise we were resolved to obey Christ's command and the Apostle's exhortation.

They said we must take the oath that we might manifest our allegiance to the king. I told them I had been formerly sent up a prisoner by Colonel Hacker, from that town to London, under pretence that I had held meetings to plot to bring in King Charles. I also desired them to read our mittimus, which set forth the cause of our commitment to be that we " were to have a meeting "; and I said Lord Beaumont could not by that act send us to jail unless we had been taken at a meeting, and found to be such persons as the act speaks of; therefore we desired that they would read the mittimus and see how wrongfully we were imprisoned.

They would not take notice of the mittimus, but called a jury and indicted us for refusing to take the oaths of allegiance and supremacy. When the jury was sworn and instructed, as they were going out, one that had been an alderman of the city spoke to them, and bade them " have a good conscience "; and one of the jury, being a peevish man, told the justices there was one affronted the jury; whereupon they called him up, and tendered him the oath also, and he took it.

While we were standing where the thieves used to stand, a cut-purse had his hand in several Friends' pockets. Friends declared it to the justices, and showed them the man. They called him up before them, and upon examination he could not deny it; yet they set him at liberty.

It was not long before the jury returned, and brought us in guilty; and after some words, the justices whispered together, and bid the jailer take us to prison again; but the Lord's power was over them, and His everlasting Truth, which we declared boldly amongst them. There being a great concourse of people, most of them followed us; so that the crier and bailiffs were fain to call the people back again to the court.

We declared the Truth as we went along the streets, till we came to the jail, the streets being full of people.

When we were in our chamber again, after some

time the jailer came to us and desired all to go forth that were not prisoners. When they were gone he said, " Gentlemen, it is the court's pleasure that ye should be set at liberty, except those that are in for tithes; and you know there are fees due to me; but I shall leave it to you to give me what you will."

Thus we were all set at liberty on a sudden, and passed every one into our services. Leonard Fell went with me again to Swannington.

I had a letter from Lord Hastings, who, hearing of my imprisonment, had written from London to the justices of the sessions to set me at liberty. I had not delivered this letter to the justices; whether any knowledge of his mind received through another hand made them discharge us so suddenly, I know not. This letter I carried to Lord Beaumont, who had sent us to prison. When he had broken it open and read it, he seemed much troubled; but at last he came a little lower, yet threatened us that if we had any more meetings at Swannington, he would break them up and send us to prison again.

But, notwithstanding his threats, we went to Swannington, and had a meeting with Friends there, and he neither came nor sent to break it up.

[After travelling through Northamptonshire, Bedfordshire and Warwickshire, he came again to London.]

I stayed not long in London, but went into Essex, and so to Norfolk, having great meetings. At Norwich, when I came to Captain Lawrence's, there was a great threatening of disturbance; but the meeting was quiet. Passing thence to Sutton, and into Cambridgeshire, I heard of Edward Burrough's decease. Being sensible how great a grief and exercise it would be to Friends to part with him, I wrote the following lines for the staying and settling of their minds:

" FRIENDS:

" Be still and quiet in your own conditions, and settled in the Seed of God, that doth not change; that in that ye may feel dear Edward Burrough among you in the Seed, in which and by which he begat you to God, with whom he is; and that in the Seed ye may all see and feel him, in which is the unity with him in the life; and so enjoy him in the life that doth not change, which is invisible.   GEORGE FOX." [2]

[Hereupon extensive travels follow, throughout the eastern counties, then through the southern as far as Land's End, and again through Wales and the English Lake district. He finally reaches Swarthmore some time in 1663, and finds that an offer of twenty-five pounds has been made to any man who would take him.

---

[2] This letter well illustrates the difficulties of George Fox's style. The letter manifests a profound and beautiful spirit, but the phraseology is none too clear. He means: " Dear Edward is living in God, who is invisible and unchangeable; settle your own lives down into that same living God whose divine presence manifested in Edward Burrough has begotten a spiritual life in you, and you will feel yourselves united in spirit and life with the dear departed one."

Out of the experiences of this long, though somewhat uneventful trip we give only the following discussion, which throws good light on Fox's " principle of truth ":

" Next morning, some of the chief of the town * desired to speak with me, amongst whom was Colonel Rouse. I went, and had a great deal of discourse with them concerning the things of God. In their reasoning they said, ' The gospel was the four books of Matthew, Mark, Luke and John '; and they called it natural. I told them, the gospel was the power of God, which was preached before Matthew, Mark, Luke or John were written; and it was preached to every creature, of which a great part might never see nor hear of those four books, so that every creature was to obey the power of God; for Christ, the Spiritual Man, would judge the world according to the gospel, that is, according to his invisible power. When they heard this, they could not gainsay; for the Truth came over them. I directed them to their Teacher, the grace of God, and showed them the sufficiency of it, which would teach them how to live, and what to deny; and being obeyed would bring them salvation. So to that grace I recommended them, and left them."]

I came over the sands to Swarthmore. There they told me that Colonel Kirby had sent his lieutenant, who had searched trunks and chests for me.

That night, as I was in bed, I was moved of the Lord to go next day to Kirby Hall, which was Colonel Kirby's house, about five miles off, to speak with him. When I came thither I found the Flemings, and sev-

* Truro.

eral others of the gentry (so called) of the country, who were come to take their leave of Colonel Kirby, he being then about to go up to London to the Parliament. I was taken into the parlour amongst them; but Colonel Kirby was not then within, being gone out a little way. They said little to me, nor I much to them.

After a little while Colonel Kirby came in, and I told him I came to visit him (understanding he was desirous to see me) to know what he had to say to me, and whether he had anything against me.

He said, before all the company, " As I am a gentleman, I have nothing against you." " But," said he, " Mistress Fell must not keep great meetings at her house, for they meet contrary to the Act."

I told him that that Act did not take hold on us, but on such as " met to plot and contrive, and to raise insurrections against the King "; whereas we were no such people: for he knew that they that met at Margaret Fell's were his neighbours, and a peaceable people.

After many words had passed, he shook me by the hand, and said again that he had nothing against me; and others of them said I was a deserving man. So we parted, and I returned to Swarthmore.

Shortly after, when Colonel Kirby was gone to London, there was a private meeting of the justices and deputy-lieutenants at Houlker Hall, where Justice Preston lived, where they granted a warrant to apprehend me. I heard over night both of their meeting and of the warrant, and could have gone out of their reach if I would, for I had not appointed any

meeting at that time, and I had cleared myself of the
north, and the Lord's power was over all. But I considered that there being a noise of a plot in the north,
if I should go away they might fall upon Friends;
but if I gave myself up to be taken, it might prevent
them, and Friends should escape the better. So I
gave myself up to be taken, and prepared for their
coming.

Next day an officer came with his sword and pistols to take me. I told him I knew his errand before,
and had given myself to be taken; for if I would have
escaped their imprisonment I could have been forty
miles off before he came; but I was an innocent man,
and so it mattered not what they could do to me. He
asked me how I heard of it, seeing the order was
made privately in a parlour. I said it was no matter
for that; it was sufficient that I heard it.

I asked him to let me see his order, whereupon he
laid his hand on his sword, and said I must go with
him before the lieutenant to answer such questions as
they should propound to me. I told him it was but
civil and reasonable for him to let me see his order;
but he would not. Then said I, " I am ready."

So I went along with him, and Margaret Fell accompanied us to Houlker Hall. When we came
thither there was one Rawlinson, a justice, and one
called Sir George Middleton, and many more that I
did not know, besides old Justice Preston, who lived
there.

They brought Thomas Atkinson, a Friend, of Cart-
mel, as a witness against me for some words which he
had told to one Knipe, who had informed them,

which words were that I said I had written against
the plotters and had knocked them down. These
words they could not make much of, for I told them
I had heard of a plot, and had written against it.

Old Preston asked me whether I had an hand in
that script. I asked him what he meant. He said,
" in the Battledore?" I answered, " Yes."

Then he asked me whether I understood languages.
I said, " Sufficient for myself," and that I knew no
law that was transgressed by it. I told them also
that to understand outward languages was no matter
of salvation, for the many tongues began but at the
confusion of Babel; and if I did understand anything
of them, I judged and knocked them down again for
any matter of salvation that was in them.

Thereupon he turned away, and said, " George Fox
knocks down all the languages; come," said he, " we
will examine you of higher matters."

Then said George Middleton, " You deny God, and
the Church, and the faith."

I replied, " Nay, I own God and the true Church,
and the true faith. But what Church dost thou
own?" said I (for I understood he was a Papist).

Then he turned again and said, " You are a rebel
and a traitor."

I asked him to whom he spoke, or whom did he call
rebel. He was so full of envy that for a while he
could·not speak, but at last he said, " I spoke it to
you."

With that I struck my hand on the table, and told
him, " I have suffered more than twenty such as
thou; more than any that is here; for I have been cast

into Derby dungeon for six months together, and
have suffered much because I would not take up arms
against this King before Worcester fight. I was sent
up a prisoner out of my own country by Colonel
Hacker to Oliver Cromwell, as a plotter to bring in
King Charles in the year 1654. I have nothing but
love and good-will to the King, and desire the eternal good and welfare of him and all his subjects."

"Did you ever hear the like?" said Middleton.
"Nay," said I. "Ye may hear it again if ye will.
For ye talk of the King, a company of you, but where
were ye in Oliver's days, and what did ye do then for
him? But I have more love to the King for his
eternal good and welfare than any of you have."

Then they asked me whether I had heard of the
plot. I said, "Yes, I have heard of it."

They asked me how I had heard of it, and whom
I knew in it. I told them I had heard of it through
the high-sheriff of Yorkshire, who had told Dr. Hodg-
son that there was a plot in the north. That was the
way I had heard of it; but I had never heard of any
such thing in the south, nor till I came into the north.
As for knowing any in the plot, I was as a child in
that, for I knew none of them.

Then said they, "Why would you write against it
if you did not know some that were in it?"

I said, "My reason was, because you are so forward to crush the innocent and guilty together;
therefore I wrote against it to clear the Truth* and to
stop all forward, foolish spirits from running into

* "Truth" is used here and often in Friends' writings for the
CAUSE which Friends represented.

such things. I sent copies of it into Westmoreland, Cumberland, Durham, and Yorkshire, and to you here. I sent another copy of it to the King and his council, and it is likely it may be in print by this time."

One of them said, " This man hath great power! "

I said, " Yes, I have power to write against plotters."

Then said one of them, " You are against the laws of the land."

I answered, " Nay, for I and my Friends direct all people to the Spirit of God in them, to mortify the deeds of the flesh. This brings them into well-doing, and away from that which the magistrate's sword is against, which eases the magistrates, who are for the punishment of evil-doers. So people being turned to the Spirit of God, which brings them to mortify the deeds of the flesh; this brings them from under the occasion of the magistrate's sword; and this must needs be one with magistracy, and one with the law, which was added because of transgression, and is for the praise of them that do well. In this we establish the law, are an ease to the magistrates, and are not against, but stand for all good government."

Then George Middleton cried, " Bring the book, and put the oaths of allegiance and supremacy to him."

Now he himself being a Papist, I asked him whether he, who was a swearer, had taken the oath of supremacy. As for us, we could not swear at all, because Christ and the Apostle had forbidden it.

Some of them would not have had the oath put to

me, but would have set me at liberty. The rest would not agree to it, for this was their last snare, and they had no other way to get me into prison, as all other things had been cleared to them. This was like the Papists' sacrament of the altar, by which they ensnared the martyrs.[3]

So they tendered me the oath, which I could not take; whereupon they were about to make my mittimus to send me to Lancaster jail; but considering of it, they only engaged me to appear at the sessions, and for that time dismissed me.

I went back with Margaret Fell to Swarthmore, and soon after Colonel West, who was at that time a justice of the peace, came to see me. He told us that he had acquainted some of the rest of the justices that he would come and see Margaret Fell and me; "but it may be," said he, "some of you will take offence at it." I asked him, what he thought they would do with me at the sessions? He said they would tender the oath to me again.

Whilst I was at Swarthmore, William Kirby came into Swarthmore meeting, and brought the constables with him. I was sitting with Friends in the meeting, and he said to me, "How now, Mr. Fox! you have a fine company here." "Yes," said I, "we meet to wait upon the Lord."

So he began to take the names of Friends, and those that did not readily tell him their names he

---

[3] Most of the Quakers who suffered in prison during the reign of Charles were imprisoned for refusing to take the oath.

committed to the constables' hands, and sent some to
prison. The constables were unwilling to take them
without a warrant, whereupon he threatened to set
them by the heels; but the constable told him that
he could keep them in his presence, but after he was
gone he could not keep them without a warrant.

The sessions coming on, I went to Lancaster, and
appeared according to my engagement. There was
upon the bench Justice Fleming, who had bid five
pounds in Westmoreland to any man that would apprehend me, for he was a justice both in Westmoreland and Lancashire. There were also Justice Spen-
cer, Colonel West and old Justice Rawlinson, the
lawyer, who gave the charge, and was very sharp
against Truth and Friends; but the Lord's power
stopped them.

The session was large, the concourse of people
great, and way being made for me, I came up to the
bar, and stood with my hat on, they looking earnestly
upon me and I upon them for a pretty space.

Proclamation being made for all to keep silence
upon pain of imprisonment, and all being quiet, I
said twice, " Peace be among you."

The chairman asked if I knew where I was. I said,
" Yes, I do; but it may be," said I, " my hat offends
you. That's a low thing; that's not the honour that
I give to magistrates, for the true honour is from
above; which," said I, " I have received, and I hope
it is not the hat which ye look upon to be the
honour."

The chairman said they looked for the hat, too,
and asked wherein I showed my respect to magis-

trates if I did not put off my hat. I replied, "In coming when they called me." Then they bade one take off my hat.

After this it was some time before they spoke to me, and I felt the power of the Lord to arise. After some pause old Justice Rawlinson, the chairman, asked me if I knew of the plot. I told him I had heard of it in Yorkshire by a Friend, who had it from the high-sheriff. They asked me whether I had declared it to the magistrates. I said, " I sent papers abroad against plots and plotters, and also to you, as soon as I came into the country, to take all jealousies out of your minds concerning me and my friends; for it is our principle to declare against such things."

They asked me if I knew not of an Act against meeting. I said I knew there was an Act that took hold of such as met to the terrifying of the King's subjects, were enemies to the King, and held dangerous principles; but I hoped they did not look upon us to be such men, for our meetings were not to terrify the King's subjects, neither are we enemies to him or any man.

Then they tendered me the oaths of allegiance and supremacy. I told them I could not take any oath at all, because Christ and His Apostle had forbidden it; and they had sufficient experience of swearers, first one way, then another; but I had never taken any oath in my life.

Then Rawlinson asked me whether I held it was unlawful to swear. This question he put on purpose to **ensnare me; for** by an Act that was made those were liable to banishment or a great fine that should say it was unlawful to swear. But I, seeing the snare, avoided it, and told him that " in the time of the law amongst the Jews, before Christ came, the law commanded them to swear; but Christ, who doth fulfil the law in His gospel-time, commands not to swear at all; and the apostle James forbids swearing, even to them that were Jews, and had the law of God."

After much discourse, they called for the jailer, and committed me to prison.

I had about me the paper which I had written as a testimony against plots, which I desired they would read, or suffer to be read, in open court; but they would not. So, being committed for refusing to swear, I bade them and all the people take notice that I suffered for the doctrine of Christ, and for my obedience to His command.

Afterwards I understood that the justices said they had private instructions from Colonel Kirby to prosecute me, notwithstanding his fair carriage and seeming kindness to me before, when he declared before many of them that he had nothing against me.

Several other Friends were committed to prison, some for meeting to worship God, and some for not swearing; so that the prison was very full. Many of them being poor men, that had nothing to maintain their families by but their labour, which now they were taken from, the wives of several went to the justices who had committed their husbands, and told them that if they kept their husbands in jail for nothing but the truth of Christ, and for good con-

science' sake, they would bring their children to them
to be maintained.

A mighty power of the Lord rose in Friends, and
gave them great boldness, so that they spoke much
to the justices. Friends also that were prisoners
wrote to the justices, laying the weight of their sufferings upon them, and showing them both their injustice and want of compassion towards their poor
neighbours, whom they knew to be honest, conscien-
tious, peaceable people, that in tenderness of conscience could not take any oath; yet they sent them to
prison for refusing to take the oath of allegiance.

Several who were imprisoned on that account were
known to be men that had served the King in his
wars, and had hazarded their lives in the field in his
cause, and had suffered great hardships, with the loss
of much blood, for him, and had always stood faithful
to him from first to last, and had never received any
pay for their service. To be thus requited for all
their faithful services and sufferings, and that by
them that pretended to be the King's friends, was
hard, unkind, and ungrateful dealing.

At length the justices, being continually attended
with complaints of grievances, released some of the
Friends, but kept divers of them still in prison.

I was kept till the assize, and Judge Turner and
Judge Twisden coming that circuit, I was brought
before Judge Twisden, the 14th of the month called
March, the latter end of the year 1663.

When I was brought to the bar, I said, " Peace be
amongst you all." The Judge looked upon me, and
said, " What! do you come into the court with your

hat on!" Upon which words, the jailer taking it off, I said, "The hat is not the honour that comes from God."

Then said the Judge to me, "Will you take the oath of allegiance, George Fox?" I said, "I never took any oath in my life, nor any covenant or engagement." "Well," said he, "will you swear or no?" I answered, "I am a Christian, and Christ commands me not to swear; so does the apostle James; and whether I should obey God or man, do thou judge."

"I ask you again," said he, "whether you will swear or no." I answered again, "I am neither Turk, Jew, nor heathen, but a Christian, and should show forth Christianity."

I asked him if he did not know that Christians in the primitive times, under the ten persecutions, and some also of the martyrs in Queen Mary's days, refused swearing, because Christ and the apostle had forbidden it. I told him also that they had had experience enough, how many had first sworn for the King and then against him. "But as for me," I said, "I have never taken an oath in my life. My allegiance doth not lie in swearing, but in truth and faithfulness, for I honour all men, much more the King. But Christ, who is the Great Prophet, the King of kings, the Saviour and Judge of the whole world, saith I must not swear. Now, must I obey Christ or thee? For it is because of tenderness of conscience, and in obedience to the command of Christ, that I do not swear and we have the word of a King for tender consciences."

Then I asked the Judge if he did own the King. "Yes," said he, "I do own the King."

"Why, then," said I, "dost thou not observe his declaration from Breda, and his promises made since he came into England, that no man should be called in question for matters of religion so long as he lived peaceably? If thou ownest the King," said I, "why dost thou call me in question, and put me upon taking an oath, which is a matter of religion; seeing that neither thou nor any one else can charge me with unpeaceable living?"

Upon this he was moved, and, looking angrily at me, said, "Sirrah, will you swear?"

I told him I was none of his Sirrahs; I was a Christian; and for him, an old man and a judge, to sit there and give nicknames to prisoners did not become either his grey hairs or his office."

"Well," said he, "I am a Christian, too."

"Then do Christian works," said I.

"Sirrah!" said he, "thou thinkest to frighten me with thy words." Then, catching himself, and looking aside, he said, "Hark! I am using the word sirrah again;" and so checked himself.

I said, "I spoke to thee in love; for that language did not become thee, a judge. Thou oughtest to instruct a prisoner in the law, if he were ignorant and out of the way."

"And I speak in love to thee, too," said he.

"But," said I, "love gives no nicknames."

Then he roused himself up, and said, "I will not be afraid of thee, George Fox; thou speakest so loud thy voice drowns mine and the court's; I must call for three or four criers to drown thy voice; thou hast good lungs."

"I am a prisoner here," said I, "for the Lord Jesus Christ's sake; for His sake do I suffer; for Him do I stand this day. If my voice were five times louder, I should lift it up and sound it for Christ's sake. I stand this day before your judgment-seat in obedience to Christ, who commands not to swear; before whose judgment-seat you must all be brought and must give an account."

"Well," said the Judge, "George Fox, say whether thou wilt take the oath, yea or nay?"

I replied, "I say, as I said before, judge thou whether I ought to obey God or man. If I could take any oath at all I should take this. I do not deny some oaths only, or on some occasions, but all oaths, according to Christ's doctrine, who hath commanded His followers not to swear at all. Now if thou, or any of you, or your ministers or priests here, will prove that ever Christ or His apostles, after they had forbidden all swearing, commanded Christians to swear, then I will swear."

I saw several priests there, but not one of them offered to speak.

"Then," said the Judge, "I am a servant to the King, and the King sent me not to dispute with you, but to put the laws in execution; therefore tender him the oath of allegiance."

"If thou love the King," said I, "why dost thou break his word, and not keep his declarations and speeches, wherein he promised liberty to tender consciences? I am a man of a tender conscience, and, in obedience to Christ's command, I cannot swear."

"Then you will not swear," said the Judge; "take him away, jailer."

I said, "It is for Christ's sake that I cannot swear, and for obedience to His command I suffer; and so the Lord forgive you all."

So the jailer took me away; but I felt that the mighty power of the Lord was over them all.

The sixteenth day of the same month I was again brought before Judge Twisden. He was somewhat offended at my hat; but it being the last morning of the assize before he was to leave town, and not many people there, he made the less of it.

He asked me whether I would "traverse, stand mute, or submit." But he spoke so fast that it was hard to know what he said. However, I told him I desired I might have liberty to traverse the indictment, and try it.

Then said he, "Take him away; I will have nothing to do with him; take him away."

I said, "Well, live in the fear of God, and do justice."

"Why," said he, "have I not done you justice?"

I replied, "That which thou hast done has been against the command of Christ."

So I was taken to the jail again, and kept prisoner till the next assizes.

Some time before this assize Margaret Fell was sent prisoner to Lancaster jail by Fleming, Kirby, and Preston, justices; and at the assize the oath was tendered to her also, and she was again committed to prison.

In the Sixth month,[4] the assizes were again held at Lancaster, and the same judges, Twisden and Turner, again came that circuit. But Judge Turner then sat on the crown bench, and so I was brought before him. Before I was called to the bar I was put among the murderers and felons for about two hours, the people, the justices and also the Judge gazing upon me.

After they had tried several others, they called me to the bar, and empanelled a jury. Then the Judge

---

[4] This would be August of our calendar. Again the pen was busy during these weeks in jail, and many epistles and documents were written. A Baptist preacher, named Wiggan, who had been a great opponent of Fox, was brought into straits over the oath which he finally took. The episode furnishes this interesting entry:

" This Wiggan was poor, and while he was prisoner at Lancaster he sent into the country, and got money gathered for relief of the poor people of God in prison; and many people gave freely, thinking it had been for us, when indeed it was for himself. But when we heard of it, we laid it upon him, and wrote into the country, that Friends might let the people know the truth of the matter, that it was not our manner to have collections made for us, and that those collections were only for Wiggan and another, a drunken preacher of his society, who was so drunk, that once he lost his breeches."

asked the justices whether they had tendered me the
oath at the sessions. They said that they had. Then
he said, " Give them the book, that they may swear
they tendered him the oath at the sessions." They
said they had. Then he said, " Give them the book,
that they may swear they tendered him the oath according to the indictment."

Some of the justices refused to be sworn; but the
Judge said he would have it done, to take away all occasion of exception. When the jury were sworn, and
the justices had sworn that they had tendered me the
oath according to the indictment, the Judge asked me
whether I had not refused the oath at the last assizes.
I said, " I never took an oath in my life, and Christ,
the Saviour and Judge of the world, said, ' Swear not
at all.' "

The Judge seemed not to take notice of my answer, but asked me whether or not I had refused to
take the oath at the last assizes.

I said, " The words that I then spoke to them were,
that if they could prove, either judge, justices, priest,
or teacher, that after Christ and the Apostle had forbidden swearing, they commanded that Christians
should swear, I would swear."

The Judge said he was not at that time to dispute
whether it was lawful to swear, but to inquire
whether I had refused to take the oath.

I told him, " Those things mentioned in the oath,
as plotting against the King, and owning the Pope's,
or any other foreign power, I utterly deny."

" Well," said he, " you say well in that, but did
you refuse to take the oath? What say you?"

" What wouldst thou have me to say?" said I; " I have told thee before what I did say."

Then he asked me if I would have these men to swear that I had taken the oath. I asked him if he would have those men to swear that I had refused the oath, at which the court burst into laughter.

I was grieved to see so much lightness in a court, where such solemn matters are handled, and thereupon asked them, " Is this court a play-house? Where is gravity and sobriety," said I; " this behaviour doth not become you."

Then the clerk read the indictment, and I told the Judge I had something to speak to it; for I had informed myself of the errors that were in it. He told me he would hear afterwards any reasons that I could allege why he should not give judgment.

Then I spoke to the jury, and told them that they could not bring me in guilty according to that indictment, for the indictment was wrong laid, and had many gross errors in it.

The Judge said that I must not speak to the jury, but he would speak to them; and he told them I had refused to take the oath at the last assizes; " and," said he, " I can tender the oath to any man now, and præmunire him for not taking it; " and he said they must bring me in guilty, seeing I refused to take the oath.

Then said I, " What do ye do with a form? Ye may throw away your form then." And I told the jury it lay upon their consciences, as they would answer it to the Lord God before His judgment-seat.

Then the judge spoke again to the jury, and I called to him to " do me justice."

The jury brought me in guilty. Thereupon I told them that both the justices and they had forsworn themselves, and therefore they had small cause to laugh, as they did a little before.

Oh, the envy, rage, and malice that appeared against me, and the lightness! But the Lord confounded them, and they were wonderfully stopped. So they set me aside, and called up Margaret Fell, who had much good service among them; and then the court broke up near the second hour.

In the afternoon we were brought in again to have sentence passed upon us. Margaret Fell desired that sentence might be deferred until the next morning. I desired nothing but law and justice at his hands, for the thieves had mercy; only I requested the Judge to send some to see my prison, which was so bad they would put no creature they had in it; and I told him that Colonel Kirby, who was then on the bench, had said I should be locked up, and no flesh alive should come to me. The Judge shook his head, and said that when the sentence was given he would leave me to the favor of the jailer.

Most of the gentry of the country were gathered together, expecting to hear the sentence; and the noise amongst the people was that I should be transported. But they were all crossed at that time; for the sentence was deferred until the next morning, and I was taken to prison again.

Upon my complaining of the badness of my prison,

some of the justices, with Colonel Kirby, went up to see it. When they came they hardly durst go in, the floor was so bad and dangerous, and the place so open to wind and rain. Some that came up said, "Surely it is a Jakes-house." When Colonel Kirby saw it, and heard what others said of it, he excused the matter as well as he could, saying that I should be removed ere long to some more convenient place.

Next day, towards the eleventh hour, we were called again to hear the sentence; and Margaret Fell, being called first to the bar, she had counsel to plead, who found many errors in her indictment. Thereupon, after the Judge had acknowledged them, she was set by.

Then the Judge asked what they could say to mine. I was not willing to let any man plead for me, but desired to speak to it myself; and indeed, though Margaret had some that pleaded for her, yet she spoke as much herself as she would. But before I came to the bar I was moved in my spirit to pray that God would confound their wickedness and envy, set His truth over all, and exalt His seed. The Lord heard, and answered, and did confound them in their proceedings against me. And, though they had most envy against me, yet the most gross errors were found in my indictment.

I having put by others from pleading for me, the Judge asked me what I had to say why he should not pass sentence upon me. I told him I was no lawyer; but I had much to say, if he would but have patience to hear. At that he laughed, and others laughed also,

and said, " Come, what have you to say ? He can say
nothing." " Yes," said I, " I have much to say; have
but the patience to hear me."

I asked him whether the oath was to be tendered
to the King's subjects, or to the subjects of foreign
princes. He said, " To the subjects of this realm."
" Then," said I, " look into the indictment; ye may
see that ye have left out the word ' subject '; so not
having named me in the indictment as a subject, ye
cannot præmunire me for not taking an oath."

Then they looked over the statute and the indictment, and saw it was as I said; and the Judge confessed it was an error.

I told him I had something else to stop his judgment, and desired him to look what day the indictment said the oath was tendered to me at the sessions
there. They looked, and said it was the eleventh day
of January. " What day of the week was the sessions held on ? " said I. " On a Tuesday," said they.
" Then," said I, " look in your almanacs, and see
whether there was any sessions held at Lancaster on
the eleventh day of January, so called."

So they looked, and found that the eleventh day
was the day called Monday, and that the sessions was
on the day called Tuesday, which was the twelfth day
of that month.

" Look now," said I, " ye have indicted me for refusing the oath in the quarter-séssions held at Lancaster on the eleventh day of January last, and the
justices have sworn that they tendered me the oath
in open sessions here that day, and the jury upon

their oaths have found me guilty thereupon; and yet
ye see there was no session held in Lancaster that
day."

Then the Judge, to cover the matter, asked
whether the sessions did not begin on the eleventh
day. But some in the court answered, " No; the session held but one day, and that was the twelfth."
Then the Judge said this was a great mistake and an
error.

Some of the justices were in a great rage at this,
stamped, and said, " Who hath done this? Somebody
hath done this on purpose; " and a great heat was
amongst them.

Then said I, " Are not the justices here, that have
sworn to this indictment, forsworn men in the face
of the country? But this is not all," said I. " I have
more yet to offer why sentence should not be given
against me." I asked, " In what year of the King
was the last assize here holden, which was in the
month called March last? " The Judge said it was in
the sixteenth year of the King. " But," said I, " the
indictment says it was in the fifteenth year." They
looked, and found it so. This also was acknowledged
to be another error.

Then they were all in a fret again, and could not
tell what to say; for the Judge had sworn the officers
of the court that the oath was tendered to me at the
assize mentioned in the indictment. " Now," said I,
" is not the court here forsworn also, who have sworn
that the oath was tendered to me at the assize holden
here in the fifteenth year of the King, when it was

in his sixteenth year, and so they have sworn a year false?"

The Judge bade them look whether Margaret Fell's indictment was so or no. They looked, and found it was not so.

I told the Judge I had more yet to offer to stop sentence; and asked him whether all the oath ought to be put into the indictment or no. "Yes," said he, "it ought to be all put in."

"Then," said I, "compare the indictment with the oath, and there thou mayest see these words: viz., 'or by any authority derived, or pretended to be derived from him or his see,' which is a principal part of the oath, left out of the indictment; and in another place the words, 'heirs and successors,' are left out."

The Judge acknowledged these also to be great errors.

"But," said I, "I have something further to allege."

"Nay," said the Judge, "I have enough; you need say no more."

"If," said I, "thou hast enough, I desire nothing but law and justice at thy hands; for I don't look for mercy."

"You must have justice," said he, "and you shall have law."

Then I asked, "Am I at liberty, and free from all that ever hath been done against me in this matter?"

"Yes," said the Judge, "you are free from all that hath been done against you. But then," starting up in a rage, he said, "I can put the oath to any man here, and I will tender you the oath again."

I told him he had had examples enough yesterday of swearing and false swearing, both in the justices and in the jury; for I saw before mine eyes that both justices and jury had forsworn themselves.

The Judge asked me if I would take the oath. I bade him do me justice for my false imprisonment all this while; for what had I been imprisoned so long for? and I told him I ought to be set at liberty.

"You are at liberty," said he, "but I will put the oath to you again."

Then I turned me about and said, "All people, take notice; this is a snare; for I ought to be set free from the jailer and from this court."

But the Judge cried, "Give him the book;" and the sheriff and the justices cried, "Give him the book."

Then the power of darkness rose up in them like a mountain, and a clerk lifted up a book to me. I stood still and said, "If it be a Bible, give it me into my hand."

"Yes, yes," said the Judge and justices, "give it him into his hand." So I took it and looked into it, and said, "I see it is a Bible; I am glad of it."

Now he had caused the jury to be called, and they stood by; for, after they had brought in their former verdict, he would not dismiss them, though they desired it; but told them he could not dismiss them yet, for he should have business for them, and therefore they must attend and be ready when they were called.

When he said so I felt his intent, that if I were

freed, he would come on again. So I looked him in the face, and the witness of God started up in him, and made him blush when he looked at me again, for he saw that I saw him.

Nevertheless, hardening himself, he caused the oath to be read to me, the jury standing by; and when it was read, he asked me whether I would take the oath or not.

Then said I, " Ye have given me a book here to kiss and to swear on, and this book which ye have given me to kiss says, ' Kiss the Son '; and the Son says in this book, ' Swear not at all '; and so says also the apostle James. Now, I say as the book says, and yet ye imprison me; why do ye not imprison the book for saying so? How comes it that the book (which bids me not swear) is at liberty amongst you, and yet ye imprison me for doing as the book bids me?"

As I was speaking this to them, and held up the Bible open in my hand, to show them the place in the book where Christ forbids swearing, they plucked the book out of my hand again; and the Judge said, " Nay, but we will imprison George Fox." Yet this got abroad over all the country as a by-word, that " they gave me a book to swear on that commanded me ' not to swear at all '; and that the Bible was at liberty, and I in prison for doing as the Bible said."

Now, when the Judge still urged me to swear, I told him I had never taken oath, covenant, or engagement in my life, but my yea or nay was more binding to me than an oath was to many others; for had they not had experience how little men regarded an oath; and how they had sworn one way and then another; and how the justices and court had forsworn themselves now? I told him I was a man of a tender conscience, and if they had any sense of a tender conscience they would consider that it was in obedience to Christ's command that I could not swear. " But," said I, " if any of you can convince me that after Christ and the apostle had commanded not to swear, they altered that command and commanded Christians to swear, then ye shall see I will swear."

There being many priests by, I said, " If ye cannot do it, let your priests stand up and do it." But not one of the priests made any answer.

" Oh," said the Judge, " all the world cannot convince you."

" No," said I, " how is it likely the world should convince me; for ' the whole world lies in wickedness'; but bring out your spiritual men, as ye call them, to convince me."

Then both the sheriff and the Judge said, " The angel swore in the Revelations." I replied, " When God bringeth His first-begotten Son into the world, He saith, ' Let all the angels of God worship Him'; and He saith, ' Swear not at all.' "

" Nay," said the Judge, " I will not dispute."

Then I spoke to the jury, telling them it was for Christ's sake that I could not swear, and therefore I warned them not to act contrary to the witness of God in their consciences, for before His judgment-seat they must all be brought. And I told them that as for plots and persecution for religion and Popery,

I do deny them in my heart; for I am a Christian, and shall show forth Christianity amongst you this day. It is for Christ's doctrine I stand." More words I had both with the Judge and jury before the jailer took me away.

In the afternoon I was brought up again, and put among the thieves some time, where I stood with my hat on till the jailer took it off. Then the jury having found this new indictment against me for not taking the oath, I was called to the bar; and the Judge asked me what I would say for myself. I bade them read the indictment, for I would not answer to that which I did not hear. The clerk read it, and as he read the Judge said " Take heed it be not false again "; but he read it in such a manner that I could hardly understand what he read.

When he had done the Judge asked me what I said to the indictment. I told him that hearing but once so large a writing read, and at such a distance that I could not distinctly hear all the parts of it, I could not well tell what to say to it; but if he would let me have a copy, and give me time to consider it, I would answer it.

This put them to a little stand; but after a while the Judge asked me, " What time would you have ? "

I said, " Until the next assize."

" But," said he, " what plea will you now make ? Are you guilty or not guilty ? "

I said, " I am not guilty at all of obstinately and wilfully refusing to swear; and as for those things mentioned in the oath, as jesuitical plots and foreign powers, I utterly deny them in my heart; and if I could take any oath, I should take that; but I never took any oath in my life."

The Judge said, " You speak well; but the King is sworn, the Parliament is sworn, I am sworn, the justices are sworn, and the law is preserved by oaths."

I told him that they had had sufficient experience of men's swearing, and he had seen how the justices and jury had sworn falsely the other day; and if he had read in the " Book of Martyrs " how many of the martyrs had refused to swear, both within the time of the ten persecutions and in Bishop Bonner's days, he might see that to deny swearing in obedience to Christ's command was no new thing.

He said he wished the laws were otherwise.

I said, " Our Yea is yea, and our Nay is nay; and if we transgress our yea and our nay, let us suffer as they do, or should do, that swear falsely." This, I told him, we had offered to the King; and the King said it was reasonable.

After some further discourse they committed me to prison again, there to lie until the next assize; and Colonel Kirby gave order to the jailer to keep me close, " and suffer no flesh alive to come at me," for I was not fit, he said, " to be discoursed with by men." I was put into a tower where the smoke of the other prisoners came up so thick it stood as dew upon the walls, and sometimes it was so thick that I could hardly see the candle when it burned; and I being locked under three locks, the under-jailer, when the smoke was great, would hardly be persuaded to come up to unlock one of the uppermost doors for fear of the smoke, so that I was almost smothered.

Besides, it rained in upon my bed, and many times, when I went to stop out the rain in the cold winter-season, my shirt was as wet as muck with the rain that came in upon me while I was labouring to stop it out. And the place being high and open to the wind, sometimes as fast as I stopped it the wind blew it out again.

In this manner I lay all that long, cold winter till the next assize, in which time I was so starved, and so frozen with cold and wet with the rain that my body was greatly swelled and my limbs much benumbed.

The assize began the sixteenth of the month called March, 1664-5. The same Judges, Twisden and Turner, coming that circuit again, Judge Twisden sat this time on the crown-bench, and before him I was brought.

I had informed myself of the errors in this indictment also; for, though at the assize before Judge Turner said to the officers in court, " Pray, see that all the oath be in the indictment, and that the word ' subject ' be in, and that the day of the month and year of the King be put in right; for it is a shame that so many errors should be seen and found in the face of the country; " yet many errors, and those great ones, were in this indictment, as well as in the former. Surely the hand of the Lord was in it, to confound their mischievous work against me, and to blind them therein; insomuch that, although, after the indictment was drawn at the former assize, the

Judge examined it himself, and tried it with the clerks, yet the word " subject " was left out of this indictment also, the day of the month was put in wrong, and several material words of the oath were left out; yet they went on confidently against me, thinking all was safe and well.

When I was brought to the bar, and the jury called over to be sworn, the clerk asked me, first, whether I had any objection to make to any of the jury. I told him I knew none of them. Then, having sworn the jury, they swore three of the officers of the court to prove that the oath was tendered to me at the last assizes, according to the indictment.

" Come, come," said the Judge, " it was not done in a corner." Then he asked me what I had to say to it; or whether I had taken the oath at the last assize.

I told him what I had formerly said to them, as it now came to my remembrance.

Thereupon the Judge said, " I will not dispute with you but in point of law."

" Then," said I, " I have something to speak to the jury concerning the indictment."

He told me I must not speak to the jury; but if I had anything to say, I must speak to him.

I asked him whether the oath was to be tendered to the King's subjects only, or to the subjects of foreign princes.

He replied, " To the subjects of this realm."

" Then," said I, " look in the indictment, and thou mayest see the word ' subject ' is left out of this indictment also. Therefore, seeing the oath is not to

be tendered to any but the subjects of this realm, and
ye have not put me in as a subject, the court is to
take no notice of this indictment."

I had no sooner spoken thus than the Judge cried,
" Take him away, jailer, take him away." So I was
presently hurried away.

The jailer and people expected that I should be
called for again; but I was never brought to the
court any more, though I had many other great errors to assign in the indictment.

After I was gone, the Judge asked the jury if they
were agreed. They said, " Yes," and found for the
King against me, as I was told. But I was never
called to hear sentence given, nor was any given
against me that I could hear of.

I understood that when they had looked more nar-
rowly into the indictment they saw it was not good;
and the Judge having sworn the officers of the court
that the oath was tendered me at the assize before,
such a day, as was set forth in the indictment, and
that being the wrong day, I should have proved the
officers of the court forsworn men again, had the
Judge suffered me to plead to the indictment, which
was thought to be the reason he hurried me away so
soon.

The Judge had passed sentence of præmunire
upon Margaret Fell before I was brought in; and it
seems that when I was hurried away they recorded
me as a præmunired person,[5] though I was never

---

[5] " A præmunired person " is one who has incurred
the penalty of being put out of the protection of the

brought to hear the sentence, or knew of it, which was very illegal. For they should not only have had me present to hear the sentence given, but should also have asked me first what I could say why sentence should not be given against me. But they knew I had so much to say that they could not give sentence if they heard it.

While I was prisoner in Lancaster Castle there was a great noise and talk of the Turk's overspreading Christendom, and great fears entered many. But one day, as I was walking in my prison chamber, I saw the Lord's power turn against him, and that he was turning back again. And I declared to some what the Lord had let me see, when there were such fears of his overrunning Christendom; and within a month after, the news came that they had given him a defeat.

Another time, as I was walking in my chamber, with my eye to the Lord, I saw the angel of the Lord with a glittering drawn sword stretched southward, as though the court had been all on fire. Not long after the wars broke out with Holland, the sickness broke forth, and afterwards the fire of London; so the Lord's sword was drawn indeed.

By reason of my long and close imprisonment in so bad a place I was become very weak in body; but the Lord's power was over all, supported me through all, and enabled me to do service for Him, and for

---

crown, of having his lands, goods and chattels forfeited to the crown and of remaining in prison during the sovereign's pleasure.

His truth and people, as the place would admit. For, while I was in Lancaster prison, I answered several books, as the Mass, the Common-Prayer, the Directory and the Church-Faith,[6] which are the four chief religions that are got up since the apostles' days.

---

[6] These " four chief religions which have been got up since the apostles' days " are respectively the Roman Catholic, the Episcopalian, Presbyterian and Independent, i. e., Congregational.

CHAPTER XVI.

𝔄 𝔜𝔢𝔞𝔯 𝔦𝔫 𝔖𝔠𝔞𝔯𝔟𝔬𝔯𝔬𝔲𝔤𝔥 ℭ𝔞𝔰𝔱𝔩𝔢.

1665-1666.

After the assize, Colonel Kirby and other justices were very uneasy with my being at Lancaster; for I had galled them sore at my trials there, and they laboured much to get me removed thence to some remote place. Colonel Kirby sometimes threatened that I should be sent beyond sea.

About six weeks after the assizes they got an order from the King and council to remove me from Lancaster; and with it they brought a letter from the Earl of Anglesey, wherein it was written that if those things with which I was charged were found true against me, I deserved no clemency nor mercy; yet the greatest matter they had against me was because I could not disobey the command of Christ, and swear.

When they had prepared for my removal, the under-sheriff and the head-sheriff's man, with some bailiffs, fetched me out of the castle, when I was so weak with lying in that cold, wet, and smoky prison, that I could hardly go or stand. They led me into the jailer's house, where were William Kirby and several others, and they called for wine to give me. I told them I would have none of their wine. Then they cried, "Bring out the horses."

I desired them first to show me their order, or a

copy of it, if they intended to remove me; but they would show me none but their swords. I told them there was no sentence passed upon me, nor was I præmunired, that I knew of; and therefore I was not made the King's prisoner, but was the sheriff's; for they and all the country knew that I was not fully heard at the last assize, nor suffered to show the errors in the indictment, which were sufficient to quash it, though they had kept me from one assize to another to the end they might try me. But they all knew there was no sentence of præmunire passed upon me; therefore I, not being the King's prisoner, but the sheriff's, did desire to see their order.

Instead of showing me their order, they haled me out, and lifted me upon one of the sheriff's horses.

When I was on horseback in the street the townspeople being gathered to gaze upon me, I told the officers I had received neither Christianity, civility, nor humanity from them.

They hurried me away about fourteen miles to Bentham, though I was so weak that I was hardly able to sit on horseback, and my clothes smelt so of smoke they were loathsome to myself. The wicked jailer, one Hunter, a young fellow, would come behind and give the horse a lash with his whip, and make him skip and leap; so that I, being weak, had much ado to sit on him; then he would come and look me in the face and say, "How do you, Mr. Fox?" I told him it was not civil in him to do so. The Lord cut him off soon after.

When we were come to Bentham, in Yorkshire, there met us many troopers and a marshal; and many of the gentry of the country were come in, and abundance of people to take a view of me. I being very weak and weary, desired them to let me lie down on a bed, which the soldiers permitted; for those that brought me thither gave their order to the marshal, and he set a guard of his soldiers upon me.

When they had stayed awhile they pressed horses, raised the bailiff of the hundred, the constables, and others, and bore me to Giggleswick that night; but exceeding weak I was. There, with their clog shoes, they raised the constables, who sat drinking all the night in the room by me, so that I could not get much rest.

The next day we came to a market-town, where several Friends came to see me. Robert Widders and divers Friends came to me upon the road.

The next night I asked the soldiers whither they intended to carry me, and whither I was to be sent. Some of them said, "Beyond sea"; others said, "To Tynemouth Castle." A great fear there was amongst them lest some one should rescue me out of their hands; but that fear was needless.

Next night we came to York, where the marshal put me into a great chamber, where most part of two troops came to see me. One of these troopers, an envious man, hearing that I was præmunired, asked me what estate I had, and whether it was copyhold or free land. I took no notice of his question, but was moved to declare the Word of life to the soldiers, and many of them were very loving.

At night the Lord Frecheville (so called), who commanded these horse, came to me, and was very civil and loving. I gave him an account of my imprisonment, and declared many things to him relating to Truth.

They kept me at York two days, and then the marshal and four or five soldiers were sent to convey me to Scarborough Castle. These were very civil men, and they carried themselves civilly and lovingly to me. On the way we baited at Malton, and they permitted Friends to come and visit me.

When we were come to Scarborough, they took me to an inn, and gave notice to the governor, who sent six soldiers to be my guard that night. Next day they conducted me into the castle, put me into a room, and set a sentry on me. As I was very weak, and subject to fainting, they sometimes let me go out into the air with the sentry.

They soon removed me out of this room, and put me into an open one, where the rain came in, and which was exceedingly thick with smoke, which was very offensive to me.[1]

One day the Governor, Sir John Crossland, came to see me, and brought with him Sir Francis Cobb. I desired the Governor to go into my room, and see

---

[1] Scarborough Castle is so nearly demolished that it is now impossible to locate the rooms in which Fox was confined. The room in which he was finally quartered was on the extreme seaside of the castle and has been entirely destroyed. This year of fearful imprisonment following the severe confinement at Lancaster nearly broke down his wonderful constitution. He never again had the same physical vigor and power. Note his healthy humor in the little joke with the Papist.

what a place I had. I had got a little fire made in it, and it was so filled with smoke that when they were in they could hardly find their way out again; and he being a Papist, I told him that this was his Purgatory which they had put me into. I was forced to lay out about fifty shillings to stop out the rain, and keep the room from smoking so much.

When I had been at that charge, and made it tolerable, they removed me into a worse room, where I had neither chimney nor fire-hearth. This being towards the sea-side and lying much open, the wind drove in the rain forcibly so that the water came over my bed, and ran so about the room that I was fain to skim it up with a platter. When my clothes were wet, I had no fire to dry them; so that my body was benumbed with cold, and my fingers swelled so that one was grown as big as two.

Though I was at some charge in this room also, I could not keep out the wind and rain. Besides, they would suffer few Friends to come to me, and many times not any; no, not so much as to bring me a little food; but I was forced for the first quarter to hire one of another society to bring me necessaries. Sometimes the soldiers would take it from her, and she would scuffle with them for it.

Afterwards I hired a soldier to fetch me water and bread, and something to make a fire of, when I was in a room where a fire could be made. Commonly a threepenny loaf served me three weeks, and sometimes longer, and most of my drink was water with wormwood steeped or bruised in it.

One time the weather was very sharp, and I had

taken great cold, I got a little elecampane beer. I
heard one of the soldiers say to the other that they
would play me a trick: they would send me up to the
deputy-governor, and in the meantime drink my
strong beer; and so they did. When I came back one
of the soldiers came to me in a jeer, and asked me for
some strong beer. I told him they had played their
pretty trick; and so I took no further notice of it.

But inasmuch as they kept me so very strait, not
giving liberty for Friends to come to me, I spoke to
the keepers of the Castle to this effect: " I did not
know till I was removed from Lancaster Castle, and
brought prisoner to this Castle of Scarborough, that I
was convicted of a præmunire; for the Judge did not
give sentence upon me at the assizes in open court.
But seeing I am now a prisoner here, if I may not
have my liberty, let my friends and acquaintances
have their liberty to come and visit me, as Paul's
friends had among the Romans, who were not Christians, but heathen. For Paul's friends had their
liberty; all that would, might come to him, and he
had his liberty to preach to them in his hired house.
But I cannot have liberty to go into the town, nor
for my friends to come to me here. So you that go
under the name of Christians, are worse in this
respect than those heathen were."

But though they would not let Friends come to
me, they would often bring others, either to gaze
upon me, or to contend with me. One time a great
company of Papists came to discourse with me. They
affirmed that the Pope was infallible, and had stood
infallible ever since Peter's time. But I showed

them the contrary by history; for one of the bishops of Rome (Marcellinus by name), denied the faith and sacrificed to idols; therefore he was not infallible. I told them that if they were in the infallible Spirit they need not have jails, swords, and staves, racks and tortures, fires and faggots, whips and gallows, to hold up their religion, and to destroy men's lives about it; for if they were in the infallible Spirit they would preserve men's lives, and use none but spiritual weapons about religion.

Another Papist who came to discourse with me said, " All the patriarchs were in hell from the creation till Christ came. When Christ suffered He went into hell, and the devil said to Him, What comest thou hither for? to break open our strongholds? And Christ said, To fetch them all out. So Christ was three days and three nights in hell to bring them out."

I told him that that was false; for Christ said to the thief, " This day thou shalt be with me in paradise "; and Enoch and Elijah were translated into heaven; and Abraham was in heaven, for the Scripture saith that Lazarus was in his bosom; and Moses and Elias were with Christ upon the Mount, before He suffered.

These instances stopped the Papist's mouth, and put him to a stand.

Another time came Dr. Witty, who was esteemed a great doctor in physic, with Lord Falconbridge, the governor of Tinmouth Castle, and several knights.

I being called to them, Witty undertook to discourse with me, and asked me what I was in prison

for. I told him, " Because I would not disobey the
command of Christ, and swear." He said I ought to
swear my allegiance to the King.

He being a great Presbyterian, I asked him
whether he had not sworn against the King and
House of Lords, and taken the Scotch covenant?
And had he not since sworn to the King? What,
then, was his swearing good for? But my allegiance,
I told him, did not consist in swearing, but in truth
and faithfulness.

After some further discourse I was taken away to
my prison again; and afterwards Dr. Witty boasted
in the town amongst his patients that he had conquered me. When I heard of it, I told the Governor it was a small boast in him to say he had conquered a bondman. I desired to bid him come to me
again when he came to the Castle.

He came again awhile after, with about sixteen or
seventeen great persons, and then he ran himself
worse on ground than before. For he affirmed before
them all that Christ had not enlightened every man
that cometh into the world; and that the grace of
God, that bringeth salvation, had not appeared unto
all men, and that Christ had not died for all men.

I asked him what sort of men those were whom
Christ had not enlightened? and whom His grace had
not appeared to? and whom He had not died for?

He said, " Christ did not die for adulterers, and
idolaters, and wicked men."

I asked him whether adulterers and wicked men
were not sinners.

He said, " Yes."

" Did not Christ die for sinners ? " said I.   " Did He not come to call sinners to repentance ? "

" Yes," said he.

" Then," said I, " thou hast stopped thy own mouth."

So I proved that the grace of God had appeared unto all men, though some turned from it into wantonness, and walked despitefully against it; and that Christ had enlightened all men, though some hated the light.

Several of the people confessed it was true; but he went away in a great rage, and came no more to me.

Another time the Governor brought a priest; but his mouth was soon stopped.

Not long after he brought two or three Parliament-men, who asked me whether I did own ministers and bishops.

I told them, " Yes, such as Christ sent; such as had freely received and would freely give; such as were qualified, and were in the same power and Spirit the apostles were in. But such bishops and teachers as yours, that will go no farther than a great benefice, I do not own; for they are not like the apostles. Christ saith to his ministers, ' Go ye into all nations, and preach the gospel '; but ye Parliament-men, who keep your priests and bishops in such great fat benefices, have spoiled them all. For do ye think they will go into all nations to preach; or any farther than a great fat benefice ? Judge yourselves whether they will or not."

There came another time the widow of old Lord Fairfax, and with her a great company, one of whom was a priest. I was moved to declare the truth to them, and the priest asked me why we said Thou and Thee to people, for he counted us but fools and idiots for speaking so.

I asked him whether they that translated the Scriptures and that made the grammar and accidence, were fools and idiots, seeing they translated the Scriptures so, and made the grammar so, Thou to one, and You to more than one, and left it so to us. If they were fools and idiots, why had not he, and such as he, that looked upon themselves as wise men, and that could not bear Thou and Thee to a singular, altered the grammar, accidence, and Bible, and put the plural instead of the singular. But if they were wise men that had so translated the Bible, and had made the grammar and accidence so, I wished him to consider whether they were not fools and idiots themselves, that did not speak as their grammars and Bibles taught them; but were offended with us, and called us fools and idiots for speaking so.

Thus the priest's mouth was stopped, and many of the company acknowledged the Truth, and were pretty loving and tender. Some of them would have given me money, but I would not receive it.

After this came Dr. Cradock, with three priests more, and the Governor and his lady (so called), and another that was called a lady, and a great company with them.

Dr. Cradock asked me what I was in prison for. I told him, " For obeying the command of Christ and the apostle, in not swearing." But if he, I said, being both a doctor and a justice of peace, could convince

me that after Christ and the Apostle had forbidden
swearing, they commanded Christians to swear, then
I would swear. "Here is the Bible," I told him,
"thou mayest, if thou canst, show me any such command."

He said, "It is written, 'Ye shall swear in truth
and righteousness.'"

"Ay," said I, "it was so written in Jeremiah's
time; but that was many ages before Christ commanded not to swear at all; but where is it written
so, since Christ forbade all swearing? I could bring
as many instances out of the Old Testament for
swearing as thou, and it may be more; but of what
force are they to prove swearing lawful in the New
Testament, since Christ and the Apostle forbade it?
Besides," said I, "in that text where it is written, Ye
shall swear, what 'ye' was this? Was it 'Ye Gentiles,' or 'Ye Jews'?"

To this he would not answer. But one of the
priests that were with him answered, "It was to the
Jews that this was spoken." Then Dr. Cradock confessed it was so.

"Very well," said I, "but where did God ever
give a command to the Gentiles to swear? For thou
knowest that we are Gentiles by nature."

"Indeed," said he, "in the gospel times everything was to be established out of the mouths of two
or three witnesses; but there was to be no swearing
then."

"Why, then," said I, "dost thou force oaths upon
Christians, contrary to thy own knowledge, in the
gospel-times? And why dost thou excommunicate my

friends?" for he had excommunicated abundance both in Yorkshire and Lancashire.

He said, " For not coming to church." " Why," said I, " ye left us above twenty years ago, when we were but young lads and lasses, to the Presbyterians, Independents, and Baptists, many of whom made spoil of our goods, and persecuted us because we would not follow them. We, being but young, knew little then of your principles. If ye had intended to keep your principles alive, that we might have known them, ye should either not have fled from us as ye did, or ye should have sent us your epistles, collects, homilies, and evening songs; for Paul wrote epistles to the saints, though he was in prison. But they and we might have turned Turks or Jews for any collects, homilies, or epistles we had from you all this while. And now thou hast excommunicated us, both young and old, and so have others of you done; that is, ye have put us out of your church before ye have got us into it, and before ye have brought us to know your principles. Is not this madness in you, to put us out before we were brought in? Indeed, if ye had brought us into your church, and when we had been in, if we had done some bad thing, that had been something like a ground for excommunication or putting out again. But," said I, " What dost thou call the Church?"

" Why," said he, " that which you call the steeple-house."

Then I asked him whether Christ shed His blood for the steeple-house, and purchased and sanctified the steeple-house with His blood. And seeing the

Church is Christ's bride and wife, and that He is the Head of the Church, dost thou think the steeple-house is Christ's wife and bride, and that He is the head of that old house, or of His people?"

"No," said he, "Christ is the head of His people, and they are the Church."

"But," said I, "You have given the title Church to an old house, which belongs to the people; and you have taught them to believe so."

I asked him also why he persecuted Friends for not paying tithes; whether God ever commanded the Gentiles to pay tithes; whether Christ had not ended tithes when He ended the Levitical priesthood that took tithes; whether Christ, when He sent His disciples to preach, had not commanded them to preach freely as He had given them freely; and whether all the ministers of Christ are not bound to observe this command of Christ.

He said he would not dispute that.

Neither did I find he was willing to stay on that subject; for he presently turned to another matter, and said, "You marry, but I know not how."

I replied, "It may be so; but why dost thou not come and see?"

Then he threatened that he would use his power against us, as he had done. I bade him take heed; for he was an old man. I asked him also where he read, from Genesis to Revelation, that ever any priest did marry any. I wished him to show me some instance thereof, if he would have us come to them to be married; "for," said I, "thou hast excommunicated one of my friends two years after he

was dead, about his marriage. And why dost thou
not excommunicate Isaac, and Jacob, and Boaz, and
Ruth? for we do not read that they were ever married by the priests; but they took one another in the
assemblies of the righteous, in the presence of God
and His people; and so do we. So that we have all
the holy men and women that the Scripture speaks
of in this practice, on our side."

Much discourse we had, but when he found he
could get no advantage over me, he went away with
his company.

With such people I was much exercised while I
was there; for most that came to the Castle would
desire to speak with me, and great disputes I had
with them. But as to Friends, I was as a man buried
alive; for though many came far to see me, yet few
were suffered to come to me; and when any Friend
came into the Castle about business, if he looked
towards me they would rage at him.

At last the Governor came under some trouble
himself; for he having sent a privateer to sea, they
took some ships that were not enemies' ships, but
their friends'; whereupon he was brought into
trouble; after which he grew somewhat more
friendly to me. For before I had a marshal set over
me, on purpose to get money out of me; but I was
not free to give him a farthing; and when they found
they could get nothing off me, he was taken away
again.

The officers often threatened that I should be
hanged over the wall. Nay, the deputy-governor
told me once that the King, knowing I had great in-

terest in the people, had sent me thither, that if there should be any stirring in the nation, they should hang me over the wall to keep the people down.

There being, a while after, a marriage at a Baptist's house, upon which occasion a great many of them were met together, they talked much then of hanging me. But I told them that if that was what they desired, and it was permitted them, I was ready, for I never feared death nor sufferings in my life; but I was known to be an innocent, peaceable man, free from all stirrings and plottings, and one that sought the good of all men.

Afterwards, the Governor growing kinder, I spoke to him when he was going to London to the Parliament, and desired him to speak to Esquire Marsh, Sir Francis Cobb, and some others; and let them know how long I had lain in prison, and for what; and he did so. When he came down again, he told me that Esquire Marsh said he would go a hundred miles barefoot for my liberty, he knew me so well; and several others, he said, spoke well of me. From which time the Governor was very loving to me.

There were, amongst the prisoners, two very bad men, that often sat drinking with the officers and soldiers; and because I would not sit and drink with them too, it made them the worse against me. One time when these two prisoners were drunk, one of them (whose name was William Wilkinson, a Presbyterian, who had been a captain), came to me and challenged me to fight with him.

Seeing what condition he was in, I got out of his way; and next morning, when he was more sober, showed him how unmanly it was in him to challenge a man to fight, whose principles, he knew, it was not to strike, but if he was stricken on one ear to turn the other. I told him, if he had a mind to fight, he should have challenged some soldiers that could have answered him in his own way.

But, however, seeing he had challenged me, I was now come to answer him with my hands in my pockets; and (reaching my head towards him), "Here," said I, "here is my hair, here are my cheeks, here is my back."

With this he skipped away from me and went into another room; at which the soldiers fell a-laughing; and one of the officers said, " You are a happy man that can bear such things." Thus he was conquered without a blow. After awhile he took the oath, gave bond, got out of prison; and not long after the Lord cut him off.[2]

There were great imprisonments in this and the former years, while I was prisoner at Lancaster and Scarborough. At London many Friends were crowded into Newgate, and other prisons, where the sickness was,[3] and many died in prison. Many also

---

[2] George Fox had a very keen eye for " judgments " which came upon persons who abused him or hindered his work. It accords completely with the ideas of the time, and is one of the things which he had not transcended.

[3] This " sickness " was the London " plague " of 1665.

were banished, and several sent on ship-board by the King's order.

Some masters of ships would not carry them, but set them on shore again; yet some were sent to Barbadoes, Jamaica, and Nevis, and the Lord blessed them there. One master of a ship was very wicked and cruel to Friends that were put on board his ship; for he kept them down under decks, though the sickness was amongst them; so that many died of it. But the Lord visited him for his wickedness; for he lost most of his seamen by the plague, and lay several months crossed with contrary winds, though other ships went on and made their voyages.

At last he came before Plymouth, where the Governor and magistrates would not suffer him nor any of his men to come ashore, though he wanted necessaries for his voyage; but Thomas Lower, Arthur Cotton, John Light, and other Friends, went to the ship's side, and carried necessaries for the Friends that were prisoners on board.

The master, being thus crossed and vexed, cursed them that put him upon this freight, and said he hoped he should not go far before he was taken. And the vessel was but a little while gone out of sight of Plymouth before she was taken by a Dutch man-of-war, and carried into Holland.

When they came into Holland, the States sent the banished Friends back to England, with a letter of passport, and a certificate that they had not made an escape, but were sent back by them.

In time the Lord's power wrought over this storm,

and many of our persecutors were confounded and put to shame.

After I had lain prisoner above a year in Scarborough Castle, I sent a letter to the King, in which I gave him an account of my imprisonment, and the bad usage I had received in prison; and also that I was informed no man could deliver me but him. After this, John Whitehead being at London, and having acquaintance also with Esquire Marsh, he went to visit him, and spoke to him about me; and he undertook, if John Whitehead would get the state of my case drawn up, to deliver it to the master of requests, Sir John Birkenhead, who would endeavor to get a release for me.

So John Whitehead and Ellis Hookes drew up a relation of my imprisonment and sufferings, and carried it to Marsh; and he went with it to the master of requests, who procured an order from the King for my release. The substance of the order was that "the King, being certainly informed that I was a man principled against plotting and fighting, and had been ready at all times to discover plots, rather than to make any, etc., therefore his royal pleasure was that I should be discharged from my imprisonment," etc.

As soon as this order was obtained, John Whitehead came to Scarborough with it, and delivered it to the Governor; who, upon receipt thereof, gathered the officers together, and, without requiring bond or sureties for my peaceable living, being satisfied that I was a man of a peaceable life, he discharged me freely, and gave me the following passport:

" Permit the bearer hereof, George Fox, late a prisoner here, and now discharged by His Majesty's order, quietly to pass about his lawful occasions, without any molestation.   Given under my hand at Scarborough Castle, this first day of September, 1666.

" JORDAN CROSLANDS,
" Governor of Scarborough Castle."

After I was released, I would have made the Governor a present for the civility and kindness he had of late shown me; but he would not receive anything; saying that whatever good he could do for me and my friends he would do it, and never do them any hurt.   And afterwards, if at any time the mayor of the town sent to him for soldiers to break up Friends' meetings, if he sent any down he would privately give them a charge not to meddle.   He continued loving to his dying day.

The officers also and the soldiers were mightily changed, and became very respectful to me, and when they had occasion to speak of me they would say, " He is as stiff as a tree, and as pure as a bell; for we could never bow him."

[Here is an interesting entry in the Journal in the year 1669: "I then visited friends at Whitby and Scarborough.   When I was at Scarborough, the governor, hearing I was come, sent to invite me to his house, saying, ' Surely, you would not be so unkind as not to come and see me and my wife.' After the meeting I went to visit him, and he received me very courteously and lovingly."]

The very next day after my release, the fire broke
out in London, and the report of it came quickly
down into the country.   Then I saw the Lord God
was true and just in His Word, which he had shown
me before in Lancaster jail, when I saw the angel
of the Lord with a glittering sword drawn southward, as before expressed.

The people of London were forewarned of this
fire; yet few laid to heart, or believed it; but rather
grew more wicked, and higher in pride.   For a Friend
was moved to come out of Huntingdonshire a little
before the fire, to scatter his money, and turn his
horse loose on the streets, to untie the knees of his
trousers, let his stockings fall down, and to un-
button his doublet, and tell the people that so should
they run up and down, scattering their money and
their goods, half undressed, like mad people, as he
was sign to them; [4] and so they did, when the city
was burning.

Thus hath the Lord exercised His prophets and
servants by His power, shown them signs of His
judgments, and sent them to forewarn the people;
but, instead of repenting, they have beaten and

---

[4] This was Thomas Ibbett, of Huntingdonshire.   He
went distracted a little later, and, standing in Cheap-
side during the great fire, he tried to stop its progress
with his outspread arms, so that he nearly perished in
the flames.   For a remarkable prophecy of the " great
plague " see " Writings of George Fox the Younger,"
1662, pages 219-221.

cruelly entreated some, and some they have imprisoned, both in the former power's days* and since.

But the Lord is just, and happy are they that obey His word.

Some have been moved to go naked in their streets, in the other power's days and since, as signs of their nakedness; and have declared amongst them that God would strip them of their hypocritical professions, and make them as bare and naked as they were. But instead of considering it, they have many times whipped, or otherwise abused them, and sometimes imprisoned them.

Others have been moved to go in sackcloth, and to denounce the woes and vengeance of God against the pride and haughtiness of the people; but few regarded it. And in the other power's days, the wicked, envious, and professing priests, put up several petitions both to Oliver and Richard, called Protectors, and to the Parliaments, judges and justices, against us, full of lies, vilifying words and slanders; but we got copies of them, and, through the Lord's assistance, answered them all, and cleared the Lord's truth and ourselves of them.

But oh! the body of darkness that rose against the Truth in them that made lies their refuge! But the Lord swept them away; and in and with His power, truth, light, and life, hedged his lambs about, and preserved them as on eagles' wings. Therefore we all had, and have, great encouragement to trust the Lord, who, we saw by His power and Spirit, overturned and brought to naught all the confederacies

* The days of Oliver Cromwell.

and counsels that were hatched in darkness against His Truth and people; and by the same truth gave His people dominion, that therein they might serve Him.

Indeed, I could not but take notice how the hand of the Lord turned against the persecutors who had been the cause of my imprisonment, or had been abusive or cruel to me in it. The officer that fetched me to Holker-Hall wasted his estate, and soon after fled into Ireland. Most of the justices that were upon the bench at the sessions when I was sent to prison, died in a while after; as old Thomas Preston, Rawlinson, Porter, and Matthew West, of Borwick. Justice Fleming's wife died, and left him thirteen or fourteen motherless children. Colonel Kirby never prospered after. The chief constable, Richard Dodgson, died soon after, and Mount, the petty constable, and the wife of the other petty constable, John Ashburnham, who railed at me in her house, died soon after. William Knipe, the witness they brought against me, died soon after also. Hunter, the jailer of Lancaster, who was very wicked to me while I was his prisoner, was cut off in his young days; and the under-sheriff that carried me from Lancaster prison towards Scarborough, lived not long after. And Joblin, the jailer of Durham, who was prisoner with me in Scarborough Castle, and had often incensed the Governor and soldiers against me, though he got out of prison, yet the Lord cut him off in his wickedness soon after.

When I came into that country again, most of those that dwelt in Lancashire were dead, and others

ruined in their estates; so that, though I did not seek
revenge upon them for their actings against me contrary to the law, yet the Lord had executed His judgments upon many of them.

CHAPTER XVII.

At the Work of Organizing.

1667–1670.

I then visited Friends till I came to York, where we had a large meeting. After this I went to visit Justice Robinson, an ancient justice of the peace, who had been very loving to me and Friends from the beginning.

There was a priest with him, who told me that it was said of us, that we loved none but ourselves. I told him that we loved all mankind, as they were God's creation, and as they were children of Adam and Eve by generation; and that we loved the brotherhood in the Holy Ghost.

This stopped him. After some other discourse we parted friendly, and passed away.

About this time I wrote a book, entitled, "Fear God, and Honour the King"; in which I showed that none could rightly fear God and honour the King but they that departed from sin and evil. This book greatly affected the soldiers, and most people.

Then I was moved of the Lord to recommend the setting up of five monthly meetings of men and women in the city of London (besides the women's meetings and the quarterly meetings), to take care of God's glory, and to admonish and exhort such as walked disorderly or carelessly, and not according to Truth. For whereas Friends had had only quarterly meetings, now Truth was spread, and Friends were grown more numerous, I was moved to recommend the setting up of monthly meetings throughout the nation.[1] And the Lord opened to me what I must do, and how the men's and women's monthly and quarterly meetings should be ordered and established in this and in other nations; and that I should write to those where I did not come, to do the same.

After things were well settled at London, and the Lord's Truth, power, seed, and life reigned and shone over all in the city, I went into Essex.

[Throughout the counties where he had preached, he now went, setting up monthly meetings, i.e., local meetings for transacting the business of the Church, and for ordering and overseeing the moral and spiritual life of the membership. We shall not follow his movements in detail, but it may here be noted that the world's records show few instances of more striking energy, and fidelity to a divine mission, than do the

---

[1] In nothing did Fox show his originality and insight more clearly than in his work of organizing the Society which his ministry had drawn together. During his long imprisonment many internal difficulties had arisen, which showed that the Society was too loosely organized for a permanent work in the world. The rest of his life—twenty-four years—was mainly devoted to this work of perfecting the system of meetings and government, though his *ministry* meantime in no way slackened. The first system of Discipline, printed in 1669 by his opponents, under the title, " Canons and Institutions," was drawn up soon after the release from Scarborough Castle.

entries of these twenty-four years. Here is one glimpse of him as he is traveling through " the frost and snow," during the winter of 1667.]

I was so exceeding weak, I was hardly able to get on or off my horse's back; but my spirit being earnestly engaged in the work the Lord had concerned me in and sent me forth about, I travelled on therein, notwithstanding the weakness of my body, having confidence in the Lord, that He would carry me through, as He did by His power.

We came into Cheshire, where we had several blessed meetings, and a general men's meeting; wherein all the monthly meetings for that county were settled, according to the gospel order, in and by the power of God.

After the meeting I passed away. But when the justices heard of it, they were very much troubled that they had not come and broken it up, and taken me; but the Lord prevented them.

Then, returning towards London by Waltham, I advised the setting up of a school there for teaching boys; and also a woman's school to be opened at Shacklewell, for instructing girls and young maidens in whatsoever things were civil and useful in the creation.[2]

Thus were the men's monthly meetings settled

---

[2] On this broad principle, of *teaching everything useful and civil in creation*, the work of Friends began in the cause of education. The subsequent history of their educational work is notable.

through the nation. [1668.] The quarterly meetings were generally settled before.

I wrote also into Ireland by faithful Friends, and into Scotland, Holland, Barbadoes, and several parts of America, advising Friends to settle their men's monthly meetings in those countries. For they had had their general quarterly meetings before; but now that Truth was increased amongst them, it was needful that they should settle those men's monthly meetings in the power and Spirit of God, that first convinced them.

Since these meetings have been settled, and all the faithful in the power of God, who are heirs of the gospel, have met together in the power of God, which is their authority, to perform service to the Lord, many mouths have been opened in thanksgiving and praise, and many have blessed the Lord God, that ever He sent me forth in this service. For now all coming to have a concern and care for God's honour and glory, and His name, which they profess, be not blasphemed; and to see that all who profess the Truth walk in the Truth, in righteousness and in holiness, as becomes the house of God, and that all order their conversation aright, that they may see the salvation of God; they may all see and know, possess and partake of, the government of Christ, of the increase of which there is to be no end.

Thus the Lord's everlasting renown and praise are set up in the heart of every one that is faithful; so that we can say the gospel order established amongst us is not of man, nor by man, but of and by Jesus Christ, in and through the Holy Ghost.

This order of the gospel, which is not of man nor by man, but from Christ, the heavenly man, is above all the orders of men in the fall, whether Jews, Gentiles, or apostate Christians, and will remain when they are gone. For the power of God, which is the everlasting gospel, was before the devil was, and will be and remain forever. And as the everlasting gospel was preached in the apostles' days to all nations, that all nations might, through the divine power which brings life and immortality to light, come into the order of it, so now the everlasting gospel is to be, and is, preached again, as John the divine foresaw it should be, to all nations, kindreds, tongues, and people.

Now * was I moved of the Lord to go over into Ireland, to visit the Seed of God in that nation. There went with me Robert Lodge, James Lancaster, Thomas Briggs, and John Stubbs.

We waited near Liverpool for shipping and wind. After waiting some days, we sent James Lancaster to take passage, which he did, and brought word the ship was ready, and would take us in at Black Rock. We went thither on foot; and it being some distance, and the weather very hot, I was much spent with walking.

When we arrived, the ship was not there; so we were obliged to go to the town and take shipping. When we were on board, I said to the rest of my company, " Come, ye will triumph in the Lord, for we shall have fair wind and weather."

* 1669.

Many passengers in the ship were sick, but not one of our company. The captain and many of the passengers were very loving; and we being at sea on the first day of the week, I was moved to declare Truth among them; whereupon the captain said to the passengers, "Here are things that you never heard in your lives."

When we came before Dublin, we took boat and went ashore; and the earth and air smelt, methought, of the corruption of the nation, so that it yielded another smell to me than England did; which I imputed to the Popish massacres that had been committed, and the blood that had been spilt in it, from which a foulness ascended.

We passed through among the officers of the custom four times, yet they did not search us; for they perceived what we were: some of them were so envious they did not care to look at us.

We did not soon find Friends; but went to an inn, and sent out to inquire for some. These, when they came to us, were exceedingly glad of our coming, and received us with great joy.

We stayed there the weekly meeting, which was a large one, and the power and life of God appeared greatly in it. Afterwards we passed to a province meeting, which lasted two days, there being one about the poor, and another meeting more general; in which a mighty power of the Lord appeared. Truth was livingly declared, and Friends were much refreshed therein.

Passing thence about four and twenty miles, we came to another place, where we had a very good, refreshing meeting; but after it some Papists that were there were angry, and raged very much. When I heard of it, I sent for one of them, who was a schoolmaster; but he would not come.

Thereupon I sent a challenge to him, with all the friars and monks, priests and Jesuits, to come forth, and " try their God and their Christ, which they had made of bread and wine," but no answer could I get from them. I told them they were worse than the priests of Baal; for Baal's priests tried their wooden god, but these durst not try their god of bread and wine; and Baal's priests and people did not eat their god as these did, and then make another.

He that was then mayor of Cork, being very envious against Truth and Friends, had many Friends in prison. Knowing I was in the country, he sent four warrants to take me; therefore Friends were desirous that I should not ride through Cork. But, being at Bandon, there appeared to me in a vision a very ugly-visaged man, of a black and dark look. My spirit struck at him in the power of God, and it seemed to me that I rode over him with my horse, and my horse set his foot on the side of his face.

When I came down in the morning, I told a friend the command of the Lord to me was to ride through Cork; but I bade him tell no man. So we took horse, many Friends being with me.

When we came near the town, Friends would have shown me a way through the back side of it; but I told them my way was through the streets. Taking Paul Morrice to guide me through the town, I rode on.

As we rode through the market-place, and by the mayor's door, he, seeing me, said, "There goes George Fox"; but he had not power to stop me. When we had passed the sentinels, and were come over the bridge, we went to a Friend's house and alighted. There the Friends told me what a rage was in the town, and how many warrants were granted to take me.

While I was sitting there I felt the evil spirit at work in the town, stirring up mischief against me; and I felt the power of the Lord strike at that evil spirit.

By-and-by some other friends coming in, told me it was over the town, and amongst the magistrates that I was in the town. I said, "Let the devil do his worst." After we had refreshed ourselves, I called for my horse, and having a Friend to guide me, we went on our way.

Great was the rage that the mayor and others of Cork were in that they had missed me, and great pains they afterwards took to catch me, having their scouts abroad upon the roads, as I understood, to observe which way I went. Scarce a public meeting I came to, but spies came to watch if I were there. The magistrates and priests sent informations one to another concerning me, describing me by my hair, hat, clothes and horse; so that when I was near an hundred miles from Cork they had an account concerning me and a description of me before I came amongst them.

One very envious magistrate, who was both a priest and a justice, got a warrant from the judge of assize to apprehend me. The warrant was to go over all his circuit, which reached near an hundred miles. Yet the Lord disappointed all their councils, defeated all their designs against me, and by His good hand of Providence preserved me out of all their snares, and gave us many sweet and blessed opportunities to visit Friends, and spread Truth through that nation.

For meetings were very large, Friends coming to them from far and near; and other people flocking in. The powerful presence of the Lord was preciously felt amongst us. Many of the world were reached, convinced, and gathered to the Truth; the Lord's flock was increased; and Friends were greatly refreshed and comforted in feeling the love of God. Oh the brokenness that was amongst them in the flowings of life! so that, in the power and Spirit of the Lord, many together broke out into singing, even with audible voices, making melody in their hearts.

After I had travelled over Ireland, and visited Friends in their meetings, as well for business as for worship, and had answered several papers and writings from monks, friars, and Protestant priests (for they were all in a rage against us, and endeavoured to stop the work of the Lord, and some Jesuits swore in our hearing that we had come to spread our principles in that nation, but should not do it), I returned to Dublin, in order to take passage for England. I stayed to the First-day's meeting there, which was very large and precious.

There being a ship ready, and the wind serving, we took our leave of Friends; parting in much tenderness and brokenness, in the sense of the heavenly

life and power manifested amongst us. Having put
our horses and necessaries on board in the morning,
we went ourselves in the afternoon, many Friends accompanying us to the ship; and divers Friends and
Friendly people followed us in boats when we were
near a league at sea, their love drawing them, though
not without danger.

A good, weighty, and true people there is in that
nation, sensible of the power of the Lord God, and
tender of His truth. Very good order they have in
their meetings; for they stand up for righteousness
and holiness, which dams up the way of wickedness.
A precious visitation they had, and there is an excellent spirit in them, worthy to be visited. Many
things more I could write of that nation, and of my
travels in it; but thus much I thought good to signify,
that the righteous may rejoice in the prosperity of
truth.

We travelled till we came to Bristol, where I met
with Margaret Fell, who was come to visit her daughter Yeomans.

I had seen from the Lord a considerable time before, that I should take Margaret Fell to be my wife.
And when I first mentioned it to her, she felt the answer of Life from God thereunto. But though the
Lord had opened this thing to me, yet I had not received a command from the Lord for the accomplishing of it then. Wherefore I let the thing rest, and
went on in the work and service of the Lord as before, according as he led me; travelling up and down
in this nation, and through Ireland.

But now being at Bristol, and finding Margaret

Fell there, it opened in me from the Lord that the thing should be accomplished. After we had discoursed the matter together, I told her, if she also was satisfied with the accomplishing of it now, she should first send for her children; which she did. When the rest of her daughters were come, I asked both them and her sons-in-law if they had anything against it, or for it; and they all severally expressed their satisfaction therein.

Then I asked Margaret if she had fulfilled and performed her husband's will to her children. She replied, "The children know that." Whereupon I asked them whether, if their mother married, they would lose by it. And I asked Margaret whether she had done anything in lieu of it, which might answer it to the children.

The children said she had answered it to them, and desired me to speak no more of it. I told them I was plain, and would have all things done plainly; for I sought not any outward advantage to myself.

So, after I had thus acquainted the children with it, our intention of marriage was laid before Friends, both privately and publicly, to their full satisfaction. Many of them gave testimony thereunto that it was of God. Afterwards, a meeting being appointed for the accomplishing thereof, in the meeting-house at Broad-Mead, in Bristol, we took each other, the Lord joining us together in honourable marriage, in the everlasting covenant and immortal Seed of life. In the sense thereof living and weighty testimonies were borne thereunto by Friends, in the movings of the heavenly power which united us.[3] Then was a certificate, relating both the proceedings and the marriage, openly read, and signed by the relations, and by most of the ancient Friends of that city, besides many others from divers parts of the nation.

We stayed about a week in Bristol, and then went together to Oldstone: where, taking leave of each other in the Lord, we parted, betaking ourselves each to our several service; Margaret returning homewards to the north, and I passing on in the work of the Lord as before. I travelled through Wiltshire, Berkshire, Oxfordshire, Buckinghamshire, and so to London, visiting Friends: in all of which counties I had many large and precious meetings.[4]

[In 1670 the so-called Conventicle Act, originally passed in 1664, was renewed with increased vigor. The Act limited religious gatherings, other than those of the Established Church, to five persons, and brought all who refused to take an oath under the penalties of the Act.]

---

[3] The "Bristol Register of Friends" shows the date of the marriage of George Fox to Margaret Fell to have been "Eighth month" 27th, 1669.

[4] During the next four years George Fox and his wife were almost continually separated from each other. About three months after their marriage Margaret Fox was thrown into Lancaster prison, where she was kept until a few weeks before her husband sailed on his memorable trip to the West Indies and the American colonies.

On the First-day after the Act came in force, I went to the meeting at Gracechurch Street, where I expected the storm was most likely to begin.

When I came there, I found the street full of people, and a guard set to keep Friends out of their meeting-house. I went to the other passage out of Lombard street, where also I found a guard; but the court was full of people, and a Friend was speaking amongst them; but he did not speak long.

When he had done, I stood up, and was moved to say, "Saul, Saul, why persecutest thou me? it is hard for thee to kick against that which pricks thee." Then I showed that it is Saul's nature that persecutes still, and that they who persecute Christ in His members now, where He is made manifest, kick against that which pricks them; that it was the birth of the flesh that persecuted the birth born of the Spirit, and that it was the nature of dogs to tear and devour the sheep; but that we suffered as sheep, that bite not again, for we were a peaceable people, and loved them that persecuted us.

After I had spoken a while to this effect, the constable came with an informer and soldiers; and as they pulled me down, I said, " Blessed are the peacemakers."

The commander put me among the soldiers, and bade them secure me, saying to me, " You are the man I looked for." They took also John Burnyeat and another Friend, and led us away, first to the Exchange, and afterwards towards Moorfields. As we went along the streets the people were very moderate; some of them laughed at the constable, and told him we would not run away.

The informer went with us unknown, till, falling into discourse with one of the company, he said it would never be a good world till all people came to the good old religion that was two hundred years ago. Whereupon I asked him, " Art thou a Papist? What! a Papist informer; for two hundred years ago there was no other religion but that of the Papists."

He saw he had ensnared himself, and was vexed at it; for as he went along the streets I spoke often to him, and manifested what he was.

When we were come to the mayor's house, and were in the courtyard, several of the people that stood about, asked me how and for what I was taken. I desired them to ask the informer, and also what his name was; but he refused to tell his name. Whereupon one of the mayor's officers, looking out at a window, told him he should tell his name before he went away; for the lord mayor would know by what authority he intruded himself with soldiers into the execution of those laws which belonged to the civil magistrate to execute, and not to the military.

After this, he was eager to be gone; and went to the porter to be let out. One of the officers called to him, saying, " Have you brought people here to inform against, and now will you go away before my lord mayor comes?" Some called to the porter not to let him out; whereupon he forcibly pulled open the door and slipped out.

No sooner was he come into the street than the people gave a shout that made the street ring again, crying out, " A Papist informer! a Papist informer! " We desired the constable and soldiers to go and rescue him out of the people's hands, fearing lest they should do him a mischief.

They went, and brought him into the mayor's entry, where they stayed a while; but when he went out again, the people received him with another shout. The soldiers were fain to go and rescue him once more, and they led him into a house in an alley, where they persuaded him to change his periwig, and so he got away unknown.

When the mayor came, we were brought into the room where he was, and some of his officers would have taken off our hats, perceiving which he called to them, and bade them let us alone, and not meddle with our hats; " for," said he, " they are not yet brought before me in judicature." So we stood by while he examined some Presbyterian and Baptist teachers; with whom he was somewhat sharp, and convicted them.

After he had done with them, I was brought up to the table where he sat; and then the officers took off my hat. The mayor said mildly to me, " Mr. Fox, you are an eminent man amongst those of your profession; pray, will you be instrumental to dissuade them from meeting in such great numbers? for, seeing Christ hath promised that where two or three are met in His name, He will be in the midst of them, and the King and Parliament are graciously pleased to allow four to meet together to worship God; why will not you be content to partake both of Christ's promise to two or three, and the King's indulgence to four?"[5]

I answered to this purpose: " Christ's promise was not to discourage many from meeting together in His name, but to encourage the few, that the fewest might not forbear to meet because of their fewness. But if Christ hath promised to manifest His presence in the midst of so small an assembly, where but two or three are gathered in His name, how much more would His presence abound where two or three hundred are gathered in His name?"

I wished him to consider whether this Act, if it had been in their time, would not have taken hold of Christ, with His twelve apostles and seventy disciples, who used to meet often together, and that with great numbers? However, I told him this Act did not concern us; for it was made against seditious meetings, of such as met under colour and pretence of religion "to contrive insurrections, as [the Act says] late experience had shown." But we had been sufficiently tried and proved, and always found peaceable, and therefore he would do well to put a difference between the innocent and the guilty.

He said the Act was made against meetings, and a worship not according to the liturgy.

I told him " according to " was not the very same thing; and asked him whether the liturgy was accord-

---

[5] In a very keen letter Fox told the magistrates that this act would have prevented the twelve apostles and the seventy disciples from meeting!

ing to the Scriptures, and whether we might not read Scriptures and speak Scriptures.

He said, " Yes."

I told him, " This Act takes hold only of such as meet to plot and contrive insurrections, as late experience hath shown; but they have never experienced that by us. Because thieves are sometimes on the road, must not honest men travel? And because plotters and contrivers have met to do mischief, must not an honest, peaceable people meet to do good? If we had been a people that met to plot and contrive insurrections, etc., we might have drawn ourselves into fours; for four might do more mischief in plotting than if there were four hundred, because four might speak out their minds more freely to one another than four hundred could. Therefore we, being innocent, and not the people this Act concerns, keep our meetings as we used to do. I believe thou knowest in thy conscience that we are innocent."

After some more discourse, he took our names, and the places where we lodged; and at length, as the informer was gone, he set us at liberty.

The Friends with me now asked, " Whither wilt thou go?" I told them, " To Gracechurch street meeting again, if it is not over."

When we came there, the people were generally gone; only some few stood at the gate. We went into Gerrard Roberts's. Thence I sent to know how the other meetings in the city were. I found that at some of the meeting-places Friends had been kept out; at others they had been taken; but these were set at liberty again a few days after.

A glorious time it was; for the Lord's power came over all, and His everlasting truth got renown. For in the meetings, as fast as some that were speaking were taken down, others were moved of the Lord to stand up and speak, to the admiration of the people; and the more because many Baptists and other sectaries left their public meetings, and came to see how the Quakers would stand.

As for the informer aforesaid, he was so frightened that hardly any informer dared to appear publicly in London for some time after. But the mayor, whose name was Samuel Starling, though he carried himself smoothly towards us, proved afterwards a very great persecutor of our Friends, many of whom he cast into prison, as may be seen in the trials of William Penn, William Mead, and others, at the Old Bailey this year.[6]

As I was walking down a hill,* a great weight and oppression fell upon my spirit. I got on my horse again, but the weight remained so that I was hardly able to ride.

* Near Rochester.

---

[6] This trial at the Old Bailey is reported in full in the Preface to the Works of William Penn. It is one of the most interesting episodes in his life, and, from a legal point of view, it is one of the most important jury trials of that century. William Penn had thrown in his lot with the Quakers definitely in 1666, though he had been influenced by the preaching of Thomas Loe while he was a student in Oxford University in 1659.

At length we came to Rochester, but I was much spent, being so extremely laden and burthened with the world's spirits, that my life was oppressed under them. I got with difficulty to Gravesend, and lay at an inn there; but could hardly either eat or sleep.

The next day John Rous and Alexander Parker went to London; and John Stubbs being come to me, we went over the ferry into Essex. We came to Hornchurch, where there was a meeting on First-day. After it I rode with great uneasiness to Stratford, to a Friend's house, whose name was Williams, and who had formerly been a captain. Here I lay, exceedingly weak, and at last lost both hearing and sight. Several Friends came to me from London: and I told them that I should be a sign to such as would not see, and such as would not hear the Truth.[7]

In this condition I continued some time. Several came about me; and though I could not see their persons, I felt and discerned their spirits, who were honest-hearted, and who were not. Divers Friends who practised physic came to see me, and would have given me medicines, but I was not to meddle with any; for I was sensible I had a travail to go through; and therefore desired none but solid, weighty Friends might be about me.

Under great sufferings and travails, sorrows and oppressions, I lay for several weeks, whereby I was brought so low and weak in body that few thought I

---

[7] This is another of the times in Fox's life when he underwent serious physical changes as a result of psychical disturbance.

could live. Some that were with me went away, saying they would not see me die; and it was reported both in London and in the country that I was deceased; but I felt the Lord's power inwardly supporting me.

When they that were about me had given me up to die, I spoke to them to get a coach to carry me to Gerrard Roberts's, about twelve miles off, for I found it was my place to go thither. I had now recovered a little glimmering of sight, so that I could discern the people and fields as I went, and that was all.

When I came to Gerrard's, he was very weak, and I was moved to speak to him, and encourage him. After I had stayed about three weeks there, it was with me to go to Enfield. Friends were afraid of my removing; but I told them I might safely go.

When I had taken my leave of Gerrard, and was come to Enfield, I went first to visit Amor Stoddart, who lay very weak and almost speechless. I was moved to tell him that he had been faithful as a man, and faithful to God, and that the immortal Seed of life was his crown. Many more words I was moved to speak to him, though I was then so weak I was hardly able to stand; and within a few days after, Amor died.

I went to the widow Dry's, at Enfield, where I lay all that winter, warring in spirit with the evil spirits of the world, that warred against Truth and Friends. For there were great persecutions at this time; some meeting-houses were pulled down, and many were broken up by soldiers. Sometimes a troop of horse, or a company of foot came; and some broke their

swords, carbines, muskets, and pikes, with beating
Friends; and many they wounded, so that their blood
lay in the streets.

Amongst others that were active in this cruel persecution at London, my old adversary, Colonel Kirby,
was one. With a company of foot, he went to break
up several meetings; and he would often inquire for
me at the meetings he broke up. One time as he
went over the water to Horsleydown, there happening some scuffle between some of his soldiers and
some of the watermen, he bade his men fire at them.
They did so, and killed some.

I was under great sufferings at this time, beyond
what I have words to declare. For I was brought
into the deep, and saw all the religions of the world,
and people that lived in them. And I saw the priests
that held them up; who were as a company of men-
eaters, eating up the people like bread, and gnawing
the flesh from off their bones. But as for true religion, and worship, and ministers of God, alack! I saw
there was none amongst those of the world that pretended to it.

Though it was a cruel, bloody, persecuting time,
yet the Lord's power went over all, His everlasting
Seed prevailed; and Friends were made to stand firm
and faithful in the Lord's power. Some sober people
of other professions would say, " If Friends did not
stand, the nation would run into debauchery."

Though by reason of my weakness I could not
travel amongst Friends as I had been used to do, yet
in the motion of life I sent the following lines as an
encouraging testimony to them:

" My dear Friends:

" The Seed is above all. In it walk; in which ye all have life.

" Be not amazed at the weather; for always the just suffered by the unjust, but the just had the dominion.

" All along ye may see, by faith the mountains were subdued; and the rage of the wicked, with his fiery darts, was quenched. Though the waves and storms be high, yet your faith will keep you, so as to swim above them; for they are but for a time, and the Truth is without time. Therefore keep on the mountain of holiness, ye who are led to it by the Light.

" Do not think that anything will outlast the Truth. For the Truth standeth sure; and is over that which is out of the Truth. For the good will overcome the evil; the light, darkness; the life, death; virtue, vice; and righteousness, unrighteousness. The false prophet cannot overcome the true; but the true prophet, Christ, will overcome all the false.

" So be faithful, and live in that which doth not think the time long.   G. F."

After some time it pleased the Lord to allay the heat of this violent persecution; and I felt in spirit an overcoming of the spirits of those men-eaters that had stirred it up and carried it on to that height of cruelty. I was outwardly very weak; and I plainly felt, and those Friends that were with me, and that came to visit me, took notice, that as the persecution ceased I came from under the travails and sufferings that had lain with such weight upon me; so that towards the spring I began to recover, and to walk up and down, beyond the expectation of many, who did not think I could ever have gone abroad again.

Whilst I was under this spiritual suffering the state of the New Jerusalem which comes down out of heaven was opened to me; which some carnal-minded people had looked upon to be like an outward city dropped out of the elements. I saw the beauty and glory of it, the length, the breadth, and the height thereof, all in complete proportion. I saw that all who are within the Light of Christ, and in His faith, of which He is the author; and in the Spirit, the Holy Ghost, which Christ and the holy prophets and apostles were in; and within the grace, and truth, and power of God, which are the walls of the city;—I saw that such are within the city, are members of it, and have right to eat of the Tree of Life, which yields her fruit every month, and whose leaves are for the healing of the nations.

Many things more did I see concerning the heavenly city, the New Jerusalem, which are hard to be uttered, and would be hard to be received. But, in short, this holy city is within the Light, and all that are within the Light, are within the city; the gates whereof stand open all the day (for there is no night there), that all may come in.

CHAPTER XVIII.
Two Years in America.
1671-1673.

When I received notice of my wife's being taken to prison again,[1] I sent two of her daughters to the King, and they procured his order to the sheriff of Lancashire for her discharge. But though I expected she would have been set at liberty, yet this violent storm of persecution coming suddenly on, the persecutors there found means to hold her still in prison.

But now the persecution a little ceasing, I was moved to speak to Martha Fisher, and another woman Friend, to go to the King about her liberty. They went in the faith, and in the Lord's power; and He gave them favour with the King, so that he granted a discharge under the broad seal, to clear both her and her estate, after she had been ten years a prisoner, and præmunired; the like whereof was scarce to be heard in England.

I sent down the discharge forthwith by a Friend; by whom also I wrote to her, to inform her how to get it delivered to the justices, and also to acquaint

---

[1] This was in 1669, about three months after their marriage. The sentence of *præmunire* was passed against Margaret Fell in 1663, so that for about seven (Fox says ten) years she was the King's prisoner, and her estate was in jeopardy.

her that it was upon me from the Lord to go beyond sea, to visit the plantations in America; and therefore I desired her to hasten to London, as soon as she could conveniently after she had obtained her liberty, because the ship was then fitting for the voyage.

In the meantime I got to Kingston, and stayed at John Rous's till my wife came up, and then I began to prepare for the voyage. But the yearly meeting [2] being near at hand, I tarried till that was over. Many Friends came up to it from all parts of the nation, and a very large and precious meeting it was; for the Lord's power was over all, and His glorious, everlastingly-renowned Seed of Life was exalted above all.

After this meeting was over, and I had finished my services for the Lord in England, the ship and the

---

[2] He speaks of " the yearly meeting " as though it were a well-established institution. Norman Penney has sent me an interesting extract from Barclay's " Letters of the Early Friends," which traces the development of the yearly meeting:

" There was a yearly meeting settled at Skipton in Yorkshire for all the northern and southern countries, ... and then the yearly meeting was removed to John Crooks, . . . and afterwards the yearly meeting was kept at Balley, in Yorkshire, and likewise at Skipton, in the year 1660. And from thence it was moved to London the next year, where it hath been kept ever since," p. 312 from a document said to have been by George Fox, but only since 1672 has it been held in London without intermission. The series of yearly meeting minutes commences 23d of Third month, 1671.

Friends that intended to go with me being ready, I went to Gravesend on the 12th of Sixth month,[3] my wife and several Friends accompanying me to the Downs.

We went from Wapping in a barge to the ship, which lay a little below Gravesend, and there we found the Friends that were bound for the voyage with me, who had gone down to the ship the night before. Their names were Thomas Briggs, William Edmundson, John Rous, John Stubbs, Solomon Eccles, James Lancaster, John Cartwright, Robert Widders, George Pattison, John Hull, Elizabeth Hooton, and Elizabeth Miers. The vessel was a yacht, called the *Industry;* the captain's name Thomas Forster, and the number of passengers about fifty.

I lay that night on board, but most of the Friends at Gravesend. Early next morning the passengers, and those Friends that intended to accompany us to the Downs, being come on board, we took our leave in great tenderness of those that came with us to Gravesend only, and set sail about six in the morning for the Downs.

Having a fair wind, we out-sailed all the ships that were outward-bound, and got thither by evening. Some of us went ashore that night, and lodged at Deal, where, we understood, an officer had orders from the governor to take our names in writing, which he did next morning, though we told him they had been taken at Gravesend.

---

[3] Which would be August by the unreformed calendar.

In the afternoon, the wind serving, I took leave of my wife and other Friends, and went on board. Before we could sail, there being two of the King's frigates riding in the Downs, the captain of one of them sent his press-master on board us, who took three of our seamen. This would certainly have delayed, if not wholly prevented, our voyage, had not the captain of the other frigate, being informed of the leakiness of our vessel, and the length of our voyage, in compassion and much civility, spared us two of his own men.

Before this was over, a custom-house officer came on board to peruse packets and get fees; so that we were kept from sailing till about sunset; during which delay a very considerable number of merchantmen, outward-bound, were several leagues before us.

Being clear, we set sail in the evening, and next morning overtook part of that fleet about the height of Dover. We soon reached the rest, and in a little time left them all behind; for our yacht was counted a very swift sailer. But she was very leaky, so that the seamen and some of the passengers did, for the most part, pump day and night. One day they observed that in two hours' time she sucked in sixteen inches of water in the well.

When we had been about three weeks at sea, one afternoon we spied a vessel about four leagues astern of us. Our master said it was a Sallee [4] man-of-war,

---

[4] A Moorish pirate ship, named from Sallee, a seaport of Morocco. This incident not only indicates Fox's simple faith in God, but it also is a good illustra-

that seemed to give us chase. He said, " Come, let us
go to supper, and when it grows dark we shall lose
him."   This he spoke to please and pacify the passengers, some of whom began to be very apprehensive
of the danger.   But Friends were well satisfied in
themselves, having faith in God, and no fear upon
their spirits.

When the sun was gone down, I saw out of my
cabin the ship making towards us. When it grew
dark, we altered our course to miss her; but she altered also, and gained upon us.

At night the master and others came into my
cabin, and asked me what they should do. I told
them I was no mariner; and I asked them what they
thought was best to do. They said there were but
two ways, either to outrun him, or to tack about, and
hold the same course we were going before. I told
them that if he were a thief, they might be sure he
would tack about too; and as for outrunning him, it
was to no purpose to talk of that, for they saw he
sailed faster than we. They asked me again what they
should do, " for," they said, " if the mariners had
taken Paul's counsel, they had not come to the dam-
age they did." I answered that it was a trial of faith,
and therefore the Lord was to be waited on for
counsel.

So, retiring in spirit, the Lord showed me that His
life and power were placed between us and the ship
that pursued us. I told this to the master and the

tion of the way in which he inspired confidence in
others. The captain believes in him.

rest, and that the best way was to tack about and steer our right course. I desired them also to put out all their candles but the one they steered by, and to speak to all the passengers to be still and quiet.

About eleven at night the watch called and said they were just upon us. This disquieted some of the passengers. I sat up in my cabin, and, looking through the port-hole, the moon being not quite down, I saw them very near us. I was getting up to go out of the cabin; but remembering the word of the Lord, that His life and power were placed between us and them, I lay down again.

The master and some of the seamen came again, and asked me if they might not steer such a point. I told them they might do as they would.

By this time the moon was quite down. A fresh gale arose, and the Lord hid us from them; we sailed briskly on and saw them no more.

The next day, being the first day of the week, we had a public meeting in the ship, as we usually had on that day throughout the voyage, and the Lord's presence was greatly among us. I desired the people to remember the mercies of the Lord, who had delivered them; for they might have been all in the Turks' hands by that time, had not the Lord's hand saved them.

About a week after, the master and some of the seamen endeavoured to persuade the passengers that it was not a Turkish pirate that had chased us, but a merchantman going to the Canaries. When I heard of it I asked them, " Why then did you speak so to me ? Why did you trouble the passengers ? and why

did you tack about from him and alter your course?"
I told them they should take heed of slighting the
mercies of God.

Afterwards, while we were at Barbadoes, there
came in a merchant from Sallee, and told the people
that one of the Sallee men-of-war saw a monstrous
yacht at sea, the greatest that ever he saw, and had
her in chase, and was just upon her, but that there
was a spirit in her that he could not take. This confirmed us in the belief that it was a Sallee-man we
saw make after us, and that it was the Lord that delivered us out of his hands.

The third of the Eighth month, early in the morning, we discovered the island of Barbadoes; but it
was between nine and ten at night ere we came to
anchor in Carlisle bay.

We got on shore as soon as we could, and I with
some others walked to the house of a Friend, a merchant, whose name was Richard Forstall, above a
quarter of a mile from the bridge. But being very ill
and weak, I was so tired, that I was in a manner spent
by the time I got thither. There I abode very ill
several days, and though they several times gave me
things to make me sweat, they could not effect it.
What they gave me did rather parch and dry up my
body, and made me probably worse than otherwise
I might have been.

Thus I continued about three weeks after I landed,
having much pain in my bones, joints, and whole
body, so that I could hardly get any rest; yet I was
pretty cheery, and my **spirit** kept above it all.

Neither did my illness take me off from the service of Truth; but both while I was at sea, and after I came to Barbadoes, before I was able to travel about, I gave forth several papers (having a Friend to write for me), some of which I sent by the first conveyance for England to be printed.

Soon after I came into the island, I was informed of a remarkable passage, wherein the justice of God did eminently appear. It was thus. There was a young man of Barbadoes whose name was John Drakes, a person of some note in the world's account, but a common swearer and a bad man, who, when he was in London, had a mind to marry a Friend's daughter, left by her mother very young, with a considerable portion, to the care and government of several Friends, whereof I was one. He made application to me that he might have my consent to marry this young maid.

I told him I was one of her overseers, appointed by her mother, who was a widow, to take care of her; that if her mother had intended her for a match to any man of another profession, she would have disposed her accordingly; but she committed her to us, that she might be trained up in the fear of the Lord; and therefore I should betray the trust reposed in me if I should consent that he, who was out of the fear of God, should marry her; and this I would not do.

When he saw that he could not obtain his desire, he returned to Barbadoes with great offence of mind against me, but without a just cause. Afterwards, when he heard I was coming to Barbadoes, he swore desperately, and threatened that if he could possibly procure it, he would have me burned to death when I came there. A Friend hearing of this, asked him what I had done to him that he was so violent against me. He would not answer, but said again, " I'll have him burned." Whereupon the Friend replied, " Do not march on too furiously, lest thou come too soon to thy journey's end."

About ten days after he was struck with a violent, burning fever, of which he died; by which his body was so scorched that the people said it was as black as a coal; and three days before I landed his body was laid in the dust. This was taken notice of as a sad example.

While I continued so weak that I could not go abroad to meetings, the other Friends that came over with me bestirred themselves in the Lord's work. The next day but one after we came on shore, they had a great meeting at the Bridge, and after that several meetings in different parts of the island; which alarmed the people of all sorts, so that many came to our meetings, and some of the chiefest rank. For they had got my name, understanding I was come upon the island, and expected to see me, not knowing I was unable to go abroad.

And indeed my weakness continued the longer on me, because my spirit was much pressed down at the first with the filth and dirt, and with the unrighteousness of the people, which lay as an heavy weight and load upon me. But after I had been above a month upon the island my spirit became somewhat easier; I began to recover my health and strength, and to get abroad among Friends.[5]

After I was able to go about, and had been a little amongst Friends, I went to visit the Governor, Lewis Morice, Thomas Rous, and some other Friends being with me. He received us very civilly, and treated us very kindly, making us dine with him, and keeping us the greater part of the day before he let us go away.

The same week I went to Bridgetown. There was to be a general meeting of Friends that week; and the visit I had made to the Governor, and the kind reception I had with him, being generally known to the officers, civil and military, many came to this meeting from most parts of the island, and those not of the meanest rank; several being judges or justices, colonels or captains; so that a very great meeting we had, both of Friends and others.

The Lord's blessed power was plentifully with us; and although I was somewhat straitened for time, three other Friends having spoken before me, yet the Lord opened things through me to the general and

---

[5] As George Fox was too ill to travel, the meetings for worship and for business were held at the house where he was staying. At these meetings he gave much valuable counsel. Here he first met with slavery and dealt with it. "I desired them also that they would cause their overseers to deal mildly and gently with their negroes, and not use cruelty towards them, as the manner of some hath been and is; and that after certain years of servitude, they would make them free."

great satisfaction of them that were present. Colonel Lewis Morice came to this meeting, and with him a neighbour of his, a judge in the country, whose name was Ralph Fretwell, who was very well satisfied, and received the Truth.

Paul Gwin, a jangling Baptist, came into the meeting, and asked me how I spelt Cain, and whether I had the same spirit as the apostles had. I told him, " Yes." And he bade the judge take notice of it.

I told him, " He that hath not a measure of the same Holy Ghost as the apostles had, is possessed with an unclean spirit." And then he went his way.

We had many great and precious meetings, both for worship and for the affairs of the Church; to the former of which many of other societies came. At one of these meetings Colonel Lyne, a sober person, was so well satisfied with what I declared that he said, " Now I can gainsay such as I have heard speak evil of you; who say, you do not own Christ, nor that He died; whereas I perceive you exalt Christ in all His offices beyond what I have ever heard before." [6]

---

[6] In order that it might be positively clear that he " exalted Christ in all His offices," he wrote an extended Letter to the Governor of Barbadoes. The Letter takes the form of a declaration of faith and is often referred to as an authoritative statement of the belief of Friends. It was, however, not written for that purpose, and it is not by any means a full statement of their belief. It does not even mention the principle which held the leading place in all Fox's teaching and preaching. The Letter to the Governor was written to

As I had been to visit the Governor as soon as I was well able, after I came thither, so, when I was at Thomas Rous's, the Governor came to see me, carrying himself very courteously.

Having been three months or more in Barbadoes, and having visited Friends, thoroughly settled meetings, and despatched the service for which the Lord brought me thither, I felt my spirit clear of that island, and found drawings to Jamaica. When I had communicated this to Friends, I acquainted the Governor also, and divers of his council, that I intended shortly to leave the island, and go to Jamaica. This I did that, as my coming thither was open and public, so my departure also might be. Before I left the island I wrote the following letter to my wife, that she might understand both how it was with me, and how I proceeded in my travels:—

" MY DEAR HEART,

" To whom is my love, and to all the children, in the Seed of Life that changeth not, but is over all; blessed be the Lord forever. I have undergone great sufferings in my body and spirit, beyond words; but

---

clear Friends from false charges, and it dwells solely on the points on which Fox is rumored to be unsound, or charged with dangerous teaching. The earliest " declaration of faith " of the Quakers was issued by Christopher Holder, John Copeland and Richard Doudney, from Boston prison in 1657. The earliest statement issued in England was Richard Farnsworth's " Confession and Profession of Faith in God," London, 1658.

the God of heaven be praised, His Truth is over all.
I am now well; and, if the Lord permit, within a few
days I pass from Barbadoes towards Jamaica; and I
think to stay but little there. I desire that ye may
be all kept free in the Seed of Life, out of all cum-
brances. Friends are generally well. Remember me
to Friends that inquire after me. So no more, but
my love in the Seed and Life that changeth not.

" G. F.

" Barbadoes, 6th of 11th Month, 1671."

I set sail from Barbadoes to Jamaica on the 8th
of the Eleventh month, 1671; Robert Widders, Wil-
liam Edmundson, Solomon Eccles and Elizabeth
Hooton going with me. Thomas Briggs and John
Stubbs remained in Barbadoes, with whom were
John Rous and William Bailey.

We had a quick and easy passage to Jamaica,
where we met again with our Friends James Lancaster, John Cartwright, and George Pattison, who had
been labouring there in the service of Truth; into
which we forthwith entered with them, travelling up
and down through the island, which is large; and a
brave country it is, though the people are, many of
them, debauched and wicked.

We had much service. There was a great convincement, and many received the Truth, some of
whom were people of account in the world. We had
many meetings there, which were large, and very
quiet. The people were civil to us, so that not a
mouth was opened against us. I was twice with the

Governor, and some other magistrates, who all carried themselves kindly towards me.

About a week after we landed in Jamaica, Elizabeth Hooton, a woman of great age, who had travelled much in Truth's service, and suffered much for it, departed this life. She was well the day before she died, and departed in peace, like a lamb, bearing testimony to Truth at her departure.

When we had been about seven weeks in Jamaica, had brought Friends into pretty good order, and settled several meetings amongst them, we left Solomon Eccles there; the rest of us embarked for Maryland, leaving Friends and Truth prosperous in Jamaica, the Lord's power being over all, and His blessed Seed reigning.

Before I left Jamaica I wrote another letter to my wife, as follows:

" MY DEAR HEART,

" To whom is my love, and to the children, in that which changeth not, but is over all; and to all Friends in those parts. I have been in Jamaica about five weeks. Friends here are generally well, and there is a convincement: but things would be too large to write of. Sufferings in every place attend me; but the blessed Seed is over all; the great Lord be praised, who is Lord of sea and land, and of all things therein. We intend to pass from hence about the beginning of next month, towards Maryland, if the Lord please. Dwell all of you in the Seed of God; in His Truth I rest in love to you all.　　　G. F.

" Jamaica, 23d of 12th Month, 1671."

We went on board on the 8th of First month,* 1671-2, and, having contrary winds, were a full week sailing forwards and backwards before we could get out of sight of Jamaica.

A difficult voyage this proved, and dangerous, especially in passing through the Gulf of Florida, where we met with many trials by winds and storms.

But the great God, who is Lord of the sea and land, and who rideth upon the wings of the wind, did by His power preserve us through many and great dangers, when by extreme stress of weather our vessel was many times likely to be upset, and much of her tackling broken. And indeed we were sensible that the Lord was a God at hand, and that His ear was open to the supplications of His people.

For when the winds were so strong and boisterous, and the storms and tempests so great that the sailors knew not what to do, but let the ship go which way she would, then did we pray unto the Lord, who graciously heard us, calmed the winds and the seas, gave us seasonable weather, and made us to rejoice in His salvation. Blessed and praised be the holy name of the Lord, whose power hath dominion over all, whom the winds and the seas obey.

We were between six and seven weeks in this passage from Jamaica to Maryland. Some days before we came to land, after we had entered the bay of Patuxent River, a great storm arose, which cast a boat upon us for shelter, in which were several people of account in the world. We took them in; but the boat was lost, with five hundred pounds' worth of goods

* March 8th, 1672.

in it, as they said. They continued on board several days, not having any means to get off; and we had a very good meeting with them in the ship.

But provisions grew short, for they brought none in with them; and ours, by reason of the length of our voyage, were well-nigh spent when they came to us; so that with their living with us too, we had now little or none left. Whereupon George Pattison took a boat, and ventured his life to get to shore; the hazard was so great that all but Friends concluded he would be cast away. Yet it pleased the Lord to bring him safe to land, and in a short time after the Friends of the place came to fetch us to land also, in a seasonable time, for our provisions were quite spent.

We partook also of another great deliverance in this voyage, through the good providence of the Lord, which we came to understand afterwards. For when we were determined to come from Jamaica, we had our choice of two vessels, that were both bound for the same coast. One of these was a frigate, the other a yacht. The master of the frigate, we thought, asked unreasonably for our passage, which made us agree with the master of the yacht, who offered to carry us ten shillings a-piece cheaper than the other.

We went on board the yacht, and the frigate came out together with us, intending to be consorts during the voyage. For several days we sailed together; but, with calms and contrary winds, we were soon separated. After that the frigate, losing her way, fell among the Spaniards, by whom she was taken and plundered, and the master and mate made prisoners. Afterwards, being retaken by the English, she was sent home to her owners in Virginia. When we came to understand this we saw and admired the providence of God, who preserved us out of our enemies' hands; and he that was covetous fell among the covetous.

Here we found John Burnyeat,[7] intending shortly to sail for England; but on our arrival he altered his purpose, and joined us in the Lord's service. He had appointed a general meeting for all the Friends in the province of Maryland, that he might see them together, and take his leave of them before he departed out of the country. It was so ordered by the good providence of God that we landed just in time to reach that meeting, by which means we had a very seasonable opportunity of taking the Friends of the province together.

A very large meeting this was, and it held four days, to which, besides Friends, came many other people, several of whom were of considerable quality in the world's account. There were five or six justices of the peace, the speaker of their assembly, one of their council, and others of note, who seemed well satisfied with the meeting. After the public meetings were over, the men's and women's meetings began, wherein I opened to Friends the service thereof, to their great satisfaction.

---

[7] John Burnyeat travelled extensively and did much valuable work in America. See the Journal of John Burnyeat, reprinted in Volume II. of Friends' Library.

After this we went to the Cliffs, where another general meeting was appointed. We went some of the way by land, the rest by water, and, a storm arising, our boat was run aground, in danger of being beaten to pieces, and the water came in upon us. I was in a great sweat, having come very hot out of a meeting before, and now was wet with the water besides; yet, having faith in the divine power, I was preserved from taking hurt, blessed be the Lord!

To this meeting came many who received the Truth with reverence. We had also a men's meeting and a women's meeting. Most of the backsliders came in again; and several meetings were established for taking care of the affairs of the Church.

After these two general meetings, we parted company, dividing ourselves unto several coasts, for the service of Truth. James Lancaster and John Cartwright went by sea for New England; William Edmundson and three Friends more sailed for Virginia, where things were much out of order; John Burnyeat, Robert Widders, George Pattison, and I, with several Friends of the province, went over by boat to the Eastern Shore,* and had a meeting there on the First-day.

There many people received the Truth with gladness, and Friends were greatly refreshed. A very large and heavenly meeting it was. Several persons of quality in that country were at it, two of whom were justices of the peace. It was upon me from the Lord to send to the Indian emperor and his kings to come to that meeting. The emperor came and

* Eastern shore of Chesapeake Bay.

was at the meeting. His kings, lying further off, could not reach the place in time. Yet they came soon after, with their cockarooses.[8]

I had in the evening two good opportunities with them; they heard the Word of the Lord willingly, and confessed to it. What I spoke to them I desired them to speak to their people, and to let them know that God was raising up His tabernacle of witness in their wilderness-country, and was setting up His standard and glorious ensign of righteousness. They carried themselves very courteously and lovingly, and inquired where the next meeting would be, saying that they would come to it. Yet they said they had had a great debate with their council about their coming, before they came.

The next day we began our journey by land to New England; a tedious journey through the woods and wilderness, over bogs and great rivers.

We took horse at the head of Tredhaven creek, and travelled through the woods till we came a little above the head of Miles river, by which we passed, and rode to the head of Wye river, and so to the head of Chester river, where, making a fire, we took up our lodging in the woods. Next morning we travelled the woods till we came to Sassafras river, which we went over in canoes, causing our horses to swim beside us.

Then we rode to Bohemia river, where, in like manner swimming our horses, we ourselves went over in canoes. We rested a little at a plantation by the

---

[8] Local word for Indian chief or headman.

way, but not long, for we had thirty miles to ride
that afternoon if we would reach a town, which we
were willing to do, and therefore rode hard for it.
I, with some others, whose horses were strong, got
to the town that night, exceedingly tired, and wet to
the skin; but George Pattison and Robert Widders,
being weaker-horsed, were obliged to lie in the woods
that night also.

The town we went to was a Dutch town, called
New Castle,* whither Robert Widders and George
Pattison came to us next morning.

We departed thence, and got over the river Delaware, not without great danger of some of our lives.
When we were over we were troubled to procure
guides, which were hard to get, and very chargeable.
Then had we that wilderness country, since called
West Jersey, to pass through, not then inhabited by
English; so that we sometimes travelled a whole day
together without seeing man or woman, house or
dwelling-place. Sometimes we lay in the woods by a
fire, and sometimes in the Indians' wigwams or
houses.

We came one night to an Indian town, and lay at
the house of the king, who was a very pretty † man.
Both he and his wife received us very lovingly, and
his attendants (such as they were) were very respectful to us. They gave us mats to lie on; but provision was very short with them, they having caught but
little that day. At another Indian town where we
stayed the king came to us, and he could speak some

---

* In Delaware.   † That is, kindly-spirited.

English. I spoke to him much, and also to his people; and they were very loving to us.

At length we came to Middletown, an English plantation in East Jersey, and there we found some Friends; but we could not stay to have a meeting at that time, being earnestly pressed in our spirits to get to the half-year's meeting of Friends at Oyster Bay, in Long Island, which was very near at hand.

We went with a Friend, Richard Hartshorn, brother of Hugh Hartshorn, the upholsterer, in London, who received us gladly at his house, where we refreshed ourselves; and then he carried us and our horses in his own boat over a great water, which occupied most part of the day getting over, and set us upon Long Island. We got that evening to Friends at Gravesend, with whom we tarried that night, and next day got to Flushing, and the day following reached Oyster Bay; several Friends of Gravesend and Flushing accompanied us.

The half-year's meeting began next day, which was the first day of the week, and lasted four days. The first and second days we had public meetings for worship, to which people of all sorts came; on the third day were the men's and women's meetings, wherein the affairs of the Church were taken care of. Here we met with some bad spirits, who had run out from Truth into prejudice, contention, and opposition to the order of Truth, and to Friends therein.

These had been very troublesome to Friends in their meetings there and thereabouts formerly, and likely would have been so now; but I would not suffer the service of our men's and women's meetings

to be interrupted and hindered by their cavils. I let
them know that if they had anything to object
against the order of Truth which we were in, we
would give them a meeting another day on purpose.
And indeed I laboured the more, and travelled the
harder to get to this meeting, where it was expected
many of these contentious people would be; because
I understood they had reflected much upon me, when
I was far from them.

The men's and women's meetings being over, on
the fourth day we had a meeting with these discontented people, to which as many of them as chose
came, and as many Friends as desired were present
also; and the Lord's power broke forth gloriously to
the confounding of the gainsayers. Then some of
those that had been chief in the mischievous work of
contention and opposition against the Truth began to
fawn upon me, and to cast the blame upon others;
but the deceitful spirit was judged down and condemned, and the glorious Truth of God was exalted
and set over all; and they were all brought down and
bowed under. Which was of great service to Truth,
and to the satisfaction and comfort of Friends; glory
to the Lord for ever!

After Friends were gone to their several habitations, we stayed some days upon the island; had meetings in several parts thereof, and good service for the
Lord. When we were clear of the island, we returned to Oyster Bay, waiting for a wind to carry us
to Rhode Island, which was computed to be about
two hundred miles. As soon as the wind served, we
set sail. We arrived there on the thirtieth day of the

Third month, and were gladly received by Friends. We went to the house of Nicholas Easton, who at that time was governor of the island; where we rested, being very weary with travelling.

On First-day following we had a large meeting, to which came the deputy-governor and several justices, who were mightily affected with the Truth. The week following, the Yearly Meeting for all the Friends of New England and the other colonies adjacent, was held in this island; [9] to which, besides very many Friends who lived in those parts, came John Stubbs from Barbadoes, and James Lancaster and John Cartwright from another way.

This meeting lasted six days, the first four days being general public meetings for worship, to which abundance of other people came. For they having no priest in the island, and so no restriction to any particular way of worship; and both the governor and deputy-governor, with several justices of the peace, daily frequenting the meetings; this so encouraged the people that they flocked in from all parts of the

---

[9] George Bishop, in " New England Judged," p. 351, says that New England Yearly Meeting was set up in 1661. John Burnyeat, who had attended it in 1671, says in his Journal, " It begins in the ninth of the Fourth month *every year;* and continues for much of a week, and is a general meeting once a year for all Friends in New England." The records for several years after its origin were destroyed by fire. They are, however, complete from 1683 to date.

island. Very good service we had amongst them, and Truth had good reception.

I have rarely observed a people, in the state wherein they stood, to hear with more attention, diligence, and affection, than generally they did, during the four days; which was also taken notice of by other Friends.

These public meetings over, the men's meeting began, which was large, precious, and weighty. The day following was the women's meeting, which also was large and very solemn.

These two meetings being for ordering the affairs of the Church, many weighty things were opened, and communicated to them, by way of advice, information, and instruction in the services relating thereunto; that all might be kept clean, sweet and savoury amongst them. In these, several men's and women's meetings for other parts were agreed and settled, to take care of the poor, and other affairs of the Church, and to see that all who profess Truth walk according to the glorious gospel of God.

When this great general meeting was ended, it was somewhat hard for Friends to part; for the glorious power of the Lord, which was over all, and His blessed Truth and life flowing amongst them, had so knit and united them together, that they spent two days in taking leave one of another, and of the Friends of the island; and then, being mightily filled with the presence and power of the Lord, they went away with joyful hearts to their several habitations, in the several colonies where they lived.

When Friends had taken their leave one of an-

other, we, who travelled amongst them, dispersed
ourselves into our several services, as the Lord
ordered us.   John Burnyeat, John Cartwright, and
George Pattison went into the eastern parts of New
England, in company with the Friends that came
from thence, to visit the particular meetings there;
whom John Stubbs and James Lancaster intended to
follow awhile after, in the same service; but they
were not yet clear of this island.   Robert Widders
and I stayed longer upon this island; finding service
still here for the Lord, through the great openness
and the daily coming in of fresh people from other
colonies, for some time after the general meeting; so
that we had many large and serviceable meetings
amongst them.

During this time, a marriage was celebrated
amongst Friends in this island, and we were present.
It was at the house of a Friend who had formerly
been governor of the island: and there were present
three justices of the peace, with many others not in
profession with us.   Friends said they had never seen
such a solemn assembly on such an occasion, or so
weighty a marriage and so comely an order.   Thus
Truth was set over all.   This might serve for an example to others; for there were some present from
many other places.

After this I had a great travail in spirit concerning
the Ranters in those parts, who had been rude at a
meeting at which I was not present.   Wherefore I
appointed a meeting amongst them, believing the Lord
would give me power over them; which He did, to
His praise and glory; blessed be His name for ever!

There were at this meeting many Friends, and divers
other people; some of whom were justices of the
peace, and officers, who were generally well affected
with the Truth. One, who had been a justice twenty
years, was convinced, spoke highly of the Truth, and
more highly of me than is fit for me to mention or
take notice of.

Then we had a meeting at Providence, which was
very large, consisting of many sorts of people. I had
a great travail upon my spirit, that it might be preserved quiet, and that Truth might be brought over
the people, might gain entrance, and have a place in
them; for they were generally above the priest in
high notions; and some of them came on purpose to
dispute. But the Lord, whom we waited upon, was
with us, and His power went over them all; and His
blessed Seed was exalted and set above all. The disputers were silent, and the meeting was quiet and
ended well; praised be the Lord! The people went
away mightily satisfied, much desiring another meeting.

This place (called Providence) was about thirty
miles from Rhode Island; and we went to it by water.
The Governor of Rhode Island, and many others,
went with me thither; and we had the meeting in a
great barn, which was thronged with people, so that
I was exceedingly hot, and in a great sweat; but all
was well; the glorious power of the Lord shone over
all; glory to the great God for ever! [10]

[10] For an account of Fox's relations with Roger Williams see note in next chapter.

After this we went to Narragansett, about twenty
miles from Rhode Island; and the Governor went
with us. We had a meeting at a justice's house,
where Friends had never had any before. It was
very large, for the country generally came in; and
people came also from Connecticut, and other parts
round about, amongst whom were four justices of the
peace. Most of these people had never heard Friends
before; but they were mightily affected with the
meeting, and a great desire there is after the Truth
amongst them; so that our meeting was of very good
service, blessed be the Lord for ever!

The justice at whose house the meeting was, and
another justice of that country, invited me to come
again; but I was then clear of those parts, and going
towards Shelter Island. But John Burnyeat and
John Cartwright, being come out of New England
into Rhode Island, before I was gone, I laid this place
before them; and they felt drawings thither, and
went to visit them.

At another place, I heard some of the magistrates
say among themselves that if they had money
enough, they would hire me to be their minister.
This was where they did not well understand us, and
our principles; but when I heard of it, I said, " It is
time for me to be gone; for if their eye were so much
on me, or on any of us, they would not come to their
own Teacher." For this thing (hiring ministers) had
spoiled many, by hindering them from improving
their own talents; whereas our labour is to bring
every one to his own Teacher *in* himself.

I went thence towards Shelter Island,[11] having with me Robert Widders, James Lancaster, George Pattison, and John Jay, a planter of Barbadoes.

We went in a sloop; and passing by Point Juda * and Block Island, we came to Fisher's Island, where at night we went on shore; but were not able to stay for the mosquitoes which abound there, and are very troublesome. Wherefore we went into our sloop again, put off for the shore, and cast anchor; and so lay in our sloop that night.

Next day we went into the Sound, but finding our sloop was not able to live in that water, we returned again, and came to anchor before Fisher's Island, where we lay in our sloop that night also. There fell abundance of rain, and our sloop being open, we were exceedingly wet.

Next day we passed over the waters called the Two Horse Races, and then by Gardner's Island; after which we passed by the Gull's Island, and so got at length to Shelter Island. Though it was but about twenty-seven leagues from Rhode Island, yet through the difficulty of passage we were three days in reaching it.

The day after, being First-day, we had a meeting there. In the same week I had another among the

* Point Judith.

---

[11] " Shelter Island " lies at the Eastern end of Long Island, between Gardiner's Bay and Little Peconic Bay. Nathaniel Sylvester was the sole proprietor of the island, and he made it a shelter for persecuted Friends from New England.

Indians; at which were their king, his council, and about a hundred Indians more. They sat down like Friends, and heard very attentively while I spoke to them by an interpreter, an Indian that could speak English well. After the meeting they appeared very loving, and confessed that what was said to them was Truth.

Next First-day we had a great meeting on the island, to which came many people who had never heard Friends before. They were very well satisfied with it, and when it was over would not go away till they had spoken with me. Wherefore I went amongst them, and found they were much taken with the Truth; good desires were raised in them, and great love. Blessed be the Lord; His name spreads, and will be great among the nations, and dreadful among the heathen.

While we were in Shelter Island, William Edmundson, who had been labouring in the work of the Lord in Virginia, came to us. From thence he had travelled through the desert-country, through difficulties and many trials, till he came to Roanoke, where he met with a tender people. After seven weeks' service in those parts, sailing over to Maryland, and so to New York, he came to Long Island, and so to Shelter Island; where we met with him, and were very glad to hear from him the good service he had had for the Lord, in the several places where he had travelled since he parted from us.

We stayed not long in Shelter Island, but entering our sloop again put to sea for Long Island. We had a very rough passage, for the tide ran so strong for several hours that I have not seen the like; and being against us, we could hardly get forwards, though we had a gale.

We were upon the water all that day and the night following; but found ourselves next day driven back near to Fisher's Island. For there was a great fog, and towards day it was very dark, so that we could not see what way we made. Besides, it rained much in the night, which in our open sloop made us very wet.

Next day a great storm arose, so that we were fain to go over the Sound, and got over with much difficulty. When we left Fisher's Island, we passed by Falkner Island, and came to the main, where we cast anchor till the storm was over.

Then we crossed the Sound, being all very wet; and much difficulty we had to get to land, the wind being strong against us. But blessed be the Lord God of heaven and earth, and of the seas and waters, all was well.

We got safe to Oyster Bay, in Long Island, which, they say, is about two hundred miles from Rhode Island, the seventh of the Sixth month, very early in the morning.

At Oyster Bay we had a very large meeting. The same day James Lancaster and Christopher Holder went over the bay to Rye,[12] on the continent, in Gov-

---

[12] Rye is now in New York State. The boundary between New York and Connecticut was long in dispute. At this time it seems Rye was in Governor Winthrop's territory.

ernor Winthrop's government, and had a meeting there.

From Oyster Bay, we passed about thirty miles to Flushing, where we had a very large meeting, many hundreds of people being there; some of whom came about thirty miles to it. A glorious and heavenly meeting it was (praised be the Lord God!), and the people were much satisfied.

Meanwhile Christopher Holder and some other Friends went to a town in Long Island, called Jamaica, and had a meeting there.

We passed from Flushing to Gravesend, about twenty miles, and there had three precious meetings; to which many would have come from New York, but that the weather hindered them.

Being clear of this place, we hired a sloop, and, the wind serving, set out for the new country now called Jersey. Passing down the bay by Coney Island, Natton Island,* and Staten Island, we came to Richard Hartshorn's at Middletown harbour,† about break of day, the twenty-seventh of the Sixth month.

Next day we rode about thirty miles into that country, through the woods, and over very bad bogs, one worse than all the rest; the descent into which was so steep that we were fain to slide down with our horses, and then let them lie and breathe themselves before they could go on. This place the people of the country called Purgatory.

We got at length to Shrewsbury, in East Jersey, and on First-day had a precious meeting there, to

* Now Governor's Island.   † In New Jersey.

which Friends and other people came from afar, and the blessed presence of the Lord was with us. The same week we had a men's and women's meeting out of most parts of New Jersey.

They are building a meeting place in the midst of them and there is a monthly and general meeting set up which will be of great service in those parts in keeping up the gospel order and government of Christ Jesus, of the increase of which there is no end, that they who are faithful may see that all who profess the holy Truth live in the pure religion, and walk as becometh the gospel.

While we were at Shrewsbury, an accident befel, which for the time was a great exercise to us. John Jay, a Friend of Barbadoes, who had come with us from Rhode Island, and intended to accompany us through the woods to Maryland, being to try a horse, got upon his back, and the horse fell a-running, cast him down upon his head, and broke his neck, as the people said. Those that were near him took him up as dead, carried him a good way, and laid him on a tree.

I got to him as soon as I could; and, feeling him, concluded he was dead. As I stood pitying him and his family, I took hold of his hair, and his head turned any way, his neck was so limber. Whereupon I took his head in both my hands, and, setting my knees against the tree, I raised his head, and perceived there was nothing out or broken that way.

Then I put one hand under his chin, and the other behind his head, and raised his head two or three times with all my strength, and brought it in. I soon

perceived his neck began to grow stiff again, and then
he began to rattle in his throat, and quickly after to
breathe.

The people were amazed; but I bade them have a
good heart, be of good faith, and carry him into the
house. They did so, and set him by the fire. I bade
them get him something warm to drink, and put him
to bed. After he had been in the house a while he
began to speak; but did not know where he had been.

The next day we passed away (and he with us,
pretty well) about sixteen miles to a meeting at Middletown, through woods and bogs, and over a river;
where we swam our horses, and got over ourselves
upon a hollow tree. Many hundred miles did he
travel with us after this.[13]

To this meeting came most of the people of the
town. A glorious meeting we had, and the Truth was
over all; blessed be the great Lord God for ever!
After the meeting we went to Middletown Harbor,
about five miles, in order to take our long journey
next morning, through the woods towards Maryland;
having hired Indians for our guides.

I determined to pass through the woods on the

---

[13] This narrative has sometimes been questioned and
sometimes been taken to prove that Fox was an instrument in working miracles. Neither solution is satis-
factory, or necessary. Recent medical annals give similar cases. A dislocated neck is not necessarily fatal.
The incident shows again Fox's readiness in dealing
coolly and skillfully with hard situations. He endeav-
ors to do what *can* be done.

other side of Delaware bay, that we might head the creeks and rivers as much as possible. On the 9th of the Seventh month we set forwards, and passed through many Indian towns, and over some rivers and bogs; and when we had ridden about forty miles, we made a fire at night, and lay down by it. As we came among the Indians, we declared the day of the Lord to them.

Next day we travelled fifty miles, as we computed; and at night, finding an old house, which the Indians had forced the people to leave, we made a fire and stayed there, at the head of Delaware Bay.[14]

---

[14] It is not easy to follow Fox's scanty itinerary. There are two Tinicum islands in the Delaware (it is called " Dinidock " in the first edition of the Journal). The crossing was probably made at the upper island, which is just in front of what is now the city of Burlington, though this would be hardly ninety miles from Middletown Harbour, as he estimates. He then travels down across the very country which Friends afterwards settled under the leadership of William Penn. There is evidence to show that the idea of forming in America a colony of Friends originated with George Fox. We learn from a letter of Josiah Coale, a Friend who had travelled extensively among the Indians, that George Fox had commissioned him to treat with the Susquehanna Indians for the purchase of a strip of territory. Fox's letter is not preserved, but Josiah Coale's answer is among the Swarthmore MSS., and is as follows: "Dear George,—As concerning Friends buying a piece of land of the Susquehanna Indians, I have spoken of it to them and told them what *thou said* concerning it, but their answer was that there is no land that is habitable

Next day we swam our horses over a river about a mile wide, first to an island called Upper Tinicum, and then to the mainland; having hired Indians to help us over in their canoes. This day we rode but about thirty miles, and came at night to a Swede's house, where we got a little straw, and stayed that night.

Next day, having hired another guide, we travelled about forty miles through the woods, and made a fire

---

or fit for situation beyond Baltimore's liberty [i. e., beyond the domain of Lord Baltimore,] till they come to or near the Susquehanna fort, and besides William Fuller, who was the chief man amongst Friends with the Indians . . . is withdrawn at present, . . . so that without him little can be done at present with the Indians; and besides, these Indians are at war with another nation of Indians, who are very numerous, and it is doubted by some that in a little space they will be so destroyed that they will not be a people. Thine in the truth,   JOSIAH COALE."

This letter was written in 1660, twelve years before this American visit. About the same time William Penn's thoughts were turning in the same direction. Writing about Pennsylvania in 1681, he says: " This I can say, that I had an *opening of joy* as to these parts in the year 1661, at Oxford twenty years since." By a purchase made through John Fenwick and Edward Byllynge, Friends obtained possession of a great section of New Jersey in 1674, the year after George Fox arrived in England. There can be no doubt that his thoughts were on future settlements here as he travelled through what is now Pennsylvania and New Jersey.

at night, by which we lay, and dried ourselves; for we were often wet in our travels.

The next day we passed over a desperate river,[15] which had in it many rocks and broad stones, very hazardous to us and our horses. Thence we came to Christiana River, where we swam over our horses, and went over ourselves in canoes; but the sides of this river were so bad and miry, that some of the horses were almost laid up.

Thence we came to New Castle,* heretofore called New Amsterdam; and being very weary, and inquiring in the town where we might buy some corn for our horses, the governor came and invited me to his house, and afterwards desired me to lodge there; telling me he had a bed for me, and I should be welcome. So I stayed, the other Friends being taken care of also.

This was on a Seventh-day; and he offering his house for a meeting, we had the next day a pretty

* In Delaware.

---

[15] The " desperate river " was probably the Brandywine, and the Christiana " River " is Christiana Creek, formed from a junction of Red Clay and White Clay Creeks. It finds the Delaware about two miles below Wilmington. The Bohemia and Sassafras Rivers are two of the many arms of Chesapeake Bay. The " Kentish Shore " is the shore of Kent County, Maryland. Tredhaven (or Thirdhaven) is farther down the Bay, where the boats were so thick it seemed like the Thames! A meeting was established here which remains until the present time.

large one; for most of the town were at it. Here had never been a meeting before, nor any within a great way; but this was a very precious one. Many were tender, and confessed to the Truth, and some received it; blessed be the Lord for ever!

The 16th of the Seventh month we set forward, and travelled, as near as we could compute, about fifty miles, through the woods and over the bogs, heading Bohemia River and Sassafras River. At night we made a fire in the woods, and lay there all night. It being rainy weather, we got under some thick trees for shelter, and afterwards dried ourselves again by the fire.

Next day we waded through Chester River, a very broad water, and afterwards passing through many bad bogs, lay that night also in the woods by a fire, not having gone above thirty miles that day. The day following we travelled hard, though we had some troublesome bogs in our way; we rode about fifty miles, and got safe that night to Robert Harwood's, at Miles River,* in Maryland.

This was the 18th of the Seventh month; and though we were very weary, and much dirtied with the bogs, yet hearing of a meeting next day, we went to it, and from it to John Edmundson's. Thence we went three or four miles by water to a meeting on the First-day following.

At this meeting a judge's wife, who had never been at any of our meetings before, was reached. She said after the meeting that she would rather hear us once

* Now St. Michael's.

than the priests a thousand times. Many others also
were well satisfied; for the power of the Lord was
eminently with us. Blessed for ever be His holy
name!

We passed thence about twenty-two miles, and had
a good meeting upon the Kentish shore, to which one
of the judges came. After another good meeting
hard-by, at William Wilcock's, where we had good
service for the Lord, we went by water about twenty
miles to a very large meeting, where were some hundreds of people, four justices of peace, the high
sheriff of Delaware, and others. There were also an
Indian emperor or governor, and two others of the
chief men among the Indians.

With these Indians I had a good opportunity. I
spoke to them by an interpreter: they heard the
Truth attentively, and were very loving. A blessed
meeting this was, of great service both for convincing and for establishing in the Truth those that were
convinced of it. Blessed be the Lord, who causeth
His blessed Truth to spread!

After the meeting there came to me a woman
whose husband was one of the judges of that country, and a member of the assembly there. She told
me that her husband was sick, not likely to live; and
desired me to go home with her to see him. It was
three miles to her house, and I being just come hot
out of the meeting, it was hard for me then to go;
yet considering the service, I got a horse, went with
her, visited her husband, and spoke to him what the
Lord gave me. The man was much refreshed, and

finely raised up by the power of the Lord; and afterwards came to our meetings.

I went back to the Friends that night, and next day we departed thence about nineteen or twenty miles to Tredhaven creek, to John Edmundson's again; whence, the 3d of Eighth month, we went to the General Meeting for all Maryland Friends.[16]

This held five days. The first three meetings were for public worship, to which people of all sorts came; the other two were men's and women's meetings. To the public meetings came many Protestants of divers sorts, and some Papists. Amongst these were several magistrates and their wives, and other persons of chief account in the country. There were so many besides Friends that it was thought there were sometimes a thousand people at one of these meetings; so that, though they had not long before enlarged their meeting-place, and made it as large again as it was before, it could not contain the people.

I went by boat every day four or five miles to it, and there were so many boats at that time passing upon the river that it was almost like the Thames. The people said there were never so many boats seen there together before, and one of the justices said he had never seen so many people together in that country before. It was a very heavenly meeting, wherein the presence of the Lord was gloriously manifested. Friends were sweetly refreshed, the people generally

---

[16] What is now called Baltimore Yearly Meeting was established in 1672.

satisfied, and many convinced; for the blessed power
of the Lord was over all; everlasting praises to His
holy name for ever!

After the public meetings were over, the men's and
women's meetings began, and were held the other two
days; for I had something to impart to them which
concerned the glory of God, the order of the gospel,
and the government of Christ Jesus.

When these meetings were over, we took our leave
of Friends in those parts, whom we left well established in the Truth.

On the 10th of the Eighth month we went thence
about thirty miles by water, passing by Crane's
Island, Swan Island, and Kent Island, in very foul
weather and much rain. Our boat being open, we
were not only very much wet, but in great danger of
being overset; insomuch that some thought we could
not escape being cast away. But, blessed be God, we
fared very well, and came safely to shore next morning.

Having got to a little house, dried our clothes by
the fire, and refreshed ourselves a little, we took to
our boat again; and put off from land, sometimes sailing and sometimes rowing; but having very foul
weather that day too, we could not get above twelve
miles forward. At night we got to land, and made a
fire; some lay by that, and some by a fire at a house a
little way off.

Next morning we passed over the Great Bay, and
sailed about forty miles that day. Making to shore at
night, we lay there, some in the boat, and some at an
ale-house.

Next morning being First-day, we went six or seven miles to the house of a Friend who was a justice of the peace, where we had a meeting. This was a little above the head of the Great Bay. We had been almost four days on the water, and were weary with rowing, yet all was very well; blessed and praised be the Lord!

We went next day to another Friend's house, near the head of Hatton's Island, where we had good service amongst Friends and others; as we had also the day following at the house of George Wilson, a Friend that lived about three miles further, where we had a very precious meeting, there being great tenderness amongst the people.

After this meeting we sailed about ten miles to the house of James Frizby, a justice of the peace, where, the 16th of the Eighth month, we had a very large meeting, at which, besides Friends, were some hundreds of people, it was supposed. Amongst them were several justices, captains, and the sheriff, with other persons of note.

A blessed heavenly meeting this was; a powerful, thundering testimony for Truth was borne therein; a great sense there was upon the people, and much brokenness and tenderness amongst them.

We stayed till about the eleventh hour in the night, when the tide turned for us; then, taking boat, we passed that night and the next day about fifty miles to another Friend's house. The next two days we made short journeys visiting Friends.

The 20th of the month we had a great meeting at a place called Severn, where there was a meeting-place, but not large enough to hold the people. Divers chief magistrates were at it, with many other considerable people, and it gave them generally great satisfaction.

Two days after we had a meeting with some that walked disorderly, and had good service in it. Then, spending a day or two in visiting Friends, we passed to the Western Shore, and on the 25th had a large and precious meeting at William Coale's, where the speaker of their assembly, with his wife, a justice of peace, and several people of quality, were present.

Next day we had a meeting, six or seven miles further, at Abraham Birkhead's, where were many of the magistrates and upper sort; and the speaker of the assembly for that country was convinced. A blessed meeting it was; praised be the Lord!

We travelled the next day; and the day following, the 28th of the Eighth month, had a large and very precious meeting at Peter Sharp's, on the Cliffs, between thirty and forty miles distant from the former. Many of the magistrates and upper rank of people were present, and a heavenly meeting it was. The wife of one of the Governor's council was convinced; and her husband was very loving to Friends. A justice of the peace from Virginia was convinced, and hath had a meeting since at his house.

Some Papists were at this meeting, one of whom, before he came, threatened to dispute with me; but he was reached and could not oppose. Blessed be the Lord, the Truth reached into the hearts of people beyond words, and it is of a good savour amongst them!

After the meeting we went about eighteen miles to

the house of James Preston, a Friend that lived on Patuxent River. Thither came to us an Indian king, with his brother, to whom I spoke, and found they understood what I spoke of.

Having finished our service in Maryland, and intending to go to Virginia, we had a meeting at Patuxent on the 4th of the Ninth month, to take our leave of Friends. Many people of all sorts were at it, and a powerful meeting it was.

On the 5th we set sail for Virginia, and in three days came to a place called Nancemond, about two hundred miles from Maryland. In this voyage we met with foul weather, storms, and rain, and lay in the woods by a fire in the night.

At Nancemond lived a Friend called the widow Wright. Next day we had a great meeting there, of Friends and others. There came to it Colonel Dewes, with several other officers and magistrates, who were much taken with the Truth declared.

After this, we hastened towards Carolina; yet had several meetings by the way, wherein we had good service for the Lord; one about four miles from Nancemond Water, which was very precious; and there was a men's and women's meeting settled, for taking care of the affairs of the Church.

Another very good one also we had at William Yarrow's, at Pagan Creek, which was so large, that we were fain to be abroad, the house not being large enough to contain the people. A great openness there was; the sound of Truth spread abroad, and had a good savour in the hearts of people; the Lord have the glory for ever!

After this our way to Carolina grew worse, being much of it plashy, and pretty full of great bogs and swamps; so that we were commonly wet to the knees, and lay abroad at nights in the woods by a fire.

One night we got to a poor house at Sommertown,* and lay by the fire. The woman of the house had a sense of God upon her. The report of our travel had reached thither, and drawn some that lived beyond Sommertown to that house, in expectation to see and hear us (so acceptable was the sound of Truth in that wilderness country); but they missed us.

The next day, the 21st of the Ninth month, having travelled hard through the woods and over many bogs and swamps, we reached Bonner's Creek; and there we lay that night by the fireside, the woman lending us a mat to lie on.

This was the first house we came to in Carolina. Here we left our horses, over-wearied with travel. Thence we went down the creek in a canoe, to Macocomocock River,† and came to Hugh Smith's house, where the people of other professions came to see us (for there were no Friends in that part of the country), and many of them received us gladly.

Amongst others came Nathaniel Batts, who had been Governor of Roanoke; he went by the name of Captain Batts, and had been a rude, desperate man. He asked me about a woman in Cumberland, who, he said he had been told, had been healed by our prayers, and by laying on of hands, after she had been long

* Now Somerton.　　　† Now Chowan.

sick, and given over by the physicians; and he desired
to know the certainty of it.   I told him we did not
glory in such things, but many such things had been
done by the power of Christ.

Not far from here we had a meeting among the
people, and they were taken with the Truth; blessed
be the Lord!   Then passing down the river Maratick *
in a canoe, we went down the bay Coney-Hoe, and
came to the house of a captain, who was very loving,
and lent us his boat, for we were much wet in the
canoe, the water splashing in upon us.   With this
boat we went to the Governor's house; but the water
in some places was so shallow that the boat, being
laden, could not swim; so we were fain to put off our
shoes and stockings, and wade through the water
some distance.

The Governor, with his wife, received us lovingly;
but a doctor there would needs dispute with us.   And
truly his opposing us was of good service, giving occasion for the opening of many things to the people concerning the Light and Spirit of God, which he denied
to be in everyone; and affirmed that it was not in the
Indians.

Whereupon I called an Indian to us, and asked him
whether when he lied, or did wrong to any one, there
was not something in him that reproved him for it.
He said there was such a thing in him, that did so
reprove him; and he was ashamed when he had done
wrong, or spoken wrong.   So we shamed the doctor
before the Governor and the people; insomuch that

* Now Roanoke.

the poor man ran out so far that at length he would not own the Scriptures.

We tarried at the Governor's that night; and next morning he very courteously walked with us himself about two miles through the woods, to a place whither he had sent our boat about to meet us. Taking leave of him, we entered our boat, and went that day about thirty miles to the house of Joseph Scott, one of the representatives of the country.

There we had a sound, precious meeting; the people were tender, and much desired after meetings. At a house about four miles further, we had another meeting, to which came the Governor's secretary, who was chief secretary of the province, and had been formerly convinced.

Having visited the north part of Carolina, and made a little entrance for Truth upon the people there, we began to return towards Virginia, having several meetings in our way, wherein we had very good service for the Lord, the people being generally tender and open; blessed be the Lord!

We lay one night at the house of the secretary, to get to which gave us much trouble; for the water being shallow, we could not bring our boat to shore; but the secretary's wife, seeing our strait, came herself in a canoe (her husband being from home) and brought us to land.

Next morning our boat was sunk; but we got her up, mended her, and went away in her that day about twenty-four miles, the water being rough, and the winds high; but the great power of God was seen, in carrying us safe in that rotten boat.

Upon our return we had a very precious meeting at Hugh Smith's; praised be the Lord for ever! The people were very tender, and very good service we had amongst them. There was at this meeting an Indian captain, who was very loving; and acknowledged it to be Truth that was spoken. There was also one of the Indian priests, whom they called a Pawaw, who sat soberly among the people.

The 9th of the Tenth month we got back to Bonner's Creek, where we had left our horses, having spent about eighteen days in the north of Carolina.

Our horses having rested, we set forward for Virginia again, travelling through the woods and bogs as far as we could well reach that day, and at night lying by a fire in the woods. Next day we had a tedious journey through bogs and swamps, and were exceedingly wet and dirty all the day, but dried ourselves at night by a fire.

We got that night to Sommertown. As we came near, the woman of the house, seeing us, spoke to her son to keep up their dogs; for both in Virginia and Carolina (living lonely in the woods) they generally keep great dogs to guard their houses. But the son said, " There is no need; our dogs will not meddle with these people." When we were come into the house, she told us we were like the children of Israel, against whom the dogs did not move their tongues. Here we lay in our clothes by the fire, as we had done many a night before.

Next day we had a meeting; for the people, having been informed of us, had a great desire to hear us; and a very good meeting we had among them, where we never had had one before; praised be the Lord for ever! After the meeting we hastened away.

When we had ridden about twenty miles, calling at a house to inquire the way, the people desired us to tarry all night with them; which we did.

Next day we came among Friends, after we had travelled about an hundred miles from Carolina into Virginia: in which time we observed great variety of climates, having passed in a few days from a very cold to a warm and spring-like country. But the power of the Lord is the same in all, is over all, and doth reach the good in all; praised be the Lord for ever!

We spent about three weeks in travelling through Virginia, mostly amongst Friends, having large and precious meetings in several parts of the country; as at the widow Wright's, where many of the magistrates, officers, and other high people came. A most heavenly meeting we had; wherein the power of the Lord was so great that it struck a dread upon the assembly, chained all down, and brought reverence upon the people's minds.

Among the officers was a major, kinsman to the priest, who told me that the priest had threatened to come and oppose us. But the Lord's power was too strong for him, and stopped him; and we were quiet and peaceable. The people were wonderfully affected with the testimony of Truth; blessed be the Lord for ever!

Having finished what service lay upon us in Virginia, on the 30th we set sail in an open sloop for Maryland. But having a great storm, and being much wet, we were glad to get to shore before night; and, walking to a house at Willoughby Point, we got lodging there that night. The woman of the house was a widow, and a very tender person; she had never received Friends before; but she received us very kindly, and with tears in her eyes.

We returned to our boat in the morning, and hoisted our sail, getting forward as fast as we could. But towards evening, a storm rising, we had much ado to get to shore; and our boat being open, the water splashed often in, and sometimes over us, so that we were completely wet. Being got to land, we made a fire in the woods to warm and dry us, and there we lay all night, the wolves howling about us.

On the 1st of the Eleventh month we sailed again. The wind being against us, we made but little headway, and were fain to get to shore at Point Comfort, where yet we found but small comfort. For the weather was so cold that though we made a good fire in the woods to lie by, the water that we had brought for our use was frozen near the fireside. We made to sea again next day; but the wind being strong and against us, we advanced but little. We were glad to get to land again, and travelled about to find some house where we might buy provisions, for our store was spent.

That night, also, we lay in the woods; and so extremely cold was the weather, the wind blowing high, and the frost and snow being great, that it was hard for some of us to abide it.

On the 3d, the wind setting pretty fair, we fetched it up by sailing and rowing, and got that night to Milford Haven, where we lay at Richard Long's, near Quince's Island.

Next day we passed by Rappahannock River, where dwell many people; and Friends had a meeting there at the house of a justice, who had formerly been at a meeting where I was.

We passed over Potomac River also, the winds being high, the water very rough, our sloop open, and the weather extremely cold; and had a meeting there also, where some people were convinced. When we parted thence, some of our company went amongst them. We next steered our course for Patuxent River. I sat at the helm the greater part of the day, and some of the night. About the first hour in the morning we reached James Preston's house, on Patuxent River, which is about two hundred miles from Nancemond in Virginia.

We were very weary; yet the next day being the first of the week, we went to the meeting not far from there. The same week we went to an Indian king's cabin, where were several of the Indians, with whom we had a good opportunity to discourse; and they carried themselves very lovingly. We went also that week to a general meeting; then about eighteen miles further to John Geary's, where we had a very precious meeting; praised be the Lord God for ever!

After this the cold grew so exceedingly sharp, the frost and snow so extreme, beyond what was usual in that country, that we could hardly endure it. Neither was it easy or safe to stir out; yet we got, with some difficulty, six miles through the snow to

John Mayor's, where we met with some Friends come from New England, whom we had left there when we came away; and glad we were to see each other, after so long and tedious travels.

By these Friends we understood that William Edmundson, having been at Rhode Island and New England, was gone thence for Ireland; that Solomon Eccles, coming from Jamaica and landing at Boston in New England, was taken at a meeting there, and banished to Barbadoes; that John Stubbs and another Friend were gone into New Jersey, and several other Friends to Barbadoes, Jamaica, and the Leeward Islands. It was matter of joy to us to understand that the work of the Lord went on and prospered, and that Friends were unwearied and diligent in the service.

The 27th of the Eleventh month we had a very precious meeting in a tobacco-house. The next day we returned to James Preston's, about eighteen miles distant. When we came there, we found his house had been burnt to the ground the night before, through the carelessness of a maid-servant; so we lay three nights on the ground by the fire, the weather being very cold.

We made an observation which was somewhat strange, but certainly true; that one day, in the midst of this cold weather, the wind turning into the south, it grew so hot that we could hardly bear the heat; and the next day and night, the wind chopping back into the north, we could hardly endure the cold.

Having travelled through most parts of that country, and visited most of the plantations, and having sounded the alarm to all people where we came, and proclaimed the day of God's salvation amongst them, we found our spirits began to be clear of these parts of the world, and draw towards Old England again. Yet we were desirous, and felt freedom from the Lord, to stay over the general meeting for the province of Maryland, which drew nigh; that we might see Friends generally together before we departed.

Spending our time in the interim in visiting Friends and Friendly people, in attending meetings about the Cliffs and Patuxent, and in writing answers to cavilling objections which some of Truth's adversaries had raised and spread abroad to hinder people from receiving the Truth, we were not idle, but laboured in the work of the Lord until that general provincial meeting came on, which began on the 17th of the Third month, and lasted four days. On the first of these the men and women had their meetings for business, wherein the affairs of the Church were taken care of, and many things relating thereto were opened unto them, to their edification and comfort.

The other three days were spent in public meetings for the worship of God, at which divers of considerable account in the government, and many others, were present. These were generally satisfied, and many of them reached; for it was a wonderful, glorious meeting, and the mighty presence of the Lord was seen and felt over all; blessed and praised for ever be His holy name, who over all giveth dominion!

After this meeting we took our leave of Friends,

parting in great tenderness, in the sense of the heavenly life and virtuous power of the Lord that was livingly felt amongst us; and went by water to the place where we were to take shipping, many Friends accompanying us thither and tarrying with us that night.

Next day, the 21st of the Third month, 1673, we set sail for England; the same day Richard Covell came on board our ship, having had his own taken from him by the Dutch.

We had foul weather and contrary winds, which caused us to cast anchor often, so that we were till the 31st ere we could get past the capes of Virginia and out into the main sea. But after this we made good speed, and on the 28th of the Fourth month cast anchor at King's Road, which is the harbour for Bristol.

We had on our passage very high winds and tempestuous weather, which made the sea exceedingly rough, the waves rising like mountains; so that the masters and sailors wondered at it, and said they had never seen the like before. But though the wind was strong it set for the most part with us, so that we sailed before it; and the great God who commands the winds, who is Lord of heaven, of earth, and the seas, and whose wonders are seen in the deep, steered our course and preserved us from many imminent dangers. The same good hand of Providence that went with us, and carried us safely over, watched over us in our return, and brought us safely back again; thanksgiving and praises be to his holy name for ever!

Many sweet and precious meetings we had on board the ship during this voyage (commonly two a week), wherein the blessed presence of the Lord did greatly refresh us, and often break in upon and tender the company.

When we came into Bristol harbour, there lay a man-of-war, and the press-master came on board to impress our men. We had a meeting at that time in the ship with the seamen, before we went to shore; and the press-master sat down with us, stayed the meeting, and was well satisfied with it. After the meeting I spoke to him to leave in our ship two of the men he had impressed, for he had impressed four, one of whom was a lame man. He said, " At your request I will."

We went on shore that afternoon, and got to Shirehampton. We procured horses and rode to Bristol that night, where Friends received us with great joy. In the evening I wrote a letter to my wife, to give her notice of my landing.[16]

---

[16] The letter began as follows:

" Dear heart,

" This day we came into Bristol, near night, from the sea; glory to the Lord God over all for ever, who was our convoy, and steered our course! who is the God of the whole earth, of the seas and winds, and made the clouds His chariots, beyond all words, blessed be His name for ever! He is over all in His great power and wisdom. Amen."

CHAPTER XIX.
The Last Imprisonment.
1673–1678.

Between this and the fair, my wife came out of the North to Bristol to me, and her son-in-law, Thomas Lower, with two of her daughters,[1] came with her. Her other son-in-law, John Rous, William Penn and his wife, and Gerrard Roberts, came from London, and many Friends from several parts of the nation, to the fair; and glorious, powerful meetings we had at that time, for the Lord's infinite power and life was over all.

I passed into Wiltshire, where also we had many blessed meetings. At Slattenford, in Wiltshire, we had a very good meeting, though we met there with much opposition from some who had set themselves against women's meetings; which I was moved of the Lord to recommend to Friends, for the benefit and

---

[1] When George Fox married Margaret Fell she had one son, George, and seven daughters, as follows: Margaret, who married John Rous; Bridget, who married John Draper; Isabel, twice married, first to William Yeomans, and then to Abraham Morrice; Sarah, who married William Mead (Penn's companion in the famous trial), Mary, who married Thomas Lower; Susanna, who married William Ingram, and Rachel, who married Daniel Abraham.

advantage of the Church of Christ,[2] " that faithful
women, who were called to the belief of the Truth,
being made partakers of the same precious faith, and
heirs of the same everlasting gospel of life and salvation with the men, might in like manner come into
the possession and practice of the gospel order, and
therein be helpmeets unto the men in the restoration,* in the service of Truth, in the affairs of the
Church, as they are outwardly in civil, or temporal
things; that so all the family of God, women as well
as men, might know, possess, perform, and discharge
their offices and services in the house of God, whereby the poor might be better taken care of, the
younger instructed, informed, and taught in the way
of God; the loose and disorderly reproved and admonished in the fear of the Lord; the clearness of
persons proposing marriage more closely and strictly
inquired into in the wisdom of God; and all the members of the spiritual body, the Church, might watch
over and be helpful to each other in love."

After a visit at Kingston, I went to London, where
I found the Baptists and Socinians, with some old
apostates, grown very rude, having printed many
books against us; so that I had a great travail in the
Lord's power, before I could get clear of that city.
But blessed be the Lord, his power came over them,

* That is, in reclaiming those who have gone astray.

---

[2] This is the beginning of a serious opposition to
Fox's system of government, which finally grew to an
open schism. It was headed by John Wilkinson and
John Story. It was one of the most trying struggles of
Fox's life.

and all their lying, wicked, scandalous books were answered.

[After a visit with William Penn at the latter's
home at Rickmansworth, he started on his journey
north towards Swarthmore, accompanied by his wife,
two of her daughters and his son-in-law, Thomas
Lower, a journey which led to more than a year's imprisonment—his last imprisonment, as it proved.]

At night, as I was sitting at supper, I felt I was
taken; yet I said nothing then to any one of it.   But
getting out next morning, we travelled into Worcestershire, and went to John Halford's, at Armscott,
where we had a very large and precious meeting in
his barn, the Lord's powerful presence being eminently with and amongst us.

After the meeting, Friends being most of them
gone, as I was sitting in the parlour, discoursing with
some Friends, Henry Parker, a justice, came to the
house, and with him one Rowland Hains, a priest of
Hunniton, in Warwickshire.   This justice heard of
the meeting by means of a woman Friend, who, being nurse to a child of his, asked leave of her mistress
to go to the meeting to see me; and she speaking of
it to her husband, he and the priest plotted together
to come and break it up and apprehend me.

But from their sitting long at dinner, it being the
day on which his child was sprinkled, they did not
come till the meeting was over, and Friends mostly
gone.   But though there was no meeting when they
came, yet I, who was the person they aimed at, being
in the house, Henry Parker took me, and Thomas

Lower for company with me; and though he had nothing to lay to our charge, sent us both to Worcester jail, by a strange sort of mittimus.

Being thus made prisoners, without any probable appearance of being released before the quarter-sessions at soonest, we got some Friends to accompany my wife and her daughter into the north, and we were conveyed to Worcester. Thence, by the time I thought my wife would reach home, I wrote her the following letter:

" DEAR HEART:

" Thou seemedst to be a little grieved when I was speaking of prisons, and when I was taken. Be content with the will of the Lord God. For when I was at John Rous's, at Kingston, I had a sight of my being taken prisoner; and when I was at Bray Doily's, in Oxfordshire, as I sat at supper, I saw I was taken, and I saw I had a suffering to undergo. But the Lord's power is over all; blessed be His holy name forever!   G. F." [3]

---

[3] Margaret Fox and her daughter were sent on under the escort of a Friend, a merchant from Bristol, who, Fox says, " seemed to have met us providentially to assist my wife and her daughter in their journey homewards, when by our imprisonment they were deprived of our company and help." Fox had just received a message that his mother was in her last illness, and it had been his intention to part from his wife in Warwickshire and have a last visit with his aged mother. This privilege never came, for Mary Fox, of Fenny Drayton, died while her son was in Worcester prison.

[This imprisonment began December 17th, 1673. The case was brought before the sessions on the 21st of January, 1674. "When we came in," he writes, "they were stricken with paleness in their faces, and it was some time before anything was spoken; insomuch that a butcher in the hall said, 'What, are they afraid? Dare not the justices speak to them?'" There was manifestly no case against them on the *mittimus*, but the judge, at the suggestion of the "priest," took the easy way to catch them. "You, Mr. Fox, are a famous man, and all this may be true which you have said; but, that we may be the better satisfied, will you take the oaths of allegiance and supremacy?" The usual refusal was given, followed with the penalty of *præmunire*. During this long imprisonment he had the promise of a pardon from the king, but he refused to get his liberty by any method which implied that he had done wrong and needed pardon. At the next sessions, in April, he got a temporary liberty, so that he went to London and attended yearly meeting, after which he returned to Worcester for a new trial, which ended in the same old way. Meantime the strong man's constitution was yielding to the incessant strain upon it.]

About this time I had a fit of sickness, which brought me very low and weak in my body; and I continued so a pretty while, insomuch that some Friends began to doubt of my recovery. I seemed to myself to be amongst the graves and dead corpses; yet the invisible power did secretly support me, and conveyed refreshing strength into me, even when I was so weak that I was almost speechless. One night, as I was lying awake upon my bed in the glory of the Lord which was over all, it was said unto me that the Lord had a great deal more work for me to do for Him before He took me to Himself.

After this [about October 1st, 1674] my wife went to London, and spoke to the King, laying before him my long and unjust imprisonment, with the manner of my being taken, and the justices' proceedings against me, in tendering me the oath as a snare, whereby they had præmunired me; so that I being now his prisoner, it was in his power, and at his pleasure, to release me, which she desired.

The King spoke kindly to her, and referred her to the Lord-Keeper; to whom she went; but she could not obtain what she desired, for he said the King could not release me otherwise than by a pardon, and I was not free to receive a pardon, knowing I had not done evil. If I would have been freed by a pardon, I need not have lain so long, for the King was willing to give me pardon long before, and told Thomas Moore that I need not scruple, being released by a pardon, for many a man that was as innocent as a child had had a pardon granted him; yet I could not consent to have one. For I would rather have lain in prison all my days, than have come out in any way dishonourable to Truth; therefore I chose to have the validity of my indictment tried before the judges.

Thereupon, having first had the opinion of a counsellor upon it (Thomas Corbet, of London, with whom Richard Davis, of Welchpool, was well acquainted, and whom he recommended to me), an habeas corpus was sent down to Worcester to bring me up once more to the King's Bench bar, for the trial of the errors in my indictment. The under-sheriff set forward with me the 4th of the Twelfth month.

We came to London on the 8th, and on the 11th I was brought before the four judges at the King's Bench, where Counsellor Corbet pleaded my cause. He started a new plea; for he told the judges that they could not imprison any man upon a præmunire.

Chief-Justice Hale said, " Mr. Corbet, you should have come sooner, at the beginning of the term, with this plea."

He answered, " We could not get a copy of the return and the indictment."

The Judge replied, " You should have told us, and we would have forced them to make a return sooner."

Then said Judge Wild, " Mr. Corbet, you go upon general terms; and if it be as you say, we have committed many errors at the Old Bailey, and in other courts."

Corbet was positive that by law they could not imprison upon a præmunire.

The Judge said, " There is summons in the statute."

" Yes," said Corbet, " but summons is not imprisonment; for summons is in order to a trial."

" Well," said the Judge, " we must have time to look in our books and consult the statutes." So the hearing was put off till the next day.

The next day they chose rather to let this plea fall and begin with the errors of the indictment; and when they came to be opened, they were so **many**

and gross that the judges were all of opinion that the
indictment was quashed and void, and that I ought
to have my liberty.

There were that day several great men, lords and
others, who had the oaths of allegiance and supremacy tendered to them in open court, just before my
trial came on; and some of my adversaries moved the
judges that the oaths might be tendered again to me,
telling them I was a dangerous man to be at liberty.

But Chief-Justice Hale [4] said that he had indeed
heard some such reports, but he had also heard many
more good reports of me; and so he and the rest of
the judges ordered me to be freed by proclamation.

Thus after I had suffered imprisonment a year and
almost two months for nothing, I was fairly set at
liberty upon a trial of the errors in my indictment,
without receiving any pardon, or coming under any
obligation or engagement at all; and the Lord's everlasting power went over all, to His glory and praise.

Counsellor Corbet, who pleaded for me, obtained
great fame by it, for many of the lawyers came to
him and told him he had brought that to light which
had not been known before, as to the not imprisoning
upon a præmunire; and after the trial a judge said to
him, " You have attained a great deal of honour by
pleading George Fox's cause so in court." [5]

Being at liberty, I visited Friends in London; and

---

[4] This is Chief Justice Sir Matthew Hale.

[5] It will be noticed that Fox is set at liberty on the
errors in his indictment, and not on a judicial decision
that it is illegal to imprison on a *præmunire*.

having been very weak, and not yet well recovered,
I went to Kingston; and having visited Friends there,
returned to London, wrote a paper to the Parliament,
and sent several books to them.

A great book against swearing had been delivered
to them a little before; the reasonableness whereof
had so much influence, that it was thought they
would have done something towards our relief if they
had sat longer. I stayed in and near London till the
yearly meeting, to which Friends came from most
parts of the nation, and some from beyond sea. A
glorious meeting we had in the everlasting power of
God.

The illness I got in my imprisonment at Worcester
had so much weakened me that it was long before I
recovered my natural strength again. For which
reason, and as many things lay upon me to write,
both for public and private service, I did not stir
much abroad during the time that I now stayed in
the north; but when Friends were not with me, I
spent much time in writing for Truth's service.
While I was at Swarthmore, I gave several books to
be printed.[6]

---

[6] George Fox was now only fifty-one years old, but
he was prematurely broken by the sufferings and expos-
ures which only such an iron constitution as he possessed could have endured for thirty years. He still
had fourteen years to live, but from now on a decided
change appears. There is no cessation of activity, but
it is activity of a quieter sort. Only one important
mission journey falls in these years—the visit to Hol-

[This letter to his " Dear Heart " from York during the winter of 1677 shows that he still had some power of endurance left.]

" DEAR HEART:

" To whom is my love, and to thy daughters, and to all Friends that inquire after me. My desires are that ye all may be preserved in the Lord's everlasting Seed, in whom ye will have life and peace, dominion and settlement, in the everlasting home or dwelling in the house built upon the foundation of God.

" In the power of the Lord I am brought to York, having had many meetings in the way. The road was many times deep and bad with snow, our horses sometimes were down, and we were not able to ride; and sometimes we had great storms and rain; but by the power of the Lord I went through all.

" At Scarhouse there was a very large meeting, and at Burrowby another, to which Friends came out of Cleveland and Durham; and many other meetings we have had. At York, yesterday, we had a very large meeting, exceedingly thronged, Friends being at it from many parts, and all quiet, and well satisfied. Oh the glory of the Lord that shone over all!

---

land and Germany. Henceforth he makes his pen speak for him. Epistles and books are the main results of these fourteen years. The Journal grows dry and devoid of dramatic interest, and our gleanings from it will be few. He is much at Swarthmore or at Kingston, near London, where Margaret Rous, a daughter of his wife, lived.

" This day we have had a large men's and women's meeting, many Friends, both men and women, being come out of the country, and all was quiet. This evening we are to have the men's and women's meeting of the Friends of the city.

" John Whitehead is here, with Robert Lodge and others; Friends are mighty glad, above measure. So I am in my holy element and holy work in the Lord; glory to His name for ever! To-morrow I intend to go out of the city towards Tadcaster, though I cannot ride as in days past; yet praised be the Lord that I can travel as well as I do!

" So with my love in the fountain of life, in which as ye all abide ye will have refreshment of life, that by it we may grow and gather eternal strength to serve the Lord, and be satisfied, to the God of all power, who is all-sufficient to preserve you, I commit you all.   G. F.

"York, the 16th of the Second month [April] 1677."

[After much service in several counties, he returns to London. The Journal proceeds:]

It pleased the Lord to bring me safe to London, though much wearied; for though I rode not very far in a day, yet, through weakness of body, continual travelling was hard to me. Besides, I had not much rest at night to refresh nature; for I often sat up late with Friends, where I lodged, to inform and advise them in things wherein they were wanting; and when in bed I was often hindered of sleep by great pains in my head and teeth, occasioned, as I thought, from cold taken by riding often in the rain. But the Lord's power was over all, and carried me through all, to His praise.

To the London Yearly Meeting* many Friends came from most parts of the nation; and some out of Scotland, Holland, etc. Very glorious meetings we had, wherein the Lord's powerful presence was very largely felt; and the affairs of Truth were sweetly carried on in the unity of the Spirit, to the satisfaction and comfort of the upright-hearted; blessed be the Lord for ever!

After the yearly meeting, having stayed a week or two with Friends in London, I went down with William Penn to his house in Sussex,† John Burnyeat and some other Friends being with us. As we passed through Surrey, hearing the quarterly meeting was that day, William Penn, John Burnyeat, and I, went from the road to it; and after the meeting returning to our other company, went with them to William Penn's that night; which is forty miles from London.

I stayed at Worminghurst about three weeks; in which time John Burnyeat and I answered a very envious and wicked book, which Roger Williams, a priest of New England (or some colony thereabouts) had written against Truth and Friends.[7]

    * 1677.   † Worminghurst.

---

[7] Fox did not see Roger Williams in Providence, though the latter had a personal tilt with John Burnyeat at Newport in 1671. After George Fox had left Providence and had gone back down the Bay with his

When we had finished that service, we went with Stephen Smith to his house at Warpledon in Surrey, where we had a large meeting. Friends thereaway had been exceedingly plundered about two months before on the priest's account; for they took from Stephen Smith five kine (being all he had) for about fifty shillings tithes.

Thence we went to Kingston, and so to London, where I stayed not long; for it was upon me from the Lord to go into Holland, to visit Friends and to preach the gospel there, and in some parts of Germany. Wherefore, setting things in order for my journey as fast as I could, I took leave of Friends at London; and with several other Friends went down to Colchester, in order to my passage for Holland.

Next day, being First-day, I was at the public meeting of Friends there, which was very large and

---

companion, Nicholas Easton, governor of Rhode Island, Roger Williams rowed to Newport with a challenge to a debate. Fox, however, had already left the island, and was well on his way toward Long Island. Williams then wrote, what Fox elsewhere calls " Roger Williams's ' Book of Lyes,' " a book bearing the grimly humorous title, " George Fox digged out of his Burrows," Boston, 1676. (See Publications of the Narragansett Club, Vol. V., pp. xx.-xlv., Providence, 1872.) Fox and Burnyeat reply to this " slanderous book " in a bulky book in two parts entitled, " A New England Fire Brand Quenched." Fox seemed not to know just where the famous " apostle of soul liberty " lived, as he says, " a priest of New England (or some colony thereabouts!) "

peaceable. In the evening I had another large one, but not so public, at John Furly's house, where I lodged. The day following I was at the women's meeting there, which also was very large.

Thence next day we passed to Harwich, where Robert Duncan, and several other Friends out of the country, came to see us; and some from London came to us there, that intended to go over with me.

The packet in which we were to go not being ready, we went to the meeting in the town, and a precious opportunity we had together; for the Lord, according to His wonted goodness, by His overcoming, refreshing power, opened many mouths to declare His everlasting Truth, to praise and glorify Him.

After the meeting at Harwich we returned to John Vandewall's, where I had lodged; and when the boat was ready, taking leave of Friends, we that were bound for Holland went on board about nine in the evening, on the 25th of the Fifth month, 1677. The Friends that went over with me, were William Penn, Robert Barclay, George Keith and his wife, John Furly and his brother, William Tallcoat, George Watts, and Isabel Yeomans, one of my wife's daughters.

About one in the morning we weighed anchor, having a fair brisk wind, which by next morning brought us within sight of Holland. But that day proving very clear and calm we got forward little, till about four in the afternoon, when a fresh gale arose which carried us within a league of land. Then being becalmed again, we cast anchor for that night, it being between the hours of nine and ten in the evening.

William Penn and Robert Barclay, understanding that Benjamin Furly was come from Rotterdam to the Briel to meet us, got two of the boatmen to let down a small boat that belonged to the packet, and row them to shore; but before they could reach it the gates were shut; and there being no house without the gates, they lay in a fisherman's boat all night.

As soon as the gates were opened in the morning, they went in, and found Benjamin Furly, with other Friends of Rotterdam, that were come thither to receive us; and they sent a boat, with three young men in it, that lived with Benjamin Furly, who brought us to the Briel, where the Friends received us with great gladness.

We stayed about two hours to refresh ourselves, and then took boat, with the Holland Friends, for Rotterdam, where we arrived about eleven that day, the 28th of the month.   I was very well this voyage, but some of the Friends were sea-sick.   A fine passage we had, and all came safe and well to land; blessed and praised be the name of the Lord for ever!

Next day, being First-day, we had two meetings at Benjamin Furly's, where many of the townspeople and some officers came in, and all were civil.   Benjamin Furly, or John Claus, a Friend of Amsterdam, interpreted, when any Friend declared.   I spent the next day in visiting Friends there.

The day following, William Penn and I, with other Friends, went towards Amsterdam with some Friends of that city, who came to Rotterdam to conduct us thither. We took boat in the afternoon, and, passing by Overkirk, came to Delft, through which we walked on foot.

We then took boat again to Leyden, where we lodged that night at an inn. This is six Dutch miles from Rotterdam, which are eighteen English miles, and five hours' sail or travelling; for our boat was drawn by a horse that went on the shore.

Next day, taking boat again, we went to Haarlem, fourteen miles from Leyden, where we had appointed a meeting, which proved very large; for many of the townspeople came in, and two of their preachers. The Lord gave us a blessed opportunity, not only with respect to Friends, but to other sober people, and the meeting ended peaceably and well. After it we passed to Amsterdam.

[After a conference, the following meetings were established or " settled."]

A monthly, a quarterly, and a yearly meeting, to be held at Amsterdam for Friends in all the United Provinces of Holland, and in Embden, the Palatinate, Hamburg, Frederickstadt, Dantzic, and other places in and about Germany; which Friends were glad of, and it has been of great service to Truth.

[One of the most interesting episodes of this journey was the visit paid by George Keith's wife and Fox's step-daughter, Isabel Yeomans, to the Princess Elizabeth, to whom Fox sent a personal letter. " Princess Elizabeth " was the daughter of the unfortunate Frederick, Elector Palatine, and granddaughter of James the first of England. She was a woman of great spiritual gifts and of considerable intellectual power. She was the friend and correspondent of the philosopher Des Cartes. She had, previous to this visit, made the acquaintance (which developed into close friendship) of William Penn and Robert Barclay. She frequently used her influence upon her uncle, King Charles, and her brother, Prince Rupert, to secure the release of Friends from the prisons of England and Scotland. Her answer to George Fox's letter is as follows:]

" Dear Friend:

" I cannot but have a tender love to those that love the Lord Jesus Christ, and to whom it is given, not only to believe in Him, but also to suffer for Him; therefore your letter and your Friends' visit have been both very welcome to me. I shall follow their and your counsel as far as God will afford me light and unction; remaining still your loving friend,

" Elizabeth.

" Hertford [Westphalia], the 30th of August, 1677."

[Twice we get glimpses of the great world movements which just then had these Low Countries for their stage. In the great struggle with Louis XIV. the dykes had been cut and much of the country was under water. Here is an experience in East Friesland:]

One of the magistrates of that city [Groningen] came with us from Leeuwarden, with whom I had some discourse on the way, and he was very loving. We walked nearly two miles through the city, and then took boat for Delfziel; and passing in the even-

ing through a town called Appingdalem, where had
been a great horse-fair that day, there came many
officers rushing into the boat, and being somewhat in
drink, they were very rude. I spoke to them, exhorting them to fear the Lord, and beware of Solomon's
vanities. They were boisterous fellows; yet somewhat more civil afterwards.

[The other circumstance which connects Fox here
with history is his epistle written to the Peace Ambassadors in the city of Nimeguen. The entry in the
Journal says: "I wrote an epistle to the ambassadors
who were treating for a peace at Nimeguen." This is
dated Amsterdam, the 21st of 7th mo. (September),
1677. It concludes with these words:]

" From him who is a lover of Truth, righteousness,
and peace, who desires your temporal and eternal
good; and that in the wisdom of God that is from
above, pure, gentle, and peaceable, you may be ordered, and order all things, that God hath committed
to you, to His glory; and stop those things among
Christians, so far as you have power, which dishon-
our God, Christ, and Christianity!

" G. F."

[Here is an incident of travel in Germany.]

Being clear of Hamburg, we took leave of Friends
there, whom we left well; and taking John Hill with
us, passed by boat to a city in the Duke of Luneburg's
country; where, after we were examined by the
guards, we were taken to the main-guard, and there

examined more strictly; but after they found we were not soldiers, they were civil, and let us pass.

In the afternoon we travelled by wagon, and the waters being much out, by reason of heavy rains, when it drew towards night we hired a boy on the way to guide us through a great water we had to pass. When we came to it, the water was so deep, before we could come at the bridge, that the wagoner had to wade, and I drove the wagon.

When we were come on the bridge, the horses broke part of it down, and one of them fell into the water, the wagon standing upon that part of the bridge which remained unbroken; and it was the Lord's mercy to us that the wagon did not run into the brook. When they had got the horse out, he lay a while as if dead; but at length they got him up, put him to the wagon again, and laid the planks right; and then, through the goodness of the Lord to us, we got safe over.

After this we came to another water. Finding it to be very deep, and it being in the night, we hired two men to help us through, who put cords to the wagon to hold it by, that the force of the water might not drive it from the way. But when we came into it, the stream was so strong that it took one of the horses off his legs, and was carrying him down the stream. I called to the wagoner to pluck him to him by his reins, which he did, and the horse recovered his legs; and with much difficulty we got over the bridge, and went to Bremerhaven, the town where the wagoner lived.

It was the last day of the Sixth month that we escaped these dangers; and it being about eleven at night when we came in here, we got some fresh straw, and lay upon it until about four in the morning. Then, getting up, we set forward again towards Bremen, by wagon and boat.

On the way I had good opportunities to publish Truth among the people, especially at a market-town, where we stayed to change our passage. Here I declared the Truth to the people, warning them of the day of the Lord, that was coming upon all flesh; and exhorting them to righteousness, telling them that God was come to teach His people Himself, and that they should turn to the Lord, and hearken to the teachings of His Spirit in their own hearts.

[While the work was going forward in these fresh fields, trouble was increasing at home, as this brief letter shows:]

Next day, feeling a concern upon my mind with relation to those seducing spirits that made division among Friends, and being sensible that they endeavoured to insinuate themselves into the affectionate part, I was moved to write a few lines to Friends concerning them, as follows:

" All these that set up themselves in the affections of the people, set up themselves, and the affections of the people, and not Christ. But Friends, your peaceable habitation in the Truth, which is everlasting, and changes not, will outlast all the habitations of those that are out of the Truth, be they ever so full of words. So they that are so keen for John Story and John Wilkinson, let them take them, and the

separation; and you that have given your testimony
against that spirit, stand in your testimony, till they
answer by condemnation.   Do not strive, nor make
bargains with that which is out of the Truth; nor
save that alive to be a sacrifice for God, which should
be slain, lest you lose your kingdom.

                                                  " G. F.

" Amsterdam, the 14th of the Seventh month, 1677."

After some time George Keith and William Penn
came back from Germany * to Amsterdam, and had a
dispute with one Galenus Abrahams (one of the most
noted Baptists in Holland), at which many professors
were present; but not having time to finish the dispute then, they met again, two days after, and the
Baptist was much confounded, and Truth gained
ground.[8]

* Whither they had gone for some religious service.

[8] This Galenus Abrahams was a Mennonite and a
man of considerable note.   Sewell, the Quaker historian, who had himself been a disciple of Abrahams, tells
us that in this discussion, which lasted five hours, the
latter maintained the position that " nobody nowadays could be accepted as a messenger of God
unless he confirmed the same by miracle."   (See
Sewell's " History of Friends," Vol. II., page 368,
edition of 1823.   See, also, Barclay's " Religious
Societies of the Commonwealth," pages 174, 251.)
During his second visit to Holland, Fox had another interview with the famous Mennonite which gives
an interesting side light on the penetrating power of
Fox's eyes, already noticed.   " Before I left I went to
visit one Galenus Abrahams, a teacher of chief note

Finding our spirits clear of the service which the Lord had given us to do in Holland, we took leave of Friends of Rotterdam, and passed by boat to the Briel, in order to take passage that day for England. Several Friends of Rotterdam accompanied us, and some of Amsterdam, who were come to see us again before we left Holland. But the packet not coming in till night, we lodged that night at the Briel; and next day, being the 21st of the Eighth month, and the first day of the week, we went on board, and set sail about ten, viz., William Penn, George Keith, and I, and Gertrude Dirick Nieson. with her children.

We were in all about sixty passengers, and had a long and hazardous passage; for the winds were contrary and the weather stormy. The boat also was very leaky, insomuch that we had to have two pumps continually going, day and night; so that it was thought there was quite as much water pumped out as the vessel would have held. But the Lord, who is able to make the stormy winds to cease, and the rag-

---

among the Mennonites, or Baptists. I had been with him when I was in Holland about seven years before and William Penn and George Keith had disputes with him. He was then very high and shy, so that he would not let me touch him, nor look upon him (by his good will), but bid me ' Keep my eyes off him, for,' he said, ' they pierced him.' But now he was very loving and tender, and confessed in some measure to truth; his wife also and daughter were tender and kind, and we parted from them very lovingly."

ing waves of the sea calm, yea, to raise them and stop them at His pleasure, He alone did preserve us; praised be His name for ever!

Though our passage was hard, yet we had a fine time, and good service for Truth on board among the passengers, some of whom were great folks, and were very kind and loving. We arrived at Harwich on the 23d, at night, having been two nights and almost three days at sea.

Next morning William Penn and George Keith took horse for Colchester; but I stayed, and had a meeting at Harwich. There being no Colchester coach there, and the postmaster's wife being unreasonable in her demands for a coach, and deceiving us of it also after we had hired it, we went to a Friend's house about a mile and a half in the country, and hired his wagon, which we bedded well with straw, and rode in it to Colchester.

I stayed there till First-day, having a desire to be at Friends' meeting that day; and a very large and weighty one it was; for Friends, hearing of my return from Holland, flocked from several parts of the country, and many of the townspeople coming in also, it was thought there were about a thousand people at it; and all was peaceable.

I stayed at Bristol all the time of the fair, and some time after. Many sweet and precious meetings we had; many Friends being there from several parts of the nation, some on account of trade, and some in the service of Truth. Great was the love and unity of Friends that abode faithful in the Truth, though some who were gone out of the holy unity, and were run into strife, division, and enmity, were rude and abusive, and behaved themselves in a very unchristian manner towards me.[9]

But the Lord's power was over all; by which being preserved in heavenly patience, which can bear injuries for His name's sake, I felt dominion therein over the rough, rude, and unruly spirits; and left them to the Lord, who knew my innocency, and would plead my cause. The more these laboured to reproach and vilify me, the more did the love of Friends that were sincere and upright-hearted, abound towards me; and some that had been betrayed by the adversaries, seeing their envy and rude behaviour, broke off from them.

About two weeks after I came to London, the yearly meeting began, to which Friends came up out of most parts of the nation, and a glorious, heavenly meeting we had. Oh, the glory, majesty, love, life, wisdom, and unity, that were amongst us! The power reigned over all, and many testimonies were borne therein against that ungodly spirit which sought to make rents and divisions amongst the Lord's people; but not one mouth was opened amongst us in its defence, or on its behalf.

Good and comfortable accounts also we had, for the most part, from Friends in other countries; of which I find a brief account in a letter which soon

---

[9] He had previously had a trying time with opponents who were "very unruly and troublesome" in some meetings held at the home of his friend Thomas Ellwood, at Hunger Hill, near London.

after I wrote to my wife, the copy whereof here follows:

"DEAR HEART:

"To whom is my love in the everlasting Seed of life that reigns over all. Great meetings here have been, and the Lord's power hath been stirring through all. The Lord hath in His power knit Friends wonderfully together, and His glorious presence did appear among them. And now the meetings are over, blessed be the Lord! in quietness and peace.

"From Holland I hear things are well there: some Friends are gone that way, to be at their Yearly Meeting at Amsterdam. At Embden, Friends that were banished are got into the city again.

"At Dantzic, Friends are in prison, and the magistrates threatened them with harder imprisonment; but the next day the Lutherans rose, and plucked down (or defaced) the Popish monastery; so they have work enough among themselves.

"The King of Poland received my letter, and read it himself; and Friends have since printed it in High Dutch.[10] By letters from the Half-Yearly Meeting in Ireland, I hear that they are all in love there.

---

[10] This is an interesting letter to John III. of Poland, in which are given many passages from the words of sovereigns, both ancient and modern, in behalf of liberty of conscience. The letter is an able and valuable document, written, as the writer says, "in love to thy immortal soul and for thy eternal good." It closes with this postscript:

"Postscript.—'Blessed be the merciful, for they shall

" At Barbadoes, Friends are in quietness, and their meetings settled in peace.   At Antigua also, and Nevis, Truth prospers, and Friends have their meetings orderly and well.   Likewise in New England and other places, things concerning Truth and Friends are well; and in those places the men's and women's meetings are settled; blessed be the Lord!

" So keep in God's power and Seed, that is over all, in whom ye all have life and salvation; for the Lord reigns over all in His glory, and in His kingdom; glory to His name forever, Amen.

"In haste, with my love to you all, and to all Friends.   G. F.

"**London, the 26th of the Third month, 1678.**"

---

obtain mercy.'   And remember, O king, Justin Martyr's two Apologies to the Roman emperors, in the defence of the persecuted Christians; and that notable Apology, which was written by Tertullian, upon the same subject; which are not only for the Christian religion, but against all persecution for religion."

CHAPTER XX.

"The Seed Reigns over Death."

1679–1691.

[The year 1679 was spent almost entirely in retirement at Swarthmore, but in 1680 the activity and
travels begin again. This last decade of Fox's life finds
him much of the time in or about London, for there
are new storms to be met, and he could not lie at ease
in the " North." The Wilkinson-Story movement in
opposition to a settled system of government and discipline made his presence in the " South " necessary.
But even more than for this was he concerned over the
fresh spasm of persecution which during the closing
years of Charles' reign filled the prisons and jails with
Quakers. Whenever or wherever the " Conventicle
Act " was enforced Friends were sure to have the large
end of the suffering to bear.]

After this I was moved of the Lord to visit
Friends in some parts of Surrey and Sussex. I went
to Kingston by water, and tarried certain days; for
while I was there, the Lord laid it upon me to write
both to the great Turk, and the Dey of Algiers, severally, to warn them, and the people under them, to
turn from their wickedness, fear the Lord, and do
justly; lest the judgments of God should come upon
them, and destroy them without remedy. To the
Algerines I wrote more particularly concerning the

cruelty they exercised towards Friends and others, whom they held captives in Algiers.

At Hertford I met with John Story, and some others of his party; but the testimony of Truth went over them, and kept them down, so that the meeting was quiet.

It was on a First-day; and the next day being the men's and women's meeting for business, I visited them also, and the rather because some in that place had let in a disesteem of them. Wherefore I was moved to open the service of those meetings, and the usefulness and benefit thereof to the Church of Christ, as the Lord opened the thing in me; and it was of good service to Friends.

I had a meeting also with some of those that were gone into strife and contention, to show them wherein they were wrong; and having cleared myself of them, I left them to the Lord.

I abode at London most part of this winter,* having much service for the Lord there, both in and out of meetings: for as it was a time of great suffering among Friends, I was drawn in spirit to visit Friends' meetings more frequently; to encourage and strengthen them both by exhortation and example. The Parliament also was sitting, and Friends were diligent in waiting upon them, to lay their grievances before them.

We received fresh accounts almost every day of the sad sufferings Friends underwent in many parts of the nation. In seeking relief for my suffering

* 1680.

brethren I spent much time; together with other
Friends, who were freely given up to that service,
attending at the Parliament-House for many days
together, and watching all opportunities to speak
with such members of either House as would hear our
just complaints.

Indeed, some of these were very courteous to us,
and appeared willing to help us if they could; but the
Parliament being then earnest in examining the
Popish plot, and contriving ways to discover such as
were Popishly affected, our adversaries took advantage against us (because they knew we could not
swear nor fight) to expose us to those penalties that
were made against Papists; though they knew in
their consciences that we were no Papists, and had
had experience of us, that we were no plotters.

Sufferings continuing severe upon Friends at London,* I found my service lay mostly there; wherefore
I went but little out of town, and not far; being frequent at the most public meetings, to encourage
Friends, both by word and example, to stand fast in
the testimony to which God had called them.

At other times I went about from house to house,
visiting Friends that had their goods taken away for
their testimony to Truth; because the wicked informers were grown very audacious, by reason that
they had too much countenance and encouragement
from some justices, who, trusting wholly to their information, proceeded against Friends without hear-

ing them; whereby many were made to suffer, not
only contrary to right, but even contrary to law also.[1]

Now I had some inclination to go into the country
to a meeting, but hearing that there would be a bustle at our meetings, and feeling a great disquietness
in people's spirits in the city about choosing sheriffs,
it was upon me to stay in the city, and go to the meeting in Gracechurch street upon the first day of the
week. William Penn went with me, and spoke; and
while he was declaring the Truth to the people, a constable came in with his great staff, and bade him give
over, and come down; but he continued, declaring
Truth in the power of God.

After a while the constable drew back, and when
William Penn had done, I stood up, and declared to

---

[1] Here is a beautiful letter to those who are suffering:

" Dear, suffering lambs, for the name and command
of Jesus; be valiant for His truth, and faithful, and ye
will feel the presence of Christ with you. Look at
Him who suffered for you, who hath bought you, and
will feed you; who saith, ' Be of good comfort, I have
overcome the world '; who destroys the devil and his
works, and bruises the serpent's head. I say, look to
Christ, your sanctuary, in whom ye have rest and peace.
To you it is given not only to believe, but to suffer for
His name's sake. They that will live godly in Christ
Jesus, shall suffer persecution by the ungodly professors of Christ Jesus, who live out of Him. Therefore
be valiant for God's truth upon the earth, and look
above that spirit that makes you suffer, up to Christ,
who was before it was, and will be when it is gone."

the people the everlasting gospel, which was preached
in the apostles' days, and to Abraham; and which the
Church in the apostles' days received, and came to
be heirs of.

As I was thus speaking, two constables came in
with their great staves, and bade me give over speaking, and come down; but, feeling the power of the
Lord with me, I spoke on therein, both to the constables and to the people. To the constables I declared
that we were a peaceable people, who meet to wait
upon God, and worship Him in spirit and in truth;
and therefore they needed not to come with their
staves amongst us, who were met in a peaceable manner, desiring and seeking the good and salvation of all
people.

Then turning my speech to the people again, I declared what further was upon me to them; and while
I was speaking, the constables drew out towards the
door; and the soldiers stood with their muskets in
the yard.

When I had done speaking, I kneeled down and
prayed, desiring the Lord to open the eyes and hearts
of all people, both high and low, that their minds
might be turned to God by His Holy Spirit; that He
might be glorified in all and over all. After prayer
the meeting rose, and Friends passed away; the constables being come in again, but without the soldiers;
and indeed, both they and the soldiers carried themselves civilly.

William Penn and I went into a room hard by, as
we used to do, and many Friends went with us; and
lest the constables should think we would shun them,

a Friend went down and told them that if they would have anything with us, they might come where we were, if they pleased.

On First-day it was upon me to go to Devonshire-House meeting in the afternoon; and because I had heard Friends were kept out there that morning (as they were that day at most meetings about the city), I went sooner, and got into the yard before the soldiers came to guard the passages. But the constables were there before me, and stood in the doorway with their staves.

I asked them to let me go in. They said they could not, durst not; for they were commanded the contrary, and were sorry for it.

I told them I would not press upon them; so I stood by, and they were very civil.

I stood till I was weary, and then one gave me a stool to sit down on; and after a while the power of the Lord began to spring up among Friends, and one began to speak.

The constables soon forbade him, and said he should not speak; and he not stopping, they began to be wroth. But I gently laid my hand upon one of the constables, and wished him to let the Friend alone. The constable did so, and was quiet; and the man did not speak long. After he had done, I was moved to stand up and speak.

I then sat down; and after a while I was moved to pray. The power of the Lord was over all; and the people, the constables and soldiers put off their hats.

When the meeting was done, and Friends began to pass away, the constable put off his hat, and desired the Lord to bless us; for the power of the Lord was over him and the people, and kept them under.

I tarried in and near London, visiting Friends' meetings, and labouring in the service of the gospel, till the yearly meeting came on, which began on the 28th of the Third month. It was a time of great sufferings; and much concerned I was lest Friends that came up out of the country on the Church's service, should be taken and imprisoned at London. But the Lord was with us; His power preserved us, and gave us a sweet and blessed opportunity to wait upon Him, to be refreshed together in Him, and to perform His services for His truth and people for which we met.

As it was a time of great persecution, and we understood that in most counties Friends were under great sufferings, either by imprisonments or spoiling of goods, or both, a concern was weightily upon me lest any Friends that were sufferers, especially such as were traders and dealers in the world, should hazard the losing of other men's goods or estates through their sufferings.

On the First-day following * I went to the meeting at Gracechurch street. When I came there, I found three constables in the meeting-house, who kept Friends out; so we met in the court.

After I had been some time there, I stood up and spoke to the people, and continued speaking some time. Then one of the constables came, and took hold of my hand, and said, " You must come down." I desired him to be patient, and went on speaking to

* In 1683.

the people; but after a little time he pulled me down, and took me into the meeting-house.

I asked them if they were not weary of this work. One of them said, " Indeed we are." They let me go into the widow Foster's house, which joined the meeting-house, where I stayed, being hot.

When the meeting was ended, for one prayed after I was taken away, the constables asked some Friends which of them would pass their words that I should appear, if they should be questioned about me. But the Friends told them they need not require that, for I was a man well known in the city to be one that would neither fly nor shrink. So they went away, and I heard no further of it.

I continued yet at London, labouring in the work and service of the Lord, both in and out of meetings; sometimes visiting Friends in prison for the testimony of Jesus, encouraging them in their sufferings, and exhorting them to stand faithful and steadfast in the testimony, which the Lord had committed to them to bear. Sometimes also I visited those that were sick and weak in body, or troubled in mind, helping to bear up their spirits from sinking under their infirmities. Sometimes our meetings were quiet and peaceable; sometimes they were disturbed and broken up by the officers.

As I was speaking in the power of the Lord,* and the people were greatly affected therewith, suddenly the constables, with the rude people, came in like a sea.

* On First-day at the Savoy.

One of the constables said to me, "Come down"; and he laid hands on me.

I asked him, "Art thou a Christian? We are Christians."

He had hold of my hand, and was very fierce to pluck me down; but I stood still, and spoke a few words to the people; desiring of the Lord that the blessings of God might rest upon them all.

The constable still called upon me to come down, and at length plucked me down, and bade another man with a staff take me and carry me to prison. That man led me to the house of another officer, who was more civil; and after a while they brought in four Friends more, whom they had taken.

I was very weary, and in a great perspiration; and several Friends, hearing where I was, came to me in the constable's house; but I bade them all go their ways, lest the constables and informers should stop them.

After a while the constables led us almost a mile to a justice, who was a fierce, passionate man. After he had asked me my name, and his clerk had taken it in writing, upon the constable's informing him that I had preached in the meeting, he said in an angry manner, "Do not you know that it is contrary to the King's laws to preach in such conventicles, contrary to the Liturgy of the Church of England?"

There was present one —— Shad (a wicked informer, who was said to have broken jail at Coventry, and to have been burned in the hand at London), who, hearing the justice speak so to me, stepped up to him and told him that he had convicted them on the Act of the 22d of King Charles the Second.

" What! you convict them?" said the justice.

" Yes," said Shad, " I have convicted them, and you must convict them too upon that Act."

With that the justice was angry with him, and said, " You teach me! what are you? I'll convict them of a riot."

The informer hearing that and seeing the justice angry, went away in a fret; so he was disappointed of his purpose.

Now had I drawings in Spirit to go into Holland, to visit the Seed of God there.* And as soon as the yearly meeting was over I prepared for my journey. There went with me from London Alexander Parker, George Watts, and Nathaniel Brassey, who also had drawings into that country.

We took coach the 31st of the Third month, 1684, and got to Colchester that night. Next day being First-day, we went to the meeting there; and though there was no notice given of my coming, yet our being there was presently spread over the town, and in several places in the country at seven and ten miles distance; so that abundance of Friends came in double-horsed, which made the meeting very large.

I had a concern and travail in my mind, lest this great gathering should stir up the town, and be more than the magistrates could well bear. But it was very quiet and peaceable, and a glorious meeting we had, to the settling and establishing of Friends both

* Spring of 1684.

in town and country; for the Lord's power was over all; blessed be His name for ever!

Truly the Lord's power and presence was beyond words; for I was but weak to go into a meeting, and my face (by reason of a cold I had taken) was sore; but God manifested His strength in us and with us, and all was well. The Lord have the glory for evermore, for His supporting power![2]

It was the latter end of the summer when I came to London, where I stayed the winter following; saving that once or twice, my wife being in town with me, I went with her to her son Rous's at Kingston. And though my body was very weak, yet I was in continual service, either in public meetings, when I was able to bear them, or in particular business amongst Friends, and visiting those that were sufferers for Truth, either by imprisonment or loss of goods.

Many things also in this time I wrote, some for the press, and some for particular service; as letters to the King of Denmark and Duke of Holstein on behalf of Friends that were sufferers in their dominions.[3]

---

[2] The journal of the second visit to Holland gives little matter of fresh interest. The visit lasted from the 31st of May to the 16th of July, 1684.

[3] This letter to the Duke of Holstein ends as follows:

" I entreat the duke to consider these things. I entreat him to mind God's grace and truth in his heart that is come by Jesus; that by his Spirit of Grace and truth he may come to serve and worship God in his

The yearly meeting coming on, I was much concerned for Friends that came up to it out of the country, lest they should meet with any trouble or disturbance in their passage up or down; and the rather because about that time a great bustle arose in the nation upon the Duke of Monmouth's landing in the West.[4] But the Lord, according to His wonted goodness, was graciously pleased to preserve Friends in safety, and gave us a blessed opportunity to meet together in peace and quietness, and accompanied our meeting with His living, refreshing presence: blessed for ever be His holy name!

Considering the hurries that were in the nation, it came upon me at the close of this meeting to write a few lines to Friends, to caution all to keep out of the spirit of the world, in which trouble is, and to dwell in the peaceable Truth.

I came back to London in the First month, 1686, and set myself with all diligence to look after

---

Spirit and truth; so that he may serve the living eternal God that made him, in his generation, and have his peace in Christ, that the world cannot take away. And I do desire his good, peace, and prosperity in this world, and his eternal comfort and happiness in the world that is everlasting. Amen. G. F.

"London, 26th of the 8th Month, 1684."

[4] The Duke of Monmouth, illegitimate son of Charles II., landed in Lyme, in Devonshire, hoping to secure the throne, but he was defeated at Sedgemoor and captured July 6th, 1685.

Friends' sufferings, from which we had now some hopes of getting relief. The sessions came on in the Second month at Hicks's-Hall, where many Friends had appeals to be tried. I was with these from day to day, to advise them, and to see that no opportunity was slipped nor advantage lost; and they generally succeeded well.

Soon after the King was pleased, upon our often laying our sufferings before him, to give order for the releasing of all prisoners for conscience' sake that were in his power to discharge. Thereby the prison-doors were opened, and many hundreds of Friends, some of whom had been long in prison, were set at liberty.[5]

Some of those who had for many years been restrained in bonds, came now up to the yearly meeting, which was in the Third month this year. This caused great joy to Friends, to see our ancient, faithful brethren again at liberty in the Lord's work, after their long confinement. And indeed a precious meet-

---

[5] On the 16th of May James II. issued a warrant commanding that all Quakers who had been convicted on charges of *præmunire*, or for not swearing, or for not going to church, should be released. By the execution of this warrant about fifteen hundred Quakers were set free. Naturally the yearly meeting which followed was a happy time. This " Order of Release " is preserved in the Archives in Devonshire House in London. It is written on eleven skins of vellum, with the king's portrait at the top. In the list is the name of John Bunyan, who got included in this Royal Pardon.

ing we had; the refreshing presence of the Lord appearing plentifully with us and amongst us.

[Gradually Fox was growing physically weaker, and, though his pen was busy with documents and letters, he records almost nothing in his Journal.]

In the Seventh month * I returned to London, having been near three months in the country for my health's sake, which was very much impaired; so that I was hardly able to stay in a meeting the whole time; and often after a meeting had to lie down on a bed. Yet did not my weakness of body take me off from the service of the Lord, but I continued to labour in and out of meetings, in His work, as He gave me opportunity and ability.

I had not been long in London before a great weight came upon me, and the Lord gave me a sight of the great bustles and troubles, revolution and change, which soon after came to pass. In the sense thereof, and in the movings of the Spirit of the Lord, I wrote " A general epistle to Friends, to forewarn them of the approaching storm, that they might all retire to the Lord, in whom is safety.⁶

About this time great exercises and weights came upon me (as they had usually done before the great revolutions and changes of government), and my strength departed from me; so that I reeled, and was ready to fall, as I went along the streets. At length

* September, 1688.

⁶ This letter was written October 17th, 1688. William landed in England November 5th, 1688.

I could not go abroad at all, I was so weak, for some time, till I felt the power of the Lord to spring over all, and had received an assurance from Him, that He would preserve His faithful people to Himself through all.

About the middle of the First month, 1688-9,* I went to London, the Parliament then sitting, and engaged about the bill for indulgence. Though I was weak in body, and not well able to stir about, yet so great a concern was upon my spirit on behalf of Truth and Friends, that I attended continually for many days, with other Friends, at the Parliament-House, labouring with the members, that the thing might be done comprehensively and effectually.

I remained at London till the beginning of the Ninth month,† being continually exercised in the work of the Lord, either in public meetings, opening the way of Truth to people, and building up and establishing Friends therein, or in other services relating to the Church of God. For the Parliament now sitting, and having a bill before them concerning oaths, and another concerning clandestine marriages, several Friends attended the House, to get those bills so worded that they might not be hurtful to Friends. In this service I also assisted, attending on the Parliament, and discoursing the matter with several of the members.

[Here follows (January 10th, 1691) the last entry in the Journal, with the letter written to the Irish Friends who were enduring almost indescribable sufferings, occasioned by the civil war in Ireland.]

* March, 1689.　　† November, 1690.

Not long after I returned to London, and was almost daily with Friends at meetings. When I had been near two weeks in town, the sense of the great hardships and sore sufferings that Friends had been and were under in Ireland, coming with great weight upon me, I was moved to write an epistle, as a word of consolation unto them.[7]

[The next day he went to Gracechurch Street Meeting, which was large and in which he preached a long and powerful sermon, " opening many deep and weighty things." He then offered prayer, and the

---

[7] This epistle, the last he ever wrote, closes with a triumphant note and an optimistic outlook on the world:

" Christ the Seed reigns; and His power is over all, who bruises the serpent's head, and destroys the devil and his works, and was before he was. So all of you live and walk in Christ Jesus; that nothing may be between you and God, but Christ, in whom ye have salvation, life, rest and peace with God.

" As for the affairs of truth in this land and abroad, I hear that in Holland and Germany, and thereaway, Friends are in love, unity, and peace: and in Jamaica, Barbadoes, Nevis, Antigua, Maryland, and New-England, I hear nothing, but Friends are in unity and peace. The Lord preserve them all out of the world (in which there is trouble) in Christ Jesus, in whom there is peace, life, love, and unity. Amen. My love in the Lord Jesus Christ to all Friends everywhere in your land, as though I named them.   G. F.

" London, the 10th of the 11th month, 1690 " (January 10th, 1691).

meeting closed. When some Friends came to his room in White-Hart-Court, later in the day, he told them he had "felt the cold strike to his heart, as he came out of meeting"; "yet," he added, "I am glad I was here (i. e., in the meeting). Now I am clear, I am fully clear!" Later, when Friends were visiting him, he said: "All is well; the Seed of God reigns over all and over death itself. And though I am weak in body, yet the power of God is over all, and the Seed reigns over all disorderly spirits." "Lying thus in a heavenly frame of mind, his spirit wholly exercised towards the Lord," he fell asleep in peace on the evening of January 13th, 1691. The funeral was attended by a very large concourse of people, and the body was laid in the burying-ground near Bunhill Fields, where the grave is now marked with a modest stone. Few men in the dying hour could say more truly, "I am clear."]